Praise for *The Neuroscience*

MU00533372

"Higher education is increasingly the focus of attention as research findings about the benefits of education contrast with information about poor completion rates, equity gaps, and affordability. Business leaders and policymakers have asked whether students are learning what they need to in colleges and universities. Faculty and educational leaders who want to help their students learn and gain the credentials they need now have a helpful resource based on current knowledge of brain functioning and how people learn in *The Neuroscience of Learning and Development: Enhancing Creativity, Compassion, Critical Thinking, and Peace in Higher Education.*"—*George R. Boggs*, PhD, president and CEO emeritus, American Association of Community Colleges; superintendent and president emeritus, Palomar College

"We have known from decades of previous research that one's ability to manage stress and well-being significantly impacts one's ability to develop and learn. The way in which the authors posit ideas for how we can redesign, deliver, and evaluate higher education with this research in 'mind' is compelling. This book provides practical evidence-based suggestions for fostering the type of learning and development that our stakeholders seek and are asking us to provide."—*Chukuka S. Enwemeka, PhD, provost and senior vice president for academic affairs, San Diego State University*

"It has been almost 20 years since *How People Learn* summarized initial insights from the new discipline of cognitive science, but until now these insights have not been turned into practical advice about how to improve teaching and learning in college. Bresciani Ludvik and her colleagues admirably remedy this situation with this far-reaching volume. Going beyond acquisition of classic content and skills proficiencies, this book addresses learning that embraces equally the development of creativity, empathy, and mindfulness and includes the importance of wellness and relaxation in sustaining mental performance. Everyone who touches students in today's institutions—from teaching faculty to student affairs professionals—will find something to learn here."—*Peter T. Ewell, vice president, National Center for Higher Education Management Systems (NCHEMS)*

"The right book at the right time. This timely and well-constructed book addresses a vital issue facing higher education today: the need to increase critical thinking, communication, creativity, and resilience for today's college graduates. Drawing on neuroscience research and the exploration of innovations in teaching and learning, this book explores exciting new approaches to improve the outcomes of the college experience. There is really nothing like this in the higher education literature—very impressive."
—*Kevin Kruger, president, NASPA—Student Affairs Administrators in Higher Education*

"As a practitioner of nonviolence, I have been exposed to and adopted principles of mindfulness in many aspects of my life. I find it difficult to consistently practice in higher education association management; however, I am convinced that the principles of change, moving from a present state to a transition state to a desired state, are best applied when adopted by people who practice mindfulness. Bresciani Ludvik challenges us to cocreate a new vision in the large and complex ecosystem of American higher education by combining the neuroscience of mindfulness methodology with systemic methods to navigate whole-systems change. This is a fascinating and provocative read that I highly recommend to my colleagues." —*Cynthia H. Love, EdD, executive director, ACPA, American College Personnel Association*

"Breakthroughs in brain science will be the major disruptive innovation in higher education. A friend and neurologist convinced me that success as a college teacher required an understanding of the developing brain's impact on capacity for learning. In turn, I regularly push student affairs to use student development theories to advance the field of learning assessment. If one believes in individual differences based on varied paths through physical and psychosocial developments (and I do), then why would we expect standardized tests administered at arbitrary points in time to work well in measuring student achievement? Bresciani Ludvik is spot-on with the topics in this book. I expect this volume to make a big impact." —*Randy L. Swing, executive director, Association for Institutional Research*

THE NEUROSCIENCE OF LEARNING
AND DEVELOPMENT

THE NEUROSCIENCE OF LEARNING AND DEVELOPMENT

Enhancing Creativity, Compassion, Critical Thinking, and Peace in Higher Education

Edited by Marilee J. Bresciani Ludvik

Foreword by Gavin W. Henning
Foreword by Ralph Wolff

1996–2016 20TH ANNIVERSARY

Sty/us
PUBLISHING, LLC.

STERLING, VIRGINIA

CO-PUBLISHED WITH ACPA

ACPA
College Student
Educators International

Published by Stylus Publishing, LLC.
22883 Quicksilver Drive
Sterling, Virginia 20166-2102

Library of Congress Cataloging-in-Publication Data
Library of Congress Cataloging-in-Publication Data
Names: Bresciani, Marilee J., editor of compilation.
Title: The neuroscience of learning and development : enhancing
creativity, compassion, critical thinking, and peace in higher
education / edited by Marilee Bresciani Ludvik ; foreword by
Gavin W. Henning, Ralph Wolff.
Description: First edition. | Sterling, Virginia : Stylus Publishing,
LLC, 2016. | Includes index.
Identifiers: LCCN 2015027721|
    ISBN 9781620362839 (cloth : alk. paper) |
    ISBN 9781620362846 (pbk. : alk. paper) |
    ISBN 9781620362853 (library networkable e-edition) |
    ISBN 9781620362860 (consumer e-edition)
Subjects: LCSH: Cognitive learning. | Cognitive neuroscience.|
Holistic education. | Mindfulness (Psychology) | Education,
Higher--Aims and objectives.
Classification: LCC LB1062 .N48 2016 | DDC 370.15/2--dc23
LC record available at http://lccn.loc.gov/2015027721

13-digit ISBN: 978-1-62036-283-9 (cloth)
13-digit ISBN: 978-1-62036-284-6 (paperback)
13-digit ISBN: 978-1-62036-285-3 (library networkable e-edition)
13-digit ISBN: 978-1-62036-286-0 (consumer e-edition)

Bulk Purchases

Quantity discounts are available for use in workshops and for
staff development.
Call 1-800-232-0223

First Edition, 2016

10   9   8   7   6   5   4

This book is dedicated to my parents, George Matthew Ludvik and Helyn Zoe McDermott Ludvik, who taught me that no matter how much adversity you experience in life—no matter how many losses—the mind journeys through all of it with you. No one can ever take your mind away from you, although you certainly can "lose it" if you don't tend to it. As such, my parents reminded me, every day, to invest deeply in the development of the mind.

This book is also dedicated to all those who taught me that my mind is much more than the pile of miraculous neural connections in my brain. Thank you for creating such freedom.

CONTENTS

FOREWORD

How many of you reading this foreword want to do the best job you can to help students succeed? I imagine each one of you is nodding your head right now. You wouldn't be reading this if you didn't, right? That same purpose—to do the best job I could for students—drove me to seek out Marilee for the first time. I began working in student affairs assessment in the late 1990s because I wanted to learn how to do the best job possible for students and teach others to do that as well. After reading all of Marilee's scholarship regarding assessment, I was compelled to meet her and thank her for her work. Some of her scholarship laid the foundation for the field of student affairs assessment.

One spring (I can't remember the actual year or location), we attended the same national conference. My goal during that conference was to attend her session and then take that opportunity to introduce myself. As luck would have it, I was presenting at the same time as her session. As I was proceeding to my session, I stopped by the room where she was presenting to briefly introduce myself, thank her for her thought leadership in assessment, and make a mad dash across the convention center to set up for my presentation. As I approached her at the front of the room, Marilee smiled that smile of hers that lights up the room and said . . . something nice. I really can't remember what she said as I was so awestruck. I was meeting a celebrity— the person whose scholarship I respected so highly. She was incredibly gracious as I nervously introduced myself. I felt like a fan seeking an autograph. Although I was interrupting her as she was setting up, she made me feel like I was the most important person in the world. I left that brief meeting thinking, "She's smart, kind, and humble. Wow!" Since that brief moment, our professional relationship and friendship has grown.

As Marilee's personal interest and scholarship evolved to focus on mindfulness, I was fascinated by this emergent topic. Naively, I thought mindfulness was simply meditation and a useful tool for reducing stress. Boy, was I wrong. As we discussed mindfulness over coffee at national conferences or assessment workshops, I discovered that mindfulness is not just another word for meditation; rather, it has many benefits in addition to stress reduction.

In fact, practicing mindfulness changes the brain. Enthralled, I began reading more about the impact of mindfulness, and I was amazed by the research findings.

My knowledge of the topic blossomed in 2014 when one of my doctoral advisees, Anne Hopkins-Gross, began researching the impact of mindfulness on student affairs practice. You learn a lot by rereading a dissertation proposal a few times. With Marilee as a committee member, Anne and I were exposed to the emergent research on the neuroscience of mindfulness. When Marilee shared a prepublication draft of this manuscript, I was intrigued to further study the neuroscience of learning and its use in higher education.

I approached *The Neuroscience of Learning and Development* from the perspective of a college student educator. My entire professional career has been spent fostering student learning in some way or another. As a residence hall director, I helped foster learning and development directly with students. As an assessment professional midway through my career, my connection to student learning and development was more indirect as I created assessment systems and taught others how to perform assessment. Now, as a faculty member and graduate preparation program director, I'm engaged in this work directly through teaching and indirectly by cultivating future student affairs practitioners who will foster learning and development in other students.

With highlighter in hand, my guiding question while reading *The Neuroscience of Learning and Development* was: What can I take away from this to do the best job I can in teaching my students and helping them foster student learning and development within the students with which they work? This book forced me to reconsider everything I knew about college student learning. To be honest, it was a little disheartening to think that I had been doing it all wrong for the past 22 years. But each chapter provided hope that I could do better.

Marilee and her coauthors provide a compelling argument that we are doing higher education wrong in the United States. While research suggests we can enhance student success (Astin, 1984; Bandura, 1986; Barr & Tagg, 1995; Dweck, 2007; Kuh, Kinzie, Schuh, & Whitt, 2010) U.S. students are being outperformed academically by their peers in other countries (OECD Research Associates, 2013). Employers also lament the lack of skills college graduates possess (Hart, 2013). If we can positively impact student success, why aren't we seeing results? The issue could be our educational structures in the U.S. colleges and universities. The contributors to this book suggest that the way we organize higher education to deliver learning and development is not aligned with how the neurological system facilitates that learning. To see an impact from the ways we foster learning we need to examine how we teach (in all its forms). We must find ways to help students integrate experiences and help them develop as whole beings.

This idea of holistic learning is not new to higher education or to student affairs. *The Student Personnel Point of View,* published in 1937 by the American Council on Education, posited the importance of developing the whole student in addition to providing educational activities outside of the classroom. This concept is also the American College Personnel Association's (ACPA) first core value: education and development of the total student (ACPA–College Student Educators International 2013). The *Neuroscience of Learning and Development* provides scientific evidence to support this notion. As we pay attention to something, even something as seemingly mundane as our breathing, our brain's structures and functions change. These changes facilitate the process of discovering how to achieve learning outcomes. College student educators must create opportunities for students to make associations between what they are learning across experiences and link their cognitive learning with their psychosocial development, ultimately allowing them to make neurological connections that will positively impact their ability to succeed. At a superficial level, colleges and universities are simply not constructed to help students make these connections. Rather, students are educated in discrete time frames: 50-minute classes, 45-minute residence hall programs, and 30-minute meetings with an adviser. These isolated activities are not the real issue, however. As I have learned, the real issue is that we are not helping students integrate these activities. By rejecting the primacy of linear learning and embracing the concept of nonlinear learning and development rooted in a neurological perspective, we can create and potentially fund educational environments and experiences that center on the whole person, thus facilitating learning. Taking this approach will enable us to do a better job helping our students learn, develop, and succeed.

In an accessible, easy-to-understand approach, the authors of *The Neuroscience of Learning and Development* help the reader understand the brain and neurological bases of learning. After this overview, authors of subsequent chapters outline approaches to help students integrate their learning experiences holistically, permitting them to create neurological connections that will help them to be academically and personally successful. After reading this book, I felt prepared to begin transforming how I design, deliver, and evaluate student learning and development to positively impact students.

The first chapters focus on the brain, neuroplasticity and neurogenesis, and strategies to change the brain. With this foundational information, the text moves to learning concepts of self-authorship and experiential learning and their impact on learning. Subsequent chapters focus on specific topics related to mind and body integration including well-being and resilience, creativity, compassion and empathy, sleep and movement, integrative inquiry, and mindfulness. To the uninformed reader, the book chapters do not appear related based on titles. However, the authors expertly weave the common thread of neurological learning and mind-body holism through each chapter, making the connections between them seamless and natural.

If you aspire to do the best job you can to foster college learning and development and support students' academic and personal success, this book is a must-read. As president of ACPA–College Students International, an association that centers on fostering student learning and development, I cannot recommend this text highly enough. This book is thought provoking, engaging, and informative. It will transform your thinking and provide strategies you can use to foster college student success.

Gavin W. Henning, PhD
President, ACPA – College Student Educators International
Associate Professor, New England College

References

ACPA–College Student Educators International. (2013). *Mission, vision, and values.* Retrieved from http://www.myacpa.org/values

American Council on Education. (1937). *The student personnel point of view. Series VI—Student Personnel Work*, vol. 13. Washington, DC: American Council on Education Studies.

Astin, A. (1984). Student involvement: A developmental theory for higher education. *Journal of College Student Personnel, 25*(4), 297–308.

Bandura A. (1986). *Social foundations of thought and action: A social cognitive theory.* Englewood Cliffs, NJ: Prentice Hall.

Barr, R., & Tagg, J. (1995). From teaching to learning: A new paradigm for undergraduate education. *Change, 27*(6), 12–25.

Dweck, C. S. (2007). *Mindset: The new psychology of success.* New York, NY: Random House.

Hart Research Associates (2013, April 10). *It takes more than a major: Employer priorities for college learning and student success.* Retrieved from https://www.aacu.org/leap/documents/2013_EmployerSurvey.pdf

Kuh, G. J., Kinzie, J., Schuh, J., & Whitt, E. (2010). *Student success in college: Creating conditions that matter.* San Francisco, CA: Jossey-Bass.

Organisation of Economic Cooperation and Development (OECD). (2013) *OECD skills outlook 2013: First results from the survey of adult skills OECD Publishing.* Retrieved from http://skills.oecd.org/documents/OECD_Skills_Outlook_2013.pdf

FOREWORD

I first met Marilee J. Bresciani Ludvik at a seminar in the rain forests of Costa Rica more than 10 years ago. Leaders in the movement to assess student learning had gathered to share experiences in this still-nascent undertaking in higher education to generate momentum for shifting the focus from teaching to the process and impact of students' learning. Since then, I have witnessed the remarkable progression of scholarship and creativity that has characterized Marilee's incredible professional and personal journey. After relocating from Texas A&M University to San Diego State University, her peer-reviewed articles and books on assessing student learning and program review earned her both tenure and the respect of professional peers.

At the same time, in dealing with a number of personal and physical hardships, Marilee turned toward a variety of spiritual disciplines and found they unleashed new forms of energy and creativity outside the normal "respectable" boundaries of higher education. Creating her own foundation (Rushing to Yoga), she began to integrate the alternative disciplines of yoga and mindfulness into the evidence-based practices of academic scholarship.

This book is a realization of Marilee's efforts and those of her colleagues. It is a much-needed and remarkably useful comprehensive approach to whole-person learning. Having the privilege to read a prepublication copy, I am deeply impressed with this first book to integrate the research on neuroscience, student learning, and student (really human) development with mindfulness, compassion, and meditation, which does so in accessible language and with practical applications in mind.

Each chapter is rich with strategies that improve learning and student development, as well as tested practices and exercises to apply the research in a classroom, field experience, cocurricular setting, or even a faculty meeting.

What makes this book so important is its contribution to addressing the deep crisis in education, especially higher education. For the past decade at least, national policy on higher education has focused on improving access, retention and completion, and quality of learning. Each area has spawned its own "expert" and literature, along with practices that might make a difference. As one who headed an institutional accrediting agency where our standards focused on these issues, I know that tremendous energy was placed on responding to external demands for accountability in these areas. Inside institutions of higher education, the focus has been on academic learning, on what is recognized by the academic disciplines as important to know. Moreover, the division of institutions of higher education into disciplines further emphasizes "knowing" as academic. Student services, designed to support students outside the classroom, was intentionally separate and held to a lesser status.

In this environment, both external policy demands and internal organization of colleges and universities left the integration of learning and the integration of personal and academic/professional development to the student. Such integration, unfortunately, happened too often by chance. Both graduates and employers continue to decry the failure of our institutions to develop the whole person; to integrate creating with "knowing"; and to help students develop the emotional and intellectual tools to handle stress, find balance, and respond to the daily challenges of their multidimensional lives. All of these tools are critical necessities to thrive in the face of the dramatically changing workplace and social context of our changing world.

In conversations with hundreds of faculty members over the years about these challenges, even the most eager to integrate emotional and intellectual development ask for effective, evidence-based tools to use in their classrooms, cocurricular settings, and student mentoring experiences. This book provides a compendium of tools for personal and spiritual development of students as much as intellectual development, and each chapter demonstrates how inner development strengthens both intellectual development and outer performance.

All of us who serve in an educational role are models to our students and our colleagues in what we do and what we say. The tools for fostering mindfulness and other desired outcomes described in this book are equally applicable for faculty, staff, and administrators in fulfilling responsibilities to develop future leaders, global citizens, and compassionate human beings. The tools are also applicable to how we treat one another in the academy; for example, how we organize and conduct meetings, undertake academic and strategic planning, and so on. In other words, the tools offered in this book are as much for us as for our students.

I urge you to dive into this book at multiple points—to use the chapters of greatest interest and applicability in your work and to consider those chapters outside your normal frame of reference to see how they can contribute to rounding out your own and your students' development. It is worth the effort and the challenge—and the results, as reflected throughout the book are demonstrable.

Ralph Wolff, JD
Former President, Western Association for Colleges and Schools, Inc.
Ralph Wolff Strategic Consulting and Accreditation Reform

ACKNOWLEDGMENTS

A book like this doesn't come together overnight. It takes a courageous publisher willing to go out on a limb and share emerging research and resulting concepts and ideas that challenge the status quo. Thank you so much John von Knorring for providing me with the opportunity, your trust, and the creative autonomy to work with such a diverse group of authors in order to invite potential innovative solutions into our current state of higher education.

A book like this also doesn't come together without an amazing support network. In addition to all those who contributed to writing these chapters, I thank all those who offered instrumental support in the background. The most concerning part of offering specific gratitude is knowing that many names will be missed, many who encouraged me to make more sense of germinating ideas, and many who challenged me to gather additional data, as well as to take time to step away from the data and move from a place of intuition. Thank you, Linda Abruzzini, Suzi Batchelor Adams, Jo Allen, Mary Allen, James Anderson, Trudy Banta, Elsa Billings, Karen Black, Melanie Booth, Pat Brady, Dean Bresciani, Marie and Bill Bresciani, John Brown, Linda Bussell, Marva Cappello, Alicia Chávez, Thomas Conway, Natasha Croom, Elizabeth Dale, Deanna Dannells, Jody Donovan, Amy Driscoll, Jeremy Dunworth, Judith Eaton, Doug Eder, Melissa Eisler, Shannon Ellis, Lisa Erwin, Peter Ewell, Jane Fried, Matthew Fuller, Jamie Gallant, Tricia Bertram Gallant, Megan Moore Gardner, Suzanne Gordon, Frank Harris III, Francie Harvey, Gavin Henning, Sara Henry, Joseph Hoey, John and Joy Hoffman, Peg Jablonski, Kendra and Jay Jeffcoat, Joe Johnson, Chris Jones, Jillian Kinzie, Kimberly Kline, Dan and Susan Krick, Paula and Jim Krist, Kevin Kruger, George Kuh, Sharon LaVoy, Susan Longerbeam, Patrick Love, Marcia Baxter Magolda, Peggy Maki, Sherry Mallory, Kathleen Manning, Fred and Cheryl McFarlane, Larry and Judy Moneta, Megan Oakleaf, Minah Oh, Eric Ono, Jessica Oyler, Lori Pettigrew, Mike and Megan Policky, Kimberlee Pottberg, Terrel Rhodes, Larry Roper, Lynn Russell, Caren Sax, John Schuh, Geoff Scott, SDSU ARPE Department team, SDSU Interwork Institute team, Karen and Joey Sedtal, Tom Shandley, Barb Snyder, Sharon Sprei, Linda Suskie, Cynthia Uline, Lauren Weiner Vaknin, Hayley Weddle,

Dan Welch, Jane Wiese, and all of you who sent encouraging e-mails, notes, and phone calls. Thank you. Thank you. Thank you.

Thank you to the teachers (especially the ones who were enrolled as "my students") who were instrumental in discovering that the mind is much more than a brain and an intellect. Thank you for helping me realize the mind is something much more messy and profound and to consider that when we take into account the measurement of learning and development. Thank you 2013 SDSU EdD cohort, Baron Baptiste and Master Teachers, Peter Bonanno, Kelly Boys, Tom Callanan, Cara Carillo, the Chopra Center for Well-Being instructors, Mark Coleman, David Conde, Core Power Yoga instructors, Victoria Couch, Laura Delizona, Amy Driscoll, Rich Fernandez, Mario Galaretta, Leslieanne Gelles, Philippe Goldin, Caro Hart, Nan Herron, Steve Hickman, Chang Yi (Lillian) Hsiang, Infineight (2014 SDSU EdD cohort), INIQ participants, Hooria Jazaieri, Cyd Jenefsky, David Ji, Dorothy Knoll, Lindsey Kugel, Jon Kabat-Zinn, Jan and Nick Kuncl, Marc Lesser, Megan Leuchers, Meg Levie, Mark Levine, Danny Lewin, Elizabeth Ludvik, George A. and Julie Ludvik and family, Vanda Marlow, Mark McGinley, Oli Mittermaier, Simon Moyes, Jessica Hickmott Oyler, Wiveka Ramel, Deborah Rana, Dave and Bonnie Rech, Cailin Bloese Robinson, Penny Rue, Kat Ryan, Saki Santorelli, Lori Schwanbeck, Shauna Shapiro, Carol Smith, Tempel Smith, Spirit Rock Insight Meditation faculty, Chade Meng Tan, Cynthia Ludvik Truckenbrod and family, the University of California–San Diego (UCSD) Center for Mindfulness instructors, Bill Weller, Kelly Werner, Jan Winniford, Ralph Wolff, and especially all the Search Inside Yourself Leadership Institute (SIYLI) team and teachers in training.

I thank my rock and foundation and ever-consistent role model for mindfulness and unconditional love, Robert. Your encouragement, commitment to additional household chores, and driving to and fro opened up the time to complete this project that you knew was so important to my heart. Thank you.

Thank you to Thomas Van Vleet, PhD, the neuroscientist from Brain Plasticity Institute at Posit Science, who was extremely generous with his time and ensured we weren't overgeneralizing or misrepresenting findings.

Thank you also to Mark Baxter, PhD, professor of neuroscience from the Icahn School of Medicine at Mount Sinai, for your expert review and for ensuring we weren't overgeneralizing or misrepresenting findings. We can't thank you enough for the generous gift of your time.

Thank you to SDSU doctoral students for their formatting work. Michelle Vogel Trautt, Charles Iyoho, and Michael McHan, thank you for helping me pull this book together and for your wisdom in technical editing and formatting. Thank you, also, Charles, for verifying original citations and helping collect author bios and contracts. Michelle, thank you for your generous gift of time in final formatting and for being a shining light throughout this process. And thank you to Victoria Couch for the final assistance with the last chapter to make sure this book could be useful. I am deeply grateful to you all.

Thank you especially to each of the amazing authors, who serve as friends, colleagues, acquaintances, and my teachers. Please be sure to consult the editor and contributors section in the back of the book to learn more about these amazing human beings.

PREFACE

Marilee J. Bresciani Ludvik

Is higher education preparing our students for a world that is increasingly complex and volatile, one in which they will have to contend with uncertainty and ambiguity? Are we addressing the concerns of employers who complain that graduates do not possess the creative, critical thinking, and communication skills needed in the workplace? In the face of the evidence that our colleges and universities are failing at precisely these preparations, this book not only harnesses what we have learned from innovations in teaching but also offers intentional out-of-classroom experiences, along with emerging neuroscience, to transform how we deliver and create new knowledge, and indeed transform our students, developing their capacities for adaptive boundary spanning.

Starting from the premise that our current linear, course-based educational practices are frequently at odds with how our neurological systems facilitate learning and personal development, the authors of *The Neuroscience of Learning and Development* set out an alternative model that emphasizes a holistic approach to education that integrates mindful inquiry practice with self-authorship and the regulation of emotion as the cornerstones of learning, while demonstrating how these align with the latest discoveries in neuroscience. This book challenges all of us in higher education to move away from the degree (made up of a combination of several courses and an accumulation of credit hours) as the commodity of higher education to focus on the learning and development process itself as the primary commodity that we organize ourselves around.

This book presents the science that informs key learning and development constructs plausibly missing from today's educational systems. In addition, this book presents the science that informs the practice of compassion and peace—the science that explains the very real benefits of intentional movement and mindful inquiry. It demonstrates their application to the classroom and to the cocurriculum, and their implications for the administrative leaders who make the decisions that affect student learning; student development; and the environment within which faculty, administrators, and students reside.

Neuroscience experts, learning and development theory experts, and health practitioners outline their research and insights into how providing seemingly unintellectual learning and development opportunities for students actually stimulates portions of the brain that are needed for students to become adaptive problem solvers; creators of knowledge; and effective, compassionate social collaborators who promote the responsible use of resources to enhance sustainable change.

The book closes by offering practical ideas for implementation, showing how simple refinements in classroom and cocurricular experiences can create foundations for students to develop key skills that will enhance adaptive problem solving; creativity; overall well-being; innovation; resilience; compassion; and, ultimately, world peace.

Introduction: Rethinking How We Design, Deliver, and Evaluate Higher Education

Many recent discoveries in neuroscience are affirming some things we knew to be true about how the brain functions, while simultaneously causing us to rethink how the brain learns and develops. These neuroscience discoveries affirm much of the previous research about how to improve student success. Other discoveries cause us to question some fundamental infrastructure design for student success. In this introduction, Marilee J. Bresciani Ludvik posits the question of whether higher education is actually organized in alignment with how the brain best learns and develops. This introduction sets the stage for what follows in this book: detailed discussions of specific practices, along with the neuroscience that informs them, that can be used to significantly improve the quality of holistic student learning and development in higher education while remaining committed to access, equity, and student success.

Chapter 1: Basic Brain Parts and Their Functions

In this chapter, authors Matthew R. Evrard, Jacopo Annese, and Marilee J. Bresciani Ludvik focus on what they understand to be true about the related functional areas of specific portions of the brain important in learning and development. Mark Baxter and Thomas Van Vleet provide review. The chapter highlights the intricacies of the brain, the interrelatedness of the brain areas, and where we currently understand key aspects of learning and development to take place.

Chapter 2: Unpacking Neuroplasticity and Neurogenesis

Matthew R. Evrard and Marilee J. Bresciani Ludvik examine neuroplasticity and neurogenesis in this chapter with review by Thomas Van Vleet. The authors highlight how changeable the connections in the brain are and emphasize the researched strategies that illustrate what we understand about our ability to intentionally change certain portions of the brain.

Chapter 3: Strategies That Intentionally Change the Brain

In this chapter, with review by Thomas Van Vleet, authors Marilee J. Bresciani Ludvik, Matthew R. Evrard, and Phillipe Goldin discuss the clinical research that highlights brain plasticity and its relevance to student learning and development. They also discuss emerging studies that provide the authors with an understanding of how educators can intentionally change the brain in manners that may heighten student learning and development. This chapter further discusses the importance of developing body awareness and compassion as key concepts in enhancing desired student learning and development outcomes.

Chapter 4: (Re)Conceptualizing Meaning Making in Higher Education: A Case for Integrative Educational Encounters That Prepare Students for Self-Authorship

Emily Marx and Lisa Gates introduce the theory of self-authorship as a theoretical learning and developmental building block for supporting students' ability to integrate their internal voices in learning and developmental contexts in higher education. The theory of self-authorship is unpacked in a manner that illustrates the importance of students' self-awareness and its relevance to their ability to learn, develop, and thrive in educational experiences. The chapter offers suggestions for promoting self-authorship in both academic and student affairs contexts and explores its relationship to enhancing students' holistic learning and critical thinking.

Chapter 5: Intentional Design of High-Impact Experiential Learning

Patsy Tinsley McGill uses James Zull's work to align neuroscience with high-impact experiential learning practices. She uses data from her research on capstone experiences to illustrate how experiential learning connects with specific learning and development theories to illustrate practical implications for enhancing overall student success.

Chapter 6: Enhancing Well-Being and Resilience

Resilience and well-being remain critical concerns of higher education faculty and administrators. Christine L. Hoey discusses the interrelationship of neuroscience with specific strategies that can be used to enhance well-being, and their potential to promote resilience, creativity, critical thinking, and several other learning and development outcomes.

Chapter 7: Enhancing Creativity

Creativity remains a desired outcome for employers who recognize that simple knowledge acquisition will not create the problem solvers needed today, let alone address the seen and unforeseen complex social, economic, and environmental problems we are facing in the future. Shaila Mulholland discusses the interrelationship of neuroscience with specific strategies that can be used to enhance creativity and foster critical thinking.

Chapter 8: Enhancing Compassion and Empathy

This chapter defines *empathy* and *compassion* and explains the underlying neuroscience of such characteristics. Sarah Schairer, educated at Stanford University's Compassion Cultivation Training Program, explains how compassion can be taught to undergraduates, graduates, faculty, and staff and further explains the importance of the practice of compassion to advancing higher education outcomes.

Chapter 9: Balance Begets Integration: Exploring the Importance of Sleep, Movement, and Nature

In this chapter, physician Bruce Bekkar offers considerations on how an individual's desire for life balance can be achieved by attending to the natural world and intentionally engaging all regions of the brain. Bekkar discusses how the typical student's and educator's persistent imbalance in brain function results paradoxically in a loss of creativity, problem-solving skills, and overall well-being. Numerous strategies are suggested to restore a more holistic, integrated distribution of brain function, including engagement with nature. Emerging research validating these concepts is cited.

Chapter 10: Enhancing and Evaluating Critical Thinking Dispositions and Holistic Student Learning and Development Through Integrative Inquiry

This chapter explores methodologies used to enhance and evaluate the efficacy of critical thinking as well as many of the proposed learning and development methodologies posited in this book. Using mindfulness methodology and mindful inquiry as a foundation, Marilee J. Bresciani Ludvik, Philippe Goldin, Matthew R. Evrard, J. Luke Wood, Wendy Bracken, Charles Iyoho, and Mark Tucker introduce a way to organize and evaluate these methodologies into something they call integrative inquiry (INIQ). INIQ uses what we know (intellect), what we sense (body), and what we don't know (curiosity) to deepen the inquiry process while embracing ambiguity, thus fostering critical thinking dispositions.

Chapter 11: Mindfulness at Work in Higher Education Leadership: From Theory to Practice Within the Classroom and Across the University

In this chapter, the reader discovers how implementing previous chapters' practices for attending to our lives moment by moment can afford us some of our most creative and productive experiences. In addition, authors Les P. Cook and Anne Beffel illustrate how to develop integrated mindfulness practices to create a compassionate campus culture where colleagues and students find the space they need to recognize themselves and their connectedness to the world they help steward.

Chapter 12: A Mindful Approach to Navigating Strategic Change

In this chapter, Laurie J. Cameron provides the reader with mindful change management methodology to move the ideas presented in this book into practice. How can leadership adopt those ideas and garner organizational buy-in? How does leadership embody the principles represented in this book as it manages organization change? This chapter addresses many of these concepts in a dynamic and strategic manner.

Afterword: Adoption, Adaptation, and Transformation

In this afterword, Marilee J. Bresciani Ludvik focuses on a summary of the key findings in this book in a manner that provides practical considerations for faculty, student affairs practitioners, academic support administrators, and other organizational leaders as they seek to adopt and adapt this research to transform their design, delivery, and evaluation of higher education to impact desirable outcomes in higher education.

INTRODUCTION

Rethinking How We Design, Deliver, and Evaluate Higher Education

Marilee J. Bresciani Ludvik

We can't solve problems by using the same kind of thinking that created them.

—Albert Einstein (www.brainyquote.com/quotes/quotes/a/alberteins385842.html)

Higher education in America is in crisis. Many thoughtful scholars have already offered explanations as to why we are in this state, providing tools to manage and solve the crisis we are in and guide us toward potential solutions (Blumenstyk, 2014; Bok, 2013; Mettler, 2014; Stevens & Kirst, 2015). This book is not intended to rehash the causes of the crisis in American higher education. Rather, by bringing to bear what we know about emerging findings from neuroscience, this book invites us to redesign how we deliver and evaluate student learning and development and, in doing so, transform higher education.

Recent discoveries in neuroscience are reaffirming some things we knew to be true about how the brain functions while also causing us to rethink how we approach learning and development. Such discoveries affirm what previous research showed us to be true about how to improve student success. Other discoveries cause us to question the fundamental infrastructure and design of education (Bok, 2013). In this introduction, and in the rest of the chapters in this book, we posit the question of whether higher education is actually organized and designed in the manner that the brain learns and develops best. Affirming that online learning knowledge acquisition is a low-cost and effective strategy for short-term memorization,

1

we suggest that what is really being called for in American higher education requires something far greater than knowledge acquisition that resides in short-term memory, whether that knowledge is delivered in a cost-effective online format, in a face-to-face modality, or something in between. We suggest that resources need to be reallocated to implement discursive, interactive inquiry and to implement holistic developmental exercises that have progressively been abandoned as enrollment grew in American higher education colleges and universities (Bok, 2013). This introduction sets the stage for what follows in this book—detailed discussions of specific practices and the neuroscience that informs them that can be used to redesign higher education delivery and significantly improve the quality of holistic student learning and development while remaining committed to access, equity, affordability, and student success.

Student Success Knowns

Thanks to many amazing researchers, we know a lot about student success in regard to student persistence and degree completion. For brevity's sake, here we share only a few citations for each recognized and evidence-based student success strategy. For example, we understand that student success is evident when students become integrated into the college's social and academic culture (A. Astin, 1993; Schlossberg, 1989; Tinto, 1975), and when the institutional environment and/or commitment of the institution's leadership to students' success is well matched with student characteristics and the commitment of students to their own success (Tinto, 1987). This may also be known as *person–environment fit* (Martin & Swartz-Kulstad, 2000; Pervin, 1968, 1989; Walsh, Craik, & Price, 2000).

We see student success when students' beliefs and attitudes about their ability to succeed exist (Bean, 1980); perhaps this state could also be known as *academic self-efficacy* (Bandura, 1989; Lent, Brown, & Larkin, 1986; Multon, Brown, & Lent, 1991; Richardson, Abraham, & Bond, 2012; Robbins et al., 2004; Schunk, 1983). When students' and institutional members' expectations for students' success align (Kuh, 2003; Rendon, 1994; Solorzano, Ceja, & Yosso, 2000) and students believe that their success is based on their dedication and hard work, evidence of their accomplishments is also seen (Dweck, 2007; Lebow, 1993; Murphy & Thomas, 2008; Sassenberg & Moskowitz, 2005).

The extent and effectiveness of students' academic, social, and financial support (Bowles & Jones, 2003; Sanford, 1966; Schlossberg, 1989), as well as the extent to which students are academically prepared, contribute to success (Kuh, Kinzie, Buckley, Bridges, & Hayek, 2007). In addition, the extent to which institutional leaders use evidence of student and organizational learning to improve student success (Angelo & Cross, 1993; Barr & Tagg, 1995) plays a key role.

We understand that different parts of the brain may be ready to learn at different times (National Research Council [NRC], 2000; Zull, 2011). In addition, the quality of the information to which one is exposed and the actual experience of learning may increase the capacity of the brain to learn (NRC, 2000; Zull, 2011). We have evidence that deep learning occurs through integration of new information via the senses, meaning-making processes, idea generation, and action (Carey, 2014; Zull, 2011). As such, engaging in high-impact practices such as service-learning, community-based learning, writing-intensive courses, research with faculty, collaborative assignments and projects, learning communities, first-year seminars and experiences, study abroad and diversity/global learning experiences, internships, common intellectual experiences, and capstone courses and projects appears to lead to greater student success (Kuh, 2008; Kuh, Kinzie, Schuh, & Whitt, 2010).

If we were to summarize all this student success research into one sentence, perhaps it would be the following: Deep learning and development requires the full engagement of the whole learner along with all those fostering the intended learning and development. While this is not a new discovery, the question remains: How well have we applied the aforementioned research into the design of what we do for students who choose to enroll in our institutions?

While we have examples upon examples of how this research has been implemented piecemeal in specific areas within higher education institutions (Brownell & Swaner, 2009, 2012; Kelly, 2012; Kuh, 2008; McNair & Albertine, 2012), we have few examples of how this research has been embraced holistically or systematically across departmental units within institutions (Hatch, 2012). For example, individual two- and four-year institutions have evidence that high-impact practices implemented in specific programs for a subset of their students advances student success. However, we don't have many examples of institutions embracing student success practices across programs of all types. Furthermore, collectively, we know very little about how implementing this research impacts direct student learning and development (Brownell & Swaner, 2009; Kuh, 2008). The most seemingly direct evidence we have about what students are learning from their higher education experience comes from a controversial study by Arum and Roksa (2011).

Arum and Roksa (2011) examined survey responses, transcripts, and results from the Collegiate Learning Assessment (a standardized test taken in the first semester and at the end of a student's second and fourth year) of more than 2,300 undergraduates at 24 institutions. Their results attracted national attention when they reported that in the first two years of an undergraduate's education, 45% of students showed no significant improvement in critical thinking, analytical reasoning, problem solving, and written communication skills. After four years, 36% still showed no improvement; however, there were greater gains for students enrolled in liberal arts. While some have rather optimistically questioned their methodology, another study that used well-respected methodology produced results as disappointing.

In 2013, the Survey of Adult Skills (PIAAC), an international survey sponsored by the Organisation for Economic Co-operation and Development (OECD), was administered to adults currently residing in each participating country who held bachelor's degrees from tertiary-type A and research programs. The survey is a direct assessment of literacy, numeracy, and problem-solving skills and has not yet been methodologically challenged.

The findings are noteworthy and humbling. While the United States ranks much higher internationally in the proportion of 25- to 34-year-olds with tertiary attainment (bachelor's degrees) than any other country in the world, the level of proficiency in literacy and numeracy of this population does not. In short, the United States of America is significantly below the world average in numeracy, literacy, and problem-solving skills (OECD, 2013). The OECD findings further revealed that social background has a major impact on literacy skills. Thus, the OECD findings call us to not only improve world literacy, numeracy, and problem solving—reporting that these are key skills for enhancing global economic well-being—but also focus on developing social outcomes such as trust, service (volunteering), political efficacy, health, and overall well-being, which are expected to reduce social background barriers and thus enhance global literacy.

While formal education plays a key role in developing foundation skills, there is more to the learning journey (NRC, 2000). The Survey of Adult Skills reported, "Much of learning takes place outside formal education . . . such as within the family, workplace, and through self-directed individual activity. For skills to retain their value, they must be continuously developed throughout life" (OECD, 2013, p. 34). This statement reinforces what our aforementioned student success research already illustrates as true, namely that students must be dynamically and holistically engaged in their learning journey for any knowledge acquisition to have lasting value. If we know this to be true, why are we significantly trailing behind? Are we delivering the kind of learning and development that is not lasting or is not desired?

Employers' Demands for Student Success

In a survey (Hart Research Associates, 2013) commissioned by the Association of American Colleges and Universities (AAC&U), data illustrated employers' demand for similar kinds of learning and development that were reported as necessary by the OECD. In this study, 95% of employers surveyed reported that they give hiring preference to college graduates with skills that enabled them to contribute to innovation in the workplace. Furthermore, 93% of employers surveyed stated that demonstrated capacities for students to think critically, communicate clearly, and solve complex problems are more important than a candidate's undergraduate major. Table I.1 illustrates the percentage of employers who want colleges and universities to place more emphasis on each specific area of learning and development.

TABLE I.1
AAC&U 2013 Employers Survey Data by Hart Research Associates

Learning Outcome Demanded	Percentage of 2013 Employers Demanding More Emphasis on the Outcome	Percentage of 2009 Employers Demanding More Emphasis on the Outcome
Critical thinking and analytical reasoning skills	82	81
Ability to analyze and solve complex problems	81	75
Ability to effectively communicate orally and in writing	80	89
Ability to apply knowledge and skills to real-world settings	78	79
Ability to innovate and be creative	71	70
Teamwork skills and ability to collaborate with others in diverse group settings	67	71
Ability to connect choices and actions to ethical decisions	64	75

The takeaway from this opinion survey is that those who employ American college graduates want higher education faculty and administrators to emphasize specific skills and abilities to a much greater extent than we currently are. While this same survey reported that the majority of employers indicated that having field-specific knowledge and skills is important for success, few employers believed that gaining field-specific knowledge and skills is most needed for college graduates' success; the ability to reason and apply and transfer knowledge to new circumstances is more critical for success in any industry, including graduate school.

All this begs the question: If we have research that tells us how we can enhance student success and we have data that inform us that we are not meeting learning and development expectations of employers and other constituents, what are we missing?

What we are discovering in neuroscience is that the way we are organized to deliver learning and development within higher education is frequently at odds with how our neurological system facilitates the learning and development process. It is now an accepted fact that the brain is designed for boundary spanning and is highly interconnective (Kaku, 2014). Our brain—which extends beyond the neural networks housed in our cranium to include all of our senses (we will also explain this in greater detail in Chapters 2 and 3)—is a dynamic learning machine (Alvarez & Emory, 2006; Chan, Shum, Toulopoulou, & Chen, 2008; Chiesa, Calati, & Serretti, 2011; Goldin & Gross, 2010; Hölzel et al., 2011; Kozasa et al., 2012; Lutz, Slagter, Dunne, & Davidson, 2008; Todd, Cunningham, Anderson, & Thompson, 2012). However, if we don't use our brain in ways that align with its dynamic structure and functions, it is unlikely we will see evidence of that use in any learning and development data we collect.

Many effective classroom pedagogies have been developed and adopted by several faculty members because educators know, intuitively, that the brain (the whole person) needs to be actively engaged to ensure the kinds of application of learning that employers expect to see. While certainly not all-inclusive, a brief summary of some of these pedagogies can be found in Table I.2.

If these pedagogies have been shown to produce the types of learning and development that employers desire, why, as a nation, do we still appear to be struggling? Why wouldn't we just invite all faculty members to adopt these pedagogies and then see a significant improvement in learning and development? Neuroscience sheds some light on a possible answer. However, before we get further into the neuroscience, we need a little higher education history.

TABLE I.2

Effective Classroom Pedagogies

Pedagogy	Definition	Helpful Citation to Learn More	Theory
Inquiry-based learning	Uses questions, problems, or scenarios, and learner develops own knowledge and solutions	Bruner (1961)	Constructivist; Piaget, Dewey, Vygotsky, and Freire
Problem-based learning	Uses student-centered pedagogy in which students learn about subjects through the experience of problem solving	Barrows (1996)	Constructivist; Dewey
Service-learning	Combines classroom instruction with community service	Eyler and Giles (2007)	Progressivism and pragmatism; Dewey and William James
Team-based learning	Uses learning teams to enhance students' engagement and learning and development	Michaelsen, Knight, and Fink, (2002)	Constructivist; Dewey
Flipped classrooms	Applies blended learning where knowledge acquisition is done online and application of knowledge is completed in a facilitated classroom learning experience	Bergmann and Sams (2012)	Constructivist; Dewey, Kolb, Lewin, and Piaget
Experiential learning	Makes meaning of learning from direct experience	Kolb (1984)	Constructivist; Dewey, Kolb, Lewin, and Piaget
Self-regulated learning	Requires taking control of and evaluating one's own learning and behavior	Nilson (2013)	Constructivist; social cognition, metacognition
Contemplative learning	Uses introspection and reflection to guide learning and development	Barbezat and Bush (2014)	Constructivist; metacognition

A Brief Higher Education History Lesson

Since the creation of the first university in Bologna in 1088, faculty members have been delivering lectures to students to promote student learning and development (Colish, 1997). However, we lost a key aspect of this "lecture" process when transferring it to present-day American higher education: the dynamic, interactive ways in which learning and development were reinforced. The student–faculty relationship spanned boundaries. Students and faculty did not confine learning or the reinforcement of the learning to the classroom (Rüegg, 2003). Dynamic learning conversations carried into the streets and the local pubs and markets, and the students themselves were key in evaluating one another's learning as well as in reinforcing and generating learning (Cohen & Kisker, 2010; Thelin, 2004). Learning was dynamic, interactive, and holistically apparent in all facets of a student's life.

In the United States, Harvard, our first college, was founded in 1636 ("Historical Facts," n.d.). As early as the colonial period (1636–1789), classroom recitations and oral disputations that were critically evaluated by fellow students, as well as the master teacher, were primary learning and development tools (Cohen & Kisker, 2010; Thelin, 2004, p. 18). Learning and its application were not confined to the classroom. This appeared to continue into the 1830s when Bennet introduced the notion of applied experience of learning as opposed to simply completing a prescribed course (Thelin, 2004).

The year 1889 saw an increase in large classrooms and a decrease of discussion (Thelin, 2004). This accelerated in the 1960s combined with the construction of large lecture halls (Cohen & Kisker, 2010; Thelin, 2004). Mass delivery of higher education continued into the 1970s, where the lecture form of knowledge acquisition took precedence over classroom teaching. The tightening economy and the growth of enrollment required higher education leaders to increase the number of students in each lecture and manage the entire delivery of learning through the course (Cohen & Kisker, 2010). Learning reinforced by out-of-classroom debates declined, or was delegated to student affairs or academic support units. As enrollment grew and the faculty-to-student ratio grew as well, informal collegial interaction between students and faculty appeared impossible, except within institutions that still valued those types of interactions, such as the liberal arts institutions or institutions with a heavy liberal arts emphasis.

To manage such immense enrollment growth, the course became the vehicle to organize higher education. In essence, the course became the driver of American higher education. A student had to have a certain amount of courses to get a degree. Grades for each course made up students' cumulative grade point averages, which allowed students to stay enrolled until they earned a degree or be placed on probation. Tuition was set based on numbers of units of which each course consisted and how many courses students were enrolled in per term. Financial aid was considered based on the number of courses students were enrolled in each term. Faculty workloads were categorized by courses taught or courses bought out by grants or contracts. Funding to institutions was based on full-time equivalent enrollment, which was calculated by students' course load each term. The course became the unit of organization—the unit on which to base the initial cost of attendance and the unit in which funding would be given to the institution. And the course is the unit that determines whether a degree is granted.

Enshrining course credit as the measure of American higher education has made it difficult for online learning to alleviate costs of higher education. Evidence of the effectiveness of distance learning was documented as early as the 1840s, when Pittman engaged students in shorthand classes via the postal service (Tait, 1996). The movement to online learning took a while longer, but by 1994, web-based delivery had begun and would soon be followed by more structured approaches using course management systems (Graziadei, 1996). Graziadei illustrated that online learning was intended to enhance the teaching–learning communication experience, almost serving as a surrogate for the out-of-classroom experience. Nonetheless, the course remained in the driver's seat perhaps because in order to get students to participate in online discussions, the online discussion assignment had to become a part of the course assignment (Graziadei, 1996).

In emphasizing the course credit model, the attainment of a course-by-course, credit-hour-generated degree became the commodity. In exchange for the selection of the course around which to organize the commodity of a degree, we lost sight of the process of student learning and development. This may explain why all of our research on student success and all of our effective classroom pedagogies aren't being taken up by the masses, thus moving the needle of aggregate improved student learning and development. Emphasis on designing and delivering education based on the course—a commodity that can be bought and traded from one institution to another—may mean a loss of practice of holistic learning and development.

Consider for a moment that it isn't the class that we need to be organized around; it is the process of learning and development that we need to focus on. What would higher education look like if we shifted to the process as the commodity? What would it look like if we, as Petrie (2014) prodded, "a) focused more on development and less on content, b) made the development and the work inseparable, c) created strong developmental networks, and d) made development a process not an event" (p. 5)? Certainly, this is what competency-based education intends to do; however, most of these competency-based conversations to date are still course credit hour or clock hour driven. How could no longer focusing on organizing ourselves around a class be supported by neuroscience?

Finally, the Neuroscience

From neuroscience, we gain a key element for advancing student success. Also from neuroscience, we get a clue into the formula for redesigning higher education as we better understand what is involved in and how to change the structure and function of the brain. The details of this will be introduced in Chapters 1 through 3, so, for now, know that the field of neuroscience has shown us that what we pay attention to literally changes the structure and function of certain portions of our brain (Alvarez & Emory, 2006; Chan et al., 2008; Chiesa et al., 2011; Goldin & Gross, 2010; Hölzel et al., 2011; Kozasa et al., 2012; Lazar et al., 2005; Lutz et al., 2008; Todd et al. 2012). Assuming students can manage their attention on demand, we know that asking students to focus on their learning one class at a time without creating opportunities for them to make connections in what they are learning across courses (e.g., connecting identity development in one course to stress management in another) reinforces students not making the neural connections that are imperative to their success. Thus, we should not be surprised to see that the learning and development we intentionally delivered and evaluated in a segmented manner is not evident in application at the end of their academic career (whether that academic career lasts for two years or more than six).

As human beings, we can focus on only one thing at a time (Orr & Weissman, 2009; Rubinstein, Meyer, & Evans, 2001; Weissman, Gopalakrishnan, Hazlett, & Woldorff, 2005; Weissman, Perkins, & Woldorff, 2008). The ability to successfully span our attention rests in our capacity to move our attention from one task to another swiftly and effectively while making connections to the important patterns needed for innovative problem solving or whatever it is we are being asked to do (Carp, Fitzgerald, Taylor, & Weissman, 2012; Carp, Kim, Taylor, Fitzgerald, & Weissman, 2010). We now understand that we can train this kind of attention in ourselves and in our students.

If we create a linear learning environment where students are focusing on one course, then another, and then another, we are reinforcing the separateness of each course and are reinforcing these types of neural pathways in their brains (keep in mind that we are using Dan Siegel's [2007] definition of the *brain*, which considered it to include much more than the mass of neural connections located in the cranium and involved all senses). What if, instead, we ensured that students knew how to direct their attention on demand? And then what if we offered specific learning and development opportunities in class and outside class that guide students to make connections between the subject matter provided to the real world, so they could solve wicked problems and do so while paying attention to who they are, what they believe, and what they value? If we create the process for learning and development that fosters reinforcing neural connections that promote students' critical thinking, creativity, analytical reasoning, and peaceful communications (Ingalhalikar et al., 2014), we may be able to "deliver" the kinds of learning and development that employers and others demand. And if we do shift the design and delivery of higher education, what would evaluation look like?

Measuring Holistic Learning and Development

In Figure I.1, we depict a linear student learning and development experience. In this figure, you will note that students have a point of entry into their higher education experience—whatever that is for each student and each type of institution. We can gather a number of preassessment inputs to gain an idea of how well students are prepared for the experience that we have designed for them. That set of preassessment information or inputs can be used to predict students' success or used for us (particularly student affairs professionals and academic support professionals who are specifically educated for such processes) to coach the student toward a more customized learning and development experience given what we know about the student's cognitive and noncognitive preparation to learn.

In Figure I.1, we illustrate that in most cases we expect students to create an integrated learning experience where they are enrolling in courses by semesters, quarters, each month, or every four or six weeks, and gaining

Figure I.1 Linear student learning and development experience.

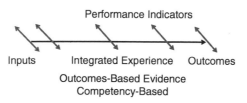

any out-of-classroom experiences that may enhance their learning. Often, however, our design of the connectedness of in-class and out-of-classroom learning experiences is not intentional. We may intentionally design a set of out-of-classroom experiences, but we don't intentionally connect them to linear in-class experiences. While we offer plenty of information to students on how to access those out-of-classroom experiences, we really expect the student to figure out the connections between in-class and out-of-class experiences.

Many institutions do not prescribe a set of out-of-classroom experiences to intentionally complement or enhance in-class experiments (whether online or face-to-face) unless students are enrolled in a specific program that does prescribe out-of-classroom experiences. Those types of prescribed out-of-classroom experiences usually cover only the first term or first year of the students' experience. There are, of course, institutions that are taking that first-year experience into the second year, but very few intentionally design a fully integrated learning and development experience across in-class and out-of-class experiences for the entire development process of the learner.

If we are able to provide guidance to the student, we may not be able to provide financial support for them to engage in the out-of-class experience. Or, my personal favorite, if they have an amazing opportunity to spend a term or another term in apprenticeship, we may not be able to arrange it for them because they already enrolled in one internship and another would increase their time to degree, a performance indicator for which there are heavy penalties for not meeting stated expectations.

Often, we don't have the institutional capacity within divisions of student affairs or academic support units to assist in the kind of advising or coaching that would allow a fully integrated model to be implemented across all the types of students on our campuses and across all the types of learning and development experiences that are possible (albeit virtual or brick and mortar). Furthermore, students are often separated academically from one another. They are not progressing together in their courses and assisting each other in order to integrate the meaning from their courses with the meaning of their lives. To progress together, the academic program must be designed such that a cohort of students proceeds through the prescribed curriculum together, facilitating each other's learning as much as or more than the professors and student affairs and academic support professionals themselves.

Furthermore, we often offer students a menu from which to select a set of courses in certain categories or we offer them a prescribed set of courses to take in each month, quarter, or semester. We advise them on how many units they may need to take in each term (whatever that means to each institution) and perhaps we even tell them when they should enroll in a subset of courses from each menu item type. We offer them complementary experiences outside of the classroom that will surely enhance their learning and we tell them that we are there to help them whenever they need our help. However, the focus on the process of learning is lost because we have scheduled the process into easy-to-manage and perhaps easy-to-evaluate isolated events.

Our biggest challenge with this linear approach is that we are not systematically guiding students in how to make sense of all of these options and how to make meaning of all of these experiences. We are not teaching them how to integrate their in-class experience with their out-of-class experience. Thus, even though we may (a) intentionally design courses with learning outcomes that align to degree-program-learning outcomes, (b) offer out-of-class experiences designed to meet desired learning outcomes, (c) implement reflective student-learning outcomes portfolios that require out-of-classroom artifacts to be collected and reflected on, and (d) place students into cohorts so they progress together through their prescribed sequence of courses, as we have in our degree programs within the department I serve in at San Diego State University, we still see noticeable gaps in employers' desired outcomes for learning and development. Why is that? Perhaps it is because we are fundamentally ignoring the actual process of learning and development. Perhaps it is because we don't train the students prior to their enrollment in how to make the connections for themselves.

Neuroscience has shed light on how the neurological system interwoven throughout one's entire body learns best and on how to create the optimum conditions for learning and development. Our brains (again, we refer to the neural structures that reside outside our cranium as well as within our cranium) are plastic (Hölzel et al., 2011), and the system we have organized to educate our brains is linear—and important to note—so is the system we are using to finance it and hold it accountable to what it produces. Our brains are complex webs of neural connections that change based on where we focus our attention (Hölzel et al., 2011). As such, we are constantly either reinforcing ways of thinking and doing, or rewiring ways of thinking and doing.

Figure I.2 illustrates what the actual student learning and development experience is like. The figure is recreated from a similar image used in Marcia Baxter Magolda's research on self-authorship, which we discuss in Chapter 4.

In essence, in this image, you see that because the student we are enrolling in a term-by-term linear course design is a human being having human experiences, her ability to pay attention and make meaning of her learning and development fluctuates based on what she is paying attention to as a student. In essence, students' learning and development might

Figure I.2 The nonlinear student learning and development experience.

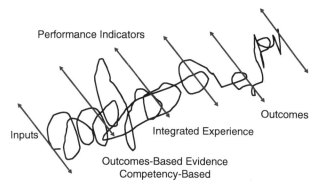

dip because they are experiencing what Baxter Magolda referred to as a "crossroads"; where an individual reaches the point where she understands that there are few absolutes in life and that she has to navigate ambiguity. Self-authorship is the process whereby a person develops the values and internal compass that will enable him or her to deal with life's challenges and deal with new information and ambiguities that may further modify beliefs and information processing. Learning may become evident when students can be focused fully on their studies. It may dip again because they are emotionally or physically distracted or rise again because they are engaged in a high-impact practice. Regardless, if we take a measurement of student success by, say, using standardized tests at a time when a student is experiencing a dip in learning and engagement because of his crossroads experience or something else, he may look as if he hasn't made any gains in his learning. However, if we have embedded the principles of neuroscience into the design of the student's experience, then the student may be able to recognize that he is at a crossroads during the key assessment period and either opt out for another testing time or request another way to demonstrate his learning.

In higher education today, we have organized ourselves so linearly that it seems we have forgotten we are human beings educating human beings. It seems we have spent more time and energy on creating a container (a commodity) that we can manage for the masses, that we forgot to honor what we know to be true about the messy, ambiguous process of human development (our actual commodity). As such, the performance indicators for which our business of higher education holds us accountable for producing are difficult to relate to employers' desired outcomes.

Employers want to see evidence of applied problem-solving skills and abilities, regardless of whether or not a student has a degree. Those holding us accountable have expectations for specific graduation rates. What is the value of a commodity in the form of a higher education credit-hour-accumulated degree if the graduate can't think critically or communicate effectively? The OECD data have already given us that answer. Why is it important to persist consistently through the degree program and in a time frame that is prescribed by government officials when doing so may not be in the best interest for a student's learning and development, let alone her well-being? Why is it important for a student to have a job if he finds no meaning in it and if the company for which he works is not making the world a more sustainable and healthier place to live?

Note that we can still use inputs assessments, reflective student learning experiences, and development portfolios that invite students to upload specific learning and development artifacts from all their learning and development opportunities, including their courses as well as the intentionally designed out-of-classroom experiences in which they are engaging. We can also still invite students to reflect on those experiences and make meaning of them in relationship to their expected degree-program-learning outcomes and their lives' purposes and goals. However, based on neuroscience findings, we must create opportunities for students to learn how to make those connections, to better make meaning out of all their experiences, and to more intentionally facilitate their *process of learning and development.*

Existing research tells us that we can teach students how to regulate stress and other emotions so that they can direct their attention, focus, and other critical thinking dispositions toward enhancing their learning and development. This all empowers the students to (a) demonstrate the expected outcomes employers desire, (b) navigate the ambiguity of applying their learning and developing holistically while requesting assistance when at a crossroads, and (c) collect the evidence that will best illustrate the achievement of employers' expected outcomes. Again, we will discuss how to do all this in greater detail later in the book. For now, we invite you to embrace the notion that the learning and development experience is quite nonlinear, and the way in which we have organized ourselves for students to learn and develop remains linear. We invite you to consider that the course-by-course, credit-hour-accumulated degree has become the commodity of higher education, rather than the process of learning and development itself. Thus, we may find it difficult to break out of the performance indicators for which we are held accountable and that have little to do with actual evidence of student learning and development. Are we able to accept Petrie's challenge—changing our focus from the organized unit of the course to the process of holistic learning and development?

From research on neuroplasticity, we know how we can intentionally change the structure and function of the brain (Hölzel et al., 2011) and we'll discuss this methodology (see mindful inquiry unpacked in Chapter 10) and how it changes the brain in more detail in Chapter 3. For now, suffice it to say that simple, yet not easy, low-cost mind-training methodology that uses focused breathing, focused movement, and other inquiry methods can improve attention (Lutz, et al., 2008; Valentine & Sweet, 1999) and reduce mind wandering (Mrazek, Franklin, Phillips, Baird, & Schooler, 2013). In addition, these training methods are known to improve psychological well-being (Brown & Ryan, 2003) and reduce levels of stress and anxiety (J. Astin, 1997; Jain et al., 2007; Rosenzweig, Reibel, Greeson, Brainard, & Hojat, 2009; Shapiro, Schwartz, & Bonner, 1998), as well as improve cognitive constructs and physiological states (Grossman, Niemann, Schmidt, & Walach, 2004). Use of these training methods has also been known to improve working memory (Mrazek et al., 2013) as well as increase performance on standardized tests (Mrazek et al., 2013). Such practices also increase creativity (Capurso, Fabbro, & Crescentini, 2014; Greenberg, Reiner, & Meiran, 2012; Langer, 2005; Ostafin & Kassman, 2012; Ren et al., 2011), problem-solving skills (Murray & Byrne, 2005; Ren et al., 2011), logic thinking (Ostafin & Kassman, 2012; Ren et al., 2011), and executive functions (Hereen, Van Broeck, & Philippot, 2009; Jha, Krompinger, & Baime, 2007; Moore & Malinowski, 2009; Zeidan, Johnson, Diamond, David, & Goolkasian, 2010).

This discovery provides us with needed information to validate what employers have told us about which applied educational practices they believe will further the outcomes they want to see realized (Hart Research Associates, 2013). Such practices include students developing research questions in their fields of expertise, engaging in evidence-based analyses, completing projects that demonstrate the culmination of their skill sets, and engaging in internships and community projects to gain direct experience, particularly collaborative experience. It also includes their working through ethical issues and debates to form their own judgments about issues at stake. All of this will be helpful in our improving the kinds of learning and development employers expect to see in our graduates, and much of it (as previously mentioned) already exists in individual classes or isolated out-of-class learning experiences.

Our challenge now is to engage students, faculty, and administrators in more conscious efforts to integrate these experiences, while adding a few other experiences that will empower the student to embrace the ambiguity of the learning and development process, rather than clinging to the linear design in which we have conditioned them to participate. In essence, employers of our students are asking us to break out of the linear design of education and implement the research around student success and high-impact practices that we already know to be true (as mentioned earlier in this introduction). When we add neuroscience discoveries to our known research in student success and high-impact practices, we have a path that leads us to the possibility of significantly improving higher education. We have a path that allows us to shift from a series of courses that focus on content to an intentional design of holistic learning and development that focuses on making meaning of applied knowledge, experience, inquiry, and solution exploration.

Contributing Value to the World

While you may be just beginning to see how a deeper understanding of the principles of neuroscience makes us rethink how we would organize the delivery of higher education to advance student learning and development, there is a little more to the story. We have already established that employers want to see better outcomes within the academy. The value of higher education is under question and has been for some time.

News media, such as *USA Today* (St. John, 2013), have reported that "kids are skipping college" because it no longer provides a guarantee of a job and they simply graduate with increased debt for a degree they don't feel they are using. *Forbes* reported in 2012 that 60% of college graduates could not get jobs in their fields (Crotty, 2012). The media has highlighted stories of successful people who have not attended college so often that it motivated people to offer young adults alternatives. Consider the billionaire founder of PayPal, Peter Thiel, who paid 20 young adults $100,000 every year to ensure that they don't go to college. This illustration provides just one example of how the overemphasized focus on collecting a series of courses to mark the achievement of a degree is not valued.

The increasing cost of higher education is also under attack. Organizations such as Harvard, the Khan Academy, and many others are providing online classes for free, allowing easy, accessible, and, in Harvard's case, accredited opportunities for knowledge acquisition. Such free and accessible learning opportunities lead the public to again question why the cost of higher education is so high. If we shift the design of higher education away from considering that the point of a higher education is the attainment of a degree created by collecting several courses (credit hours) with various degrees of content that could and arguably should be provided for free, we would have resources to invest in facilitating the ambiguous, nonlinear process of learning and development. We could also create opportunities, highlighted in this book, that are currently systematically missing from higher education and that are needed in order to engage all aspects of the brain—all aspects of the holistic student learning and development process.

So, to underscore the extent of the social movement away from content and merely amassing commodities that have no meaning, it is not just the value of higher education that is under question with the public. In the context of global sustainability conversations, many are questioning the value that specific companies add to their lives and to the world. Havas Media (2011) conducted a study of consumer engagement that drew on 50,000 consumers in France, Spain, the United Kingdom, Germany, Italy, Mexico, Brazil, Colombia, Chile, Argentina, China, Japan, India, and the United States. The survey results reported "companies that aren't making a difference—to the world and to consumers—aren't going to be around much longer" (Clendaniel, 2011). Since that study was completed in 2011, doors of businesses have been closing annually, and some colleges and universities have been struggling to stay viable. Havas Media consultancy reports that the way to make a difference to the consumer and to the world is to focus on outcomes, rather than outputs. The study further reported that consumers "found that only 20% of the brands they interact with have a positive impact on their lives. And they feel that 70% of brands could disappear entirely without them noticing" (Clendaniel, 2011). Havas Media concluded that the only way a company can thrive is if what it produces has a positive impact on the consumers' lives and on their well-being.

In America, we continue to focus on the way we organize higher education (e.g., the course and clock hours) and on its outputs, such as how many students have graduated and how quickly they have graduated, rather than on the outcomes of what graduates can actually do and who they have become. We focus on the comparable outputs of test scores, rather than on evidence of employers' desired outcomes of students' ability to creatively problem solve, engage in compassionate communication, and embrace ambiguity. We focus on the output of how much our graduates will be earning, rather than how much meaning they are able to make out of what they have learned and how they will apply that to making a difference in the world in which they are working.

The invitation here is to use the principles of neuroscience to consider not only how we are organized within higher education but also how we approach the holistic learning and development process overall. The agricultural and industrial ages have ended, yet we continue to organize and design learning and development opportunities in accordance with those frameworks. Business giants like Bill Ford of Ford Motor Company, Tony Hsieh of Zappos, Chade-Meng Tan of Google, and Jeff Weiner of LinkedIn would argue that the information age and knowledge revolution are in decline and it is time for wisdom and compassion to abound for us to make a difference in businesses, to make a difference in the world, and to create the sustainability so desperately needed to save lives, let alone empower humans to thrive in the world. Using findings from neuroscience, we know now how to better design learning experiences where we can teach students how to access wisdom and compassion to advance knowledge and information and its use (Cozolino, 2014; Hollis-Walker & Colosimo, 2011; Keng, Smoski, Robins, Ekblad, & Brantley, 2012). But to do this, we have to intentionally shift our focus from content and organization around content to organizing ourselves to advance what we know to be true about the process of learning and development. We need to exchange the commodity of a course-by-course, credit-hour-accumulated degree for the commodity of the process of ongoing meaningful learning and development.

In this book, we walk you through the basics of neuroscience to gain an overview of how different parts of the brain interact with other parts of the brain and how that relates to student learning and development. We then introduce the methods that can be used to intentionally change certain parts of the brain for you to implement and design these processes on your own campus. We also include additional research around the importance of providing out-of-classroom experiences to strengthen the learning and development you are intentionally creating via new and stronger neural connections in your students' brains. And we close with some practical tips and questions for you to consider.

This book includes emerging research and provocative opinions to encourage your thinking about your own organization's possibilities. We believe that when you see how we currently understand the brain functions, and how we can intentionally change the structure and function of the brain, we can then make some significant changes in the organization of higher education and realize the learning and development outcomes our employers desire us to "produce."

Editor's Summary Points and Questions to Consider

1. Evidence points to the possibility that we are not consistently delivering all the types of learning and development employers expect at the level that is expected. Where on your campus (within classes and outside classes) might you have the most room to improve these types of expected learning and development?

2. From neuroscience, we are gaining an understanding of how we can change certain portions of the structure and function of the brain to heighten desired learning outcomes using mindfulness methodology and intentional inquiry. How does the notion of neuroplasticity create new opportunities for you to rethink the design, delivery, and evaluation of your students' learning and development?

3. Findings from neuroscience may suggest that course-by-course delivery of learning and development may not lead to our ability to deliver the most effective and desired learning and development outcomes. How might we rethink the way we organize ourselves to deliver higher education? How would our current financing models need to be adjusted to accommodate the appropriate investment in this new learning and development design?

4. Classroom learning pedagogies that have proven to be effective in the classroom could be considered as we rethink the entire design and delivery of American higher education. How could we expand service-learning, experiential learning, flipped classrooms, and the implementation of other student-centered learning pedagogies and high-impact practices beyond a classroom structure?

5. Neuroscience illustrates how we can teach students to regulate their attention and emotions to reduce their stress and anxiety and increase their attention, focus, and overall well-being. How might implementing these kinds of teachings for students cause us to rethink how we might be able to redesign higher education learning and development opportunities?

6. Reflective student learning and development portfolios may be viable options to illustrate applied evidence of holistic student learning and development. How could your organization use the principles of neuroscience to help students create portfolios that would demonstrate meaningful evidence of student learning and development?

7. Industry research shows that only the brands that provide meaning to consumers and to the world will continue to survive and thrive. If we apply this notion to our own campuses, would our institution be among the top 20% of brands of experiences or products that students feel brought them the most meaning to their lives? Would employers of our college or university graduates consider our organizations among their top 20% for brands that made the world a better place?

8. How can we assist those who design the performance indicators that hold higher education accountable to shift their thinking away from the course-by-course, credit-hour-accumulated degree as the commodity to understanding that the process of learning and development is the commodity? What would meaningful performance indicators look like with this shift in mind?

References

Alvarez, J., & Emory, E. (2006). Executive function and the frontal lobes: A meta-analytic review. *Neuropsychology Review, 16*(1), 17–42.

Angelo, T., & Cross, P. (1993). *Classroom assessment techniques: A handbook for college teachers.* San Francisco, CA: Jossey-Bass.

Arum, R., & Roksa, J. (2011). *Academically adrift: Limited learning on college campuses.* Chicago, IL: University of Chicago Press.

Astin, A. (1993). *What matters in college?* San Francisco, CA: Jossey-Bass.

Astin, J. (1997). Stress reduction through mindfulness meditation. Effects on psychological symptomatology, sense of control, and spiritual experiences. *Psychotherapy and Psychosomatics, 66*(2), 97–106.

Bandura, A. (1989). *Social foundations of thought and action: A social cognitive theory.* Englewood Cliffs, NJ: Prentice Hall.

Barbezat, D. P., & Bush, M. (2014). *Contemplative practices in higher education.* San Francisco, CA: Jossey-Bass.

Barr, R., & Tagg, J. (1995). From teaching to learning: A new paradigm for undergraduate education. *Change: The Magazine of Higher Learning, 27*(6), 12–25.

Barrows, H. S. (1996). Problem-based learning in medicine and beyond: A brief overview. *New Directions for Teaching and Learning, 68,* 3.

Bean, J. (1980). Dropouts and turnover: The synthesis and test of a causal model of student attrition. *Research in Higher Education, 12*(2), 155–187.

Bergmann, J., & Sams, A. (2012). *Flip your classroom: Reach every student in every class every day.* Arlington, VA: International Society for Technology in Education.

Blumenstyk, G. (2014). *American higher education in crisis: What everyone needs to know.* New York, NY: Oxford University Press.

Bok, D. C. (2013). *Higher education in America.* Princeton, NJ: Princeton University Press.

Bowles, T., & Jones, J. (2003). The effect of supplemental instruction on retention: A bivariate probit model. *Journal of College Student Retention: Research, Theory and Practice, 5*(4), 431–437.

Brown, K., & Ryan, R. (2003). The benefits of being present: Mindfulness and its role in psychological well-being. *Journal of Personality and Social Psychology, 84*(4), 822–848.

Brownell, J., & Swaner, L. (2009). High-impact practices: Applying the learning outcomes literature to the development of successful campus programs. *Peer Review, 11*(2), 26–30.

Brownell, J., & Swaner, L. (2012). Five high-impact practices: Research on learning outcomes, completion, and quality. *Peer Review, 14*(3), 29.

Bruner, J. S. (1961). The act of discovery. *Harvard Educational Review, 31*(1), 21–32.

Capurso, V., Fabbro, F., & Crescentini, C. (2014). Mindful creativity: The influence of mindfulness meditation on creative thinking. *Frontiers in Psychology, 4,* 1020–1021.

Carey, B. (2014). *How we learn: The surprising truth about when, where, and why it happens.* New York, NY: Random House.

Carp, J., Fitzgerald, K. D., Taylor, S. F., & Weissman, D. H. (2012). Removing the effect of response time on brain activity reveals developmental differences in conflict processing in the posterior medial prefrontal cortex. *NeuroImage, 59*, 853–860.

Carp, J., Kim, K., Taylor, S. F., Fitzgerald, K. D., & Weissman, D. H. (2010). Conditional differences in mean reaction time explain effects of response congruency, but not accuracy, on posterior medial prefrontal cortex activity. *Frontiers in Human Neuroscience.* Retrieved from http://journal.frontiersin.org/article/10.3389/fnhum.2010.00231/abstract

Chan, R., Shum, D., Toulopoulou, T., & Chen, E. (2008). Assessment of executive functions: Review of instruments and identification of critical issues. *Archives of Clinical Neuropsychology, 23*(2), 201–216.

Chiesa, A., Calati, R., & Serretti, A. (2011). Does mindfulness training improve cognitive abilities? A systematic review of neuropsychological findings. *Clinical Psychology Review, 31*(3), 449–464.

Clendaniel, M. (2011, November 7). *The brands that survive will be the brands that make life better.* Retrieved from www.fastcoexist.com/1678768/the-brands-that-survive-will-be-the-brands-that-make-life-better

Cohen, A. M., & Kisker, C. B. (2010). *The shaping of American higher education: Emergence and growth of the contemporary system* (2nd ed.). San Francisco, CA: John Wiley.

Colish, M. L. (1997). *Medieval foundations of the western intellectual tradition, 400–1400.* New Haven, CT: Yale University Press.

Cozolino, L. (2014). *The neuroscience of human relationships* (2nd ed.). New York, NY: W. W. Norton.

Crotty, J. (2012, March 1). *60% of college grads can't find work in their field. Is a management degree the answer?* Retrieved from www.forbes.com/sites/jamesmarshallcrotty/2012/03/01/most-college-grads-cant-find-work-in-their-field-is-a-management-degree-the-answer/

Dweck, C. S. (2007). *Mindset: The new psychology of success.* New York, NY: Random House.

Eyler, J., & Giles, D. E. (2007). *Where's the learning in service-learning?* San Francisco, CA: Jossey-Bass.

Goldin, P., & Gross, J. (2010). Effects of mindfulness-based stress reduction (MBSR) on emotion regulation in social anxiety disorder. *Emotion, 10*(1), 83–91.

Graziadei, W. D. (1996). VICE in REST Part IV. In T. M. Harrison & T. D. Stephen (Eds.), *Computer networking and scholarship in the 21st century university* (pp. 257– 276). New York, NY: SUNY Press.

Greenberg, J., Reiner, K., & Meiran, N. (2012). Mind the trap: Mindfulness practice reduces cognitive rigidity. *PLOS ONE, 7*(5), e36206–e36207.

Grossman, P., Niemann, L., Schmidt, S., & Walach, H. (2004). Mindfulness-based stress reduction and health benefits. A meta-analysis. *Journal of Psychosomatic Research, 57*(1), 35–43.

Hart Research Associates. (2013, April 10). *It takes more than a major: Employer priorities for college learning and student.* Retrieved from www.aacu.org/leap/documents/2013_EmployerSurvey.pdf

Hatch, D. (2012). Unpacking the black box of student engagement: The need for programmatic investigation of high impact practices. *Community College Journal of Research and Practice, 36*(11), 903–915.

Havas Media. (2011). *Meaningful brands: Havas media launches global results.* Retrieved from http://www.havasmedia.com/press/press-releases/2011/meaningful-brands-havas-media-launches-global-results

Hereen, A., Van Broeck, N., & Philippot, P. (2009). The effects of mindfulness on executive processes and autobiographical memory specificity. *Behaviour Research and Therapy, 47*(5), 403–409.

Historical facts: Harvard University archives. (n.d.). Retrieved from www.harvard.edu/historical-facts

Hollis-Walker, L., & Colosimo, K. (2011). Mindfulness, self-compassion, and happiness in non-meditators: A theoretical and empirical examination. *Personality and Individual Differences, 50*(2), 222–227.

Hölzel, B., Carmody, J., Vangel, M., Congleton, C., Yerramsetti, S., Gard, T., & Lazar, S. W. (2011). Mindfulness practice leads to increases in regional brain gray matter density. *Psychiatry Research Neuroimaging, 191*(1), 36–43.

Ingalhalikar, M., Smith, A., Parker, D., Satterthwaite, T., Elliott, M., Ruparel, K., . . . Varma, R. (2014). Sex differences in the structural connectome of the human brain. *Proceedings of the National Academy of Sciences of the United States of America, 111*(2), 823–828.

Jain, S., Shapiro, S., Swanick, S., Roesch, S., Mills, P., Bell, I., & Schwartz, G. E. (2007). A randomized controlled trial of mindfulness meditation versus relaxation training: Effects on distress, positive states of mind, rumination, and distraction. *Annals of Behavioral Medicine, 33*(1), 11–21.

Jha, A., Krompinger, J., & Baime, M. (2007). Mindfulness training modifies subsystems of attention. *Cognitive, Affective, & Behavioral Neuroscience, 7*(2), 109–119.

Kaku, M. (2014). *The future of the mind: The scientific quest to understand, enhance, and empower the mind.* New York, NY: Random House.

Kelly, R. (2012, August 23). *Implementing high-impact learning across the institution.* Retrieved from www.facultyfocus.com/articles/academic-leadership/implementing-high-impact-learning-across-the-institution/

Keng, S., Smoski, M., Robins, C., Ekblad, A., & Brantley, J. (2012). Mechanisms of change in mindfulness-based stress reduction: Self-compassion and mindfulness as mediators of intervention outcomes. *Journal of Cognitive Psychotherapy, 26*(3), 270–280.

Kolb, D. (1984). *Experiential learning as the science of learning and development.* Englewood Cliffs, NJ: Prentice Hall.

Kozasa, E., Sato, J., Lacerda, S., Barreiros, M., Radvany, J., Russell, T., . . . & Amaro, E. (2012). Meditation training increases brain efficiency in an attention task. *NeuroImage, 59*(1), 745–749.

Kuh, G. J. (2003). What we're learning about student engagement from NSSE. *Change: The Magazine of Higher Learning, 35*(2), 24–32.

Kuh, G. J. (2008). High-impact educational practices. *Peer Review, 10*(4), 30.

Kuh, G. J., Kinzie, J., Buckley, J. A., Bridges, B. K., & Hayek, J. C. (2007). Piecing together the student success puzzle: Research, propositions, and recommendations. *ASHE-ERIC Higher Education Report, 32*(5). Washington, DC: George Washington University.

Kuh, G. J., Kinzie, J., Schuh, J., & Whitt, E. (2010). *Student success in college: Creating conditions that matter.* San Francisco, CA: Jossey-Bass.

Langer, E. (2005). *On becoming an artist: Reinventing yourself through mindful creativity.* New York, NY: Ballantine Books.

Lazar, S. W., Kerr, C. E., Wasserman, R. H., Gray, J. R., Greve, D. N., Treadway, M. T., . . . & Fischl, B. (2005). Meditation experience is associated with increased cortical thickness. *NeuroReport, 16*(17), 1893–1997.

Lebow, D. (1993). Constructivist values for instructional systems design: Five principles toward a new mindset. *Educational Technology Research and Development, 41*(3), 4–16.

Lent, R. W., Brown, S. D., & Larkin, K. C. (1986). Self-efficacy in the prediction of academic performance and perceived career options. *Journal of Counseling Psychology, 33*, 265–269.

Lutz, A., Slagter, H., Dunne, J., & Davidson, R. (2008). Attention regulation and monitoring in meditation. *Trends in Cognitive Sciences, 12*(4), 163–169.

Martin, W. E., Jr., & Swartz-Kulstad, J. L. (Eds.). (2000). *Person-environment psychology and mental health: Assessment and intervention.* Mahwah, NJ: Erlbaum.

McNair, T., & Albertine, S. (2012). Seeking high-quality, high-impact learning: The imperative of faculty development and curricular intentionality. *Peer Review, 14*(3), 4–5.

Mettler, S. (2014). *Degrees of inequality: How the politics of higher education sabotaged the American dream.* Philadelphia, PA: Basic Books.

Michaelsen, L. K., Knight, A. B., & Fink, L. D. (2002). *Team-based learning: A transformative use of small groups.* New York, NY: Praeger.

Moore, A., & Malinowski, P. (2009). Meditation, mindfulness and cognitive flexibility. *Consciousness & Cognition, 18*(1), 176–186.

Mrazek, M., Franklin, M., Phillips, D., Baird, B., & Schooler, J. (2013). Mindfulness training improves working memory capacity and GRE performance while reducing mind wandering. *Psychological Science, 24*(5), 776–781.

Multon, K. D., Brown, S. D., & Lent, R. W. (1991). Relation of self-efficacy beliefs to academic outcomes: A meta-analytic investigation. *Journal of Counseling Psychology, 38*, 30–38.

Murray, M. A., & Byrne, R. M. J. (2005). Attention and working memory in insight problem solving. In B. G. Bara, L. Barsalou, & M. Bucciarelli (Eds.), *Proceedings of the XXVII Annual Conference of the Cognitive Science Society* (pp. 1571–1575). Mahwah, NJ: Erlbaum.

Murphy, L., & Thomas, L. (2008). Dangers of a fixed mindset: Implications of self-theories research for computer science education. In S. Ceci & W. Williams (Eds.), *Proceedings of the 13th Annual Conference on Innovation and Technology in Computer Science Education* (pp. 271–275). New York, NY: Association for Computing Machinery.

National Research Council. (2000). *How people learn: Brain, mind, experience, and school* (Expanded ed.). Washington, DC: National Academies Press.

Nilson, L. (2013). *Creating self-regulated learners: Strategies to strengthen students' self-awareness and learning skills.* Sterling, VA: Stylus.

OECD skills outlook. First results from the survey of adult skills. OECD Publishing. Retrieved from skills.oecd.org/documents/OECD_Skills_Outlook_2013.pdf

Orr, J. M., & Weissman, D. H. (2009). Anterior cingulate cortex makes two contributions to minimizing distraction. *Cerebral Cortex, 19*, 703–711.

Ostafin, B., & Kassman, K. (2012). Stepping out of history: Mindfulness improves insight problem solving. *Consciousness and Cognition, 21*(2), 1031–1036.

Pervin, L. A. (1968). Performance and satisfaction as a function of individual-environment fit. *Psychological Bulletin, 69*(1), 56–68.

Pervin, L. A. (1989). Persons, situations, interactions: The history of a controversy and a discussion of theoretical models. *Academy of Management Review, 14*(3), 350–360.

Petrie, N. (2014). *Vertical leadership development, part 1: Developing leaders for a complex world.* Retrieved from www.ccl.org/Leadership/pdf/research/Vertical-LeadersPart1.pdf

Ren, J., Huang, Z., Luo, J., Wei, G., Ying, X., Ding, Z., . . ., & Luo, F. (2011). Meditation promotes insightful problem-solving by keeping people in a mindful and alert conscious state. *Science China Life Sciences, 54*(10), 961–965.

Rendon, L. I. (1994). Validating culturally diverse students: Toward a new model of learning and student development. *Innovative Higher Education, 19*(1), 13–52.

Richardson, M., Abraham, C., & Bond, R. (2012). Psychological correlates of university students' academic performance: A systematic review and meta-analysis. *Psychological Bulletin, 138*(2), 353–387.

Robbins, S. B., Lauver, K., Le, H., Davis, D., Langley, R., & Carlstrom, A. (2004). Do psychosocial and study skill factors predict college outcomes? A meta-analysis. *Psychological Bulletin, 130*(2), 261–288.

Rosenzweig, S., Reibel, D., Greeson, J., Brainard, G., & Hojat, M. (2009). Mindfulness-based stress reduction lowers psychological distress in medical students. *Teaching and Learning in Medicine, 15*(2), 88–92.

Rubinstein, J. S., Meyer, D. E., & Evans, J. E. (2001). Executive control of cognitive processes in task switching. *Journal of Experimental Psychology: Human Perception and Performance, 27*(4), 763–797.

Rüegg, W. (2003). Mythology and historiography of the beginnings. In H. de Ridder-Symoens (Ed.), *A history of the university in Europe: Volume 1: Universities in the Middle Ages* (pp.4–8). Cambridge, UK: Cambridge University Press.

Sanford, N. (1966). *Self and society.* New York, NY: Atherton Press.

Sassenberg, K., & Moskowitz, G. (2005). Don't stereotype, think different! Overcoming automatic stereotype activation by mindset priming. *Journal of Experimental Social Psychology, 41*(5), 506–514.

Schlossberg, N. (1989). Marginality and mattering: Key issues in building community. *New Directions for Student Services, 1989*(48), 5–15.

Schunk, D. H. (1983). Ability versus effort attributional feedback: Differential effects on self-efficacy and achievement. *Journal of Educational Psychology, 75*, 848–856.

Shapiro, S., Schwartz, G., & Bonner, G. (1998). Effects of mindfulness-based stress reduction on medical and premedical students. *Journal of Behavioral Medicine, 21*(6), 581–599.

Siegel, D. J. (2007). *The mindful brain: Reflection and attunement in the cultivation of well-being.* New York, NY: W. W. Norton.

Solorzano, D., Ceja, M., & Yosso, T. (2000). Critical race theory, racial microaggressions, and campus racial climate: The experiences of African American college students. *Journal of Negro Education, 69*(1/2), 60–73.

St. John, O. (2013). *Kids skip college: Not worth the money.* Retrieved from www .usatoday.com/story/money/personalfinance/2013/04/21/avoiding-college-avoiding-debt/1987309/.

Stevens, M., & Kirst, M. (2015). *Remaking college: Ecology of higher education.* Stanford, CA: Stanford University Press.

Tait, A. (1996). Conversation and community: Student support in open and distance learning. In R. Mills & A. Tait (Eds.), *Supporting the learner in open and distance learning* (pp. 59–72). London, UK: Pitman.

Thelin, J. R. (2004). *A history of American higher education* (2nd ed.). Baltimore, MD: Johns Hopkins University Press.

Tinto, V. (1975). Dropout from higher education: A theoretical synthesis of recent research. *Review of Educational Research, 45*(1), 89–125.

Tinto, V. (1987). *Leaving college: Rethinking the causes and cures for student attrition* (2nd Ed.). Chicago, IL: University of Chicago Press.

Todd, R., Cunningham, W., Anderson, A., & Thompson, E. (2012). Affect-biased attention as emotion regulation. *Trends in Cognitive Sciences, 16*(7), 365–372.

Valentine, E., & Sweet, P. (1999). Meditation and attention: A comparison of the effects of concentrative and mindfulness meditation on sustained attention. *Mental Health, Religion & Culture, 2*(1), 59–70.

Walsh, W. B., Craik, K. H., & Price, R. H. (2000). *Person-environment psychology: New directions and perspectives.* Mahwah, NJ: Erlbaum.

Weissman, D. H., Gopalakrishnan, A., Hazlett, C., & Woldorff, M. (2005). Dorsal anterior cingulate cortex resolves conflict from distracting stimuli by boosting attention toward relevant events. *Cerebral Cortex, 15*(2), 229–237.

Weissman, D. H., Perkins, A. P., & Woldorff, M. G. (2008). Cognitive control in social situations: A role for the dorsolateral prefrontal cortex. *NeuroImage, 40*, 955–962.

Zeidan, F., Johnson, S. K., Diamond, B. J., David, Z., & Goolkasian, P. (2010). Mindfulness meditation improves cognition: Evidence of brief mental training. *Conscious Cognition, 19*(2), 597–605.

Zull, J. E. (2011). *From brain to mind: Using neuroscience to guide change in education.* Sterling, VA: Stylus.

BASIC BRAIN PARTS AND THEIR FUNCTIONS

Matthew R. Evrard, Jacopo Annese, and Marilee J. Bresciani Ludvik
with review by Mark Baxter and Thomas Van Vleet

Everything we do, every thought we've ever had, is produced by the human brain. But exactly how it operates remains one of the biggest unsolved mysteries, and it seems the more we probe its secrets, the more surprises we find.

—Neil deGrasse Tyson (www.brainyquote.com/quotes/quotes/n/neildegras531089.html)

Many of the traditional student learning and development theories used in higher education are based in developmental theories in psychology and cognitive neuroscience, along with a number of other disciplines (Ansari & Coch, 2006; Coch & Ansari, 2009; Goswami, 2006; Meltzoff, Kuhl, Movellan, & Sejnowski, 2009). With emerging findings, educational neuroscientists are affirming previous assumptions about the brain's role in reading, numerical comprehension, attention, and particular types of learning disabilities such as dyslexia and attention deficit/hyperactivity disorder (Ansari, 2008; Carey, 2014; Davis, 2004; Gabrieli, 2009; Howard-Jones, Pickering, & Diack, 2007; McCandliss & Noble, 2003; Petitto & Dunbar, 2004; Price, Holloway, Räsänen, Vesterinen, & Ansari, 2007). The fascination with the brain is all around us, and so it is indeed time to intentionally incorporate neuroscience discoveries into the design, delivery, and evaluation of higher education.

This chapter sets out to provide a brief framework of the brain. We intend to describe various regions of the brain and generalize their primary functions. But first allow me to share how I, Matthew R. Evrard, arrived at the gates of an emerging field.

Have you ever had the experience of suddenly realizing a past memory—perhaps as a child or teenager—that helped explain why you are who you are? I can recall multiple memories from my early childhood where my mother took me to a store and told me to choose a gift. I always chose books on scientific theory. Such books were well above my comprehension level, but I was unyielding in my attempts to understand as much as I could. If there was a puzzle, I wanted to solve it. Memories such as these, as well as my imperishable love of science, strengthened my belief that I was born a self-challenging scientist, proudly mom-accredited.

Determined to become an academically accredited scientist, I pursued my bachelor of science in psychology at SUNY Buffalo State College, where I became involved with undergraduate neuroscience research. And so it began for me, the linkage of neuroscience and higher education. Just like many who later choose student affairs as a profession, my undergraduate experience was transformational in more ways than I have space to share. This transformation occurred because of the many student leadership roles I took on, which allowed me to facilitate others' meaning making out of class. With each new term, I became more inspired to engage in my academic community. The only thing that was more difficult than turning down a new opportunity was choosing between neuroscience and higher education for graduate school. I recall being questioned by many on how I could even be considering two such "unrelated" fields. Conversation after conversation, the question was deceptively simple: Are you a science guy, or are you a student development guy? It seems ironic that such dichotomous questions came from colleagues who were also emphasizing the importance of integration across majors.

Mentally, I was living a civil war. The part of me that wanted to pursue neuroscience wanted to split from the part of me that wanted to pursue higher education. How could I choose? More to the point, why did I have to choose? I remember asking myself these questions often between late-night phone calls from freshmen locked out of their dorm rooms. Needless to say, I continued to battle this war with no clear victor.

My decision was abruptly put off during my senior year when my mother was diagnosed with cancer and had just a few months to live. In the time I spent with my mother, watching her health deteriorate, memories of the young scientist came flooding back while the nurturing development aspects came into play daily. As I began to contemplate my authentic self, I realized I was neither a "research science guy" nor a "student development guy." How could society demand I pursue only one? Truly, I was both: a man of science and education. So I did both. I pursued my master of arts in student affairs at San Diego State University, where I was able to conduct neuroscience research in a number of labs. That led me to pursue my doctorate in neuroscience at SUNY Downstate, where I continue to explore the interconnections of neuroscience and learning and development. There is no "or" anymore; it is all about the "and."

The way I look to the brain is how I imagine Copernicus looked to the skies as he tried to prove that the center of the universe was, in fact, the sun. It is amazing to think that literally right in front of me (as I am drafting this chapter while in the lab), almost a trillion cells coalesce into the brain. Within these cells, I see the potential to answer some of life's biggest questions. While intimidating to some, I find it empowering to know that scientists have barely scratched the surface of brain science, leaving so much to be discovered. Even so, there have been tremendous achievements in what scientists do "know." The first thing that comes to mind when someone asks me, "What do we know about the brain?" is its ability to change. That is, the brain is an adaptable organ that alters its own structure and function in response to experience. This adaptability has caused some to suspect, with merit, that these changes in the brain can explain many of the learning and behavioral processes. With a better understanding of the brain and its underlying mechanisms, scientists can then ask better, more pointed, questions permitting larger pieces of the puzzle to be revealed. In this way, higher education professionals and others may be able to advance the quality of higher education and its students by providing environments that foster meaningful learning and development.

The field of advertising has already turned to neuroscience to better inform its practices (Plassman, Ambler, Braeutigam, & Kenning, 2007; Ramsoy, 2014). Several companies, such as Twitter, have utilized emerging brain science to quantifiably assess social constructs such as attention (Lindstrom, 2010). The information they gather can be used to design marketing campaigns and assess their effectiveness. The field of advertising is among the first to intentionally incorporate emerging neuroscience research and has allegedly increased its profitability as a result, causing other fields to follow (Duhigg, 2014; Hazeldine, 2013). If advertising and other business practices are reaping the rewards of neuroscience, then why shouldn't higher education?

We feel that higher education's most inspiring characteristic is the potential to engender change in an individual and society. In the current state, it may be hindered by ineffective and/or outdated strategies. What if higher education leaders implemented emerging neuroscience findings into their own practices? Take, for example, a student who has been placed on academic probation because of poor grades; the very essence and existence of "academic probation" may elevate his or her stress and anxiety (Reesor, MacDonald, & Wertkin, 1992; Ross, Niebling, & Heckert, 1999; Winn, 1995; Yaworski, Weber, & Ibrahim, 2000). Chronic stress and anxiety may impede students' ability to perform, consequently curtailing their potential (Sharkin, 2004; Torres & Solberg, 2001; Turner & Berry, 2000; Zajacova, Lynch, & Espenshade, 2005). In such a case, neuroscience can be applied to better the practices in higher education. One example could be introducing practices that reduce acute stress and anxiety while improving the capacity to learn. Another example may be providing students with strategies to improve their grades while concurrently incorporating stress and anxiety reduction techniques. And yet another example could be engaging in strategies to increase activity in specific areas of the brain associated with attention and critical thinking.

These are just a few examples of the presumed benefits that integrating neuroscience into higher education could achieve; there are many others, some of which are proposed in this book. If those working within or with higher education integrate just a few of them, we remain confident that together with the work from leaders in neuroscience and higher education the quality and effectiveness of the higher education learning system can improve. We may even be able to lower the overall cost of higher education or, at the very least, reallocate resources to design effective solutions.

What follows in this chapter is a brief introduction to the brain so readers can navigate the content in the forthcoming chapters with relative ease. Hopefully, this chapter will generate additional ideas of how neuroscience can be integrated into higher education design, delivery, and evaluation. Although this is a complex topic, we have attempted to introduce this material in a manner that is accessible and yet avoids overgeneralization, leading to inaccurate assumptions and uses.

Neuroscience offers new ideas and concepts that can maximize and facilitate meaningful student learning and development. First we offer a brief history of neuroscience showcasing paradigm shifts in theories and modalities used to investigate the brain. Then we introduce basic neuroanatomical structures and their respective functions while emphasizing their interconnectedness. Next we discuss popular modalities used to investigate the brain and explain what those results may mean when interpreted. Finally, we integrate neuroscience knowledge with the forthcoming themes in the book.

How Do We Know About the Brain?

Who are you? What are your aspirations, values, and goals? What do you know? How do you know what you know? What are you currently feeling and sensing? How aware of all of this are you? Tribes in Papua New Guinea believed that the answers to these questions lay in a gray, rather squishy material that was inside your skull (Glasse, 1967). When a member of a tribe died, they would ceremoniously eat this organ with the belief that a person's wisdom, experiences, and personality could be passed down to those who participated in the ceremony. What these people ate is what we now call the human brain. Although this may seem morbid and outrageous to modern Western sensibilities, modern science is confirming the tribe's belief that the brain is the organ that processes who you are.

Questions like "Who are you?" can produce an endless variety of responses that are, at the scientific level, all the result of the brain's processing abilities (Kandel, Schwartz, Jessell, Siegelbaum, & Hudspeth, 2013; Levitin, 2014). Because the brain is an elaborate system of networks forged from 90 billion neurons interacting with each other, we humans are able to experience existence (Kandel et al., 2013; Seung, 2012). Equally important is that the brain is adaptive and interacts with its surrounding environment on a molecular, cellular, systemic, and behavioral level. This interaction between the environment and the brain/body—which we are denoting as the entire nervous system—enables behavior, personality, survival, learning, and just about everything else you can do or imagine (Kandel et al., 2013). Although scientists have just begun revealing pieces of the mystery, studies correlating the brain to behavior have been traced back to ancient societies.

Fundamental shifts have been made in the science that studies brains in both the tools used to deduce knowledge (e.g., microscope) and the underlying ideology. Scientists are now able to empirically test ideas that have been previously hypothesized or overlooked. Relatively new concepts such as neuroplasticity (the altering of existing neural connections) and neurogenesis (the birth of new neurons) have profoundly advanced the understanding of the brain (Draganski et al., 2004; Kandel et al., 2013). Today, it is widely accepted that the brain is a malleable and an adaptive organ—a paradigm shift from the early twentieth-century ideology that the brain is a static organ (Hanson, 2009; Kandel et al., 2013; Levitin, 2014).

These discoveries would have been impossible without the advent of modern technology to provide data along with new conceptual insights to interpret (and extrapolate) their significance. Both neuroimaging and microscopy have unveiled the increasingly complex and intricate ways in which the brain works. In interpreting these data in novel approaches, scientists have come to understand that these connections between neurons, or neuronal pathways, are endlessly changing and are essential in normal brain functioning, specifically for learning and development (Wickens, 2014).

History of the Brain

For almost as long as there have been written records, there has been an acknowledgment of the brain's role in cultivating the sense of being (Hanson, 2009; Kandel et al., 2013; Siegel, 2007). Currently, the oldest written report of the brain's function with a sense of "behavior" dates back more than 5,000 years ago, somewhere around 3,000 BCE, and was written by the ancient Egyptians (Kandel et al., 2013). Of all the known papyruses, the Edwin Smith Surgical Papyrus is the first to depict two cases where an injury to the brain correlated with psychological and physiological changes. In these reports, two individuals suffered injuries to the head and developed aphasia, the loss of the ability to produce or understand speech. People with aphasia may forget specific words or may be unable to speak, write, or even read. Let us quickly note that aphasia affects the ability to access thoughts and ideas through language, not the thought or idea in and of itself (intelligence). The type and extent of aphasia, we now know, can be predicted by damage to specific areas in the brain (Kandel et al., 2013). For as much as these early accounts seem elementary, they are the first systemically written medical records of the brain.

Advancements in technology permitted new inventions that allowed a deeper look into the brain. The advent of the microscope and procedures that could stain neurons allowed for a closer view of the brain and permitted scientists, like Santiago Ramón y Cajal, to classify different types of neurons (Wickens, 2014). Santiago Ramón y Cajal, who is considered one of the founding fathers of modern neuroscience, was the first to illustrate the single functional unit of the brain: the neuron (Carter, 2014; Wickens, 2014). His work earned him the 1906 Nobel Prize in Physiology. Neurons are the cells in the brain that allow parts of the brain to communicate with other areas in the brain and the body. Santiago Ramón y Cajal published the first illustrations of the neuron in 1899. Today, it is estimated the human brain has roughly 90 billion neurons that collectively work together (Seung, 2012). However, in the nineteenth century the neuron was just emerging and much science exclusively focused on sections of the brain and their potential associated responsibilities for behavior.

Modern neuroscience is beginning to understand how the brain operates and the intimate relationship it has with behavior, decision making, and even learning. These discoveries would not have been possible without advances in technology that are able to actually measure these changes. A radical invention in modern neuroscience was conceived at SUNY Downstate Medical Center, in 1972 by Raymond Damadian (Imperato, 2011). Damadian invented the magnetic resonance scanning machine. These machines provided the first methods that could produce a look at the anatomical structure of the human brain in vivo (Wickens, 2014). Today a magnetic resonance image (MRI; the abbreviation can also stand for magnetic resonance imaging) provides a physician or scientist with a black-and-white image of the brain's structure, which can then determine if any abnormalities are present and provide metrics like volume and density while the patient is awake. The advent of the MRI has been the foundation of many other neuroimaging modalities, such as functional MRI (fMRI) and diffusion tensor imaging (DTI), which directly measure function and connections, respectively (Assaf & Pasternak, 2008).

These technologies have thus provided a base for which scientists can begin to investigate how the brain and behavior complement each other. Researchers have, for almost as long as the brain has been studied, debated the importance between structure and function. Park and Friston (2013) suggested,

> (I) the relationship between structure and function is an integration problem, (II) the organization of structural networks supports local and global integration, (III) the inherent context sensitivity of functional integration mandates a divergence of functional connectivity from structural connectivity, and (IV) understanding the dynamic configuration of connectivity will benefit from theoretically informed and realistic neuronal models. (p. 1238411)

In other words, current and future research should seek to champion the integration problem between structure and function by focusing on neuronal pathways at the macro (connections between structures) and micro (connections within structures) levels rather than the traditional anatomical approach, which associates specific regions of the brain with single functions. Just think what following a line of inquiry like this could mean for advancing how we design, deliver, and evaluate higher education.

We next deal with the nuances of neuroimaging and address some common and important questions. Is more activity a good thing? Do I want to increase the size or density of my cortex? And, more important, how do we know that such answers are good or bad?

How Scientists Examine the Brain

The way we think about the brain is influenced by neuroimaging technologies because they are the sole source of images representing the elusive object of cognitive research. Anatomists and pathologists have been immune to this dependency because they observe and handle the real thing. For these scholars, neuroscience begins at autopsy. Upon the removal of the calvarium—the portion of a skull including the braincase and excluding the lower jaw or lower jaw and facial portion—the brain presents itself as a squishy, bloodshot, gelatinous blob encased in a thin membrane (the meninges), just like the egg's yolk. Only after fixation with the preservative formalin—a clear aqueous solution of formaldehyde containing a small amount of methanol—does the brain assume the familiar pale and rubbery appearance and lend itself to neurological scrutiny.

What has been learned about the brain from gross dissection? A great deal. Every neuronal structure or fiber tract was identified and classified post-mortem long before computed tomography (CT) and nuclear magnetic resonance (NMR) technologies afforded views of soft tissue inside of our skull (Wickens, 2014). Bear with us as we return to the main idea of this chapter, but consider this—new powerful telescopes have revealed the existence of new moons and solar systems, just as deep oceanic vessels have picked up new marine species and showed us ecosystems worthy of science fiction; conversely, MRI has not led to the discovery of any previously unknown brain structure. Arguably, the giant leap forward (indeed, a giant step for mankind) afforded by MRI was not in the realm of discovery, but in the field of diagnostics as we discovered how the brain functioned.

Noninvasive imaging has been extremely valuable in localizing pathological phenomena underlying neurological symptoms. Leveraging large-scale population-based imaging studies, we have identified markers of neurodegenerative and (far less reliably) psychiatric disease. Lesion and electrode localization studies in the cerebral cortex (Lashley, 1950; Penfield & Jasper 1954; Penfield & Milner, 1958; Penfield & Roberts, 1959) not only established a topography of cortical function (foretold by Franz Gall—yes, the phrenology guy) but also provided the conceptual foundations for modern brain mapping. In recent times, the MRI became the tool of choice not only to investigate structural markers of neurological disease but also to study the functional architecture of the brain.

A structural MRI (occasionally abbreviated as sMRI) relies on a strong, stable magnetic field (the strength of which is measured in Tesla, or "T" units) surrounding the body and the excitation of hydrogen atoms by pulses that gradient coils produce at different angles (Kandel et al., 2013). The technique targets hydrogen atoms of water molecules that are present in "soft" tissue (as opposed to "hard" tissue such as bone or enamel that can be seen with X-rays). Image contrast distinguishing between gray and white matter in the brain is created by the different rates of relaxation of hydrogen atoms toward the original state of alignment with the main magnetic field. If hydrogen atoms were a crowd of cadets being trained on a field and the main magnetic field was the sergeant keeping them at attention, then the gradients would be lieutenants loudly giving them alternate orders to face this or the other direction. If after they face one side of the field they are allowed to spontaneously relax back into their original stance, they would do it at different speeds depending on whether they are standing deeply in sand (white matter) or on cement (gray matter). A tougher, more authoritative sergeant (a stronger magnet), means a more uniform assembly and clearer relaxation effect—and better image quality from higher-strength magnets in MRI machines.

Anatomical images acquired by sMRI provide the topographic substrate for mapping brain activity—that is, determining where particular motor, perceptual, and associative cognitive functions, including learning, are supported in the brain. The fMRI localizes signal related to neuronal activity based on the relative paramagnetic properties of oxygenated versus deoxygenated hemoglobin as blood perfuses areas that are metabolically active and oxygen is exchanged (Jezzard, Matthew, & Smith, 2001). In other words, when an individual engages in a specific activity or thought, an fMRI is able to distinguish between the areas of your brain that are being used and those that are not.

Since the mid-1990s, widespread access to research scanners spurred a "land run" to map functions in the human cerebral cortex combining sMRI, fMRI, and a variety of paradigms that emulated and validated earlier data from electrode or lesion mapping in experimental primates. The cortical surface of the brain gradually subdivided into distinct parcels that "activated" in response of specific tasks or conditions. Often the experimental paradigm involved comparing a condition where a particular element or attribute was present with one where it was absent (a "subtraction" paradigm); this is, for example, how several visual areas specific to color, motion, or faces were identified in the occipital lobes (Tootell et al., 1995; Zeki, 1993). The parcellation of the cerebral cortex by fMRI validated classical anatomical studies of the early twentieth century, such as those of Korbinian Brodmann (1909), where he charted cortical fields based on microscopic features. Actual overlap between functional fields defined by MRI and areas identified in classical monographs and a few modern revivals of the architectonic method that defines cortical areas based on microscopic features of neuronal morphology (Annese, Pitiot, Dinov, & Toga, 2004; Zilles et al., 1995) was a topic of debate, crucial because the human brain, and the cerebral cortex in particular, shows a very large degree of variability across different individuals. It is important to know if there is a common design in spite of differences in shape. In other words, can one predict the position of a specific function based on anatomical landmarks? Neurosurgeons surely would like to know.

In neurosurgeons' pursuit of understanding localized function, we should acknowledge contributions made by a few celebrity lesion patients. We begin with Phineas Gage, the man who survived a metal rod that blasted through his left eye socket and frontal lobe and was left with a bizarre change in character, especially a lack of restraint in social interaction. If Gage's long-term symptoms might have been exaggerated (Macmillan, 1996), Monsieur Leborgne's were pervasive. Leborgne was described by Dr. Paul Broca in 1881 as another lesion patient who suffered from seizures and lost the ability to utter any sound but "tan" after age 30. Moreover, in Leborgne's case, the patient's brain was actually preserved at autopsy. The lesion discovered on the middle part of the patient's left frontal lobe led Broca to the first convincing case of localization of function. Broca's name—and, thus, this cortical region—is indelibly synonymous with language, or, to be more precise, with speech.

In the 1950s, Henry Molaison, formerly known as Patient HM, underwent removal of a portion of his hippocampus and amygdala, a surgery intended to put an end to his life-threatening seizures. However, Molaison's seizures were not the only thing that ended; so, too, did his ability to form any new memories, a condition referred to as anterograde amnesia. While Henry could effortlessly recall events from his entire preoperative life, he could not remember anything just prior to his operation or anything that happened to him after his operation. From this landmark case, scientists have determined that the hippocampus has a fundamental role in memory. Henry was able to learn new skills, such as tracing a five-pointed star while only being able to watch his hand in a mirror. He became better at mirror drawing across the days, achieving a skill equivalent to that of anyone his age with intact temporal lobes, but could not consciously recall that he knew how to perform those new skills (Milner, 1962).

So far, we have talked only about gray matter; truth be told, gray matter mattered most to brain mappers until very recently. That is, until a new application of MRI was used to measure water diffusion in the brain, specifically in the white matter, hence the name of the method, diffusion weighted imaging (DWI). The white matter is principally composed of myelinated fibers (explained in more detail in Chapter 2); therefore, the diffusion of water molecules is at least theoretically restricted (termed *anisotropic* or exhibiting properties with different values when measured in different directions) unless events such as a stroke or tumor disrupt the fabric of the tissue. For this reason, DWI is used as a diagnostic tool; however, if water molecules move uniformly in one major direction, it could be assumed that the restriction follows the trajectory of axonal bundles (movement away from the cell body). Diffusion tensor imaging (DTI) measures the diffusion of water molecules along multiple axes and calculates the predominant orientation of diffusion. The results are displayed as color-coded orientation maps and "solid" connectivity maps. Interesting to note is that the content of the frame also approximates the size of a single pixel in an MRI image.

In highlighting how scientists study the brain, we are hoping you will move into the next section with an awareness of *how* we know *what* we know today. Emerging technology will likely provide us with new understandings in the future. And as Park and Friston (2013) asserted, the important question for higher education leaders revolves around understanding the integration of structure and function and aligning that understanding with design, delivery, and evaluation of higher education.

Regions and Structures of Interest

As we mentioned, at this point, there is agreement among scientists that to experience (or to become aware of) anything (emotional, physical, computational) it must be processed through the brain, the entirety of the nervous system (Hanson, 2009; Levitin, 2014; Siegel, 2008). While we can hope to increase our understanding of which specific structures have specific functions, particularly when it comes to learning and development, there is still a lot we don't know. Perhaps, it is easier to convey this by using a house as an analogy.

Houses have multiple rooms, and the bigger the house, the more rooms; the more rooms, the more specific each room function becomes. That is to say, most houses have a bedroom, and in that bedroom is a closet for clothes and in that closet are drawers for underwear, socks, and so on. However, there are those houses in well-off places like Beverly Hills that have not only a bedroom but also an additional room for clothes and perhaps another for shoes and coats and so on. Imagine the human brain as a mansion that sits at the summit of Beverly Hills with so many rooms one begins to lose count. However, the "rooms" in the brain have functions that have developed from other functions or behaviors, or "rooms." In addition, the more rooms, the more hallways connecting the rooms in the mansion. The separation of all primary functions into specific rooms ensured our survival, safety, and creativity, among other functions (Penfield & Rasmussen, 1950). So, in the house in Beverly Hills, someone may have pants in the room whose function is to store coats or they may have socks in the room where the hats are kept. That wouldn't make much sense, but it happens and we don't really know why.

Throughout history, many neuroanatomists tried to divide the brain into specific structures that could then be localized for a unique and specific function. However, as we have touched on, that may be an impossible and fruitless endeavor (Hanson, 2009; Seung, 2012; Siegel, 2008). The relationship between structure and function of the brain is now considered to be more about connections between individual neurons and structure (referred to as the *connectome*) and less about attributing a specific function to a specific area (Seung, 2012). While it is common for neuroscience literature to assign a function or set of functions to a specific structural region of the brain, it is important to understand that the connections that lie between and within these regions influence both the function and structure. Thus, neural connections have an equally important role in determining behavior than any isolated structure (in most cases). However, research on the neural connections has just started to emerge and therefore scientists have been able to determine only certain structures, or rooms, and their primary function based on the most common item in that room. Imagine walking into a room and seeing a twin-sized bed, a small fridge, and a Taylor Swift poster. Your first thought may be that this room is a student's dorm room. However, after you spend a little more time in the room other items like a motorcycle and a dishwasher emerge, and the twin-sized bed is actually a long table. Perhaps your first thought was wrong; this isn't a dorm room! It's someone's bedroom. However, what is the dishwasher doing in a bedroom; let alone the motorcycle? This is similar to current methods in neuroscience. We have been to almost all the rooms in the mansion and have attributed a function based on initial observations, and in some areas, scientists are beginning to take a fourth or fifth look, but still have questions about some of the smaller anomalies, like the dishwasher. So, for simplicity, we only discuss relevant structures pertaining to this book.

Toga (2013) provided a comprehensive resource of basic neuroanatomy. The brain is divided into two nearly identical sides: the right hemisphere and the left hemisphere. These two hemispheres are able to communicate with each other via commissures—bundles of fibers that propagate an electrical message between hemispheres—most notably the corpus callosum. The most prominent characteristic of the brain is the cerebral cortex, which is the outmost shell of the brain that covers both hemispheres. This convolving layer, which looks similar to a walnut, is often referred to as gray matter within the literature (Carter, 2014). As previously mentioned, there are two types of "matter" in the brain, gray and white matter. There are two different colors of matter because every neuron has both a "gray" and "white" part, which will be discussed in more detail in Chapter 2. The size of the cerebral cortex distinguishes humans apart from other species, and the convoluted nature of the cerebral cortex permits more neurons to fit into a smaller area. For example, if you take a piece of paper and crunch it into a ball, it fits into a much smaller area. Having more neurons then allows a larger capacity for learning, remembering, and thinking (Roth & Dicke, 2005).

Additionally, the brain is divided into four lobes: frontal, parietal, occipital, and temporal. Figure 1.1 provides a visualization of the location of these lobes. The frontal lobe (notated as 1 in Figure 1.1) is the latest in the evolution of the human brain and is responsible for higher-level thinking such as critical thinking, problem solving, planning, production of speech, and other executive functions. The parietal lobe (2) is responsible for understanding

Figure 1.1 Lobes and structures of the human brain.

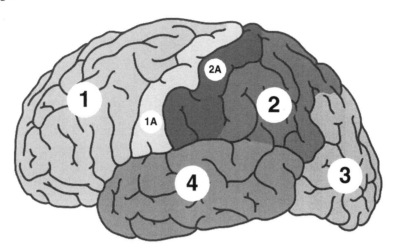

Note. Each number represents a certain area of the human brain that is of interest to this study: (1) prefrontal cortex/frontal lobe; (1A) primary motor cortex; (2) parietal lobe; (2A) primary somato-sensory cortex; (3) occipital lobe; (4) temporal lobe. Created by Matthew R. Evrard, 2014, and reproduced with his permission.

language, integrating visual processes related to "where" an object is, and facets of attention. The occipital lobe (3) is localized primarily for vision. Finally, the temporal lobe (4) subserves memory, navigation, hearing, and the integration of visual processes related to "what" an object is.

However, it is important to understand that at this level of division there are many other areas of the brain such as the midbrain, hindbrain, insula, and limbic system (Toga, 2013). (See Figure 9.1 for an image of these parts of the brain.) It might be helpful to understand that the cerebral cortex covers the entire surface of the brain—the insula is a division of the cerebral cortex hidden in the lateral fissure. The midbrain has many sensory tracts (bundles of nerves) that travel between your brain and body; in addition, it is responsible for reflexes, addiction, reward, and motivation (Kandel et al., 2013; Toga, 2013). On the other hand, the hindbrain controls basic functions like breathing, heart rate, and correcting various motor behaviors (Toga, 2013). In the following sections, we discuss specific brain structures, their function, and how these structures connect to other areas of the brain.

The limbic system (Figure 1.2) refers to a collection of subcortical brain structures that, anatomically, lie in the middle of the brain (medial, beneath the cerebral cortex). The entire system has far-reaching functionality, having a prominent role in emotion, stress, anxiety, memory, learning, navigation, and motivation. Interestingly, while all other senses project through the

Figure 1.2 The limbic system of the human brain.

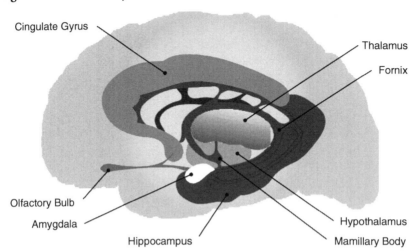

thalamus, smell is the only sense that has direct limbic system projections. This explains why certain smells can trigger more intense and vivid emotions than other stimuli (Binder, Hirokawa, & Windhorst 2009). Additional structures related to the limbic system include the amygdala, hippocampus, cingulate cortex, fornix, thalamus, and hypothalamus.

As we have mentioned time and time again, the brain is expansively complex with 90 billion neurons and 10 times the amount of connections, called synapses, between those neurons. As such, scientists are just beginning to understand how the brain operates. But what remains evident is that the connections between neurons matter and can influence learning. This means that scientists may finally understand why there is a Britney Spears album or a dishwasher in what they thought was the bedroom. *Connectionism*, the study of the connections between neurons, attempts to describe how areas of the brain work by examining the intricate pattern of neuronal networks (Fodor & Pylyshyn, 1988; Seung, 2012).

Through everyday experiences, the connections between neurons can change, which is one current theory as to why humans are able to learn and remember (Seung, 2012). It is likely that your neurons are reorganizing themselves at this very moment because you are reading this book. As exciting as that is, the connections between neurons are not entirely shaped by experience, but also by genes. In Sebastian Seung's (2012) book, *Connectome*, he describes the brain and its neurons as a forest where the trees are the neurons; the roots and branches are the connections between the neurons. With that example, it becomes easier to envision how the brain's neurons are expansively connected to one another, and how certain experiences can alter the paths between.

We have explained the importance of the connectivity of the brain while also explaining that functional areas are not necessarily completely regulated by specific areas of the brain. We now explain our operational understanding of what scientists know to be true today. As we describe each section of the brain relevant to the content of this book, keep in mind that you have, in essence, two of each section, one in the right hemisphere of the brain and one in the left hemisphere. As you read, also remember the house analogy; shoes can be found in the coat closet.

The Amygdala

The amygdala is one of the primary structures of the limbic system and is the emotional processor of the brain; therefore, its relevant function to the material in this book relates to regulating perceptions, reactions to fear and aggression, reward, and positive affect (LeDoux, 2003). It is located medially in the temporal lobes and is widely connected to other areas of the brain related to fear, facial responses, stress, and aggression (Coccaro, McCloskey, Fitzgerald, & Phan, 2007; Pare & Duvarci, 2012; Roozendaal, McEwen, & Chattarji, 2009). Accordingly, as an area responsible for orchestrating anxiety and the fight-or-flight response (LeDoux, 2003), to what extent the amygdala's activity can be modified is of primary interest. Another interesting point we should mention is that the amygdala resides right in front of the hippocampus; the two share many intimate connections to determine and drive some behaviors associated with memory (Richter-Levin, 2004).

The amygdala is the output of the emotion center. It receives sensory information almost immediately from the thalamus, which provides the amygdala with so-called low-resolution information (Kandel et al., 2013). Sensory information also projects from the thalamus to the cortex and from the cortex to the amygdala, providing so-called high-resolution information (Kandel et al., 2013). While the high-resolution sensory information takes longer to arrive in the amygdala, it carries more information that is beneficial for an emotional response. However, low-resolution sensory information moves quickly to the amygdala and can signal for us to immediately react to threatening situations.

The Hippocampus

The hippocampus is located within the temporal lobes of the brain, immediately behind the amygdala. Additionally, the hippocampus is connected to various areas of the brain important to the regulation of emotion including the prefrontal cortex, amygdala, entorhinal cortex, and hypothalamus

(Amaral & Lavenex, 2006). The primary function of the hippocampus is in learning systems, navigation, and memory, specifically conscious memories for facts and events (Andersen et al., 2007; Bliss & Collingridge, 1993; Jacobs et al., 2013; Kandel et al., 2013; McClelland, McNaughton, & O'Reilly, 1995; Squire, 1992).

The 2014 Nobel Prize in Physiology and Medicine was shared by John O'Keefe, May-Britt Moser, and Edvard Moser for their work connecting the hippocampus to navigation. The hippocampus is also a part of the limbic system (the brain's emotional processor), so when a memory is stored, the context (e.g., emotion) can remain associated with it. The hippocampus has bidirectional projection to the cortex and amygdala (Andersen et al., 2007). The connections between the hippocampus and amygdala are thought to be a mechanism undergirding contextual fear (Andersen et al., 2007). In this way, the amygdala is activated due to a perceived threat and the hippocampus then can associate this fear with other contexts in that moment (Andersen et al., 2007). Accordingly, there is general agreement that the stress response can be modulated by memory, among other things, (Kim & Diamond, 2002; Kim, Lee, Han, & Packard, 2001). Take, for example, the ability of certain memories to elicit an emotion, even if that emotion isn't happening in that exact moment. Memories have the potential to heighten or suppress stress.

The Thalamus

Located between the cerebral cortex and the midbrain, the thalamus is the major relay station for neural connections from one area of the nervous system to another, and because of its pervasive role it has many connections to other areas of the brain (Carter, 2014). The thalamus screens, sorts, and preprocesses sensory information (e.g., movement, vision, touch, pain) and then sends it to the cerebral cortex for integration and decision making (Carter, 2014). As a part of the limbic system, the thalamus regulates sensory information and controls sleep and awake states of consciousness (Kandel et al., 2013). With the exception of smell, all other senses project to the thalamus before reaching the neocortex (Kandel et al., 2013).

The Hypothalamus

The hypothalamus has a major role to play in conscious behaviors, emotions, and instincts (Carter, 2014) and is located between the thalamus and brain stem. It integrates information from the nervous and endocrine system via the pituitary gland, which sits below it (Carter, 2014). (Note that the adrenal glands, parts of the endocrine system that sit atop the kidneys, are responsible for releasing hormones in response to stress, including cortisol, adrenaline, and noradrenaline.) The hypothalamus is known to commonly control fleeing, fighting, feeding, and reproducing (Joseph, 1996). It communicates with the endocrine system by releasing and receiving hormones in the bloodstream (Joseph, 1996). The secretion of hormones into the bloodstream has extensive and long-lasting psychological and physiological responses as the body breaks down these hormones at a slow rate (De Kloet, Karst, & Joëls, 2008). Because hormones influence feelings and the rate of secretion and absorption of hormones can influence stress, the hypothalamus is also a player in the regulation of emotion.

The Prefrontal Cortex

The prefrontal cortex refers to the frontal lobe without the motor or premotor cortex, the most anterior part of the brain. The prefrontal cortex is the most recent lobe of the brain to evolve and is responsible for executive functions such as higher-level thinking and cognitive processes such as attention, planning, focusing, problem solving, comparing and evaluating, judgment, and decision making (Engle, Kane, & Tuholski, 1999; Kane & Engle, 2002; Koster, De Lissnyder, Derakshan, & De Raedt, 2011; Miller & Cohen, 2001; Newman, Carpenter, Varma, & Just, 2003; Shallice, 1982; Shallice & Burgess, 1991).

Markedly, neuroscientists have observed extensive neural connections from this region of the brain to almost all areas of the brain, including the hippocampus, amygdala, thalamus, hypothalamus, and corticocortical connections (e.g., to regions of the parietal and temporal cortex) (Carmichael & Price, 1995; Fuster, 1988; Goldman-Rakic, Selemon, & Schwartz, 1984; Uylings, Van Eden, De Bruin, Corner, & Feenstra, 1991). This has led researchers to believe that the connections of the prefrontal cortex with the limbic system are what lead to prioritization, the linkage of memory and sensory input, and the ability to manage emotions, and thus the ability to self-regulate. Our interest in this part of the brain is most evident. Interestingly, in many psychological diagnoses such as attention deficit disorder, post-traumatic stress disorder, and schizophrenia abnormal prefrontal cortex activity is displayed in some way (Drevets et al., 1997; Raine, Lencz, Bihrle, LaCasse, & Colletti, 2000).

Anterior Cingulate Cortex

The anterior cingulate cortex is the frontal part of the cingulate cortex located in the frontal lobe of the brain. It runs parallel to the corpus callosum (the major pathway that connects the two hemispheres) and is sometimes referred to as the cingulate gyrus. The anterior cingulate cortex has a role in rational cognitive functions, such as emotional control and associating emotional states with behavioral outcomes. In other words, let's imagine that in your reading of this book that the behavioral activity of reading elicited a feeling of joyful inquiry (of happily wanting to know more). What should follow is associative learning between the behavioral act of reading and the feeling of joyful inquiry. It may also signal a need for cognitive control over this association (Hadland, Rushworth, Gaffan & Passingham, 2003; Hayden & Platt, 2010; Kozlovskiy et al., 2012).

Insula

The insula, sometimes referred to as the insular cortex, is an additional layer of cortex (or gray matter) that lies underneath the external cerebral cortex. In fact, the insula cannot be seen from just looking at a human brain. The insula is beneath the temporal lobe, occipital lobe, and parietal lobe and lies posterior to the frontal lobe. The insula has a specific area where it topographically represents sound and has been connected to a host of functions that center on emotion regulation and homeostasis maintenance (Kandel et al., 2013). Such functions as perception, self-awareness, body awareness, sensing or awareness of "gut" feelings, empathy, activation of mirror neurons, and the ability to integrate sensation and emotion have all been associated with this area of the brain.

Sensory-Motor Areas

The sensory-motor areas of the brain reside anterior to the poscentral sulcus. In Figure 1.1, 1A is the primary motor cortex and 2A is the primary somatosensory cortex between these. Where the cerebral cortex convolutes inward is the central sulcus. The motor cortex, which resides anterior to the central sulcus, controls voluntary muscle movement (Kandel et al., 2013). That is to say, the motor cortex is sending messages to your body's muscles telling them to move or not to move. The somatosensory cortex, which resides after the central sulcus, evaluates all the incoming messages from your body (Kandel et al., 2013). In other words, it receives and analyzes a variety of messages from touch to pain.

As you recall, the brain has two hemispheres (right and left), which means the somatosensory cortex can be divided into left and right halves. The right side of your body has neurons that travel to the left side of your brain, and the left side of your body has neurons that travel to the right side of your brain (Kandel et al., 2013).

Basal Ganglia

The basal ganglia were originally believed to be solely involved with movement (the sensory-motor area), primarily because diseases such as

Parkinson's compromise the structure and consequently the function of the basal ganglia (Kandel et al., 2013). But this view is rapidly changing as the basal ganglia also have connections to other areas of the brain, such as the cerebral cortex, thalamus, and brain stem, making them a prominent structure in learning and development (Kandel et al., 2013). Together these structures are involved with not only movement, but also higher-level behaviors, including learning (procedural, habit formation, and developing routines), emotion regulation, executive function, and mood (Kandel et al., 2013). Think back to Henry Molaison, who had lost the ability to form new memories, but his basal ganglia remained untouched. Perhaps this can explain why he was able to learn new skills and procedures without any explicit recollection of having done them before.

There are five smaller subcortical structures (gray matter) that together make up the basal ganglia: the caudate nucleus, putamen, globus pallidus, subthalamic nucleus, and the substantia nigra. In emerging research, you may read about one of these subcortical structures; we thought it might be helpful for you to have this reference.

Language and Communication Centers

Most of language processing occurs in the cerebral cortex (the convoluted exterior on the surface of the brain). There are two distinct centers of the brain that are used in language and communication; both reside in the temporal lobe of the brain (Figure 1.3). Understanding both written and spoken language is made possible by Wernicke's area, which is located in the back of the temporal lobe close to where the occipital and parietal lobes meet (Kandel et al., 2013). The area associated with the ability to produce speech is also on the temporal lobe but located near the front of the brain (Kandel et al., 2013). While up to now you have had two of every structure, comprehension seems to be localized to a single side, and for an overwhelming majority of people it is the left. Thus, comprehension (oral, written, object recognition) appears to be a left-hemisphere process (Kandel et al., 2013).

Table 1.1 correlates the structures we've discussed with their respective area and function in the brain. Moreover, these structures all have a role in regulating emotion (Lupien, McEwen, Gunnar, & Heim, 2009). And we understand that the hippocampus and prefrontal cortex are associated with cognitive regulation.

There are many other structures in the brain, along with endless subdivisions of the ones we have mentioned. Again, we have shared only a few owing to their relevance to the topics in this book. What is important to remember beyond structure and function is that the neural connections between parts of the brain are incredibly dynamic.

Figure 1.3 Sensory-motor and language-processing centers in the brain.

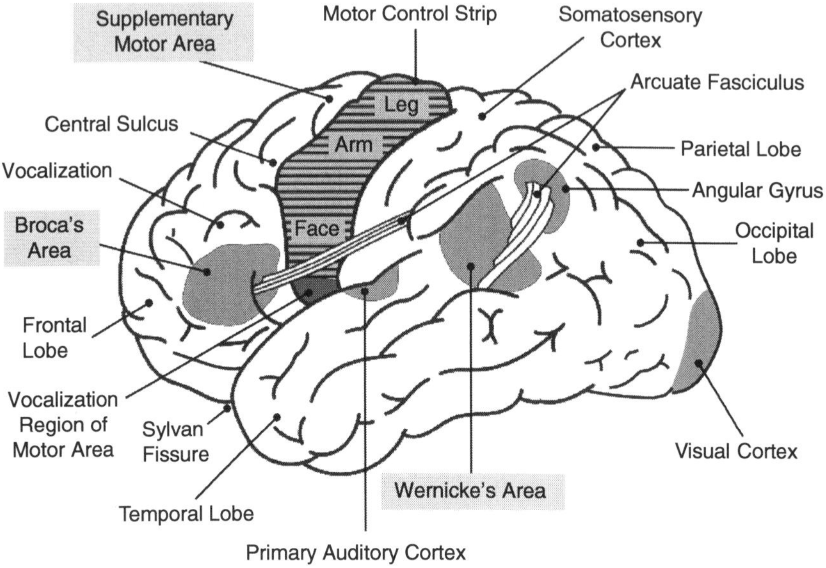

TABLE 1.1
Neurocorrelates of Function

Brain Structure	Brain Lobe	Functions of Interest
Amygdala	Limbic system	Flight-or-flight response, stress, anxiety
Hippocampus	Limbic system	Memory consolidation (short term to long term)
Prefrontal cortex	Frontal	Executive functions, attention, decision making
Hypothalamus	Limbic system	Communication between brain and body, four Fs (fleeing, feeding, fighting, and mating)
Basal ganglia	Subcortical	Movement, emotion regulation, learning, mood
Sensory-motor areas	Frontal/parietal	Input from environment/voluntary movement
Insula	Subcortical	Emotion regulation and maintaining homeostasis
Broca's area	Temporal	Production of speech
Wernicke's area	Temporal	Understanding speech, writing

Note. Adapted from Joseph, 1996; Kandel et al., 2013; LeDoux, 2003; Shallice & Burgess, 1991; Squire, 1992.

Neuroplasticity and Neurogenesis

As you are most likely aware, emerging research has demonstrated that our brains are malleable; in fact, they can change signficantly in response to our environment, behavior, and/or injury (Alvarez & Emory, 2006; Chan, Shum, Toulopoulou, & Chen, 2008; Chiesa, Calati, & Serretti, 2011; Goldin & Gross, 2010; Hölzel et al., 2011; Kozasa et al., 2012; Lutz, Slagter, Dunne, & Davidson, 2008; Pascual-Leone et al., 2011; Todd, Cunningham, Anderson, & Thompson, 2012). Notably, through intentional (or unintentional) actions, an individual is able to produce functional and structural changes in his or her brain. *Neurogenesis* is the brain's ability to produce new neurons, whereas *neuroplasticity* refers to the brain's ability to modify its connections with other neurons (Taupin, 2006). Granted, neurogenesis and neuroplasticity have not been identified in all regions of the brain, but these processes have been shown to be integral to many of the structures we mentioned such as the hippocampus (Kokaia & Lindvall, 2003; Pittenger & Duman, 2008). Consequently, neurogenesis and neuroplasticity in the hippocampus and prefrontal cortex are disrupted by chronic stress and anxiety (Lucassen et al., 2010; Lupien et al., 2009). We discuss this in more detail in Chapters 2 and 6.

In summary, considering that the amygdala, hippocampus, prefrontal cortex, and hypothalamus all have a role in regulating emotion, and that unregulated emotion may negatively affect neurogenesis and neuroplasticity (specifically in regions localized for memory and executive functions), a training program that seeks to regulate students' emotion as well as cognition, thus promoting critical thinking dispositions, may be effective if these regions can be targeted in the training process.

Editor's Summary Points and Questions to Consider

1. The brain's structure and functions are quite complex. Still, there are specific regions of the brain that can be associated primarily with specific functions. What specific structures and functions are compelling to your design, delivery, and evaluation of all learning and development opportunities?
2. The structures and functions of the brain that integrate emotion, memory, and thought are also quite complex and interrelated. How does reflecting on these integrated aspects motivate you to consider them when you design, deliver, and evaluate your courses and cocurricular programs?

3. Neural connections and pathways between and within functional areas of the brain are dynamic and can be changed. How does this motivate you to explore all of the ways in which you can intentionally design opportunities for students to change their brains in class and out of class?

4. The behavior, emotions, and activities we give our attention to become stronger and more automatic as we strengthen those neural pathways. What neural networks are you strengthening? What have you intentionally and unintentionally directed your attention toward?

References

Andersen, P., Morris, R., Amaral, D., Bliss, T., & O'Keefe, J. (Eds.). (2006). *The hippocampus book.* New York, NY: Oxford University Press.

Alvarez, J. A., & Emory, E. (2006). Executive function and the frontal lobes: A meta-analytic review. *Neuropsychology Review, 16*(1), 17–42.

Amaral, D., & Lavenex, P. (2006). Hippocampal neuroanatomy. In P. Andersen, R. Morris, D. Amaral, T. Bliss, & J. O'Keefe (Eds.), *The hippocampus book (pp. 37–114).* Oxford, UK: Oxford University Press.

Annese, J., Pitiot, A., Dinov, I. D., & Toga, A. W. (2004). A myelo-architectonic method for the structural classification of cortical areas. *NeuroImage, 21*(1), 15–26.

Ansari, D. (2008). Effects of development and enculturation on number representation in the brain. *Nature Reviews Neuroscience, 9*(4), 278–291.

Ansari, D., & Coch, D. (2006). Bridges over troubled waters: Education and cognitive neuroscience. *Trends in Cognitive Sciences, 10*(4), 146–151.

Assaf, Y., & Pasternak, O. (2008). Diffusion tensor imaging (DTI)–based white matter mapping in brain research: A review. *Journal of Molecular Neuroscience, 34*(1), 51–61.

Binder, M. D., Hirokawa, N., & Windhorst, U. (2009). *Encyclopedia of neuroscience* (Vol. 1). Berlin, Germany: Springer Verlag.

Bliss, T. V., & Collingridge, G. L. (1993). A synaptic model of memory: Long-term potentiation in the hippocampus. *Nature, 361*(6407), 31–39.

Brodmann, K. (1909). *Vergleichende Lokalisationslehre der Grosshirnrinde in ihren Prinzipien dargestellt auf Grund des Zellenbaues.* London, UK: Smith-Gordon.

Carey, B. (2014). *How we learn: The surprising truth about when, where, and why it happens.* New York, NY: Random House.

Carmichael, S. T., & Price, J. L. (1995). Limbic connections of the orbital and medial prefrontal cortex in macaque monkeys. *Journal of Comparative Neurology, 363*(4), 615–641.

Carter, R. (2014). *The human brain book.* New York, NY: DK Publishing.

Chan, R. C. K., Shum, D., Toulopoulou, T., & Chen, E. Y. H. (2008). Assessment of executive functions: Review of instruments and identification of critical issues. *Archives of Clinical Neuropsychology, 23*(2), 201–216.

Chiesa, A., Calati, R., & Serretti, A. (2011). Does mindfulness training improve cognitive abilities? A systematic review of neuropsychological findings. *Clinical Psychology Review, 31*(3), 449–464.

Coccaro, E. F., McCloskey, M. S., Fitzgerald, D. A., & Phan, K. L. (2007). Amygdala and orbitofrontal reactivity to social threat in individuals with impulsive aggression. *Biological Psychiatry, 62*(2), 168–178.

Coch, D., & Ansari, D. (2009). Thinking about mechanisms is crucial to connecting neuroscience and education. *Cortex, 45*(4), 546–547.

Davis, A. (2004). The credentials of brain-based learning. *Journal of the Philosophy of Education, 38*(1), 21–36.

De Kloet, E. R., Karst, H., & Joëls, M. (2008). Corticosteroid hormones in the central stress response: Quick-and-slow. *Frontiers in Neuroendocrinology, 29*(2), 268–272.

Draganski, B., Gaser, C., Busch, V., Schuierer, G., Bogdahn, U., & May, A. (2004). Neuroplasticity: Changes in grey matter induced by training. *Nature, 427*(6972), 311–312.

Draganski, B., Gaser, C., Kempermann, G., Kuhn, H. G., Winkler, J., Büchel, C., & May, A. (2006). Temporal and spatial dynamics of brain structure changes during extensive learning. *Journal of Neuroscience, 26*(23), 6314–6317.

Drevets, W. C., Price, J. L., Simpson, J. R., Todd, R. D., Reich, T., Vannier, M., & Raichle, M. E. (1997). Subgenual prefrontal cortex abnormalities in mood disorders. *Nature, 386*(6627), 824–827.

Duhigg, C. (2014). *The power of habit: Why we do what we do in life and business.* New York, NY: Random House.

Engle, R. W., Kane, M. J., & Tuholski, S. W. (1999). Individual differences in working memory capacity and what they tell us about controlled attention, general fluid intelligence, and functions of the prefrontal cortex. In A. Miyake & P. Shah (Eds.), *Models of working memory: Mechanisms of active maintenance and executive control,* (pp. 102–134). New York, NY: Cambridge University Press.

Fodor, J. A., & Pylyshyn, Z. W. (1988). Connectionism and cognitive architecture: A critical analysis. *Cognition, 28*(1), 3–71.

Fuster, J. M. (1988). *Prefrontal cortex.* Boston, MA: Birkhäuser.

Gabrieli, J. D. (2009). Dyslexia: A new synergy between education and cognitive neuroscience. *Science, 325*(5938), 280–283.

Glasse, R. (1967). Cannibalism in the Kuru region of New Guinea. *Transactions of the New York Academy of Sciences, 29*(6), 748–754.

Goldin, P. R., & Gross, J. J. (2010). Effects of mindfulness-based stress reduction (MBSR) on emotion regulation in social anxiety disorder. *Emotion, 10,* 83–91.

Goldman-Rakic, P. S., Selemon, L. D., & Schwartz, M. L. (1984). Dual pathways connecting the dorsolateral prefrontal cortex with the hippocampal formation and parahippocampal cortex in the rhesus monkey. *Neuroscience, 12*(3), 719-743.

Goswami, U. (2006). Neuroscience and education: From research to practice? *Nature Reviews Neuroscience, 7*(5), 406–413.

Hadland, K., Rushworth, M., Gaffan, D., & Passingham, R. (2003). The effect of cingulate lesions on social behaviour and emotion. *Neuropsychologia, 41*(8), 919–931.

Hanson, R. (2009). *Buddha's brain: The practical neuroscience of happiness, love, and wisdom.* Oakland, CA: New Harbinger Publications.

Hayden, B., & Platt, M. (2010). Neurons in anterior cingulate cortex multiplex information about reward and action. *Journal of Neuroscience, 30*(9), 3339–3346.

Hazeldine, S. (2013). *Neuro-sell: How neuroscience can power your sales success.* London, UK: Kogan Page.

Hölzel, B. K., Carmody, J., Vangel, M., Congleton, C., Yerramsetti, S. M., Gard, T., & Lazar, S. W. (2011). Mindfulness practice leads to increases in regional brain gray matter density. *Psychiatry Research: Neuroimaging, 191*(1), 36–43.

Howard-Jones, P., Pickering, S., & Diack, A. (2007). *Perception of the role of neuroscience in education.* Summary Report for the DfES Innovation Unit. University of Bristol, UK: Neuroscience and Education Network.

Imperato, P. J. (2011). Downstate at 150: A celebration of achievement. Honoring the sesquicentennial of the College of Medicine, Downstate Medical Center, State University of New York, 1860–2010. *Journal of Community Health, 36*(6), 1055–1056.

Jacobs, J., Weidemann, C. T., Miller, J. F., Solway, A., Burke, J. F., Wei, X. X., . . . & Kahana, M. J. (2013). Direct recordings of grid-like neuronal activity in human spatial navigation. *Nature Neuroscience, 16,* 1188–1190. doi:10.1038/nn.3466

Jezzard, P., Matthews, P. M., & Smith, S. M. (Eds.). (2001). *Functional MRI: An introduction to methods* (Vol. 61). Oxford, UK: Oxford University Press.

Joseph, R. (1996). *Neuropsychiatry, neuropsychology, and clinical neuroscience: Emotion, evolution, cognition, language, memory, brain damage, and abnormal behavior.* Philadelphia, PA: Williams & Wilkins.

Kandel, E. R., Schwartz, J. H., Jessell, T. M., Siegelbaum, S. A., & Hudspeth, A. J. (Eds.). (2013). *Principles of neural science* (Vol. 5). New York, NY: McGraw-Hill

Kane, M. J., & Engle, R. W. (2002). The role of prefrontal cortex in working-memory capacity, executive attention, and general fluid intelligence: An individual-differences perspective. *Psychonomic Bulletin & Review, 9*(4), 637–671.

Kim, J. J., & Diamond, D. M. (2002). The stressed hippocampus, synaptic plasticity and lost memories. *Nature Reviews Neuroscience, 3*(6), 453–462.

Kim, J. J., Lee, H. J., Han, J. S., & Packard, M. G. (2001). Amygdala is critical for stress-induced modulation of hippocampal long-term potentiation and learning. *Journal of Neuroscience, 21*(14), 5222–5228.

Kokaia, Z., & Lindvall, O. (2003). Neurogenesis after ischaemic brain insults. *Current Opinion in Neurobiology, 13*(1), 127–132.

Koster, E. H., De Lissnyder, E., Derakshan, N., & De Raedt, R. (2011). Understanding depressive rumination from a cognitive science perspective: The impaired disengagement hypothesis. *Clinical Psychology Review, 31*(1), 138–145.

Kozasa, E. H., Sato, J. R., Lacerda, S. S., Barreiros, M. A., Radvany, J., Russell, T. A., & Amaro, E., Jr. (2012). Meditation training increases brain efficiency in an attention task. *NeuroImage, 59*(1), 745–749.

Kozlovskiy, S. A., Vartanov, A. V., Nikonova, E. Y., Pyasik, M. M., & Velichkovsky, B. M. (2012). The cingulate cortex and human memory processes. *Psychology in Russia: State of the Art, 5*(1).

Lashley, K. S. (1950). Physiological mechanisms in animal behavior. *Academic Press, Society for Experimental Biology*, (Society's Symposium IV), pp. 454–482.

LeDoux, J. (2003). The emotional brain, fear, and the amygdala. *Cellular and Molecular Neurobiology, 23*(4-5), 727–738.

Levitin, D. (2014). *The organized mind: Thinking straight in the age of information overload*. New York, NY: Penguin.

Lindstrom, M. (2010). *Buyology: Truth and lies about why we buy*. New York, NY: Random House.

Lucassen, P. J., Meerlo, P., Naylor, A. S., Van Dam, A. M., Dayer, A. G., Fuchs, E., & Czeh, B. (2010). Regulation of adult neurogenesis by stress, sleep disruption, exercise and inflammation: Implications for depression and antidepressant action. *European Neuropsychopharmacology, 20*(1), 1–17.

Lupien, S. J., McEwen, B. S., Gunnar, M. R., & Heim, C. (2009). Effects of stress throughout the lifespan on the brain, behaviour and cognition. *Nature Reviews Neuroscience, 10*(6), 434–445.

Lutz, A., Slagter, H. A., Dunne, J. D., & Davidson, R. J. (2008). Attention regulation and monitoring in meditation. *Trends in Cognitive Sciences, 12*(4), 163–169.

McMillan, M. B. (1996). Phineas Gage: A case for all reasons. In C. Code, C.-W. Wallesch, Y. Joanette, & A.-R. Lecours (Eds.), *Classic Cases in Neuropsychology* (pp. 245–262). New York, NY: Psychology Press.

McCandliss, B. D., & Noble, K. G. (2003). The development of reading impairment: A cognitive neuroscience model. *Mental Retardation and Developmental Disability Research Review, 9*(3), 196–204.

McClelland, J. L., McNaughton, B. L., & O'Reilly, R. C. (1995). Why there are complementary learning systems in the hippocampus and neocortex: Insights from the successes and failures of connectionist models of learning and memory. *Psychological Review, 102*(3), 419–457.

Meltzoff, A. N., Kuhl, P. K., Movellan, J., & Sejnowski, T. J. (2009). Foundations for a new science of learning. *Science, 325*(5938), 284–288.

Miller, E. K., & Cohen, J. D. (2001). An integrative theory of prefrontal cortex function. *Annual Review of Neuroscience, 24*(1), 167–202.

Milner, B (1962). In P. Passouant (Ed.), *Physiologie de l'hippocampe* (pp. 257–272). Paris, France: Centre National de la Recherche Scientifique.

Newman, S. D., Carpenter, P. A., Varma, S., & Just, M. A. (2003). Frontal and parietal participation in problem solving in the Tower of London: fMRI and computational modeling of planning and high-level perception. *Neuropsychologia, 41*(12), 1668–1682.

Pare, D., & Duvarci, S. (2012). Amygdala microcircuits mediating fear expression and extinction. *Current Opinion in Neurobiology, 22*(4), 717–723.

Park, H.-J., & Friston, K. (2013, November 1). Structural and functional brain networks: From connections to cognition. *Science, 342*(6158). doi.org/10.1126/science.1238411

Pascual-Leone, A., Freitas, C., Oberman, L., Horvath, J. C., Halko, M., Eldaief, M., . . . & Rotenberg, A. (2011). Characterizing brain cortical plasticity and network dynamics across the age-span in health and disease with TMS-EEG and TMS-fMRI. *Brain Topography, 24*, 302–315.

Penfield, W., & Jasper, H. (1954). Epilepsy and the functional anatomy of the human brain. *Neurology, 4*(6), 483.

Penfield, W., & Milner, B. (1958). Memory deficit produced by bilateral lesions in the hippocampal zone. *AMA Archives of Neurology & Psychiatry, 79*(5), 475–497.

Penfield, W., & Rasmussen, T. (1950). The cerebral cortex of man: A clinical study of localization of function. *Journal of the American Medical Association, 144*(16), 1412.

Penfield, W., & Roberts, L. (1959). Speech and brain mechanisms. *Neurology, 9*(11), 797.

Petitto, L. A., & Dunbar, K. (2004). *Building usable knowledge in mind, brain, & education* (K. Fischer & T. Katzir, Eds.). Cambridge, UK: Cambridge University Press.

Pittenger, C., & Duman, R. S. (2008). Stress, depression, and neuroplasticity: A convergence of mechanisms. *Neuropsychopharmacology, 33*(1), 88–109.

Plassmann, H., Ambler, T., Braeutigam, S., & Kenning, P. (2007). What can advertisers learn from neuroscience? *International Journal of Advertising, 26*(2), 151–175.

Price, G. R., Holloway, I., Räsänen, P., Vesterinen, M., & Ansari, D. (2007). Impaired parietal magnitude processing in developmental dyscalculia. *Current Biology, 17*(24), R1042–R1043.

Raine, A., Lencz, T., Bihrle, S., LaCasse, L., & Colletti, P. (2000). Reduced prefrontal gray matter volume and reduced autonomic activity in antisocial personality disorder. *Archives of General Psychiatry, 57*(2), 119–127.

Ramsoy, T. (2014). *Introduction to neuromarketing & consumer neuroscience*. Rørvig, Denmark: Neurons Inc ApS.

Reesor, L. C., MacDonald, F., & Wertkin, R. A. (1992). Enhancing student coping and modifying the stressful academic environment: Advice from students and faculty. *Journal of Teaching in Social Work, 6*, 87–97.

Richter-Levin, G. (2004). The amygdala, the hippocampus, and emotional modulation of memory. *Neuroscientist, 10*(1), 31–39.

Roozendaal, B., McEwen, B. S., & Chattarji, S. (2009). Stress, memory and the amygdala. *Nature Reviews Neuroscience, 10*(6), 423–433.

Ross, S. E., Niebling, B. C., & Heckert, T. M. (1999). Sources of stress among college students. *College Student Journal, 33*(2), 312–318.

Roth, G., & Dicke, U. (2005). Evolution of the brain and intelligence. *Trends in Cognitive Sciences, 9*(5), 250–257.

Seung, S. (2012). *Connectome: How the brain's wiring makes us who we are*. Boston, MA: Houghton Mifflin Harcourt.

Shallice, T. (1982). Specific impairments of planning. *Philosophical Transactions of the Royal Society B: Biological Sciences, 298*(1089), 199–209.

Shallice, T. I. M., & Burgess, P. W. (1991). Deficits in strategy application following frontal lobe damage in man. *Brain, 114*(2), 727–741.

Sharkin, B. S. (2004). College counseling and student retention: Research findings and implications for counseling centers. *Journal of College Counseling, 7*(2), 99–110.

Siegel, D. J. (2007). *The mindful brain*. Louisville, CO: Sounds True.

Squire, L. R. (1992). Memory and the hippocampus: A synthesis from findings with rats, monkeys, and humans. *Psychological Review, 99*(2), 195–231.

Taupin, P. (2006). Adult neurogenesis and neuroplasticity. *Restorative Neurology and Neuroscience, 24*(1), 9–15.

Todd, R. M., Cunningham, W. A., Anderson, A. K., & Thompson, E. (2012). Affect-biased attention as emotion regulation. *Trends in Cognitive Sciences, 16*(7), 365–372.

Toga, A. W. (2013). Anatomy of the brain. In A. L. C. Runehov, L. Oviedo, (Eds.), *Encyclopedia of Sciences and Religions*. London, UK: Routledge.

Tootell, R. B., Reppas, J. B., Kwong, K. K., Malach, R., Born, R. T., Brady, T. J., & Belliveau, J. W. (1995). Functional analysis of human MT and related visual cortical areas using magnetic resonance imaging. *Journal of Neuroscience, 15*(4), 3215–3230.

Torres, J. B., & Solberg, V. S. (2001). Role of self-efficacy, stress, social integration, and family support in Latino college student persistence and health. *Journal of Vocational Behavior, 59*(1), 53–63.

Turner, L., & Berry, T. (2000). Counseling center contributions to student retention and graduation: A longitudinal assessment. *Journal of College Student Development, 4*(6), 627–637.

Uylings, H. B. M., Van Eden, C. G., De Bruin, J. P. C., Corner, M. A., & Feenstra, M. G. P. (1991). The anatomical relationship of the prefrontal cortex with the striatopallidal system, the thalamus and the amygdala: Evidence for a parallel organization. *Prefrontal Cortex: Its Structure, Function and Pathology 85*, 95.

Wickens, A. P. (2014). *A history of the brain: From Stone Age surgery to modern neuroscience*. New York, NY: Psychology Press.

Winn, T. D. (1995). Attributional differences between successful and unsuccessful college students on academic probation. *Dissertation Abstracts International, 57*(2), 582.

Yaworski, J., Weber, R., & Ibrahim, N. (2000). What makes students succeed or fail? The voices of developmental college students. *Journal of College Reading and Learning, 30*(2), 195–221.

Zajacova, A., Lynch, S. M., & Espenshade, T. J. (2005). Self-efficacy, stress, and academic success in college. *Research in Higher Education, 46*(6), 677–706.

Zeki, S. (1993). *A vision of the brain*. Hoboken, NJ: Wiley-Blackwell.

Zilles, K., Schlaug, G., Matelli, M., Luppino, G., Schleicher, A., Qü, M., & Roland, P. E. (1995). Mapping of human and macaque sensorimotor areas by integrating architectonic, transmitter receptor, MRI and PET data. *Journal of Anatomy, 187*(3), 515–537.

2

UNPACKING NEUROPLASTICITY AND NEUROGENESIS

Matthew R. Evrard and Marilee J. Bresciani Ludvik,
with review by Thomas Van Vleet

Of all the resources you have within your community, your family, your work, and your personal
life that are available to you to make your life fuller, happier, more productive, and healthier—
your own mind is the only one of these resources that you have the capacity to change, at will, in
any given moment of time.
—Rick Hanson (*Hardwiring Happiness*, 2013, pp. 8–9)

The knowledge that our experiences, or how we intentionally direct our attention, can modify the structure and function of the human brain causes us to question structural relevance to learning and development. While we have known for quite some time that learning and development are dynamic processes (Erwin, 1991), demonstrating evidence in a manner that could inform an accountability conversation has been most challenging. However, remarkable advancements in neuroscience have led to a better understanding of the brain and the specific structures that undergird learning and development. Specifically, certain brain areas involved in learning and development exhibit a marked ability to respond to experience, attention, and other facets of our environment. That being the case, students can be trained to take on greater responsibility for their own intentional brain development.

The prevalent view has historically been that either you "have it"— "it" being intellect, talent, personality, or ability—or you "don't have it"; it was all determined by a genetic predisposition or mind-set (Dweck, 2007). That being said, whatever you "have," then you have to make the most of it, because that was just the way "you were wired." You know, that whole "I'm a people person; I'm not really cut out to be in a lab, studying microscopic organisms all day." "Okay, we will find you something to major in where you work with people and don't have to focus on a microscope." Or another one of our favorites, "I don't do math." "Okay, you don't do math—we'll find something else you can do."

Studies indicate that students with poor math fluency have certain areas of the brain with reduced activity unlike those who are fluent in math (Delazar et al., 2005; Meintjes et al., 2010; Smedt, Holloway, & Ansari, 2011) Neuroplasticity may circumvent this apparent structural difference. Those previously deficient in math may be able to become proficient in math not just because they choose to believe they can but because they can train their brain in specific ways. This is incredibly liberating for both teacher and student. Some of the neural wiring, once thought to be genetically predetermined, can actually change (Carter, 2014; Draganski et al., 2004; Kandel, Schwartz, & Jessell, 2013; Lazar et al., 2005; Mechelli et al., 2004; Sampaio-Baptista et al., 2014). And as we learned in the Introduction and Chapter 1, a change in structure supports a change in function (Carter, 2014; Kandel et al., 2013; Sampaio-Baptista et al., 2014).

While there is benefit to practicing positive psychology, as well as having a positive mind-set, a change in brain structure is something we can identify and something we may be able to intentionally design for in our educational systems. For example, engaging in specific brain-training practices means students may be able to create new possibilities for their lives. In neuroplasticity, we see all the unlocked potential within every prospective student in the world.

What if prospective or current students knew that just because they struggled with math or science in high school, it did not mean they couldn't master it in college? What if they knew that the pain and suffering caused by the bully in middle school that kept them in the shadows could be used to transform them into the next class president who could speak confidently to large audiences? What if they were told that their creative selves had just as much importance as their emotional selves, their analytical selves, and their shy selves? What if they knew that integrating the knowledge they were discovering in and out of classrooms was key to their overall success as human beings? What if they knew this was possible but involved more than simply choosing to believe it was possible?

William James has been attributed with the quote, "If you can change your mind, then you can change your life" (James, n.d.). We have research that illustrates the importance of our mind-set (Dweck, 2007). We understand that when the brain commands the body to do anything, it does so by sending electrochemical signals from neuron to neuron, traveling through multiple regions (Abeles, 1991; Carter, 2014; Kandel et al., 2013; Penfield

& Rasmussen, 1950; Sokolov & Sokolov, 1963). For example, the ability to move must pass from the primary motor cortex, to the thalamus, down the spinal cord, and then to the muscles. However, who is commanding the brain? Many believe it is the mind.

We have no unanimous scientific definition of what the *mind* is. Perhaps the mind commands the brain and the body. Or perhaps the brain commands the body and the mind. Or perhaps the body commands the brain and the mind. *Merriam-Webster* defines the *mind* as "the element or complex of elements in an individual that feels, perceives, thinks, wills, and especially reasons" (www.merriam-webster.com/dictionary/mind). There are a lot of ideas about what the mind is or what that "element" referred to by *Merriam-Webster* is; for example, spirit, consciousness, God, the universe, or ancestors. From a neuroscience perspective, we don't know, so we leave it to the reader to determine what it is for you, just as we leave it to our students to determine what it is for them.

While you will see the term *mind* used in the remaining chapters of the book, some of the authors use the term somewhat interchangeably with the "element, complex of elements, or entity" that is integrating all the sensing, beliefs, emotions, and thoughts into an awareness that is acknowledged and apparently processed in the brain. Some authors use the term *mind* to refer to the awareness that there is a self or the awareness that is integrating experience with beliefs and thoughts and emotions. Others use the term when they may be referring to the brain. In any event, we invite you to keep an open "mind" as you read. Perhaps consider an operational definition of the *mind* to mean the awareness that arises when you are aware that you are integrating your senses, thoughts, emotions, and intuition into discerning whether to use what is presented in this book or not.

Defining Neuroplasticity and Neurogenesis

The term *neuroplasticity* is derived from the Greek words for neuron and plastic. The prefix *neuro-* comes from the root word *nervus*, which means "of the nervous system, nerves, or nerve" (dictionary.reference.com/browse/neuro-). The suffix *-plastic* comes from the root word *plastikös*, which means "to mold, form" (en.wikipedia.org/wiki/List_of_Greek_and_Latin_roots_in_English). Together, the term *neuroplasticity* refers to the brain's ability to be fashioned by its own processes, which then support, facilitate, and promote behavior (Kandel et al., 2013; Zilles, 1992). Paillard (2008) defines *neuroplasticity* as "the ability of a system to achieve novel functions, either by transforming its internal connectivity or by changing the elements of which it is made" (p. 162).

Neurogenesis is another process by which the brain is able to respond to its environment. *Neurogenesis* refers to the birth of new neurons generated from neural stem and progenitor cells (Kandel et al., 2013). In 1998, *Nature Medicine* published a paper by Eriksson et al. concluding that "cell genesis occurs in human brains and that the human brain retains the potential for self-renewal throughout life" (p. 1315). However, the focus of research (and thus this book) is on *neuroplasticity*, the change of existing neurons, rather than *neurogenesis*, the birth of neurons.

The concept of neuroplasticity has been around since Santiago Ramón y Cajal (see Chapter 1) noticed that cells die, which challenged the notion that there were a fixed number of cells in the brain (Stahnisch & Nitsch, 2002). Ramón y Cajal did not believe in modern interpretations of neuroplasticity or neurogenesis, explaining that once development is complete, the sources of growth and regeneration of axons and dendrites are irretrievably lost (Stahnisch & Nitsch, 2002). Ramón y Cajal believed that the nerve paths in the adult brain were fixed and unchangeable. He believed that everything could die and nothing could be regenerated. Decades later, other scientists noticed how neural pathways changed in response to stimuli or training (Draganski, Gaser, Kempermann, Kuhn, Winkler, Büchel, & May, 2006; Raisman, 1969; Watanabe, Gould, & McEwen, 1992). One of the landmark studies that informed today's understanding of neuroplasticity was published in 2000 by a group of scientists in London. Using magnetic resonance images (MRI)—a methodologically accepted imaging assay used to study how the brain functions during specific tasks (see Chapter 1 for of MRIs)—Maguire and her colleagues (2000) investigated how the hippocampus (primary role in memory and navigation) differed between 16 taxi drivers and 50 non–taxi drivers in London.

Taxi drivers in London undergo extensive training to learn how to navigate more than 25,000 streets between thousands of places that are not laid out in a grid. In fact, cab drivers who wish to effectively navigate the streets of London require an immense amount of time studying for their written exam. The average preparation time is a little less than three years. Maguire and colleagues (2000) discovered that the gray matter of the anterior hippocampus was significantly denser in London taxi drivers than it was in non–taxi drivers in London. Remember from Chapter 1 that the hippocampus is the structure within the brain that facilitates the storage of memories, so it should be no surprise that those who passed displayed a marked increase of neuronal density in this area of the brain.

Intrigued by their findings, Maguire and colleagues published two articles in 2006 that further examined memory and its role in neuroplasticity in the hippocampus. The first study compared 18 taxi drivers and 17 bus drivers in London (Maguire, Woolette, & Spiers, 2006). At first glance, the groups seem similar; however, taxi drivers must have a larger memory bank for navigating the complexities of the London streets than London bus drivers, who have a regular route to drive. Maguire and colleagues (2006) determined that London taxi drivers (those who had to remember) had much larger hippocampi than London bus drivers (those who did not). The second study compared the hippocampi of novice taxi drivers and experienced taxi drivers, concluding that the gray matter within the hippocampus was significantly denser in experienced cabdrivers than it was in novices.

In addition to Maguire's work, another landmark study came from Sara Lazar (2005) and her team. The article documented the effect that focused attention training to internal experiences can have on the human brain. Twenty longtime meditation (intense focused attention) practitioners were recruited and analyzed. Lazar and colleagues (2005) concluded that brain regions associated with attention, sensory perception, and processing were thicker in longtime meditators than they were in matched controls. The regions of the brain that showed increased cortical thickening in this study included the anterior insula (associated with self-awareness), a portion of the prefrontal cortex (associated with executive functions), and another portion of the brain (associated with sensory perception processing). This study provided additional support for the theory that more than the hippocampus can be impacted by education and training in order to intentionally change the structure and function of the brain.

In essence, the training that the London cabdrivers participated in increased the structure and function of their hippocampus—specifically in their ability to recall exact streets in London—allowing the cabdrivers to transport their passengers efficiently to their destinations. For Lazar et al.'s study, the demonstrated structural changes occurred in the same areas associated with attention regulation (AR), emotion regulation (ER), and cognitive regulation (CR). AR, ER, and CR are discussed at length in Chapter 3. For now, suffice it to say that long-term meditation practitioners are able to pay attention to their inner experiences, including bodily sensations and emotions (AR). (This makes them desired participants for functional imaging studies, as their accurate self-awareness reports are essential to accurate reading of MRIs.) Further, as these meditation practitioners are able to cognitively reappraise the thoughts that arise from paying attention to these bodily sensations and emotions (CR), they can, on demand, regulate stress and anxiety (ER). Other studies and compilations of studies have affirmed Lazar and colleagues' findings (Begley, 2007; Davidson & Lutz, 2008; Hölzel et al., 2011; Lutz et al., 2004). Some of these studies use experienced medita-tors as subjects, while others did not.

How Is Neuroplasticity Possible?

Around 90 billion neurons and 100 billion connections come together to form an elaborate neural network that we call the brain (Seung, 2012). As you consider this neural network, think of the United States and its transportation infrastructure. Its cities and states are all intricately con-nected. Highways and interstates connect major cities and states, with local streets and highways further connecting smaller parts of cities. The brain is no different; the neural network allows the brain to communicate with and within specific structures. These pathways are the foundation of neuroplasticity because when the number of connections between neu-rons increases, so do available routes to travel (Carter, 2014; Kandel et al., 2013; Seung, 2012).

In regard to neural regeneration, consider the same metaphor. When we are traveling and a road has been damaged by a flood or is simply under repair, we are rerouted to another path. We can get to the same destination but must use a different route. In some instances, it may take us longer to get to the destination we intended to go, but we do get there. When the original route is repaired, if it is repairable, we can then travel along that route once again. Further, certain routes that have more traffic are allocated a larger proportion of resources to ensure the safety, efficiency, and effectiveness of the route. The brain is no different; the more a certain pathway is used, the stronger the pathway and the easier it is to activate that neural pathway in the future (Kandel & Hawkins, 1992; Miller & Cohen, 2001; Tye, Stuber, de Ridder, Bonci, & Janak, 2008). Scientists refer to this phenomenon as *synaptic plasticity* (Kandel et al., 2013).

Neural communication, through either restructuring or regeneration, is an electrochemical process (Carter, 2014; Kandel et al., 2013). This means that communication involves chemical and electrical signals to relay mes-sages to itself and the body. Neural communication can be described in three steps: presynaptic, synaptic transmission, and postsynaptic. First, the presyn-aptic neuron sends an electrical signal down its axon until it reaches the synaptic terminals, which are located at the end of a neuron (Figure 2.1). To illustrate, imagine leaving your house in the morning for work—you pull out of your driveway and continue down the road. At some point, you will have to stop. This is the first step in neural communication, the electrical signal traveling down its "road."

Figure 2.1 Neuron and dendrite.

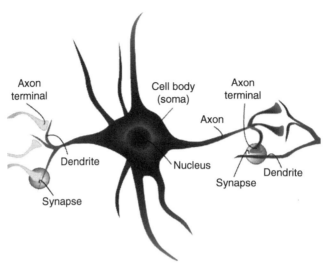

Note. Extracted from www.braingamereview.com/wp-content/uploads/2012/08/neuroplasti city-neurogenesis.png on December 21, 2014.

Once the electrical message reaches the presynaptic terminals, the electrical message stimulates the release of chemical messengers called neurotransmitters, which are released into the synaptic cleft and mark the beginning of the second step of neural communication (Kandel et al., 2013). The synaptic cleft is a microscopically small aqueous area between the two neurons communicating (the presynaptic neuron, where the message originated, and postsynaptic neuron, where the message is headed). Because in most cases the two neurons are not directly connected, the second step of neuronal communication must be chemical rather than electrical (Kandel et al., 2013). Going back to our example of driving down the road, this would be the equivalent of waiting until it is safe to proceed through the intersection. Imagine that you are stopped and are now relying on another signal for permission to continue—such as sitting at a red stoplight and waiting for the green "go" signal.

The third and final step involves binding of the neurotransmitter to the postsynaptic neuron. After the presynaptic neuron releases its neurotransmitters, they bind to specific receptors on a postsynaptic neuron. This causes the postsynaptic cell to generate an electrical signal. If the signal is strong enough, it will travel to the next neuron (Kandel et al., 2013). This would be the equivalent of pushing on the gas pedal and continuing to travel until you have to stop again.

This cascading process of electrochemical neural transmission is the basis of functioning. It forms our memories; permits breathing, digestion, movement, emotions, and reasoning; and so on. The point is that electro-chemical communication is the "language" of neurons. If this language is disrupted, remarkable changes emerge in behavior and the structure and function of the brain. Given its pervasive nature, neuronal communication is exceptionally specific; some neurotransmitters increase the probability of an electrical signal continuing in the postsynaptic neuron (excitatory); others decrease the probability (inhibitory).

In addition to exogenous chemicals, emotions and thoughts can influence neural communication (Kandel et al., 2013). For example, if the fight-or-flight response is activated, a profound increase in the release of certain transmitters occurs in the synaptic cleft. The same is true if the reward pathway is activated. Dopamine (a specific neurotransmitter) is often associated with this pathway. The more a certain pathway is activated, the easier it is for it to become activated again. To illustrate, imagine having to meet another person in a building with which you are unfamiliar. If you are anything like the authors of this chapter, this is not a simple automatic process. It requires intentional direction of our attention to navigate the unfamiliar hallways. However, after you repeatedly visit this person, there comes a point when you go to the building and you know exactly where to go; thus, your attention is directed elsewhere.

How does this all occur? How can certain pathways become stronger? The process has been called *long-term potentiation*. Rapidly activating two neurons (presynaptic and postsynaptic) triggers a cascading effect that makes it easier for those two synapses to communicate again. Scientists have determined that with repeated excitation of a neuron, calcium flows into the postsynaptic neuron and triggers other messengers to continue the process. Calcium levels are kept relatively low in neurons and are therefore exceptionally sensitive to the smallest fluctuations. Because of the influx of calcium, two fundamental changes occur. First, in the postsynaptic neuron, various protein kinases add more receptors. The more receptors on a specific post-synaptic neuron, the more transmitters it can collect. Think of it as adding more garages (receptors) to your house; that is, the more garages, the more cars you can store (neurotransmitters). Second, the postsynaptic neuron retroactively communicates back to the presynaptic neuron, telling it to release more neurotransmitters. Think of it as telling the car dealership to order more cars because you now have more garages. Interestingly, influxes of calcium trigger the changes to the genetic code carried by RNA. While scientists are still working to fully explain the molecular and cellular underpinnings of long-term potentiation, it is clear that changes occur to both the pre- and postsynaptic neurons by increasing the amount of neurotransmitters released and adding more receptors, respectively.

Have you heard the phrase "Neurons that wire together fire together"? This phrase encapsulates the process we just described (Hanson, 2013; Kandel et al., 2013). Often this concept is referred to as *Hebbian theory* within the neuroscience literature. Based on what you focus on, you literally are strengthening (long-term potentiation) or weakening the synaptic connections between the neurons of your brain. When the neural connections are strengthening, certain areas of the brain's gray matter increase (neuroplasticity). In addition, the creation of new neural connections is also possible because of the genetic changes induced by long-term potentiation. Similarly, when connections are weakened, the gray matter can also thin and become less dense (Hanson, 2013; Kandel et al., 2013).

Although this pithy "wiring and firing" phrase may accurately describe learning and development, it also may not be entirely true. For example, experts in math do indeed have increased cortical thickness in an area of the brain (intraparietal sulcus [IPS]) that is associated with acuity of the approximate number system (Emerson & Cantlon, 2014). Still, some people who are better at math have shown a less dense area of the IPS portion of the brain, which may mean that neurons have been pruned, allowing faster, more efficient synaptic communication (Emerson & Cantlon, 2014). In other words, if you are on the road with 100 different ways to get where you are going but you keep taking the same route, the other roads will appear less traveled. Similarly, a neuron not used may actually reduce in size because the message found the fastest route.

Let's consider a math example. What is 1 plus 1? You likely didn't need to pull out a calculator or count out tokens to answer this question. The neurological route to produce the answer is fast and efficient because you use this information more than you may even be aware. But what if we asked you what 7,593 plus 68,649 is? How about 9,483 times 67,579? How about 637 divided by 48? You likely had to calculate those answers in your head, on paper, or with a calculator because you don't use this information regularly. You learned it, you can still "do" it, but it may not come as quickly.

Let's consider another example. Do you remember learning to ride a bicycle? It seemed nearly impossible at first, right? Likely you began with training wheels. After due time, you removed them. Scientifically, your brain was undergoing neuroplasticity, slowly adapting itself by altering and creating new neural connections. What followed was your becoming increasingly familiar with all the mental facilities it takes to ride a bike without training wheels. As these nascent neural networks strengthened, so too did your confidence in your ability to ride the bicycle. This process goes well beyond learning to ride a bike and can be affected by even the most innocuous factors (Corbetta & Shulman, 2002; Wulf & Prinz, 2001).

Each and every day, our brains undoubtedly change as a result of what we experience and how we process the experience (via thought, emotion, and/or bodily sensation). Mostly, these changes occur through neuroplasticity (Carter, 2014; Hanson, 2013; Kandel et al., 2013). What seems to be a commonly accepted truth is that in order for us to learn, we must pay attention to what we want to learn (Hallahan & Sapona, 1983; Harris, Todorov, & Fiske, 2005; Treisman & Gelade, 1980; Weiss, 2013). In 2004, *Nature* published a landmark study by Draganski et al., comparing volunteers who learned how to juggle with those who had not. The authors found actual structural change in the areas associated with visual motion and attention in those who learned to juggle. This study underscored the importance that what we pay attention to and focus on literally changes the structure and function of our brain. Hölzel and colleagues (2011) further emphasized the correlation (and, in some studies, cause and effect) of attention and functional and structural changes in a meta-analysis of literature.

While it is evident that what we pay attention to each and every day literally changes the structure and function of our brains, we are also beginning to understand that there are many influences on how the brain can change and how much of that change may be evident in the moment (state) or how much of it becomes an entrained characteristic or behavior (trait) (Geiger, Achermann, & Jenni, 2010; Goodman, Rietschel, Lo, Costanzo, & Hatfield, 2013).

Influencers on Neuroplasticity

There are three notable points that can affect the degree of and the extent to which neuroplasticity occurs. There are likely others, but we will focus our discussion on aging; glial cells (another type of brain cell); and the interplay among genetics, environment, and behavior/experience (technically a component of environment, but for purposes of this book we are subdividing). First, as we mentioned, the brain never stops changing; however, it is susceptible to aging (Arriagada, Growdon, Hedley-Whyte, & Hyman, 1992; Craik & Salthouse, 2008; Dickson et al., 1992; Gunning-Dixon & Raz, 2000; Price & Morris, 1999; Raz et al., 2005; Terry, DeTeresa, & Hansen, 1987; Terry et al., 1991). As the brain ages, its ability to rewire existing neurons and birth new neurons diminishes (Drapeau et al., 2003; Gallagher & Rapp, 1997; Morrison & Hof, 1997). In addition, the aging brain experiences a wide range of changes that may impair and affect learning and development (Hof & Morrison, 2004). For instance, certain structures lose volume but some appear to be safeguarded from atrophy (Fjell et al., 2009; Good et al., 2002).

One example is the hippocampus, which you may remember has a large role in memory. It appears to have certain subregions within it that deteriorate with age (Buckner et al., 2005; West, 1993). If the hippocampus were removed, making new memories would be impossible (McClelland, McNaughton, & O'Reilly, 1995; Scoville & Milner, 1957); however, all memory prior to the removal of the hippocampus would still exist (Scoville & Milner, 1957). That leads scientists to believe that memories are actually stored all over our cortex (i.e., the gray matter; also see Chapter 1 and the many rooms in the house analogy). The hippocampus does not appear to be required to recall long-term memories (McClelland et al., 1995), but forming new short-term memory is dependent on the hippocampus (Scoville & Milner, 1957). So this may be why as we age we have more trouble remembering little things, such as where the keys are or telephone numbers (Drapeau et al., 2003; Mohapel, Mundt-Petersen, Brundin, & Frielingsdorf, 2006).

Conversely, the occipital lobe (i.e., the part of your brain that processes vision) experiences very few changes with age (Raz et al., 2005). Given that the brain does shrink with age, so do the number of receptors (Kemperman, Gast, & Gage, 2002) and the amount of white matter (Craik & Salthouse, 2008). If that wasn't enough, with age, certain plaques and tangles begin to form in the brain (Dickson et al., 1992). The accumulation of plaques and tangles is believed to be the underlying cause of many forms of dementia, such as Alzheimer's (Arriagada et al., 1992; Price & Morris, 1999; Terry et al., 1987; Terry et al., 1991). One of the most relevant aspects to learning and development is that the brain's ability to generate new neurons (neurogenesis) declines as age increases, alongside the declining probability of healthy functioning adult neurons (Shors, Anderson, Curlik, & Nokia, 2012).

There is evidence to suggest that the normal process of aging can contribute to cortical thinning (Lazar et al., 2005). This idea, perhaps, is the origin of the phrase "use it or lose it." In the aforementioned study, Lazar and colleagues (2005) discovered what would be considered normal thinning of the neocortex in the group that was older. However, in the group that practiced longtime meditation (e.g., focused breathing and/or mindfulness, which we explain in detail in Chapter 3 as AR, ER, and CR), cortical thinning was not present when compared with age-matched controls. This suggests that the normal aging process and its influence on brain density can also be intentionally changed through engaging in a specific daily practice of focused breathing.

Let us go even deeper than a cellular level and present a few studies that investigated mindfulness at a molecular level. Chromosomes, which carry our genetic code, have caps on each of their ends to protect them (Richter & von Zglinicki, 2007). These small structures are called *telomeres* and bind to each of the four ends of a chromosome; think of a telomere as the little aglet on the end of a shoelace that keeps your shoelaces from unraveling. The telomeres are the aglet and the shoestring is the chromosome; now imagine the shoestring is in the shape of an X with four aglets. As your chromosomes replicate (the shoestring begins to divide itself into replicas of itself), the aglets become smaller and smaller with each cell division. When the telomeres or aglets become too small, the cell dies. Generally, an enzyme called *telomerase reverse transcriptase* controls the rate at which aglets are broken down, trying to avoid leaving the shoestring vulnerable to the environment (imagine your shoestring fraying with no aglet to keep the ends together). In addition to normal aging, chronic stress expedites the shortening of telomeres (Richter & von Zglinicki, 2007). Chronic stress can induce the same changes in a healthy adult's telomeres that would be characteristic of someone who is elderly.

The link between focused-breathing meditation and mindfulness (the practice of becoming aware of what you are paying attention to right here and right now without being attached to your judgment of your experience) and its ability to reduce stress and prevent the shortening of telomeres has been researched. A recent meta-analysis reviewed four studies. Schutte and Malouff (2014) contended that mindfulness training had a significant effect on increasing the activity of the enzyme (telomerase reverse transcriptase), responsible for maintaining telomere length. However, this research is still hotly debated. The debate highlights the need for more randomized controlled studies, as the few studies currently published do not contain a standardized intervention and include a low number of participants.

We understand that neuroplasticity involves more than just neurons. Neuroplasticity is dependent on other cells in the brain called glial cells. The story of the glial cell is one of the underdog. It was once believed to have no function in the brain apart from being the "glue" that held all the "important" neurons together. After all, the word *glial* is derived from the Latin word for glue (www.merriam-webster.com/dictionary/glial). Because they were once thought to be of only "little importance" to neural function, glial cells have only recently begun to be studied. What science has revealed so far is that the number of glial cells mirrors the number of neurons in the brain, thus making the total number of glial cells around 90 billion, although the proportion of glial cells to neurons varies in different brain regions (Azevedo et al., 2009). Glial cells support healthy brain functioning as they provide essential nutrients (e.g., glucose, oxygen) to the neurons—which is vital if a neuron is to remain or grow to be healthy and functioning. Additionally, glial cells destroy infection pathogens, remove nonfunctioning neurons to create room for neurogenesis, and help recycle certain neurotransmitters (Azevedo et al., 2009; Kandel et al., 2013). As if those functions were not enough, scientists have recently discovered that glial cells are a primary player in the "formation, maturation, function, and elimination of synapses" (Clarke & Barres, 2013, p. 311). Thus, glial cells are an intricate part of neuroplasticity and thus also an intricate part of learning and development.

Further, myelin (the "insulation" that covers the axon of the neuron) speeds up communication between neurons (Carter, 2014). Myelin is actually the "leg" of an oligodendrocyte (a glial cell).

> Previously of interest in demyelinating diseases such as multiple sclerosis, myelin is attracting new interest as an unexpected contributor to a wide range of psychiatric disorders, including depression and schizophrenia. This is stimulating research into myelin involvement in normal cognitive function, learning, and [intelligence quotient] IQ. Myelination continues for decades in the human brain; it is modifiable by experience, and it affects information processing by regulating the velocity and synchrony of impulse conduction between distant cortical regions. (Fields, 2008, p. 362)

Our point is that myelin may be modified by experience.

Neuroplasticity can also be induced or limited as a result of damage in the brain. Someone who experiences brain damage, such as a stroke or traumatic brain injury, will experience an increase in neuroplasticity, because the brain is trying to repair itself (Doidge, 2007). The brain is a self-healer; however, the extent to which neurons are able to grow and then survive depends on myriad factors—genes, environment, time of treatment, and behavior/experience/choices (Doidge, 2007). Understanding that helps explain why recovery varies person to person.

When it comes to this area of the research and our ability to intentionally influence neurological change, there is very little research that is consistent. Pharmaceutical research has focused on understanding the conditions that promote and facilitate neuroplasticity post–brain injury (Font, Arboix, & Krupinski, 2010). The majority of the research we have to share that doesn't use pharmaceuticals comes in the form of mindfulness-based stress reduction (MBSR) (Kabat-Zinn, 2013). In this research, there are several studies that illustrate that participants in eight-week MBSR training programs were able to better manage the stress created from traumatic injury and the resulting emotional losses of injury.

We hope you have come to understand that our neurons process our experiences through a complex electrochemical reaction. We just have one more key piece of information to share, and it involves the connection of genetics and the environment (including behavior/experience). How do certain genes turn themselves off and on? Why do identical twins have nonidentical outcomes? The answer, in part, is that the neurotransmitters released during the chemical phase of neural communication (think back to part two of neural communication) can turn specific genes on or off; they can even inhibit or activate surrounding neurons. The actual mechanisms by which this change occurs are much more complex. But, in essence, these changes occur because of the release of neurotransmitters that signal a change in epigenetic markers that then change which genes will be expressed as the genetic code is replicated (Nestler, 2011). Interestingly, mindfulness meditation training has been associated with decreased expression of proinflammatory genes (Kaliman et al., 2014), thus illustrating its potential to influence gene expression.

We have provided you with an overview of how we know the brain can change. In Chapter 3, we talk more specifically about the specific training methodology that has been used in correlation with structural and functional changes of the brain.

Editor's Summary Points and Questions to Consider

1. The brain has the amazing ability to respond to external stimuli through neurogenesis and neuroplasticity. How does knowing all the ways that the brain can regenerate and change influence how you view the design, delivery, and evaluation of all the opportunities you provide students to learn and develop within higher education (including in-class and out-of-class opportunities)?

2. There are specific training methodologies that promote neuroplasticity and even appear to decrease the effects of normal aging. How does knowing this information influence how you view the design, delivery, and evaluation of all the opportunities you provide students to learn and develop within higher education (including in-class and out-of-class opportunities)? How does it influence how and when students access higher education at your institution?

3. Mind-set is a malleable factor that contributes to student success. How might neuroscience findings inform intentional design changes to shift students' mind-set?

References

Abeles, M. (1991). The auditory cortex: Structural and functional bases of auditory perception. *Trends in Neurosciences, 14*(5), 214.

Arriagada, P. V., Growdon, J. H., Hedley-Whyte, E. T., & Hyman, B. T. (1992). Neurofibrillary tangles but not senile plaques parallel duration and severity of Alzheimer's disease. *Neurology, 42*(3), 631–639.

Azevedo, F. A., Carvalho, L. R., Grinberg, L. T., Farfel, J. M., Ferretti, R. E., Leite, R. E., & Herculano-Houzel, S. (2009). Equal numbers of neuronal and non-neuronal cells make the human brain an isometrically scaled-up primate brain. *Journal of Comparative Neurology, 513*(5), 532–541.

Begley, S. (2007). *Change your mind, change your brain: How a new science reveals our extraordinary potential to transform ourselves.* New York, NY: Random House.

Buckner, R., Snyder, A., Shannon, B., LaRossa, G., Sachs, R., Fotenos, A. F., . . . Mintun, M. A. (2005). Molecular, structural, and functional characterization of Alzheimer's disease: Evidence for a relationship between default activity, amyloid, and memory. *Journal of Neuroscience, 25*(34), 7709–7717.

Carter, R. (2014). *The human brain book.* New York, NY: DK Publishing.

Clarke, L. E., & Barres, B. A. (2013). Emerging roles of astrocytes in neural circuit development. *Nature Reviews Neuroscience, 14*(5), 311–321.

Corbetta, M., & Shulman, G. L. (2002). Control of goal-directed and stimulus-driven attention in the brain. *Nature Reviews Neuroscience, 3*(3), 201–215.

Craik, F. I. M. & Salthouse, T. A. (Eds.), (2008). *Handbook of aging and cognition.* (3rd ed.). New York, NY: Psychology Press.

Davidson, R. J., & Lutz, A. (2008). Buddha's brain: Neuroplasticity and meditation. *IEEE Signal Processing Magazine, 25*(1), 174–176.

Dickson, D. W., Crystal, H. A., Mattiace, L. A., Masur, D. M., Blau, A. D., Davies, P., & Aronson, M. K. (1992). Identification of normal and pathological aging in prospectively studied nondemented elderly humans. *Neurobiology of Aging, 13*(1), 179–189.

Doidge, N. (2007). *The brain that changes itself: Stories of personal triumph from the frontiers of brain science.* New York, NY: Viking.

Draganski, B., Gaser, C., Busch, V., Schuierer, G., Bogdahn, U., & May, A. (2004). Neuroplasticity: Changes in grey matter induced by training. *Nature, 427*(6972), 311–312.

Drapeau, E., Mayo, W., Aurousseau, C., Le Moal, M., Piazza, P. V., & Abrous, D. N. (2003). Spatial memory performances of aged rats in the water maze predict levels of hippocampal neurogenesis. *Proceedings of the National Academy of Sciences of the United States of America, 100*(24), 14385–14390.

Dweck, C. S. (2007). The perils and promises of praise. *Educational Leadership, 65*(2), 34–39.

Emerson, R. W., & Cantlon, J. F. (2014). Continuity and change in children's longitudinal neural responses to numbers. *Developmental Science, 18*(2), 314–326.

Eriksson, P. S., Perfilieva, E., Björk-Eriksson, T., Alborn, A. M., Nordborg, C., Peterson, D. A., & Gage, F. H. (1998). Neurogenesis in the adult human hippocampus. *Nature Medicine, 4*(11), 1313–1317.

Erwin, T. D. (1991). *Assessing student learning and development: A guide to the principles, goals, and methods of determining college outcomes.* Ann Arbor, MI: ProQuest Info & Learning.

Fields, R. D. (2008). White matter in learning, cognition, and psychiatric disorder. *Trends in Neurosciences, 31*(7), 361–370.

Fjell, A. M., Walhovd, K. B., Fennema-Notestine, C., McEvoy, L. K., Hagler, D. J., Holland, D., & Dale, A. M. (2009). One-year brain atrophy evident in healthy aging. *Journal of Neuroscience, 29*(48), 15223–15231.

Font, M. A., Arboix, A., & Krupinski, J. (2010). Angiogenesis, neurogenesis and neuroplasticity in ischemic stroke. *Current Cardiology Reviews, 6*(3), 238–244.

Gallagher, M., & Rapp, P. R. (1997). The use of animal models to study the effects of aging on cognition. *Annual Review of Psychology, 48*(1), 339–370.

Geiger, A., Achermann, P., & Jenni, O. G. (2010). Sleep, intelligence and cognition in a developmental context: Differentiation between traits and state-dependent aspects. *Progress in Brain Research, 185*(3), 167–179.

Good, C., Johnsrude, I., Ashburner, J., Henson, R., Friston, K., & Frackowiak, R. S. J. (2002). A voxel-based morphometric study of ageing in 465 normal adult human brains. *NeuroImage, 14*(1), 21–36.

Goodman, R. N., Rietschel, J. C., Lo, L. C., Costanzo, M. E., & Hatfield, B. D. (2013). Stress, emotion regulation and cognitive performance: The predictive contributions of trait and state relative frontal EEG alpha asymmetry. *International Journal of Psychophysiology, 87*(2), 115–123.

Gunning-Dixon, F. M., & Raz, N. (2000). The cognitive correlates of white matter abnormalities in normal aging: A quantitative review. *Neuropsychology, 14*(2), 224–232.

Hallahan, D. P., & Sapona, R. (1983). Self-monitoring of attention with learning-disabled children past research and current issues. *Journal of Learning Disabilities, 16*(10), 616–620.

Hanson, R. (2013). *Hardwiring happiness: The new brain science of contentment, calm, and confidence.* New York, NY: Harmony.

Harris, L. T., Todorov, A., & Fiske, S. T. (2005). Attributions on the brain: Neuroimaging dispositional inferences, beyond theory of mind. *NeuroImage, 28*(4), 763–769.

Hof, P. R., & Morrison, J. H. (2004). The aging brain: Morphomolecular senescence of cortical circuits. *Trends in Neurosciences, 27*(10), 607–613.

Hölzel, B. K., Carmody, J., Vangel, M., Congleton, C., Yerramsetti, S. M., Gard, T., & Lazar, S. W. (2011). Mindfulness practice leads to increases in regional brain gray matter density. *Psychiatry Research: Neuroimaging, 191*(1), 36–43.

James, W. (n.d.). Retrieved from http://www.goodreads.com/author/quotes/15865. William_James

Kabat-Zinn, J. (2013). *Full catastrophe living, revised edition: How to cope with stress, pain and illness using mindfulness meditation.* New York, NY: Bantam.

Kaliman, P., Alvarez-Lopez, M. J., Cosín-Tomás, M., Rosenkranz, M. A., Lutz, A., & Davidson, R. J. (2014). Rapid changes in histone deacetylases and inflammatory gene expression in expert meditators. *Psychoneuroendocrinology, 40*, 96–107.

Kandel, E. R., & Hawkins, R. D. (1992). The biological basis of learning and individuality. *Scientific American, 267*(3), 78–86.

Kandel, E. R., Schwartz, J. H., & Jessell, T. M. (Eds.). (2013). *Principles of neural science* (Vol. 5.) New York, NY: McGraw-Hill.

Kempermann, G., Gast, D., & Gage, F. H. (2002). Neuroplasticity in old age: Sustained fivefold induction of hippocampal neurogenesis by long-term environmental enrichment. *Annals of Neurology, 52*(2), 135–143.

Lazar, S. W., Kerr, C. E., Wasserman, R. H., Gray, J. R., Greve, D. N., Treadway, M. T., & Fischl, B. (2005). Meditation experience is associated with increased cortical thickness. *Neuroreport, 16*(17), 1893–1897.

Lutz, A., Greischar, L., Rawlings, N., Ricard, M., & Davidson, R. (2004). Long-term meditators self-induce high-amplitude gamma synchrony during mental practice. *Proceedings of the National Academy of Sciences of the United States of America, 101*(46), 16369–16373.

Maguire, E. A., Gadian, D. G., Johnsrude, I. S., Good, C. D., Ashburner, J., Frackowiak, R. S. J., & Frith, C. D. (2000). Navigation-related structural change in the hippocampi of taxi drivers. *Proceedings of the National Academy of Sciences of the United States of America, 97*(8), 4398–4403.

Maguire, E. A., Woollett, K., & Spiers, H. J. (2006). London taxi drivers and bus drivers: A structural MRI and neuropsychological analysis. *Hippocampus, 16*(12), 1091–1101.

McClelland, J. L., McNaughton, B. L., & O'Reilly, R. C. (1995). Why there are complementary learning systems in the hippocampus and neocortex: Insights from the successes and failures of connectionist models of learning and memory. *Psychological Review, 102*(3), 419.

Mechelli, A., Crinion, J. T., Noppeney, U., O'Doherty, J., Ashburner, J., Frackowiak, R. S., & Price, C. J. (2004). Neurolinguistics: Structural plasticity in the bilingual brain. *Nature, 431*(7010), 757.

Meintjes, E. M., Jacobson, S. W., Molteno, C. D., Gatenby, J. C., Warton, C., Cannistraci, C. J., . . . & Jacobson, J. L. (2010). An fMRI study of magnitude comparison and exact addition in children. *Magnetic Resonance Imaging, 28*(3), 351–362.

Miller, E. K., & Cohen, J. D. (2001). An integrative theory of prefrontal cortex function. *Annual Review of Neuroscience, 24*(1), 167–202.

Mohapel, P., Mundt-Petersen, K., Brundin, P., & Frielingsdorf, H. (2006). Working memory training decreases hippocampal neurogenesis. *Neuroscience, 142*(3), 609–613.

Morrison, J. H., & Hof, P. R. (1997). Life and death of neurons in the aging brain. *Science, 278*(5337), 412–419.

Nestler, E. (2011). Hidden switches in the mind. *Scientific American, 305*(6), 76–83.

Paillard, T. (2008). Combined application of neuromuscular electrical stimulation and voluntary muscular contractions. *Sports Medicine, 38*(2), 161–177.

Penfield, W., & Rasmussen, T. (1950). The cerebral cortex of man: A clinical study of localization of function. *Journal of the American Medical Association, 144*(16), 1412.

Price, J. L., & Morris, J. C. (1999). Tangles and plaques in nondemented aging and preclinical Alzheimer's disease. *Annals of Neurology, 45*(3), 358–368.

Raisman, G. (1969). Neuronal plasticity in the septal nuclei of the adult rat. *Brain Research, 14*(1), 25–48.

Raz, N., Lindenberger, U., Rodrigue, K. M., Kennedy, K. M., Head, D., Williamson, A., & Acker, J. D. (2005). Regional brain changes in aging healthy adults: General trends, individual differences and modifiers. *Cerebral Cortex, 15*(11), 1676–1689.

Richter, T., & von Zglinicki, T. (2007). A continuous correlation between oxidative stress and telomere shortening in fibroblasts. *Experimental Gerontology, 42*(11), 1039–1042.

Sampaio-Baptista, C., Scholz, J., Jenkinson, M., Thomas, A. G., Filippini, N., Smit, G., & Johansen-Berg, H. (2014). Gray matter volume is associated with rate of subsequent skill learning after a long-term training intervention. *NeuroImage, 96,* 158–166.

Schutte, N. S., & Malouff, J. M. (2014). The relationship between perceived stress and telomere length: A meta-analysis. *Stress and Health.* Retrieved from http://www.ncbi.nlm.nih.gov/pubmed/25393133. doi.org/10.1002/smi.2607

Scoville, W. B., & Milner, B. (1957). Loss of recent memory after bilateral hippocampal lesions. *Journal of Neurology, Neurosurgery, and Psychiatry, 20*(1), 11–21.

Seung, S. (2012). *Connectome: How the brain's wiring makes us who we are.* Boston, MA: Houghton Mifflin Harcourt.

Shors, T. J., Anderson, M. L., Curlik, D. M., & Nokia, M. S. (2012). Use it or lose it: How neurogenesis keeps the brain fit for learning. *Behavioural Brain Research, 227*(2), 450–458.

Smedt, B. D., Holloway, I. D., Ansari, D. (2011). Effects of problem size and arithmetic operation on brain activation during calculation in children with varying levels of arithmetical fluency. *Neuroimage, 57,* 771–781.

Sokolov, E. N. (1963). *Perception and the conditioned reflex* (S. W. Waydenfield, Trans.). Oxford, UK: Pergamon Press.

Stahnisch, F. W., & Nitsch, R. (2002). Santiago Ramón y Cajal's concept of neuronal plasticity: The ambiguity lives on. *Trends in Neurosciences, 25*(11), 589–591.

Terry, R. D., DeTeresa, R., & Hansen, L. A. (1987). Neocortical cell counts in normal human adult aging. *Annals of Neurology, 21*(6), 530–539.

Terry, R. D., Masliah, E., Salmon, D. P., Butters, N., DeTeresa, R., Hill, R., & Katzman, R. (1991). Physical basis of cognitive alterations in Alzheimer's disease: Synapse loss is the major correlate of cognitive impairment. *Annals of Neurology, 30*(4), 572–580.

Treisman, A. M., & Gelade, G. (1980). A feature-integration theory of attention. *Cognitive Psychology, 12*(1), 97–136.

Tye, K. M., Stuber, G. D., de Ridder, B., Bonci, A., & Janak, P. H. (2008). Rapid strengthening of thalamo-amygdala synapses mediates cue–reward learning. *Nature, 453*(7199), 1253–1257.

Watanabe, Y., Gold, E., & McEwen, B. S. (1992). Stress induces atrophy of apical dendrites of hippocampal CA3 pyramidal neurons. *Brain Research, 588*(2), 341–345.

Weiss, S. L. (2013). Learning-related behaviors small group reading instruction in the general education classroom. *Intervention in School and Clinic, 48*(5), 294–302.

West, M. J. (1993). Regionally specific loss of neurons in the aging human hippocampus. *Neurobiology of Aging, 14*(4), 287–293.

Wulf, G., & Prinz, W. (2001). Directing attention to movement effects enhances learning: A review. *Psychonomic Bulletin & Review, 8*(4), 648–660.

Zilles, K. (1992). Neuronal plasticity as an adaptive property of the central nervous system. *Annals of Anatomy, 174*(5), 383–391.

3

STRATEGIES THAT INTENTIONALLY CHANGE THE BRAIN

Marilee J. Bresciani Ludvik, Matthew R. Evrard, and Philippe Goldin,
with review by Thomas Van Vleet

Between stimulus and response there is a space. In that space is our power to choose our
response. In our response lies our growth and our freedom.

—Victor Frankl (www.brainyquote.com/quotes/quotes/v/viktorefr160380.html)

We took a bit of time in Chapter 2 to define *neuroplasticity* and explain the influences on it. In this chapter, we discuss the importance of harnessing what we have learned from neuroscience to create educational opportunities that enhance student success. To theoretically frame the connection of neuroscience to learning and development, we borrow from the field of clinical psychology (Ochsner, Bunge, Gross, & Gabrieli, 2002). Specifically, we posit that higher education administrators (e.g., student affairs staff, academic support staff) and faculty can use strategies known to structurally and functionally change portions of the brain in order to foster students' ability to do the following:

- Become aware of how and to what students pay attention (attention regulation; AR).
- Become aware of how students regulate their emotions (emotion regulation; ER).
- Become aware of students they use their cognitive processes for inquiry and then direct their attention toward whatever it is they desire, while regulating their emotions on demand (cognitive regulation; CR).

- Become aware of how AR, ER, and CR are key to fostering students' learning and development success.

In particular, CR empowers students to make meaning of their experiences and who they are relative to what is being experienced. Further, it is expected that the combination of AR, ER, and CR training methodology promotes critical thinking dispositions as well as creativity, resilience, and emotional intelligence, along with other outcomes desired by employers and faculty alike, such as conscious choice making and the ability to own the consequences of choice.

Hölzel, Carmody, and colleagues' (2011) meta-analysis exemplified the effectiveness that specific training interventions can have on cultivating body awareness, AR, ER, and CR. Participants in this study were able to improve their own AR, ER, and CR abilities by engaging in the specific training methodologies provided. Similarly, Hölzel, Lazar, and colleague's (2011) research further confirmed these findings using functional and structural neuroimaging (functional magnetic resonance imaging [fMRI] and MRI; see Chapter 1). These publications were some of the first to provide empirical evidence that specific AR, ER, and CR training methodologies are associated with neuroplasticity changes in the brain. Markedly, the brain regions affected parallel those in learning and development. A few examples include the anterior cingulate cortex, insula, temporoparietal junction (the division between the temporal lobe and parietal lobe), frontolimbic network, and default mode network (structures within the prefrontal cortex that communicate during resting states). Together with Hölzel and colleagues' work, many publications continue to replicate (and extend) these initial findings, substantially validating the power these training methodologies have on inducing structural and functional changes in the brain (Converse, Ahlers, Travers, & Davidson, 2014).

Research in clinical psychology and neuroscience reinforces the significance of extrapolating these findings to guide the design, delivery, and evaluation of higher education. For example, clinical psychology research tells us that negative self-thoughts are inversely related to self-efficacy and positively related to stress (Multon, Brown, & Lent, 1991; Schunk, 1985; Zimmerman, 2000). CR, which is the ability to observe, analyze, focus, and reflect on thoughts, allows an individual to choose which thoughts he or she reflects and subsequently acts on. This regulatory strategy has been shown to decrease anxiety (Mahone, Bruch, & Heimberg, 1993) as well as enhance overall well-being (Kabat-Zinn, 2013; Segal, Williams, & Teasdale, 2013).

The launching point in this entire process appears to be AR. AR refers to processes of regulation attention that modify alerting, orienting, and executive attention. AR does not involve training in reasoning or linguistic processing. Instead, AR involves training in the ability to focus on a selected object while inhibiting irrelevant distracter stimuli. Because attention is the gateway to all other higher-order cognitive abilities and emotional responses, slight modifications in attentional deployment may have large effects on emotion generation (Fan & Posner, 2004).

Emotion generation and regulation are important for two primary reasons. First, the amygdala appears to modulate the strength of conscious memory for events according to emotional importance, regardless of whether the emotion is pleasant or aversive (Hamann, Ely, Grafton, & Kilts, 1999). Second, the amygdala's influences on memory storage are not mediated by lasting neural changes within the amygdala (Packard, Cahill, & McGaugh, 1994). It could be that not training ourselves to become aware of our emotions or not training ourselves to be able to regulate them on demand may negatively impact our ability to store and potentially recall memories.

Goldin and Gross (2010) reported that subjects who experienced social anxiety and engaged in breath-focused attention tasks (a form of AR) actually reduced their amygdala activity (reported reduced levels of anxiety) and subjects increased the level of activity in other brain areas localized for attention and other executive functions (including the prefrontal cortex). Goldin and Gross are not alone in reporting such liberating findings; focused breathing's correlation with abating anxiety and expanding attention has been validated and extended in various studies (Arch & Craske, 2006, 2010; Batten & Hayes, 2005; Hocking & Koenig, 1995; Luders, 2014; Luders et al., 2012; Mankus, Aldao, Kerns, Mayville, & Mennin, 2013; Roemer, Orsillo, & Salters-Pedneault, 2008). For example, a report by Chiesa, Calati, and Serretti (2011) posited that attention is associated with a decrease in stress and significant improvements in selective and executive attention. We can postulate that such reported changes in improved attention and decreased stress and anxiety likely increases students' overall well-being and their overall success.

To further emphasize the importance of AR, ER, and CR in a training model that promotes student success, Goldin's and others' research (Anderson, Goldin, Kurita, & Gross, 2008; Goldin & Gross, 2010; Goldin, Hakimi, Manber, Canli, & Gross, 2009; Goldin, Manber-Ball, Werner, Heimbert, & Gross, 2009; Goldin, McRae, Ramel, & Gross, 2008; Goldin, Ramel, & Gross, 2009; Hutcherson, Goldin, Ramel, McRae, & Gross, 2008) posited that emotions coordinate a human's experiential, behavioral, and physiological responses to perceived challenges and opportunities. In other words, emotions dictate perception and thus emotions dictate how one responds to events. If left untrained, these emotions interfere with a student's cognitive processing ability.

Hanson (2013) argued that because of our evolution of survival (further unpacked in Chapter 9), our brain is hardwired to detect threat first. When a student is given a cognitively challenging problem to attend to (inside or outside the classroom), the brain may see the assignment or the task as a threat; thus, the fight-or-flight system is activated. The *unaware* activation of the limbic system, as we have shown, can impede cognitive reasoning. So, in addition to students bringing whatever emotions life had already presented them with into the learning and development opportunity provided to them, they may now be in a learning or developmental situation where further emotional activation occurs. As highlighted in the previous paragraph, this emotional activation can influence how they see the learning opportunity and how they interact with it if the emotions are left untrained. It may even impact memory storage of the learning activity.

There is good news, however. Emotions are exceptionally subject to diverse regulatory processes, which can modulate their intensity, duration, expression, and neural profile (Gross, 2002; Gross & Thompson, 2007). Through the use of AR and ER training, students can be taught how to regulate their emotions in a manner that allows them to experience their emotions, rather than suppress them. The training also empowers students to engage cognitively with the material that may have activated the emotional response, fostering more conscious choices and awareness of potential consequences of their choices. Rather than reacting to whatever stressful or emotional circumstances students find themselves in (whether it is an assigned activity or an elected one), students can choose a response. How?

CR uses language-based reasoning strategies to reconstruct the meaning of an emotion-eliciting situation in order to up- or downmodulate specific features of emotion (Ochsner & Gross, 2005). Compared with less adaptive regulation strategies (e.g., behavioral avoidance, expressive suppression), CR is broadly applicable and effective across situations without physiological or cognitive costs. Together, the AR, ER, and CR processes initiate, maintain, and monitor the implementation of cognitive linguistic strategies that reinterpret an emotional situation (Ochsner & Gross, 2005).

Without AR, ER, and CR, some may experience emotion dysregulation. In essence, we refer to *emotion dysregulation* as what happens when we are not aware of our emotions and not engaged in cognitive reappraisal processes and other types of inquiry training (CR). Emotion dysregulation is thought to play a crucial role in anxiety and mood disorders (Goldin & Gross, 2010; Goldin, Hakimi, et al., 2009). A growing body of empirical work is beginning to illuminate the neural correlates and behavioral sequelae of emotion dysregulation in individuals suffering from anxiety and mood disorders (Campbell-Sills & Barlow, 2007).

We understand that fostering student success requires tending to the whole person (Abes, Jones, & McEwen, 2007; Evans, Forney, Guido, Patton, & Renn, 2009; Goleman, 2001; Kegan, 1982, 1994; Kohlberg, 1969; Baxter Magolda, 1999, 2001; Pizzolato, 2008; Pizzolato & Ozaki, 2007; E. W. Taylor, 2008). Students take their emotional selves with them everywhere they go, and they interact with what is presented to them with emotions, aware of them or not. As such, our ability to intentionally train students' AR, ER, and CR in and out of the classroom may be a primary component for students' success.

How Do We Change the Structure and Function of Our Brains?

We have highlighted seminal research that demonstrates specific training methodologies do, in fact, exert a changeable force over certain portions of the structure and function of the brain, areas known to be associated with AR, ER, and CR. The question remains: How can we leverage this research in a practical way? Adapted from Hölzel, Lazar, and colleagues (2011), Table 3.1 illustrates the research-informed training methodologies that are used in a specific training program called integrative inquiry (INIQ; see Chapter 10 and www.integrativeinquiry.org for more details).

INIQ uses mindfulness methodology and mindful inquiry (outlined in Table 3.1) to influence particular areas of the brain known for developing traits of AR, ER, and CR in order to decrease stress and anxiety as well as heighten executive functions. In this chapter, we unpack these training methodologies one by one and then relate them back to AR, ER, and CR. Some of the measurements—the ones that could be used easily in higher education settings to determine the efficacy of these approaches via outcomes-based assessment—are discussed in Chapter 10.

For the sake of brevity and to ensure inclusivity in our language, we are not providing the rich history of these training methodologies. Many of the training methodologies originated in wisdom traditions. We have great respect for the origins of these methodologies and intend to present them here so that those who may not find an affinity with the origin of these methodologies may still find them quite accessible and useful without the practices being harmful to their own personal beliefs and values.

TABLE 3.1

Integrative Inquiry (INIQ) Training Methodology and Associated Brain Areas

Regulation Strategy		Instructions	Associated Brain Areas
Attention Regulation			
I	Focused breathing	Sustain attention on the breath; whenever distracted, return attention to the breath without judgment	• Prefrontal cortex • Anterior cingulate cortex
II	Focused movement or body scan	Focus on internal sensory experiences of breathing, emotions, or other bodily sensations	• Prefrontal cortex • Cingulate cortex • Insula
Emotion Regulation			
I	Body awareness, cognitive reappraisal, and journaling	Approach ongoing emotional reactions using awareness, attention, and inquiry (nonjudgmentally, with acceptance)	• Dorsal prefrontal cortex • Cingulate cortex • Insula • Temporoparietal junction • Hippocampus
II	Exposure, extinction, reconsolidation, and journaling	Expose oneself to whatever is present in the field of awareness; letting oneself be affected by it; refraining from internal reactivity	• Ventromedial prefrontal cortex • Cingulate cortex • Temporoparietal junction • Hippocampus • Amygdala
Cognitive Regulation			
I	Exploring sense of self, self-regulation, and journaling	Use inquiry, language, and emotional regulation; detach from identification with a static sense of self; remain aware of relationship with experiences within and around oneself	• Medial prefrontal cortex • Posterior cingulate cortex • Temporoparietal junction • Hippocampus • Amygdala • Insula

Focused Breathing

One of the most researched brain-changing methods is meditation (Kabat-Zinn, 2013). According to *Merriam-Webster*, *meditation* is "the act or process of spending time in quiet thought" (www.merriam-webster.com/inter?dest=/dictionary/meditation). There are several different types of meditation. In this book, we often refer to meditation as *focused breathing*, partly because we want to remain as inclusive as possible with our language. (It is not our intent to alienate or dishonor the wisdom traditions from where the practice of meditation originates; rather, we intend to invite in as many people as possible to this rich conversation.) In addition, focused breathing (concentration meditation) (Kabat-Zinn, 2013) is an effective method to train attention.

The definition we are using for *focused breathing* is quite simple—the process of focusing on a single object of concentration, such as the breath. The practice invites the participant to sit as still as possible and to sit in a relaxed yet alert posture. Then the participant is invited to quietly focus her attention on her own breath, whatever that means to her (Tan, 2012). Perhaps the participant has her eyes open or closed. If the eyes are open, the participant is invited to focus on something that is not moving, as if she is looking but not really seeing. Regardless of eyes open or closed, the participant is invited to notice without judgment and with the simplicity of a curious child seeing something for the first time. For example: How does it feel to pay attention to my breath? Can I feel my breath moving in and out of my body? Can I feel my breath moving in and out of my nose or mouth?

In this manner, attention begins to be trained—neural connections are literally physiologically changing as the practitioner of focused breathing consistently and repeatedly invites her attention to the breath. When attention is drawn away from the breath, such as becoming distracted by a sound in the environment, a bodily sensation, or a thought such as "I wonder if I am doing this right," the practitioner simply invites her attention back to the breath—gently and kindly and without judgment around how well she is practicing focused breathing (Tan, 2012).

Some of the meditation practices that are described in the neuroscience literature go beyond focused breathing as just described and invite the participant to focus on a phrase or a word, often called a *mantra*. In addition, some types of meditation will invite participants to move from focused attention to open attention and notice their surroundings in detail, perhaps in a way they have never noticed their surroundings before. Studies using these specific types of mental training are being replicated to ascertain whether other parts of the brain (other than those already identified in the focused attention literature) are consistently recruited. In INIQ, all of these practices are embedded into the training program so that students can explore, within their own inquiry, what works best for them.

Intentionally focusing on the breath alters the body's physiology, decreasing emotional reactivity of the amygdala and sending soothing chemicals to relieve the body of stress and anxiety. It also provides many other health benefits (Brook et al., 2013; Chen et al., 2012; Cramer, Haller, Lauche, & Dobos, 2012; Desbordes et al., 2012; Fang et al., 2010; Goldstein, Josephson, Xie, & Hughes, 2012; Goyal et al., 2014; Greeson et al., 2011; Jedel et al., 2014; Lakhan & Schofield, 2013; Lerner, Kibler, & Zeichner, 2013; Luders et al., 2009; Morgan, Irwin, Chung, & Wang, 2014; Nidich et al., 2009; Reiner et al., 2013; Rosenkranz et al., 2013; Rubia, 2009; Segal et al., 2013; Tang, Tang, & Posner, 2013; Westbrook et al., 2013; Zeidan, Grant, Brown, McHaffie, & Coghill, 2012). Thus, we recommend focused breathing as a foundational AR and ER practice for any postsecondary educational learning and development environment (see Chapter 10 for details).

Another form of training that has been researched a great deal is a practice called *mindfulness* (Hanson, 2013; Kabat-Zinn, 2013). This practice involves becoming aware, without judgment, of one's thoughts, feelings, and sensations as they arise and pass in any given situation or moment (Kabat-Zinn, 2013). By building the capacity to witness one's own experience without attachment or reactivity, one slowly begins to add inquiry (CR) to distinguish fact from interpretation. Mindfulness methodology is intended to train awareness of what a person may be experiencing in any given moment, while also paying attention to thoughts and emotions that are arising within. With additional CR training, the person can delineate her relationship to her experience (whether it be an internal experience or an external experience) and then act in empowered thoughtful awareness of emotion, rather than from a place of emotion devoid of awareness and reasoning.

Although the practices for achieving focus and mindfulness are simple, they are deceptively so. Many people find it difficult to apply the practices in a way that results in characteristic traits associated with long-term practice. Why? As we mentioned, according to our evolution, the brain is hardwired to constantly search our surroundings and protect ourselves against threats (Carter, 2014; Chiesa & Seretti, 2009; Hanson, 2013; Siegel, 2012). Because many (but not all) of us no longer need to search our environments constantly to stay aware of what will harm us, we seek other distractions, often unaware we are doing so. For instance, how many times did you check your e-mail, phone messages, or text messages while reading this chapter? How many times were you—without really being aware of why and or how—getting distracted, drifting off to other thoughts, getting up to move? We are hardwired to look for something other than what is in front of us right here and now. Just think about what training awareness toward where our attention is placed would do to increase student success.

Attention training through focused breathing can create neural connections that potentiate access on demand to the parts of the brain that foster creativity, innovation, well-being, compassion, nonviolent communication, resilience, problem solving, critical thinking, and happiness and reduce stress and anxiety (Arch & Craske, 2006; Hanson, 2013; Hölzel, Carmody, et al., 2011; Hölzel, Lazar, et al., 2011; Kerr et al., 2011; Levitin, 2014; Lutz et al., 2009; MacCoon, MacLean, Davidson, Saron, & Lutz, 2014; Meiklejohn et al., 2012; Oman et al., 2007; Pace et al., 2009; Tan, 2012).

In training attention, we must also train awareness of where our attention resides (Kabat-Zinn, 2013; Picciano, Dziuban, & Graham, 2014). Neuroscience validates the importance of the role of awareness in attention training. In a recent study by Levinson, Stoll, Kindy, Merry, and Davidson (2014), four independent studies were conducted on more than 400 participants, who engaged in a randomized controlled trial of focused breathing. However, rather than simply focusing on the breath, participants counted their breaths while they directed their attention on their breaths. Thus, participants had to cognitively become aware of their breath as they breathed by counting the number of breaths they took. Researchers found those who practiced breath counting were associated with more meta-awareness, less mind wandering, better mood, and greater nonattachment to distractions than those who had been paired with an award, and far better than their matched controls.

In essence, without awareness of where our attention resides, it is difficult to apply trained attention or acknowledge emotions that arise in the present moment. Without awareness of emotions that are arising in the present moment, it is difficult to train the cognitive processes that would allow students to differentiate fact from interpretation and to access language processes that would promote the kinds of inquiry into what is actually happening and what is possible next. Without inquiry into what is actually happening in the present moment, students can't differentiate fight-or-flight processes ignited in order to gain access to the executive functions found in the prefrontal cortex that promote analytical reasoning, problem solving, conscious choice making, and other necessary enhancers for student success. This is where mindfulness methodology comes into the picture—training awareness, attention, emotions, and cognition (Kabat-Zinn, 2013; Tan, 2012).

Mindfulness Methodology

As a matter of principle, focused breathing is the foundational practice for mindfulness methodology (Arch & Craske, 2006; Hölzel, Carmody, et al., 2011; Kabat-Zinn, 2013; Lutz et al., 2009). However, mindfulness—the awareness that arises when we pay attention in a particular way in the present moment—can be applied to anything that anyone does at any time in his or her day (Kabat-Zinn, 2013). In other words, I can become aware that I am brushing my teeth in a particular way or I can become aware that I am drinking water in a particular way. And when I become aware of an action in the moment, I do so inquisitively, like a small child. I suspend my judgment of whether I am brushing my teeth well or not. I just observe what I am doing and become aware that I am observing what I am doing right here and right now. When I notice what I am doing in the moment, I can make choices to do something the same or differently in the next moment. Using focused breathing as the foundational practice of mindfulness training may elicit what might be considered a more concerted focus of attention and a more cognitively recognized process of awareness (Gross & Thompson, 2007; Hölzel, Carmody, et al., 2011). What do we mean by that?

Research illustrates which parts of the brain are structurally changed among those who are seasoned practitioners of focused breathing and among those who have just been trained in focused breathing compared with those who have not (Brefczynski-Lewis, Lutz, Schaefer, Levinson, & Davidson, 2007; Dickenson, Berkman, Arch, & Lieberman, 2012; Hölzel, Carmody, et al., 2011; Hölzel, Lazar, et al., 2011; Lutz, Slagter, Dunne, & Davidson, 2008). As we discovered in Chapter 1, the parts of the brain that are activated by those trained in focused breathing are associated with increased attention and increased awareness of bodily sensations (insula, hippocampus, prefrontal cortex, amygdala, parietal lobe). Neuroplasticity then leads us to understand that if we use training methodologies associated with parts of the brain that are functionally associated with decreased stress and anxiety, alongside those associated with increased attention and awareness of bodily sensations and memory, then attention, awareness, and performance can be trained as these parts of the brain overlap (Kabat-Zinn, 2013; Tan, 2012).

We understand that the simple (but not easy) practice of sitting and focusing on the breath for around 30 minutes a day for eight weeks in a row will garner fMRI evidence of structural and functional changes in the parts of the brain that strengthen attention, emotion, and cognitive regulation (Holzel, Carmody, et al., 2011; Holzel, Lazar, et al., 2011; Kilpatrick et al., 2011; V. A. Taylor et al., 2012). However, what if your students and/or colleagues have no interest in practicing focused breathing for 30 minutes a day to literally change the structure and function of their brains?

Focused Movement

Recognizing that many of the students, faculty, and administrators with whom we work (and we used to count ourselves among them) are not really interested in sitting down, sitting still, and quietly paying attention to how their breath moves in and out of their bodies, we have also explored the use of focused movement as an AR, ER, and CR training methodology.

The research reveals that participants who engaged in a 15-week tai chi course—a form of focused movement—significantly improved their attention as compared with those in the control group (Converse et al., 2014). Focused movement has been shown to engage the brain more fully (Cotman & Berchtold, 2002; Cotman, Berchtold, & Christie, 2007; Strong et al., 2005; Taras, 2005; Wulf & Prinz, 2001). Running (Creer, Romberg, Saksida, van Pragg, & Bussey, 2009; Winter et al., 2007, Creer et al., 2009), brisk walking (Colcombe et al., 2006), and other types of exercise (Cotman & Berchtold, 2002; Cotman, et al., 2007) appear to also increase learning, although the specifics in terms of brain function are unclear. These practices and additional associated research will be further described in Chapters 6 and 9.

In INIQ, we often use focused movement to slowly invite participants into feeling more comfortable with engaging in focused breathing. For those not interested in focused breathing or focused movement yet still want to improve their capacity for learning, there are many more practices to explore, a few of which are further described in this chapter. Many more will be outlined in the remaining chapters of this book.

Journaling

Journaling practices are known to engage the brain in specific ways. While we are unsure how journaling specifically changes the brain, we are synthesizing research as to the portions of the brain that are significantly engaged in potentially enhancing student success. For example, reflective journaling by hand increases neural activity that may lead to improved literacy (Berninger, 2012; Berninger, Robert, Amy, & Noelia, 2009; Lotze, Erhard, Neumann, Eickoff, & Langner, 2014).

Engagement in cursive handwriting increases functional specialization/ sensory-motor activity—that is, it fosters the capacity for optimal efficiency, a desired outcome by many (James & Atwood, 2009). When learning cursive writing, for example, the brain develops functional specialization that integrates sensation, movement control, and thinking (James & Atwood, 2009).

Reflective journal writing is a key training methodology in INIQ as students are invited to explore emotions, thoughts, and awareness of where their attention is placed. They are also invited to explore connections among thoughts, physiological sensations of emotions expressed in their bodies, and their personal beliefs and values.

Cognitive Appraisal and Reappraisal and Exposure

We don't have a great deal of neuroscience to support the psychological practices of cognitive appraisal, reappraisal, and exposure in an educational environment, but we understand that they are important in training AR, ER, and CR (Gross, 2002, 2007; Gross & Thompson, 2007; Hölzel, Carmody, et al., 2011). *Cognitive appraisal* refers to how a person interprets a situation or how one views a situation. The appraisal process involves direct, immediate, and intuitive evaluations made on the environment in reference to personal well-being utilized to make sense of events or daily experiences. In our day-to-day practice, this is commonly referred to as the process of meaning making, values clarification, and/or cognitive awareness of choices we make based on our values, among other titles. This is a practice that many may engage in without awareness.

Cognitive behavioral therapy (CBT; note that most faculty and administrators are not trained to administer CBT) uses cognitive reappraisal among many other practices, and it has a great deal of neurological research. CBT has been shown to be a highly effective treatment for anxiety, depression, and other common neurological disorders (Butler, Chapman, Forman, & Beck, 2006; Hoffman et al., 2012). CBT refers to a number of structured, directed types of psychotherapy that focus on the thoughts behind a patient's feelings. This category often includes exposure therapy and other activities. We are not advocating that faculty and administrators engage in administering exercises they are not trained to administer; we simply note that the practice of cognitive reappraisal—a strategy that involves changing the trajectory of an emotional response by reinterpreting the meaning of the emotional trigger—is a practice that trains ER and is also a practice that may advance learning and development, particularly that of critical thinking.

We are intentionally avoiding a detailed discussion of the practice of exposure, which involves exposing the student to or confronting the student with a simulation that triggers an unwelcomed emotion, as this practice is quite complex. While highly effective in training AR, ER, and CR, it can also be quite dangerous for the student if proper assessment of the student's psychological well-being is not attended to prior to the practice. Thus, we emphasize here that if you have not received training to engage in these practices, and if you are not able to properly assess the participant prior to your planned administration of training, refrain from engaging in this practices even though it is highly effective in regulating attention, emotion, and cognition.

Self-Regulation

One's sense of identity, of self, of belonging, of community, of making meaning out of the experiences that surround one all emerge from an orchestra of neural communication that influences choice making (Keenan, Nelson, O'Connor, & Pascual-Leone, 2001; Keenan, Wheeler, Gallup, & Pascual-Leone, 2000; Morin, 2002). While, for now, we are oversimplifying self-regulation, note that the value of connecting learners with themselves to cultivate awareness of choice is considered an integral part of the learning process and has been described in a number of ways, including: self-authorship (Baxter Magolda, 2001), reflexivity (Goodall, 2000), contemplative inquiry (Barbezat & Bush, 2014; Palmer & Zajonc, 2010), integrative education (Palmer & Zajonc, 2010), emotional intelligence (Goleman, 1994), and mindfulness.

INIQ contains a great deal of self-inquiry, self-referential, and other-referential processing. We understand that the cognitive processing of distinguishing self from others is complex and that the regions of the brain involved in these distinctions are recruited in the decision-making process (De Brigard, Sprend, Mitchell, & Schacter, 2015; Moran, Jolly, & Mitchell, 2014; Zaki, López, & Mitchell, 2014). In order for students to be empowered to engage in their learning journey and the choices required to foster their own development, they may need to become aware of when they are distinguishing self from others—objects or people—particularly when fantasizing about the future or ruminating over the past (Contreras, Schirmer, Banaji, & Mitchell, 2013; De Brigard et al., 2015).

Furthermore, when differentiating self from other, people tend to use their own mental states to make sense of others', particularly when they consider the "other" as similar to them (Tamir & Mitchell, 2012).

Without awareness that others may be different from them or without awareness that people are making choices under the assumption that others are the same as them, choices may create a great deal of dysregulation, discomfort for self and others, and potentially hardship. Research illustrates that specific regions of the brain are recruited when one is differentiating whether another is different from self (Contreras, Banaji, & Mitchell, 2013). Zaki and Mitchell (2014) argued that we have an intuitive desire toward prosocial choices. Nonetheless, we understand that if we do not see others as similar to ourselves, we may engage in harmful behavior such as bullying, macro- and microaggressions, discrimination, and violence. The ability to *become aware* of when others are similar to ourselves and when they are not and use that awareness to engage in prosocial behavior can be trained. We will unpack the details of this neurology and its training in Chapter 8.

We may be able to infer that the more we invite students to interact with whomever and/or whatever they are experiencing—the more likely they are to engage their memory (hippocampus) (Goldberg, Harel, & Malach, 2006; Vogeley et al., 2001; Wolf, 1988). Because we know the hippocampus is very responsive to neuroplasticity (see earlier research in this chapter), this may also be a positive finding for fostering holistic learning and development.

Implications for Critical Thinking

Critical thinking has been an elusive learning outcome and a challenge in terms of designing activities or courses to promote it (Paul, Elder & Bartell, 1997). Thus, convergence on anatomical correlates remains equally elusive. Still, there are overwhelming similarities between what neuroscientists call *executive functions* and what social scientists call *critical thinking*. Take, for example, that working memory and attentional control are both fundamental to the definition of *executive functions* and *critical thinking*. Neuroscientists have begun to correlate certain anatomical structures with certain behaviors integral to critical thinking; knowing these parameters could theoretically result in a mutually agreeable and understandable definition. Nonetheless, scientists are still fastidiously working to understand how critical thinking, as a collective process, is achieved (Paul et al., 1997).

Turning back to what we do know, students arrive and move through college with stress and anxiety—critical conditions that reduce available attention (Orthner, Jones-Sanpei, & Williamson, 2004). Stress and anxiety limit the ability to analyze and synthesize, which are cornerstones of critical thinking—regardless of which definition one prefers (Paul et al., 1997). Therefore, regulating attention and emotion via mindfulness methodology appears to be essential to fostering critical thinking.

Based on the research shared in this chapter, we hypothesize that enhanced AR, ER, and CR resulting from mindfulness methodology and mindful inquiry will lead to decreased perceived stress and anxiety, increased executive functions, and increased self-regulation or conscious (i. e., aware) choice making. With decreased stress and anxiety and increased executive functions and conscious choice making as demonstrated outcomes of mindfulness methodology and mindful inquiry, it therefore seems permissible to assert that using these methodologies in higher education might have implications for the development of critical thinking.

Other Skill-Based Training Methodologies

Of course, the aforementioned training tools and techniques are not an exhaustive or inclusive list. Research by Torkel Klingberg (2010) demonstrated another method shown to induce structural and functional changes in the brain. The working memory training program improves performance in nontrained tasks that rely on working memory and control of attention. *Control of attention* is the ability to hold on to information for a relatively short amount of time. Klingberg's (2010) research stated that to achieve a significant effect, participants must commit to 30 minutes a day, five days a week, fully engaged in the various exercises that are designed to identify and then push the limit of an individual's specific working memory. Remarkably, improvements in working memory remained for six months after completing the training program (Klingberg, 2010). This specific methodology has been shown to be exceptionally successful in children diagnosed with attention deficit/hyperactivity disorder, which is hallmarked by a deficiency in working memory (Klingberg, 2010). But does this working memory training program differ from those previously discussed? If you were looking for a clear answer, we don't have one. The answer is both yes and no.

There are a host of other training programs that change the structure and function of the brain. The working memory training program and those similar seek to improve attention (a facet of working memory) and, in this way, train for only one of the three regulation strategies that we assert are fundamental in improving student learning and development. Tang and Posner

(2009) compare attention training (working memory training program) and attention state training (those aforementioned in this book) and further delineate the differences between the two:

> Attention training: [1] trains executive attention networks, [2] requires directed attention and effortful control, [3] targets non-autonomic control systems, [4] produces mental fatigue easily, and [5] training transfers to other cognitive abilities [whereas] attention state training: [1] produces changes of body-mind state, [2] requires effort control (early stage) and effortless exercise (later), [3] involves the autonomic system, [4] aims at achieving a relaxed and balanced state, and [5] training transfers to cognition, emotion, and social behaviors. (Tang & Posner, 2009, p. 226)

Being mindful of what kind of attention training we are designing in education is key to fostering greater student success.

Other training methodologies are unpacked in the chapters that follow, and we invite the readers to critically analyze each one with reference to whether trait changes or state changes may be occurring.

Editor's Summary Points and Questions to Consider

1. Focused breathing, focused movement, mindfulness methodology, mindful inquiry, and other practices are known to change the structure and function of certain portions of the brain. How might you incorporate these methodologies into the design, delivery, and evaluation of your higher education programs and curricula? How could student affairs practitioners use this methodology in their programming for orientation, summer bridge programming, and other key student success programs and interventions?

2. If we are aware of what we are paying attention to, we can intentionally change the structure and function of our brain. How do you want to train your personal awareness? How do you want to train the awareness of your students?

3. We are beginning to discover the differences between training trait attention and state attention. How might you become more aware of which methodologies to embed in your programs and curricula to intentionally train trait changes?

4. If we are aware of what we are paying attention to, we can become aware of our emotions and how they may be influencing our decisions. How do you want to train your personal emotional awareness? How do you want to train the emotional awareness of your students?

5. If we are aware of how our emotions may be influencing our choices, we can become aware that we have an opportunity to choose a response. How do you want to train your personal choice awareness? How do you want to train the choice awareness of your students?

References

Abes, W. S., Jones, S. R., & McEwen, M. K. (2007). Reconceptualizing the model of multiple dimensions of identity: The role of meaning-making capacity in the construction of multiple identities. *Journal of College Student Development, 48*(1), 1–22.

Anderson, B., Goldin, P., Kurita, K., & Gross, J. J. (2008). Self-representation in social anxiety disorder: Linguistic analysis of autobiographical narratives. *Behavior Research and Therapy, 46*, 1105–1192.

Arch, J. J., & Craske, M. G. (2006). Mechanisms of mindfulness: Emotion regulation following a focused breathing induction. *Behaviour Research and Therapy, 44*(12), 1849–1858.

Arch, J. J., & Craske, M. G. (2010). Laboratory stressors in clinically anxious and non-anxious individuals: The moderating role of mindfulness. *Behaviour Research and Therapy, 48*(6), 495–505.

Barbezat, D. P., & Bush, M. (2014). *Contemplative practices in higher education: Powerful methods to transform teaching and learning.* San Francisco, CA: Jossey-Bass.

Batten, S. V., & Hayes, S. C. (2005). Acceptance and commitment therapy in the treatment of comorbid substance abuse and post-traumatic stress disorder: A case study. *Clinical Case Studies, 4*(3), 246–262.

Baxter Magolda, M. B. (1999). *Creating contexts for learning and self authorship: Constructive-developmental pedagogy.* Nashville, TN: Vanderbilt University Press.

Baxter Magolda, M. B. (2001). *Making their own way: Narratives for transforming higher education to promote self-development.* Sterling, VA: Stylus.

Berninger, V. (2012). *Evidence-based, developmentally appropriate writing skills K to 5: Teaching the orthographic loop of working memory to write letters so developing writers can spell words and express ideas.* Retrieved from www.hw21summit .com/media/zb/hw21/H2937N_Berninger_presentation.pdf

Berninger, V., Robert, A., Amy, A., & Noelia, G. (2009). Comparison of pen and keyboard transcription modes in children with and without learning disabilities. *Learning Disability Quarterly, 32*(3), 11–18.

Brefczynski-Lewis, J. A., Lutz, A., Schaefer, H. S., Levinson, D. B., & Davidson, R. J. (2007). Neural correlates of attentional expertise in long-term meditation practitioners. *Proceedings of the National Academy of Sciences of the United States of America, 104*(27), 11483–11488.

Brook, R. D., Appel R. J., Rubenfire, M., Ogedegbe, G., Bisognano, J. D., Elliott, W. J., . . . & Rajagopalan, S. (2013). Beyond medications and diet: Alternative approaches to lowering blood pressure: A scientific statement from the American Heart Association. *Hypertension, 61*(6), 1360–1383.

Butler, A. C., Chapman, J. E., Forman, E. M., & Beck, A. T. (2006). The empirical status of cognitive-behavioral therapy: A review of meta-analyses. *Clinical Psychology Review, 26*(1), 17–31.

Campbell-Sills, L., & Barlow, D. H. (2007). Incorporating emotion regulation into conceptualizations and treatments of anxiety and mood disorders. In J. J. Gross (Ed.), *Handbook of emotion regulation* (pp. 542–559). New York, NY: Guilford Press.

Carter, R. (2014). *The human brain book.* New York, NY: DK Publishing.

Chen, K. W., Berger, C. C., Manheimer, E., Forde, D., Magidson, J., Dachman, L., & Lejuez, C. W. (2012). Meditative therapies for reducing anxiety: A systematic review and meta-analysis of randomized controlled trials. *Depression and Anxiety, 29*(7), 545–562.

Chiesa, A., Calati, R., & Serretti, A. (2011). Does mindfulness training improve cognitive abilities? A systematic review of neuropsychological findings. *Clinical Psychology Review, 31*(3), 449–464.

Chiesa, A., & Serretti, A. (2009). Mindfulness-based stress reduction for stress management in healthy people: A review and meta-analysis. *Journal of Alternative and Complementary Medicine, 15*(5), 593–600.

Colcombe, S. J., Erickson, K. I., Scalf, P. E., Kim, J. S., Prakash, R., McAuley, E., & Kramer, A. F. (2006). Aerobic exercise training increases brain volume in aging humans. *Journal of Gerontology Series A: Biological Sciences and Medical Sciences, 61*(11), 1166–1170.

Contreras, J. M., Banaji, M. R., & Mitchell, J. P. (2013). Multivoxel patterns in fusiform face area differentiate faces by sex and race. *PLOS ONE, 8*(7), e69684.

Contreras, J. M., Schirmer, J., Banaji, M. R., & Mitchell, J. P. (2013). Common brain regions with distinct patterns of neural responses during mentalizing about groups and individuals. *Journal of Cognitive Neuroscience, 25*(9), 1406–1417.

Converse, A. K., Ahlers, E. O., Travers, B. G., & Davidson, R. J. (2014). Tai chi training reduces self-report of inattention in healthy young adults. *Frontiers in Human Neuroscience, 8*(13), 1–7.

Cotman, C. W., & Berchtold, N. C. (2002). Exercise builds brain health: Key roles of growth factor cascades and inflammation. *Trends in Neuroscience, 25*(6), 295–301.

Cotman, C. W., Berchtold, N. C., & Christie, L. A. (2007). Exercise: A behavioral intervention to enhance brain health and plasticity. *Trends in Neuroscience, 30*(9), 464–472.

Cramer H., Haller, H., Lauche, R., & Dobos, G. (2012). Mindfulness-based stress reduction for low back pain: A systematic review. *BMC Complementary and Alternative Medicine, 12*(162), 1–8.

Creer, D. J., Romberg, C., Saksida, L. M., van Pragg, H., & Bussey, T. J. (2009). Running enhances spatial pattern separation. *Proceedings of the National Academy of Sciences of the United States of America, 107*(5), 2367–2372.

De Brigard, F., Sprend, R. N., Mitchell, J. P., & Schacter, D. L. (2015). Neural activity associated with self, other, and object-based counterfactual thinking. *NeuroImage, 109*(2015), 12–26.

Desbordes, G., Negi, L. T., Pace, T. W. W., Wallace, B. W., Raison, C. L., & Schwartz, X. (2012). Effects of mindful-attention and compassion meditation training on amygdala response to emotional stimuli in an ordinary, non-meditative state. *Frontiers in Human Neuroscience, 6*, 292–306.

Dickenson, J., Berkman, E., Arch, J., & Lieberman, M. (2012). Neural correlates of focused attention during a brief mindfulness induction. *Social Cognitive and Affective Neuroscience, 8*(1), 40–47.

Evans, N. J., Forney, D. S., Guido, F. M., Patton, L. D., & Renn, K. A. (2009). *Student development in college: Theory, research, and practice.* Hoboken, NJ: Wiley.

Fan, J., & Posner, M. (2004). Human attentional networks. *Psychiatrische Praxis 31*(Suppl. 2), 210–214.

Fang, C. Y., Reibel, D. K., Longacre, M. L., Rosenzweig, S., Campbell, D. E., & Douglas, S. D. (2010). Enhanced psychosocial well-being following participation in a mindfulness-based stress reduction program is associated with increased natural killer cell activity. *Journal of Complementary and Alternative Medicine, 16*(5), 531–538.

Goldberg, I. I., Harel, M., & Malach, R. (2006). When the brain loses its self: Prefrontal inactivation during sensorimotor processing. *Neuron, 50*(2), 329–339.

Goldin, P. R., & Gross, J. J. (2010). Effects of mindfulness-based stress reduction (MBSR) on the emotion regulation in social anxiety disorder. *Emotion, 10*, 83–91.

Goldin, P. R., Hakimi, S., Manber, T., Canli, T., & Gross, J. J. (2009). Neural bases of social anxiety disorder: Emotional reactivity and cognitive regulation during social and physical threat. *Archives of General Psychiatry, 66*, 170–180.

Goldin, P. R., Manber-Ball, T., Werner, K., Heimberg, R., & Gross, J. J. (2009). Neural mechanisms of cognitive reappraisal of negative self-beliefs in social anxiety disorder. *Biological Psychiatry, 66*, 1091–1099.

Goldin, P. R., McRae, K., Ramel, W., & Gross, J. J. (2008). The neural bases of emotion regulation: Reappraisal and suppression of negative emotion. *Biological Psychiatry, 63*, 577–586.

Goldin, P. R., Ramel, W., & Gross, J. J. (2009). Mindfulness meditation training and self-referential processing in social anxiety disorder: Behavioral and neural effects. *Journal of Cognitive Psychotherapy, 23*, 242–257.

Goldstein, C., Josephson, R., Xie, S., & Hughes, J. (2012). Current perspectives on the use of meditation to reduce blood pressure. *International Journal of Hypertension, 2012*, 578397. Retrieved from www.hindawi.com/journals/ijhy/2012/578397/.

Goleman, D. (1994). *Emotional intelligence: Why it can matter more than IQ.* New York, NY: Random House.

Goleman, D. (2001). *An EI-based theory of performance. The emotionally intelligent workplace: How to select for, measure, and improve emotional intelligence in individuals, groups, and organizations.* San Francisco, CA: Jossey-Bass.

Goodall, H. L. (2000). *Writing the new ethnography.* Lanham, MD: AltaMira.

Goyal, M., Singh, S., Sibinga, E. M., Sibinga, E. M. S., Gould, N. F., Rowland-Seymour, A., . . . & Haythornthwaite, H. A. (2014). Meditation programs for psychological stress and well-being: A systematic review and meta-analysis. *JAMA Internal Medicine, 174*(3), 357–368.

Greeson, J. M., Webber, D. M., Smoski, M. J., Brantley, J., G., Ekblad, A. G., Suarez, E. C., & Wolever, R. Q. (2011). Changes in spirituality partly explain health-related quality of life outcomes after mindfulness-based stress reduction. *Journal of Behavioral Medicine, 34*(6), 508–518.

Gross, J. J. (2002). Emotion regulation: Affective, cognitive, and social consequences. *Psychophysiology, 39*(3), 281–291.

Gross, J. J. (Ed.) (2007). *Handbook of emotion regulation.* New York, NY: Guilford Press.

Gross, J. J., & Thompson, R. A. (2007). Emotion regulation: Conceptual foundations. In J. J. Gross (Ed.), *Handbook of emotion regulation* (pp. 3–24). New York, NY: Guilford Press

Hamann, S. B., Ely, T. D., Grafton, S. T., & Kilts, C. D. (1999). Amygdala activity related to enhanced memory for pleasant and aversive stimuli. *Nature Neuroscience, 2*(3), 289–293.

Hanson, R. (2013). *Hardwiring happiness: The new brain science of contentment, calm, and confidence.* New York, NY: Harmony.

Hocking, L. B., & Koenig, H. G. (1995). Anxiety in medically ill older patients: A review and update. *International Journal of Psychiatry in Medicine, 25*(3), 221–238.

Hoffman, S. G., Anu, A., Imke, J. J., Vonk, M. A., Sawyer, A. T., & Fang, A. (2012). The efficacy of cognitive behavioral therapy: A review of meta-analyses. *Cognitive Therapy and Research, 36*(5), 427–440.

Hölzel, B. K., Carmody, J., Vangel, M., Congleton, C., Yerramsetti, S. M., Gard, T., & Lazar, S. W. (2011). Mindfulness practice leads to increases in regional brain gray matter density. *Psychiatry Research: Neuroimaging, 191*(1), 36–43.

Hölzel, B. K., Lazar, S. W., Gard, T., Schuman-Olivier, Z., Vago, D. R., & Ott, U. (2011). How does mindfulness meditation work? Proposing mechanisms of action from a conceptual and neural perspective. *Perspectives on Psychological Science, 6*(6), 537–559.

Hutcherson, C. A., Goldin, P. R., Ramel, W., McRae, K., & Gross, J. J. (2008). Attention and emotion influence the relationship between extraversion and neural response. *Social Cognitive and Affective Neuroscience, 3*, 71–79.

James, K. H., & Atwood, T. P. (2009). The role of sensorimotor learning in the perception of letter-like forms: Tracking the causes of neural specialization for letters. *Cognitive Neuropsychology, 26*(1), 91–110.

Jedel, S., Hoffman, A., Merriman, P., Swanson, B., Voigt, R., Shaikh, M., . . . & Keshavarzian, A. (2014). A randomized controlled trial of mindfulness-based stress reduction to prevent flare-up in patients with inactive ulcerative colitis. *Digestion, 89*, 142–155.

Kabat-Zinn, J. (2013). *Full catastrophe living, revised edition: How to cope with stress, pain and illness using mindfulness meditation.* New York, NY: Bantam Books.

Keenan, J. P., Nelson, A., O'Connor, M., & Pascual-Leone, A. (2001). Self-recognition and the right hemisphere. *Nature, 409*(6818), 305.

Keenan, J. P., Wheeler, M. A., Gallup, G. G., Jr., & Pascual-Leone, A. (2000). Self-recognition and the right prefrontal cortex. *Trends in Cognitive Sciences, 4*(9), 338–344.

Kegan, R. (1982). *The evolving self: Problem and process in human development.* Cambridge, MA: Harvard University Press.

Kegan, R. (1994). *In over our heads: The mental complexity of modern life.* Cambridge, MA: Harvard University Press.

Kerr, C. E., Jones, S. R., Wan, Q., Pritchett, D. L., Wasserman, R. H., Wexler, A., & Moore, C. I. (2011). Effects of mindfulness meditation training on anticipatory alpha modulation in primary somatosensory cortex. *Brain Research Bulletin, 85*(3), 96–103.

Kilpatrick, L. A., Suyenobu, B. Y., Smith, S. R., Bueller, J. A., Goodman, T., Creswell, J. D., & Naliboff, B. D. (2011). Impact of mindfulness-based stress reduction training on intrinsic brain connectivity. *NeuroImage, 56*(1), 290–298.

Klingberg, T. (2010). Training and plasticity of working memory. *Trends in Cognitive Sciences, 14*(7), 317–324.

Kohlberg, L. (1969). *Stage and sequence: The cognitive-developmental approach to socialization.* New York, NY: Rand McNally.

Lakhan, S. E., & Schofield, K. L. (2013). Mindfulness-based therapies in the treatment of somatization disorders: A systematic review and meta-analysis. *PLOS ONE, 8*(8), e71834.

Lerner, R., Kibler, J. L., & Zeichner, S. B. (2013). Relationship between mindfulness-based stress reduction and immune function in cancer and HIV/AIDS. *Cancer and Clinical Oncology, 2*(1), 62–72.

Levinson, D. B., Stoll, E. L., Kindy, S. D., Merry, H. L., & Davidson, R. J. (2014). A mind you can count on: Validating breath counting as a behavioral measure of mindfulness. *Frontiers in Psychology, 5,* 1202.

Levitin, D. J. (2014). *The organized mind: Thinking straight in the age of information overload.* New York, NY: Penguin.

Lotze, M., Erhard, K., Neumann, N., Eickoff, S. B., & Langner, R. (2014). Neural correlates of verbal creativity: Differences in resting-state functional connectivity associated with expertise in creative writing. *Frontiers in Human Neuroscience, 8,* 516.

Luders, E. (2014). Exploring age-related brain degeneration in meditation practitioners. *Annals of the New York Academy of Sciences, 1307*(1), 82–88.

Luders, E., Kurth, F., Mayer, E., Toga, A., Narr, K., & Gaser, C. (2012). The unique brain anatomy of meditation practitioners: Alterations in cortical gyrification. *Frontiers in Human Neuroscience, 6,* 34.

Luders, E., Toga, A. W., Lepore, N., & Gaser, C. (2009). The underlying anatomical correlates of long-term meditation: Larger hippocampal and frontal volumes of gray matter. *NeuroImage, 45*(3), 672–678.

Lutz, A., Slagter, H. A., Dunne, J. D., & Davidson, R. J. (2008). Attention regulation and monitoring in meditation. *Trends in Cognitive Sciences, 12*(4), 163–169.

Lutz, A., Slagter, H. A., Rawling, N., Francis, A., Greischar, L. L., & Davidson, R. J. (2009). Mental training enhances attentional stability: Neural and behavioral evidence. *Journal of Neuroscience, 29*(42), 13418–13427.

MacCoon, D. G., MacLean, K. A., Davidson, R. J., Saron, C. D., & Lutz, A. (2014). No sustained attention differences in a longitudinal randomized trial comparing mindfulness based stress reduction versus active control. *PLOS ONE, 9*(6). Retrieved from http://journals.plos.org/plosone/article?id=10.1371/journal.pone.0097551

Mahone, E. M., Bruch, M. A., & Heimberg, R. G. (1993). Focus of attention and social anxiety: The role of negative self-thoughts and perceived positive attributes of the other. *Cognitive Therapy and Research, 17*(3), 209–224.

Mankus, A. M., Aldao, A., Kerns, C., Mayville, E. W., & Mennin, D. S. (2013). Mindfulness and heart rate variability in individuals with high and low generalized anxiety symptoms. *Behaviour Research and Therapy, 51*(7), 386–391.

Meiklejohn, J., Phillips, C., Freedman, M. L., Griffin, M. L., Biegel, G., Roach, A., & Saltzman, A. (2012). Integrating mindfulness training into K–12 education: Fostering the resilience of teachers and students. *Mindfulness, 3*(4), 291–307.

Moran, J. M., Jolly, E., & Mitchell, J. P. (2014). Spontaneous mentalizing predicts the fundamental attribution error. *Journal of Cognitive Neuroscience, 26*(3), 569-576.

Morgan, N., Irwin, M., Chung, M., & Wang, C. (2014). The effects of mind-body therapies on the immune system: Meta-analysis. *PLOS ONE, 9*(7), e100903–e100913.

Morin, A. (2002). Right hemispheric self-awareness: A critical assessment. *Consciousness and Cognition, 11*(3), 396–401.

Multon, K. D., Brown, S. D., & Lent, R. W. (1991). Relation of self-efficacy beliefs to academic outcomes: A meta-analytic investigation. *Journal of Counseling Psychology, 18,* 30–38.

Nidich, S., Rainforth, M., Haaga, D., Hagelin, J., Salerno, J., Travis, F., . . . Schneider, R. H. (2009). A randomized controlled trial on effects of the Transcendental Meditation program on blood pressure, psychological distress, and coping in young adults. *American Journal of Hypertension, 22*(12), 1326–1331.

Ochsner, K. N., Bunge, S. A., Gross, J. J., & Gabrieli, J. D. E. (2002). Rethinking feelings: An fMRI study of the cognitive regulation of emotion. *Journal of Cognitive Neuroscience, 14*(8), 1215–1229.

Ochsner, K. N., & Gross, J. J. (2005). The cognitive control of emotion. *Trends in Cognitive Sciences, 9*(5), 242–249.

Oman, D., Shapiro, S. L., Thoresen, C. E., Flinders, T., Driskill, J. D., & Plante, T. G. (2007). Learning from spiritual models and meditation: A randomized evaluation of a college course. *Pastoral Psychology, 55*(4), 473–493.

Orthner, D. K., Jones-Sanpei, H., & Williamson, S. (2004). The resilience and strengths of low-income families. *Family Relations, 53*(2), 159–167.

Pace, T. W., Negi, L. T., Adame, D. D., Cole, S. P., Sivilli, T. I., Brown, T. D., & Raison, C. L. (2009). Effect of compassion meditation on neuroendocrine, innate immune and behavioral responses to psychosocial stress. *Psychoneuroendocrinology, 34*(1), 87–98.

Packard, M. G., Cahill, L., & McGaugh, J. L. (1994). Amygdala modulation of hippocampal-dependent and caudate nucleus-dependent memory processes. *Proceedings of the National Academy of Sciences of the United States of America, 91,* 8477–8481.

Palmer, P. J., & Zajonc, A. (2010). *The heart of higher education: A call to renewal.* San Francisco, CA: Jossey-Bass.

Paul, R. W., Elder, L., & Bartell, T. (1997). *California teacher preparation for instruction in critical thinking: Research findings and policy recommendations* (pp. 18–19). Sacramento, CA: California Commission on Teacher Credentialing.

Picciano, A. G., Dziuban, C. D., & Graham, C. R. (Eds.). (2014). *Blended learning: Research perspectives* (Vol. 2.) New York, NY: Routledge.

Pizzolato, J. E. (2008). Advisor, teacher, partner: Using the learning partnerships model to reshape academic advising. *About Campus, 13*(1), 18–25.

Pizzolato, J. E., & Ozaki, C. C. (2007). Moving toward self-authorship: Investigating outcomes of learning partnerships. *Journal of College Student Development, 48*(2), 196–214.

Roemer, L., Orsillo, S. M., & Salters-Pedneault, K. (2008). Efficacy of an acceptance-based behavior therapy for generalized anxiety disorder: Evaluation in a randomized controlled trial. *Journal of Consulting and Clinical Psychology, 76*(6), 1083–1084.

Rosenkranz, M., Davidson, R., MacCoon, D., Sheridan, J., Kalin, N., & Lutz, A. (2013). A comparison of mindfulness-based stress reduction and an active control in modulation of neurogenic inflammation. *Brain Behavior and Immunity, 27*(1), 174–184.

Rubia, K. (2009). The neurobiology of meditation and its clinical effectiveness in psychiatric disorders. *Biological Psychology, 82*(1), 1–11.

Schunk, D. H. (1985). Self-efficacy and classroom learning. *Psychology in the Schools, 22*(2), 208–223.

Segal, Z. V., Williams, M. G., & Teasdale, J. D. (2013). *Mindfulness-based cognitive therapy for depression* (2nd Ed.). New York, NY: Guilford Press.

Siegel, D. J. (2012). *Pocket guide to interpersonal neurobiology: An integrative handbook of the mind.* New York, NY: W. W. Norton.

Strong, W. B., Malina, R. M., Blimkie, C. J., Daniels, S. R., Dishman, R. K., Gutin, B., . . . & Trudeau, F. (2005). Evidence based physical activity for school-age youth. *Journal of Pediatrics, 146*(6), 732–737.

Tamir, D. I., & Mitchell, J. P. (2012). Anchoring and adjustment during social inferences. *Journal of Experimental Psychology: General,* 1–12.

Tan, C. M. (2012). *Search inside yourself: The unexpected path to achieving success, happiness, and world peace.* New York, NY: HarperCollins.

Tang, Y. Y., & Posner, M. I. (2009). Attention training and attention state training. *Trends in Cognitive Science, 13*(5), 222–227.

Tang, Y. Y., Tang, R., & Posner, M. I. (2013). Brief meditation training induces smoking reduction. *Proceedings of the National Academy of Sciences, 110*(34), 13971–13975.

Taras, H. (2005). Physical activity and student performance at school. *Journal of School Health, 75*(6), 214–218.

Taylor, E. W. (2008). Transformative learning theory. *New Directions for Adult and Continuing Education, 119,* 5–15.

Taylor, V. A., Daneault, V., Grant, J., Scavone, G., Breton, E., Roffe-Vidal, S., & Beauregard, M. (2012). Impact of meditation training on the default mode network during a restful state. *Social Cognitive and Affective Neuroscience, 8*(1), 4–14.

Vogeley, K., Bussfeld, P., Newen, A., Herrmann, S., Happe, F., Falkai, P., . . . & Zilles, K. (2001). Mind reading: Neural mechanisms of theory of mind and self-perspective. *NeuroImage, 14,* 170–181.

Westbrook, C., Creswell, J. D., Tabibnia, G., Hulson, E., Kober, H., & Tindle, H. A. (2013). Mindful attention reduces neural and self-reported cue-induced craving in smokers. *Social Cognitive and Affective Neuroscience, 8*(1), 73–84.

Winter, B., Breitenstein, C., Mooren, F. C., Voelker, K., Fobker, M., Lechtermann, A., Krueger, K., . . . & Knecht, S. (2007). High impact running improves learning. *Neurobiology of Learning and Memory, 87*(4), 597–609.

Wolf, E. (1988). *Treating the self.* New York, NY: Guilford Press.

Wulf, G., & Prinz, W. (2001). Directing attention to movement effects enhances learning: A review. *Psychonomic Bulletin & Review, 8*(4), 648–660.

Zaki, J., López, G., & Mitchell, J. P. (2014). Activity in ventromedial prefrontal cortex covaries with revealed social preferences: Evidence for person-invariant value. *Social Cognitive and Affective Neuroscience, 9*(4), 464–469.

Zeidan, F., Grant, J., Brown, C., McHaffie, J., & Coghill, R. (2012). Mindfulness meditation-related pain relief: Evidence for unique brain mechanisms in the regulation of pain. *Neuroscience Letters, 520*(2), 165–173.

Zimmerman, B. J. (2000). Self-efficacy: An essential motive to learn. *Contemporary Educational Psychology, 25*(1), 82–91.

4

(RE)CONCEPTUALIZING MEANING MAKING IN HIGHER EDUCATION

A Case for Integrative Educational Encounters That Prepare Students for Self-Authorship

Emily Marx and Lisa Gates

"For the meaning of life differs from man to man [sic], from day to day, and from hour to hour. What matters, therefore, is not the meaning of life in general but rather the specific meaning of a person's life at a given moment."

—Viktor E. Frankl (www.brainyquote.com/quotes/keywords/meaning
.html#1R57F8zLTtoeVRL1.99)

It is a very big and challenging thing to become a *self*—a whole person— particularly in the context of higher education today. Over the course of our careers in student affairs and academic affairs, we have frequently observed students hitting the pause button on matters of the self in order to push through the crucible of their competitive academic programs. Colleges often provide so many prescriptive formulas for "success" with the intention of offering support that they may unwittingly prevent students from wrestling with deeply engaging questions necessary to develop a sense of self (Baxter Magolda, 1999, 2001; Pizzolato, 2008).

Our Shared Vision for Higher Education

This chapter seeks to inspire a vision for encounters in higher education that embraces students in all their multidimensionality (Palmer & Zajonc, 2010), promote students' development of self-authorship, and propose a number of corresponding practices to that end. Specifically, it examines possibilities for faculty and staff to create "high-impact moments" that further challenge college students to develop a more integrated sense of self and, in doing so, a set of complex reasoning skills (Baxter Magolda, 1999, 2001), integrity (Appel-Silbaugh, 2007; Keeling, 2006), and independence (Baxter Magolda, 2001). Colleges and universities have traditionally focused on students' cognitive development in higher education. Current national standards such as those developed by the Association of American Colleges and Universities' Liberal Education and America's Promise (AAC&U's LEAP), which identified "Essential Learning Outcomes" for education in a new century (AAC&U, 2007), *Learning Reconsidered 2* (Keeling, 2006), and the Council for the Advancement of Standards (CAS) in Higher Education demand that we pay attention, to not only the intellect but also the "whole person." For students (or any learners, for that matter), educating the whole person involves paying attention to what can be learned and what is happening within the self in the context and process of learning.

Similar to the integrative movement in medicine that includes mind, body, and spirit in promoting health and wellness, there is an urgent need to consider the whole student in higher education. We view "self" as central to what it means to be a whole person, including the epistemological, intrapersonal, and interpersonal domains that are associated with self-authorship development (Baxter Magolda, 2001). *Self-authorship* is the ability to internally define one's own beliefs, identities, and relationships (Baxter Magolda, 2001). Fostering self-authorship offers insights about how to connect with the development of the whole person. Thus, the concept of "whole person" includes the essential elements of a self: intellectual, emotional, social, cultural, spiritual, and personal—all of what we bring to the table in the process of meaning making. We advocate for an integrative approach to educational encounters—interactions with students both in and out of the classroom—as one of many ways of promoting self-authorship development during the college years.

By connecting scholarly research on self-authorship with research on mindfulness and mindful learning, it is our contention that we can adopt a philosophy and apply strategies that will better meet students' developmental needs in college. To connect a view of the whole person with the theory of self-authorship, this chapter describes the need for further inclusion of the self in higher education, reviews literature on self-authorship, explores intersections between self-authorship development and integrative education, and proposes a series of tangible actions to promote self-authorship that are applicable in both student affairs and academic contexts.

Rationale

Developing a broader understanding of self requires having opportunities to identify one's voice, wrestle with perspectives, and critically engage with one's own lived experiences. It begins by awakening to the personal authority necessary to make decisions for oneself. Scholars term the ability to internally define one's own beliefs, identities, and relationships the capacity for *self-authorship* (Baxter Magolda, 2001; Kegan, 1982; Pizzolato, 2005). Self-authorship typically occurs after young adults leave the supportive college environment and begin to experience the challenges of leading more independent lives (Baxter Magolda, 2001). However, research indicates that it may be possible to facilitate self-authorship during the students' college career (Baxter Magolda, 2001; Hodge, Baxter Magolda, & Haynes, 2009; Parks, 2000; Pizzolato, 2005). Since college students often experience challenging experiences during college, student affairs administrators and faculty are "particularly well positioned for self-authorship interventions" (Pizzolato, 2005, p. 638). Consistent with the research on self-authorship is the idea that students have the capacity to rise to the level of complexity in their environment (Baxter Magolda, 2003). Campuses can promote self-authorship development through revamped curricula, cocurricular experiences, and campus structures that support knowledge creation; programs that challenge students to identify with the well-being of others; and advising and mentoring relationships that promote development of the self (Baxter Magolda, 2001).

Students in higher education face many immediate complex challenges, including increasing expectations to ensure postgraduation jobs; an intense culture of competition for test scores, grades, and achievements and, as a result of this culture, delays in developmental stages traditionally marking adulthood (Arnett, 2004; Settersten & Ray, 2010); premature commitment to academic, career, and personal decisions (Huerta, 2013); and lack of preparation for life after college (Baxter Magolda, 2003). With respect to the latter, in the Job Outlook 2011 report from the National Association of Colleges and Employers (2010), analytical and problem-solving skills were ranked among the most important skills by employers. In another national survey, 64% of employers wanted colleges to place greater emphasis on complex problem–solving skills (AAC&U, 2007). As mentioned earlier, a recent four-year longitudinal study assessing college student learning conducted by Arum and Roksa (2011) made national headlines. More than 4,000 college students at 29 diverse institutions took the Collegiate Learning Assessment. The study found that 45% of the students in the sample made no statistically significant increases in critical thinking, complex reasoning, and writing skills during their college years (Arum & Roksa, 2011). Collectively, such reports suggest the need to focus on and improve our effectiveness in promoting student growth and development during the college years. These studies also suggest that campuses would benefit from placing greater emphasis on practices known to promote such essential learning outcomes.

Teaching and advising through the lens of self-authorship offers educators the opportunity to foster critical learning outcomes through practices that support the development of the whole person in everyday educational encounters. More than 30 years of research have linked self-authorship with achievement of a number of critical learning outcomes, summarized here. The capacity to self-author is crucial to the development of complex reasoning skills, healthy relationships, and sense of identity described in higher education learning outcomes. In 2005, the AAC&U launched LEAP, a decade-long initiative, that identified "Essential Learning Outcomes" for education in a new century (AAC&U, 2007). Similarly, *Learning Reconsidered 2* (Keeling, 2006) and the CAS in Higher Education (2006) describe a number of learning outcomes for higher education. Many of these learning outcomes are advanced by the development of self-authorship in the cognitive, intrapersonal, and interpersonal domains. These include cognitive–cognitive complexity (Baxter Magolda, 2001; Keeling, 2006; Pizzolato, 2008; Pizzolato & Ozaki, 2007); inquiry and analysis, critical and creative thinking, and problem solving (AAC&U, 2007; Baxter Magolda, 2001; Pizzolato, 2008; Pizzolato & Ozaki, 2007); foundations and skills for lifelong learning (AAC&U, 2007; Baxter Magolda & King, 2004); synthesis and advanced accomplishment across general and specialized studies (AAC&U, 2007; Baxter Magolda & King, 2004); knowledge acquisition (Baxter Magolda, 2001; Keeling, 2006; Pizzolato, 2008); interpersonal–intercultural knowledge and competence (AAC&U, 2007; Abes, Jones, & McEwen, 2007; Kegan, 1994; Taylor, 2008); civic knowledge and engagement (AAC&U, 2007; Baxter Magolda & King, 2004); meaningful interpersonal relationships (Baxter Magolda, 2001; CAS in Higher Education, 2006; Pizzolato, 2008); independence (Baxter Magolda, 2001; CAS in Higher Education, 2006); intrapersonal–ethical reasoning and action (AAC&U, 2007; Appel-Silbaugh, 2007; Baxter Magolda & King, 2004); integrity acquisition, integration, and application (Appel-Silbaugh, 2007; Keeling, 2006); clarified values (Baxter Magolda, 2001; CAS in Higher Education, 2006; Pizzolato, 2008; Pizzolato & Ozaki, 2007); and career choices (Baxter Magolda, 2001; CAS in Higher Education, 2006; Creamer & Laughlin, 2005). Achieving such a wide range of learning outcomes is clearly a tall order for colleges and universities. Promoting self-authorship so that it occurs more frequently in college may advance achievement of these vital outcomes.

In our collective experiences in higher education, we frequently encounter even high-achieving students who express a lack of confidence navigating the complex social milieu on and off campus and limited readiness to meet the demands of the professional world awaiting them. We hear widespread reports about students' fear of participating in class and initiating interactions with their professors. A top administrator/faculty member from a large public research institution estimated that a mere 10% of students show up as fully engaged participants in the classroom (A. Havis, personal communication, September 11, 2014). In addition to limitations around career preparation, a dearth of critical thinking skill development, and an observed deficit of student engagement, there is a related, though lesser-addressed, outcome worthy of discussion: deeper engagement of the whole self (Baxter Magolda & King, 2004; Brooks, 2014). We wonder about the degree to which students are invited to identify their own voices in conversations throughout their college experiences. In what ways might student development and engagement be enhanced if such conversations were pervasive in higher education? And how do we maintain a keen focus on achieving student learning outcomes while engaging students' hearts and minds in an era of decreasing budgets and increasingly larger class sizes?

Collectively, with more than 40 years in professorial, administrative, and student affairs roles, we, the authors of this chapter, remain passionate believers in the transformative possibilities of higher education for what it is possible for students and ourselves to know, do, create, or become. And yet we join the decades-long chorus of other scholars and practitioners who have articulated the need to adopt a more integrated view of our students and therefore modify our pedagogical approaches in order to enhance student engagement and learning (Baxter Magolda, 1999, 2001; Deresiewicz, 2014; Holba & Noyes, 2013; Langer, 1989; Lewis, 2007; Nash & Murray, 2010; Palmer & Zajonc, 2010; Parks, 2000). As discussed in this book's introduction, especially in light of extensive conversation around high-impact practices and experiential learning ("High-Impact Educational Practices," 2014), traditional approaches focusing primarily on students' knowledge acquisition may need additional rethinking. Such a shift requires a collective and fundamental reconsideration of current practices, resulting in educators considering whole-student engagement in the learning process. As also mentioned in the introduction, we realize that some educators are already approaching teaching, learning, and advising in this way. However, given the high degree of privacy in educational encounters (i.e., office hours, advising sessions, classroom instruction, mentoring meetings, etc.), the extent to which educators employ integrative approaches is difficult to ascertain. Marx (2012) underscores that among new professionals in student affairs, educational practices that promote self-authorship are often the exception and not the rule. The evidence related to learning outcomes and research on self-authorship development in college presented previously calls us to do something different.

William Deresiewicz (2014) recently received significant press for his critique of educational practices in elite colleges and universities. In his *New York Times* best-selling book, *Excellent Sheep: The Miseducation of the American Elite and the Way to a Meaningful Life*, Deresiewicz challenges Ivy League colleges in particular to reconsider their hyperfocus on the corporatization of education in favor of a more holistic, critical approach. Such a turn supports a view of education for education's sake, the hallmark of a liberal arts education. He argues for the need to consider the development of the self when he says that "everyone is born with a mind, but it is only through this act of introspection, of self-examination, of establishing communication between the mind and the heart, the mind and experience, that you become an individual, a unique being—a soul. And that is what it means to develop a self" (p. 84). Deresiewicz's view bolsters an essential purpose of the university: to foster and uncover our common humanity, offering us opportunities to explore questions such as "What is it possible to know?" and "How shall we live?" We believe it is essential to contend with questions about career in the college years, and it is possible to do so with a sense of personal development that considers broadly what it means to be a self in context with others.

Authoring a Self

Developing an integrated, holistic view of students requires considering what our goals in student encounters ought to be. Self-authorship offers a framework for understanding the developmental process of identifying a self and our role in transforming everyday encounters with students. In order to better conceptualize whole-student engagement, this section describes the phases of self-authorship. Further, we describe strategies for promoting self-authorship from the literature and propose integrative educational approaches as an additional way to help students access their internal voices and prepare for self-authorship.

The theory of self-authorship describes a complex process by which young adults develop a strong sense of self. The framework of self-authorship was developed by Robert Kegan (1982, 1994). Kegan (1994) described self-authorship as:

> A new whole, an internal identity . . . that can coordinate, integrate, act upon, or invent values, beliefs, convictions, generalizations, ideals, abstrac-

tions, interpersonal loyalties and intrapersonal states. It is no longer authored by them. It authors them and thereby achieves a personal authority. (p. 185)

The concept of self-authorship was later applied to college students by Marcia Baxter Magolda (1999), a prolific author in this area. Baxter Magolda describes self-authorship as a developmental process in which young adults in their 20s and 30s move from reliance on others for decision making and knowledge generation into a period in which they integrate their own knowledge and judgment with that acquired from others (Baxter Magolda, 2001). This does not mean that students' ideas, understandings, or beliefs necessarily supersede existing knowledge or authority, but rather that students' voices are incorporated into decision making and are actively engaged in cocreating knowledge. Grounded in the constructivist development tradition, research on self-authorship focuses on *how* people know rather than *what* they know (Abes et al., 2007; Baxter Magolda, 2001; Kegan, 1982, 1994; Parks, 2000). The ability to self-author is the result of the resolution of disequilibrium caused by cognitive dissonance between external and internal voices (Baxter Magolda, 2001; Kegan, 1982; Pizzolato, 2005). It requires the ability to think logically through multiple points of view in a way that also recognizes and respects one's internal voice, goals, values, and beliefs, and the ability to act in alignment with that reasoning (Pizzolato, 2005). "The ability of the internal voice to coordinate external influences in making choices is a hallmark of self-authorship" (Baxter Magolda, personal communication, June 8, 2015).

Students who develop the ability to self-author during college are also more likely to make more informed career, academic, relationship, and life decisions that take into account their internal voices. Self-authorship involves young adults' abilities to be reflective and purposeful and thus be more able to make decisions that reconcile input from outside sources with their own perspectives. The University of Nevada–Las Vegas instituted a community standards program based on the tenets of self-authorship development. Students in the program reported having become more self-aware, responsible, confident, capable of standing up for what they believed, and understanding of others than before starting the program (Baxter Magolda, 2003). Additionally, based on results of her longitudinal study and research on promising practices for self-authorship development, Baxter Magolda (2003) concludes that if campus administrators surround students with experiences that make the self central to learning in college, students may choose a major or career path based on their skills and interests rather than the wishes of their parents, for example. Students' abilities to make decisions based on their internal voices may result in deeper engagement with their coursework and cocurricular involvement (Baxter Magolda, 2003). They may courageously choose relationships based on a sense of what is right for them rather than the desire to please others, thus fostering students' intra- and interpersonal development in the process.

In addition to the practical outcomes of self-authoring during college, there are intrinsic benefits as well. Developing a stronger and more finely tuned internal voice may allow students to more deeply pursue questions of meaning and purpose in their lives. Parks (2000) calls for campuses to provide opportunities for students to reflect on big questions that are "both deeply intimate and ultimate" (p. 25). Reflective conversations with professors, advisers, and mentors can prompt these questions, including those that promote self-authorship and help students in their process of "becoming at home in the Universe" (Parks, 2000, p. 34). Not surprisingly, such intrinsic gains have other benefits as well. In one study of 344 undergraduate students at a large midwestern university, students who scored highly on the Purpose in Life Scale (which may be more characteristic of self-authoring students) also persisted at a higher rate in college than those who did not (DeWitz, Woolsey, & Walsh, 2009).

Foundations of the Self-Authorship Process

Before addressing strategies for promoting self-authorship in educational encounters, we must first understand the developmental process of self-authorship. Baxter Magolda's (2001, 2009a) longitudinal study of self-authorship development among young adults identified a three-phase process. In the first phase, called external formulas, young adults rely on experts for decision making and knowledge creation. The pivotal second phase, the crossroads, occurs as a result of cognitive dissonance that young adults must reconcile (Baxter Magolda, 2001; Parks, 2000). For some, it may take multiple experiences of cognitive dissonance to move from feeling dissatisfied with external definitions to experiencing a catalyst that leads them to search for internal ones (Pizzolato, 2005). In the third phase of self-authorship, they explore beliefs, identities, and their relationships with others in a way that simultaneously honors their own internal voice as well as the perspectives of others (Baxter Magolda, 2001, 2009a). Individuals have the capacity to take in others' ideas, but remain critical of them until they see how they align with their own values and ideas.

The self-authorship phase includes three elements, or developmental capacities (Baxter Magolda, 2008). First, young adults must begin *trusting their internal voice*, which involves realizing that while no one can control what happens one's reaction to it can be controlled. Recognizing the difference between occurrences in the world and one's reaction to them provides the opportunity for individual reflection, agency, and choice. Second, young adults must *build an internal foundation* that begins to collate their choices into commitments that form a guiding life philosophy. Participants in Baxter Magolda's longitudinal study rarely arrived at this phase before age 30 (Baxter Magolda, 2001). Third, young people must solidify these philosophies so that they become second nature, which Baxter Magolda terms *securing internal commitments* (Baxter Magolda, 2009a, 2009b; King, Baxter Magolda, Perez, & Taylor, 2009). These often-unconscious road maps help young adults navigate life's challenges, informed by an empowered sense of self. The ability to develop these internal road maps has an impact on multiple dimensions of a young adult's experience. While developing the sort of coherent life philosophy described in these elements may be a stretch for many college students, young adults can make significant developmental strides from opportunities to practice integrating their voices with those of others during the college years, the goal of which is to integrate external knowledge with internal ways of knowing for whole-student development (Baxter Magolda, 2001).

The work of self-authorship calls for approaches and practices that challenge us to take into account a more integrative view of student development. Research-based strategies to support self-authorship described in Table 4.1 are predicated on assumptions about knowledge and learning. These assumptions may influence our teaching and advising approaches and ultimately the growth and development of students. Teaching and advising assumptions supporting self-authorship development, described in Baxter Magolda and King's learning partnership model, view knowledge as complex and socially constructed, the self as central to knowledge generation, expertise and authority as shared among peers in knowledge creation, learners as having the capacity to know, learning as situated in the learner's experience, and meaning as mutually constructed with the learner (Baxter Magolda & King, 2004).

In order to demonstrate how a more integrative view of student development may set the stage for self-authorship, we propose a way of thinking about student engagement that incorporates Ellen Langer's concept of mindful learning and discuss its possibilities for supporting students' self-authorship development.

TABLE 4.1
Strategies for Promoting Self-Authorship

Assumptions About Learning and Development	Strategies for Promoting Self-Authorship From the Literature	Proposed Integrative Education Strategies to Prepare Students for Self-Authorship
Recognize that knowledge is complex and socially constructed.	• Prompt students to compare alternatives. • Prompt students to explore multiple frameworks or lenses. • Explore assumptions about knowledge as universal. • Encourage critique of existing theories. • Encourage taking a stand on an issue or a topic (Baxter Magolda & King, 2004). • Encourage feedback (Brown, 2004). • Ask students sufficiently big and complex questions (Brown, 2004; Hodge et al., 2009; Parks, 2000).	• Contextualize everything: What do we know? What do we need to know? Why is it important? How does it connect to students and their larger purpose? How is it possible to think about this in a different way? From a different point of view? • Commit to inquiry—in our discipline, with others in the community, and with the self (epistemological, interpersonal, intrapersonal) (Baxter Magolda, 2001). • Focus on questions, not necessarily answers—educators and students raise big and small questions. • Disrupt the status quo, challenge assumptions.
Recognize that the self is central to knowledge construction.	• Ask reflective questions. • Ask students to identify their perspectives. • Encourage students to reflect on their personal values (Baxter Magolda & King, 2004). • Encourage students to reflect on their level of satisfaction with relying on external definitions/sources for decision making. • Ask clarifying questions about whether the students' decisions were driven by internal or external forces (promotes behavior regulation/self-regulation). • Ask students to distinguish and weigh internal versus external factors for decision making and behavior regulation (Pizzolato, 2005).	• Encourage students to spend time alone (Deresiewicz, 2010). • Open classes with a moment of silence or internal reflection to invite students to go within. • Aim for reflexivity in writing assignments. • Utilize mindfulness practices, such as focused attention, mindfulness meditation, and breathing techniques, to expand capacities to hear and trust internal voices.

(Continues)

TABLE 4.1 (Continued)

Assumptions About Learning and Development	Strategies for Promoting Self-Authorship From the Literature	Proposed Integrative Education Strategies to Prepare Students for Self-Authorship
Recognize that expertise and authority are mutually shared among peers in knowledge construction.	• Promote confidence by validating students' voices. • Encourage discussion with peers with diverse perspectives. • Transfer authority from adviser to students to empower them to make their own decisions (Baxter Magolda & King, 2004). • Facilitate interpersonal collaboration (Brown, 2004). • Counsel students toward cognitive interdependence in which students successfully manage conflicting expectations in a way that considers their needs and the needs of others (Pizzolato & Ozaki, 2007).	• Connect the conversation to a broader context. • Validate and call out the self in interactions. • Discourage blind alignment with traditional practices and prescribed formulas.
Validate learners' capacity to know.	• Promote confidence by validating students' voices. • Prompt students to identify their own viewpoints, values, and worldviews. • Ask students to expand on their initial views of experiences (Baxter Magolda & King, 2004).	• Connect the conversation to a broader context. • Validate and call out the self in interactions. • Discourage blind alignment with traditional practices and prescribed formulas.
Situate learning in learner's experience.	• Redirect conversation toward learner's experience. • Encourage students to apply what they learned in a given situation to another situation. • Encourage students to apply what they learned in another situation to a current situation (Baxter Magolda & King, 2004). • Encourage students to make sense of their experience, rather than having the educator make sense of it for them (Baxter Magolda & King, 2008).	• Adopt a student-centered view of interaction. • Remember that students are in a variety of developmental stages; faculty and staff advisers should address all three self-authorship domains (cognitive, intrapersonal, and interpersonal) in assignments, projects, and advising. • Assign writing to discover the self (e.g., ethnographic writing projects).

(Continues)

TABLE 4.1 (Continued)

Assumptions About Learning and Development	Strategies for Promoting Self-Authorship From the Literature	Proposed Integrative Education Strategies to Prepare Students for Self-Authorship
Construct meaning mutually with the learner.	• Display curiosity. • Ask students to reflect on their own assumptions, rather than always adopting the expert, guide, authority role (Baxter Magolda & King, 2004).	• Listen with deep respect for students' intellect and life experience. Validate contributions. Draw from their passions whenever possible. • Show up as "fully human." Sharing your own journey and how you make sense of it may offer students an understanding of the human side of their explorations.
Promote volitional efficacy, or the belief in one's ability to persist in goal-oriented behavior despite challenges.	• Ask probing questions to encourage reflection about possible challenges and the student's ability to persist despite them (Pizzolato, 2005). • Emphasize action and engagement (Brown, 2004).	• Ask questions to uncover unrecognized steps they have already taken toward the goal.
Promote coping skills.	• Work with students to identify appropriate coping skills (i.e., identifying personal strengths, relaxation techniques, support systems, exercising options) (Pizzolato, 2005).	• Share mindfulness practices such as cognitive regulation, emotional regulation, and meditation with students to help them learn to identify their voices. • Help students identify stressors and the need for finding coping strategies.

Toward an Integrative Educational Experience

The value of connecting learners with themselves as an integral part of the learning process through self-authorship has been described in a number of additional ways, including reflexivity; personally and academically reflecting on lived experiences revealing deep connections between writer and subject (Goodall, 2000); emotional intelligence, awareness of one's own and others' emotions (Goleman, 1995); intellectual entrepreneurship, inviting students' innovative thinking into the learning process (Gates, 2014); mindful learning, strategies to encourage deep engagement with learning (Langer, 1989); and integrative education (Palmer & Zajonc, 2010). An integrative view of education encourages students to "bring all of who they are and what they know into each class" (Palmer & Zajonc, 2010, pp. 90–91). Further, this approach "embraces every dimension of what it means to be human . . . honors the varieties of human experience, looks at us and our world through a variety of cultural lenses, and educates our young people in ways that enable them to face the challenges of our time" (Palmer & Zajonc, 2010, p. 20). Integrative approaches to education empower students to use their lived experiences and inner resources to make sense of the world around them. When students become integral to meaning making, they may more acutely identify disparities between the perspectives of others and their internal voices. A student wrestling with such discrepancies may experience a challenging crossroads experience.

Attempting to reconcile the cognitive dissonance associated with crossroads experiences is often unsettling for students. Mindfulness practices may help prepare students to manage the inevitable internal stress during such times by helping them persist in the difficult yet developmental self-authorship process rather than retreating to reliance on experts, so typical of students in the early stages of self-authorship. Additionally, concepts of mindfulness and mindful learning have a lot to offer as we grapple with the question of how to create integrative learning environments that support self-authorship development. Before discussing Langer's concept of mindful learning, we first address what is meant by mindfulness. The term *mindfulness* is often associated with philosophical and religious traditions and practices such as yoga. It is defined by Kabat-Zinn (2009) as "moment-to-moment awareness. It is cultivated by purposefully paying attention to things we ordinarily never give a moment's thought to" (p. 2). Ritchhart and Perkins (2000) describe mindfulness as "an open and creative state of consciousness" (p. 28). Mindfulness, then, involves a present awareness of the situation, self, and other that, according to Kabat-Zinn (2009), points us toward the "poignant enormity of our life experience" (p. 6). While specific mindfulness techniques may differ, they "share the common goal of training an individual's attention and awareness so that consciousness becomes more finely attuned to events and experiences in the present" (Shapiro, Brown, & Astin, 2008, pp. 6–7). A focus on the present moment may lead to greater awareness of the self in context and a deeper engagement with the learning process (Goleman, 1995). It may also support self-authorship by giving students experience with assessing their internal states.

The practice of mindfulness has several important implications that may foster learning and engagement essential to self-authorship, including "increased creativity, flexibility, and use of information as well as memory and retention" (Ritchhart & Perkins, 2000, p. 29). Therefore, mindfulness may develop traditional academic skills as well as support important affective and interpersonal communication skills that are developed through the self-authorship process (Abes et al., 2007; Baxter Magolda, 2001; Kegan, 1994; Pizzolato, 2008; Taylor, 2008). Other benefits of mindfulness connected to more classical notions of learning, according to Ritchhart and Perkins (2000), include "the flexible transfer of knowledge and skills to new contexts, the development of deep understanding, student motivation and engagement, the ability to think critically and creatively, and the development of more self-directed learners" (p. 29). Similarly, a number of studies suggest links among self-authorship development, critical thinking, and independence (Baxter Magolda, 2001; Baxter Magolda & King, 2004; Keeling, 2006; Pizzolato, 2008; Pizzolato & Ozaki, 2007).

There are clear connections between the strategies that can be used to promote mindfulness and those that promote self-authorship development. Additional mindfulness practices such as cognitive regulation, attention, and emotional regulation also may help young adults learn to identify their voices amid the barrage of perspectives and social formulas they encounter in higher education. By connecting us to ourselves, such mindfulness practices allow us to remain open to new challenges and new ways of seeing. Therefore, mindfulness may help students become more open to the possibilities embedded in crossroads experiences. We propose that mindfulness can set the stage for and foster self-authorship. Developing regular mindfulness practices, such as meditation, breathing techniques, or exercises that bring present awareness, may help students develop the inner knowing that will serve them when they encounter challenging crossroads essential to the development of self-authorship.

For decades, Ellen Langer and her colleagues have researched innovative ways to deeply engage learners in their learning contexts. Langer's work on mindful learning practices returns us to the reason we may have originally pursued life in the academy. According to Langer (1997), "Continually re-experiencing life from a fresh vantage point is part of being truly alive." Mindfulness inspires novel ways of seeing through keen interpretive work and reflexive reframing. It is an enlarged set of possibilities offering new ways of noticing. Mindful education means paying attention to what connects us to learning and therefore opens the possibilities for developing the whole person in our everyday encounters with our students. Such integrative approaches to education invite students to engage in learning with an additional awareness that helps them identify their internal voices, and to ultimately self-author.

Langer's (1997) three qualities of mindfulness are "a) the continuous creation of new categories; b) openness to new information; and c) an implicit awareness of more than one perspective" (p. 73). These three qualities support the development of self-authorship by creating an environment where young adults must identify multiple perspectives, including their own (Baxter Magolda & King, 2004). For Langer, the cornerstone of mindful learning is the idea that there could always be a different way to come at an idea, a new way of thinking about it, and/or an invitation to more deeply engage learners. For professionals in higher education, a mindful approach to learning situates learners as essential cocreators of knowledge (Baxter Magolda & King, 2004; Gates, 2014).

Applying Teaching and Advising Strategies That Support Self-Authorship Development

As educators, how can we begin to foster self-authorship for our students? There are no formulas to ensure students will show up with their wholehearted selves; some students are more reluctant than others. Table 4.1 describes concrete ways to foster self-authorship development among college students. We encourage you to adopt and adapt these strategies as you determine what works best for you, your students, and your campus programs.

In Table 4.1, the first column describes underlying assumptions about learning and development necessary to support self-authorship. The second column offers concrete strategies derived from the literature for promoting self-authorship both in and out of the classroom. During challenging crossroads experiences, students often face disorienting feelings of disequilibrium. It is often unsettling to rely on internal voices for guidance; therefore, college students may eagerly seek direction from others in order to reconcile the discomfort. The third column in the table identifies integrative education strategies that may help students practice accessing their internal voices throughout the college experience.

While Table 4.1 is not meant to provide an exhaustive list of strategies for promoting self-authorship, it offers intentional opportunities for meaning making and deeper, mindful, whole-student engagement. To demonstrate the ways some of the aforementioned strategies may be applied, we now offer some specific examples from our experiences in both student affairs and academic affairs.

Emily's Example: Educator Development Is Linked to Student Development

Over my 14 years in the field of student affairs, I have witnessed students struggling to make meaning of their lives, grappling with career decisions, individuating from their parents' expectations, making academic choices, experiencing relationship challenges, managing roommate issues, working through questions of sexuality, addressing leadership challenges, and exploring their values. In talking with students during everyday experiences and major crossroads, I developed an interest in identifying mentoring strategies that would lead to the richest learning experiences for students as they search for authentic and engaged places in the world. My search prompted me to conduct a study investigating the degree to which new professionals in student affairs, who often have the most one-on-one contact with students, use strategies known to promote self-authorship (see Table 4.1). The study also sought to identify adviser characteristics that may influence the advising practices they use, such as gender, education, and the adviser's own level of self-authorship development.

Among the study's findings, advisers in earlier stages of self-authorship development gave more concrete direction and instruction to students—strategies that are less likely to promote the cognitive dissonance necessary for self-authored thinking (Marx, 2012). These same professionals often longed to provide support and definitive answers for students. This more directive approach is often well received by students, who may welcome relief from the uncertainty and related struggles associated with big "crossroads" decisions. For example, in an effort to support a Greek student managing a tough judicial issue in her chapter, one new Greek adviser in the early stage of self-authorship made a challenging phone call for the student. To better support the student leader's self-authorship development, the adviser might have worked with the student to prepare her to make the difficult phone call herself. An example of a new professional in the late stage of self-authorship, however, demonstrates more challenging advising approaches that support self-authorship development. Aaron, a new career adviser, said students who often "come to me to seek particular career advice turn out to have many other underlying issues related to the situation. . . . Instead of giving direct advice on the specific question, I often encourage the students to elaborate their thoughts and feelings about the situation" (Marx, 2012, p. 97). Aaron's use of probing and reflective questions challenges students to identify their own perspectives, needs, and values. These strategies, while often uncomfortable for students, offer them an opportunity to practice self-authored thinking. The link between new professionals' stage of self-authorship and the advising strategies they use with students calls us to be mindful of our own developmental process as educators. Supervisors, graduate preparation programs, mentors, and other confidants have a unique opportunity to utilize the strategies suggested in this chapter with educators themselves, thus bolstering educators' internal capacities and expanding their ability to create developmentally rich contexts for students (Baxter Magolda, 2014; Drago-Severson, 2010).

The preceding story demonstrates that as educators, our own stage of development influences our ability to support student development. Next, Lisa's story illustrates the simultaneous coconstruction of knowledge and self and the relationship between whole-student engagement and the achievement of academic rigor, both of which contribute to creating contexts for self-authorship development.

Lisa's Story: Integrative Learning Through Writing-Intensive Courses

As a professor, my view of students has always been one of great reverence. I see students as "intellectual entrepreneurs" with tremendous capacity for innovative thought (Gates, 2014). My teaching experience has covered broad institutional ground: community colleges, large and small private colleges, and large public research institutions. Regardless of the type of institution, I have found that creating safe yet demanding learning spaces and inviting students to share their lived experiences, knowledge, and points of view promote deep student engagement, enhance class participation, increase the likelihood students visit my office hours, and often lead to student work that far surpassed expectations. Nothing, however, in my two decades of classroom instruction has more deeply drawn students into their learning than a writing-intensive course called "Ethnography." The course met several key programmatic objectives: It was a capstone course, it was the upper-division writing-intensive course, and it satisfied one of three methodological requirements for the communication undergraduate major.

The primary assignment for the course required students to employ qualitative research methods to investigate a culture or subculture of their choosing and write up their findings in a 30-page paper. Students knew well in advance that they would need to commit to their chosen culture by week two of the semester. The course had a reputation on campus for being rigorous. The rigor (or fear) of the course played a role in their engagement, no doubt. Because the assignment employed academic prose and narrative, it played to varying strengths in students' writing abilities. This allowed students who had perhaps not performed as well in traditional academic writing to shine in their creation of evocative narratives and vice versa. Further, the process of learning was made even more complex through the weekly sharing of scaffolded student writing assignments. Often some of the most raw and therefore memorable narratives were written by students who were not among the typically top-performing students. Narrative writing, including autoethnographic tales (autobiographical narratives that connect the students to the concepts under investigation), facilitated deep student engagement inviting students to personally and academically connect with their own and their peers' stories.

My previous experience in the classroom did not prepare me for managing the deep levels of engagement students invested in their research. Navigating students' vulnerability proved to be a challenge when some elected to write about their experiences of past sexual abuse, domestic violence, racism, the loss of both parents to cancer, and other profound life experiences. If it is deep engagement we desire from our students, we may need to be better prepared for what they might share. Such conversations can be difficult to navigate in traditional academic spaces. I decided that if they were willing to step that deeply and vulnerably into their work, I needed to write my own story along with them. We moved through that semester together and discovered something fundamental about what it means to be human; about finding hope when we may feel different; and, most profoundly, about our connections to the participants we studied, and our connections to one another as a unified learning community. The improvement in students' writing was remarkable. Students became aware of the research process, creative and academic writing strategies, and literary structure and coherence. They also developed critical thinking and project and time management skills. They learned that members of the cultures they studied—victims of human trafficking, the homeless, veterans, refugees, leaders in corporate and nonprofit organizations, among others—were more similar to them than they had realized. Even after a year-long ethnographic project, they learned that academic writing often involves self-imposed stopping points that bring us to a conclusion even though we may sense that there is much more to discover in the field.

The experiences from this assignment primarily demonstrate a pedagogy of integrative learning through the process of reflexivity, and students' discoveries of their place in the coconstruction of knowledge. The story also illustrates the developmental power of revisiting and making new meaning of crossroads experiences. In Lisa's pedagogical example, students were not passive recipients of information, but were actively and collaboratively engaged in meaning making and rediscovering something about their lived experiences. This is consistent with Langer's (1997) view that interaction with our environment is not merely a matter of aligning ourselves with our environment but "a process by which we give form, meaning, and value to our world" (p. 1161). Our examples of integrative education underscore the necessity for a fierce commitment to reflective inquiry and an epistemological humility that allows educators to coconstruct knowledge with students.

Overcoming Resistance

As with any change, there is likely to be some resistance to adopting new ways of seeing and the practices that accompany them (DuFon & Christian, 2013). Chapters 11 and 12 address this specific challenge directly. Mindfulness can be interpreted in many ways, including what some may perceive as unconventional and even spiritual. One could argue that an educator who does not come from a spiritual perspective nevertheless can apply integrative strategies to encounters in order to foster whole-student engagement. Other sources of resistance may be a reluctance to include learners as cocreators of knowledge. To be sure, knowledge acquisition is an expected and essential element of the higher education experience. A range of traditional teaching and learning strategies, including lectures and experiential and collaborative learning, are well established in higher education. Traditional faculty members may be inclined to leave more integrated approaches to student learning and development professionals in the realm of student affairs. Designating institutional domains that leave cognitive growth to academic affairs and intra- and interpersonal development to student affairs is, by definition, dis-integrating for the student.

In order to support development of the whole student, an integrated view of students must occur at the institutional level as well as in daily practices with students that foster both "a movement toward the truth and toward the self" (Deresiewicz, 2014, p. 85). There are many practices that can move us toward this integrated approach; many were described in this chapter and also mentioned in the introduction. More are described in the chapters that follow.

This chapter reviewed literature on self-authorship, advocated an integrative view of higher education through mindful learning, and proposed strategies for practical application to promote whole-student engagement in everyday student encounters. Our vision for higher education is largely transformative. This vision includes establishing learning spaces where students have plenty of opportunities to practice self-authored thinking, where they can courageously bring their deeply held beliefs to the conversation, take risks to pose critical questions, both large and small, and connect meaningfully with other students, faculty, and staff who do the same.

Viewing whole-student development through the lens of self-authorship contributes to an education where students "won't be damned to go through life at second hand, thinking other people's thoughts and dreaming other people's dreams. It's been said that people go to monasteries to find out why they have come, and college ought to be the same" (Deresiewicz, 2014, pp. 85–86). We invite educators to create rigorous, safe learning spaces that allow for radical inquiry and prompt students to think deeply along with us as we do the work of transforming what is possible to know, create, do, and become. It is possible to build universities that provide students the opportunity to take their places in the economy and connect themselves authentically to a self that has a sense of heart, purpose, and agency. We believe, after all, that the life of the mind is also a life of the heart and perhaps even the soul.

Editor's Summary Points and Questions to Consider

1. Fostering self-authorship may help faculty, administrators, and student affairs professionals provide holistic student learning and development. How do you see yourself adopting and adapting some of the key self-authorship strategies mentioned in this chapter?
2. Various regions of the brain need to become activated and then upregulated and/or downregulated in accordance with each moment for students to demonstrate self-awareness and ultimately self-regulation. In essence, in the crossroads stage of self-authorship, students may need to be able to down-regulate their limbic system and upregulate their prefrontal and medial cortex to pay attention to what is happening in the moment, and then choose to focus on discerning what is true for them in the moment. Consistent mindfulness methodology practice thickens the insula and may increase opportunities for students to sense what is happening in their own selves while discerning the difference between what is another's experience. Training in compassion and empathy (explored further in Chapter 8) that influences the insula, prefrontal cortex, limbic system, and anterior cingulate cortex also helps students take in others' ideas while monitoring their own thoughts, feelings, and sensations without attachment to the judgment of what they are feeling, hearing, observing, or thinking. Neuroplasticity illustrates how mindfulness can change the structure and function of key areas of the brain that are associated with attention, emotion, and cognitive regulation (refer to Chapter 3). These same brain regions may be associated with self-authorship development. How can

you envision using mindfulness practices on your campus (in and out of the classroom) to determine how well they may foster self-authorship?

References

Abes, E. S., Jones, S. R., & McEwen, M. K. (2007). Reconceptualizing the model of multiple dimensions of identity: The role of meaning-making capacity in the construction of multiple identities. *Journal of College Student Development, 48*(1), 1–22.

Appel-Silbaugh, C. (2007). *Acting out integrity and honor: Student Honor Council cultural influence on members' development.* (Doctoral dissertation) University of Maryland, College Park.

Arnett, J. J. (2004). *Emerging adulthood: The winding road from the late teens through the twenties.* New York, NY: Oxford University Press.

Arum, R., & Roksa, J. (2011). *Academically adrift: Limited learning on college campuses.* Chicago, IL: University of Chicago Press.

Association of American Colleges & Universities. (2007). *College learning for the new global century.* Washington, DC: Author.

Baxter Magolda, M. B. (1999). *Creating context for learning and self-authorship: Constructive-developmental pedagogy.* Nashville, TN: Vanderbilt University Press.

Baxter Magolda, M. B. (2001). *Making their own way: Narratives for transforming higher education to promote self-authorship.* Sterling, VA: Stylus.

Baxter Magolda, M. B. (2003). Identity and learning: Student affairs' role in transforming higher education. *Journal of College Student Development, 44*(2), 231–247.

Baxter Magolda, M. B. (2008). Three elements of self-authorship. *Journal of College Student Development, 49*(4), 269–284.

Baxter Magolda, M. B. (2009a). The activity of meaning making: A holistic perspective on college student development. *Journal of College Student Development, 50*(6), 621–639.

Baxter Magolda, M. B. (2009b). *Authoring your life: Developing an internal voice to meet life's challenges.* Sterling, VA: Stylus.

Baxter Magolda, M. B. (2014). Enriching educators' learning experience. *About Campus: Enriching the Student Learning Experience, 19*(2), 2–10.

Baxter Magolda, M. B., & King, P. (Eds.). (2004). *Learning partnerships: Theory and models of practice to educate for self-authorship.* Sterling, VA: Stylus.

Baxter Magolda, M. B., & King, P. (2008). Toward reflective conversations: An advising approach that promotes self-authorship. *Peer Review, 10*(11), 8–11.

Brooks, D. (2014, September 8). Becoming a real person. *New York Times.* Retrieved from www.nytimes.com/2014/09/09/opinion/david-brooks-becoming-a-real-person.html?_r=0

Brown, S. C. (2004). Learning across the campus: How college facilitates the development of wisdom. *Journal of College Student Development, 45*(2), 134–148.

Council for the Advancement of Standards in Higher Education. (2006). *CAS professional standards for higher education* (6th ed.). Washington, DC: Author.

Creamer, E. G., & Laughlin, A. (2005). Self-authorship and women's career decision making. *Journal of College Student Development, 46*(1), 13–27.

Deresiewicz, W. (2010, March 1). *Solitude and leadership.* Retrieved from theamericanscholar.org/solitude-and-leadership/#.VDWezytdWQY

Deresiewicz, W. (2014). *Excellent sheep: The miseducation of the American elite and the way to a meaningful life.* New York, NY: Free Press.

DeWitz, S. J., Woolsey, M. L., & Walsh, W. B. (2009). College student retention: An exploration of the relationship between self-efficacy beliefs and purpose in life among college students. *Journal of College Student Development, 50*(1), 19–34.

Drago-Severson, E. (2010). *Leading adult learning.* Thousand Oaks, CA: Corwin.

DuFon, M. A., & Christian, J. (2013). The formation and development of the mindful campus. *New Directions for Teaching and Learning, 134,* 65–72.

Gates, L. R. (2014, March 19). *Students as intellectual entrepreneurs: The case for instructors as transformational leaders.* Lecture conducted from San Diego State University Department of Communication, San Diego, CA, March 19.

Goleman, D. (1995). *Emotional intelligence: Why it can matter more than IQ.* New York: Bantam Books.

Goodall, H. L. (2000). *Writing the new ethnography.* Lanham, MD: Altamira Press.

High-Impact Educational Practices. (2014, June 24). Retrieved from www.aacu.org/leap/hips

Hodge, D. C., Baxter Magolda, M. B., & Haynes, C. A. (2009). Engaged learning: Enabling self-authorship and effective practice. *Liberal Education, 95*(4), 16–23.

Holba, A. M., & Noyes, C. M. (2013). *Mindfulness learning and contemplative inquiry in online environments.* Retrieved from www.nyu.edu/classes/keefer/waoe/holbaa.pdf.

Huerta, E. (2013, August 16). *Why I left Google: Thoughts on trading in pride and security for authenticity.* Retrieved from medium.com/this-happened-to-me/why-i-left-google-c02f1ff471c6

Kabat-Zinn, J. (2009). *Full catastrophe living: Using the wisdom of your body and mind to face stress, pain, and illness.* New York, NY: Bantam Dell.

Keeling, R. P. (2006). *Learning reconsidered 2: A practical guide to implementing a campus-wide focus on the student experience.* Washington, DC: NASPA.

Kegan, R. (1982). *The evolving self: Problem and process in human development.* Cambridge, MA: Harvard University Press.

Kegan, R. (1994). *In over our heads: The mental demands of modern life.* Cambridge, MA: Harvard University Press.

King, P. M., Baxter Magolda, M. B., Perez, R. J., & Taylor, K. B. (2009). *Refining the journey toward self-authorship: Developmental steps within the crossroads.* Paper presented at the Association for the Study of Higher Education, Vancouver, BC.

Langer, E. J. (1989). *Mindfulness.* Reading, MA: Addison-Wesley.

Langer, E. J. (1997). *The power of mindful learning* [Kindle version]. Reading, MA: Addison-Wesley. Retrieved from Amazon.com

Lewis, H. (2007). *Excellence without a soul: Does liberal education have a future?* New York, NY: Public Affairs.

Marx, E. (2012). *Advising to promote self-authorship: Exploring advising strategies and advisor characteristics among new student affairs professionals.* ProQuest, UMI Dissertations Publishing. UMI: 3528182

Nash, R., & Murray, M. (2010). *Helping college students find purpose: The campus guide to meaning-making.* San Francisco, CA: Jossey-Bass.

National Association of Colleges and Employers. (2010). *Job outlook 2011: November 2010.* Bethlehem, PA: NACE Research.

Palmer, P. J., & Zajonc, A. (2010). *The heart of higher education: A call to renewal.* San Francisco, CA: Jossey-Bass.

Parks, S. D. (2000). *Big questions, worthy dreams: Mentoring young adults in their search for meaning, purpose, and faith.* San Francisco, CA: Jossey-Bass.

Pizzolato, J. (2005). Creating crossroads for self-authorship: Investigating the provocative moment. *Journal of College Student Development, 46*(6), 624–641.

Pizzolato, J. (2008). Meaning making inside and outside the academic arena: Investigating the contextuality of epistemological development in college students. *Journal of General Education, 56*(3–4), 228–251.

Pizzolato, J., & Ozaki, C. (2007). Moving toward self-authorship: Investigating outcomes of learning partnerships. *Journal of College Student Development, 48*(2), 196–214.

Ritchhart, R., & Perkins, D. N. (2000). Life in the mindful classroom: Nurturing the disposition of mindfulness. *Journal of Social Issues, 56,* 27–47.

Settersten, R., & Ray, B. E. (2010). *Not quite adults: Why 20 somethings are choosing a slower path to adulthood, and why it's good for everyone.* New York, NY: Bantam.

Shapiro, S. L., Brown, K. W., & Astin, J. A. (2008). *Toward the integration of meditation into higher education: A review of research.* Prepared for the Center for Contemplative Mind in Society. Unpublished research report. Retrieved from www.contemplativemind.org/archives/830

Taylor, K. (2008). Mapping the intricacies of young adults' developmental journey from socially prescribed to internally defined identities, relationships, and beliefs. *Journal of College Student Development, 49*(3), 215–234.

Vogeley, K., Bussfeld, P., Newen, A., Herrmann, S., Happé, F., Falkai, P., . . . Ziles, K. (2001). Mind reading: Neural mechanisms of theory of mind and self-perspective. *NeuroImage, 14*(1), 170–181.

INTENTIONAL DESIGN OF HIGH-IMPACT EXPERIENTIAL LEARNING

Patsy Tinsley McGill

Give me, O Lord, an ever watchful heart.
—Saint Thomas Aquinas (*Prayer for All Virtues to a Christian Man*, 1866)

S o far in this book, you have read how higher education has changed over the decades and you are being introduced to ideas that will invite even further change—change that will hopefully be positively trans-formational for many. Have you ever considered whether you were one of the fortunate few in college, any level of college, to experience learning that changed your life— learning that made you view yourself and your place in this world differently? I know I was not that fortunate as an undergraduate student or as a graduate student in my master's program. In my doctoral program, however, I experienced the kind of learning that Zull (2002) said "can be almost like a religious experience" (p. 9). This religious experience kind of learning transformed the very essence of who I was and continue to be. I know from experience that this kind of education can be intentionally designed and evaluated. Based on my experience and my research, I present in this chapter a framework that can be used to intentionally design high-impact experiential learning—the kind of learning that leads to personal transformation—and make it an achievable outcome. But first, I share my own story of transformation.

I can use the term *luck* to describe the circumstances that led me to be in the right physical place at the right point in time for me to experi-ence life-changing learning. Beyond that, luck had little, if anything, to do with it. Considering my mental place at that time, it's a miracle it happened at all. My personal transformation was the outcome of a series of learning experiences designed by Ernie Stringer, a community ethnographer from Australia. My path to writing this chapter can be traced back to the intersection of my life's journey with Ernie's, because everything I have done as a researcher and teacher over the past decade was directly influenced by his constructivist community-based approach to teaching and learning.

Ernie is no "sage on the stage" or "guide on the side" (Johnson, Johnson, & Smith, 1991, p. 81); Ernie is an architect of high-impact experiential learning, a structure that transforms the lives of many who study with him. About the time I was experiencing my first course with Ernie, Robert Barr and John Tagg (1995) wrote about the shift from an instruction-based paradigm to a learning-based paradigm in higher education in the article "From Teaching to Learning: A New Paradigm for Undergraduate Education." They also discussed the shift by instructors from a focus on the transmission of information through disassociated activities to the design of integrated learning experiences. Ernie's intentional design of how we would learn and experience the community-based ethnography course we experienced with him was a perfect example of the power of this shift in the classroom. Because of Ernie, as a student I experienced the power of transformative learning in my own education. Because of Ernie, as a professor I have observed the power of transformative learning in the lives of many of my own students. And because of Ernie, I have become a student and architect of high-impact experiential learning as a researcher. I hope this will enable me to impact teaching and learning beyond my own classroom.

Charting the Path to Transformation and Understanding

I was a 40-something southern female whose professional identity was my dominant identity at the time I was accepted by the College of Education at Texas A&M University to earn a PhD in educational human resources development. I had built an international reputation as a pioneer and innovator in satellite-based distance learning in the 1980s and 1990s. The apex of my career had been founding the first private satellite network in the nation to offer live, interactive high school credit courses and professional development programs to students and teachers in rural schools across the continental United States. My story as an entrepreneur and my life-altering experiences throughout that part of my life journey is for another book. The chapter in that book that is critical to this story is the intersection of my life as a professional with my life as a returning adult student. I was running two companies—a publishing company and an international consulting company—while earning my PhD, and I was commuting three hours both to and from classes. I was a basket case, to say the least. Friends described me not just as a type A personality; they described me as an extreme-A or a triple-A personality.

The last thing I needed to encounter at this point in my life and career was a professor who began our first class by asking his students to cocreate the course syllabus, deliverables, assignments, due dates, you name it, with him. That was Ernie Stringer. Enter the first of about a dozen meltdowns that I experienced over the first semester I studied with him! As my time with Ernie and with my classmates progressed (and as my stomach ulcers literally increased in number and severity), I began to realize that the way he was teaching and the way I was experiencing learning were changing the way I viewed my self, and just about everything in my world. And this was not just happening to me. My classmates reported that they were also fundamentally changing both as learners and as professionals. Our ways of being in the world were transforming. The experience was so profound that many of us stayed together to study with Ernie in a series of courses over the next several semesters; we even wrote and published a book about the experience, *Community-Based Ethnography: Breaking Traditional Boundaries of Research, Teaching, and Learning* (Stringer et al., 1997). It was a turning point in my life and in my career. Two years later, I left a successful career, as well as my family, my friends, and everything I loved about my home state, and moved halfway across the country to experience a new way of working, living, and being in the world. That part of my life journey, again, is for another chapter in another book.

A few years after my move, I had the opportunity to join the faculty of California State University, Monterey Bay (CSUMB). I knew little about the university at the time except that it was only about a decade old, had been built on a former military base, and had a profound vision statement. CSUMB was also known as a learner-centered outcomes-based institution (Tagg, 2003). I was hired to teach the strategic management senior capstone course in the College of Business. Senior capstone is a high-impact educational practice that serves as a culminating experience as well as a bridge to graduate school and careers for students. The CSUMB College of Business capstone course is experiential learning at its utmost. It is a project-based course in which teams of students work as consultants with local firms to determine how the firms can achieve greater success in serving their clients or customers. My experience and qualifications as a teacher were very thin, but at least I was equipped with a PhD in education and more than 20 years of experience as a student. Even though my studies with Ernie covered fewer than 2 of the 20 years I had spent as a student, it was definitely my experiences in his courses that had the greatest influence on how I designed the capstone experience for my students.

Well, I quickly discovered that CSUMB students were no more prepared to experience Ernie's way of teaching and learning in my undergraduate capstone courses than I had been in my doctoral courses. In spite of that (and my students' meltdowns), I quickly began to observe students experiencing and talking about the kind of personal transformation I had experienced in my studies with Ernie. Students' views of their selves and their futures were changing as they completed their capstone course requirements. Because this usually happened at or very near the end of each semester, I could only confirm what I was observing through student feedback in course evaluations; in statements made at capstone festival; and/or in what students sent me in follow-up e-mails, cards, and notes. This was enough, however, to convince me that there was definitely something to the Ernie way of teaching and learning that was worth examining more closely.

Deconstructing Ernie's Intentional Course Design

From the moment I entered the classroom on the first night of the first course I took with Ernie, I felt an uncomfortable difference. He was moving tables out of the way and arranging chairs in a circle. He had no syllabus to give us, no deliverables to assign us, and no textbook for us to buy. There was absolutely no structure! It was all so unexpected. For an extreme type A personality who was running two companies and who organized her life around schedules and deliverables, it was crazy! I remember thinking that Ernie was probably just not prepared to teach that first night. After all, he was from Australia and maybe he just didn't know what was expected of a professor at Texas A&M.

Having had many opportunities since that time not only to deconstruct that experience with my fellow classmates, but also to discuss teaching and learning with Ernie himself, I know with certainty that he knew exactly what he was doing and why he was doing it. It was all very constructivist! I had studied constructivist learning theory, as well as the other learning theories referenced in this book, but this was my first time to experience a class truly based on constructivist principles. What were the essential elements of that experience that most influenced my own course design?

- He relinquished control: As indicated previously, in Ernie's class we collaboratively developed our syllabus, decided on our course deliverables, and built our course schedule. By rearranging our chairs in a circle each week, there was no focal point of authority; we were all learning from each other. By not dictating what we were to produce in the course, how we would produce it, and on what schedule, Ernie was giving us, as students, the power the instructor typically retains.

- He built community: In each of Ernie's courses, we experienced learning in community. From the way he had us rearrange our chairs to remove the focal authority to our collective decision to bring and share food each evening and weekend class, Ernie was intentionally building a community of learners.

- He emphasized acquiring and applying new knowledge and skills: Each activity we did in class, even as simple as interviewing a classmate and introducing that classmate to the other students, was modeling a skill we would use in our community-based project. Each qualitative research skill we learned through the stories Ernie told, the readings he assigned, and the activities we did in class provided foundation knowledge and skills we later used in our field-based research projects.

- He required reflective practice: One of the deliverables our class agreed on with Ernie was to keep a reflective journal of not only our fieldwork but also our class experiences. This became the basis of the book we wrote together as our class project in our third course together.

- He deemphasized grades: As hard as it was for me to understand at the time, Ernie's approach to grading was one that made each of us work even harder. As I recall, Ernie did not give any grades until the end of the semester. For the first time in all of my years in school, however, it didn't matter to me. I worked hard not to make an A, but rather to meet his expectations.

While this is a simplistic analysis of a very complex learning environment, I've discovered over time that the implications of these instructional design elements for my own teaching and on my own students' learning experiences have been significant. This became most apparent when I learned how widely students' capstone experiences vary across my own campus, particularly since some lack any experiential focus.

Listening to Student Voices Across Campus

During the early years of my teaching, I received a request from the provost to serve on a three-member educational effectiveness research team that spent several years examining the capstone experience across majors at CSUMB. Through this study, it became clear to me that not all capstone experiences are created equal. I began to see that my students' capstone experiences were very different from those of students in other majors at CSUMB; nevertheless, there were consistent messages coming from capstone students across the majors regarding what they believed they needed to be successful in a capstone experience.

Because this was not the focus of our educational effectiveness study, I reexamined the data collected from students, analyzed and categorized what students said they needed to be successful, and wrote an article summarizing those findings. In the *Journal of General Education* article, "Understanding the Capstone Experience Through the Voices of Students" (Tinsley McGill, 2012), I presented the four most essential elements needed to support success as reported by students in the study: preparation, communication, support, and structure. In explaining the meaning of these elements, suffice it to say that capstone instructors often require students to spend much more time and effort on their coursework than instructors in other courses do; therefore, students frequently enter capstone neither expecting nor prepared to spend as much time or effort as their capstone instructors require. Students also frequently confront a much higher level of rigor in an experiential capstone and find themselves unprepared to think, write, or present at the level of excellence required to succeed. This is particularly the case when the final capstone report is prepared for, and the capstone festival presentation is made to, a community client. Students expressed the need for open and timely communication with their instructors, which relates to their need for access to and the support of faculty, advisers, and staff at levels they hadn't experienced in other courses. This support included instructor and/or adviser feedback at critical points in the semester. Finally, the students across campus expressed the need for enough structure to guide them through the process and keep them on schedule to successfully complete their projects.

While findings were consistent across the majors in the data analyzed from the CSUMB educational effectiveness capstone study, the data did not reveal insights into the transformative quality of capstone that I had personally observed among my students. To further explore how capstone experiences can change a student's view of the world and her place in it, I took a semester-long sabbatical in 2012 and turned to sources beyond my own campus as well as within my own classrooms for answers.

Moving to Theory- and Science-Informed Design

In 2008, the Association of American Colleges & Universities (AAC&U) published what has become a key reference for understanding how to help students achieve outcomes they will need to succeed in their careers in the new global economy. *High-Impact Educational Practices: What They Are, Who*

Has Access to Them, and Why They Matter (Kuh, 2008) named a culminating senior experience, generally referred to as capstone, as one of 10 effective high-impact active learning practices that can increase student engagement, retention, and success. In that report, Kuh made the point that "to engage students at high levels, these practices must be done well" (p. 20). But what does it mean for these practices to be done well?

Since 2008, other researchers and educators have asked similar questions regarding what makes high-impact activities, practices, experiences, and courses effective. In 2010, AAC&U published a follow-on report to *High-Impact Educational Practices* (Brownell & Swaner) that examined factors contributing to positive student outcomes in five of the practices originally highlighted by Kuh. As recently as 2012, Randy Bass stated that "we need to ask what gives these practices high impact, and then we need to look at ways to integrate those kinds of strategies into course design and classroom pedagogy" (p. 26). Kuh (2008) actually began to answer his own question about what it means for such practices to be done well by identifying student behaviors that are influenced when students participate in the LEAP high-impact practices. When these behaviors are viewed from the perspective of how they impact course design, an instructor would do the following:

- Give assignments that require significant time and effort from students.
- Ensure substantive interaction among students and with the instructor.
- Involve a cycle of assignments with instructor feedback and student response to that feedback.
- Involve substantive reflection and integration of learning by students.
- Require that students apply learning to real-world cases, projects, simulations, and so on.

While I can certainly affirm that my capstone course design includes these elements, they do not provide a complete picture of what I believe a course must entail for it to lead to transformative learning among students. For example, there are key experiences from Ernie's way of teaching missing from this list—experiences that make significant contributions to the transformative power of his classes. Realizing this, I shifted my focus to learn everything I could about learning. I went back to reexamine the adult learning theories I had studied in my doctoral program, this time with a focus on how those theories translate to action in the classroom. It was around this time that a colleague referred me to the work of James E. Zull (2002) and his book *The Art of Changing the Brain: Enriching the Practice of Teaching by Exploring the Biology of Learning*. This led me to rich discoveries (presented later in this chapter) that provided some of the what, why, and how answers that had eluded me. Finally, I turned to my qualitative research roots for answers in the words of students who had experienced my own capstone course. My students' reflections and words were more insightful than I could have ever imagined they would be and provided answers to many of my lingering questions about my own learning experience with Ernie, as well as my students' learning experiences with me.

Reexamining Learning Theories in Action

Since the first semester I began teaching senior capstone in 2005, I have focused my course design on having students apply their knowledge and skills to real-world projects and on supporting my students' successful transitions from college to career or graduate school. In the course, students must integrate what they have learned across their general education courses and business curriculum, apply their integrated knowledge and skills in experiential-based research projects in which they work with a company or nonprofit organization in the community, and synthesize their findings into a professional written report and oral presentation. The course design moves students along the continuum from experiencing passive learning to becoming engaged learners who have the potential to achieve deep understanding. Table 5.1 provides definitions and examples of how I use each learning theory in designing a continuum of learning experiences in capstone.

What I hope students achieve after progressing through this continuum of activities is deep understanding. Zull (2002) believes that deep understanding equates to deep learning, which is learning that changes lives. How does this differ from transformative learning, or learning that changes the way a person views her self and her place in the world (Schneider, personal communication, June 14, 2011)? And might these be the applications of learning theories that, as referred to in the introduction, change the learner herself, rather than simply trying to fill the learner with knowledge (Petrie, 2013)?

To understand how this progression can effect the kind of change that I experienced and that I have observed in students, I turned again to Zull's (2002) early work, *The Art of Changing the Brain: Enriching the Practice of Teaching by Exploring the Biology of Learning*. In this book, Zull focused on helping educators understand "what conditions, what environments, and what practices make learning work better" (p. 6). His work helped me realize that understanding how the brain physically changes when deep learning occurs is much more important than following any particular

TABLE 5.1
Continuum of Learning Theories Applied in Class

Learning Theories	Class Activities
Passive learning: Learning "in which students receive the ideas and information" (Bean, 2011, p. 202) transmitted by the instructor or acquired through other sources.	Students read assignments and study new information, tools, processes, examples, and so on, presented in class and acquired through experience and study.
Reflective learning: Learning in which students "make meaningful connections about their learning" (Bain & Bass, 2012, p. 202).	Students individually reflect on ways to apply the tools and processes in sample scenarios.
Active learning: Learning in which "the mind is actively engaged," and students "make information or a concept their own by connecting it to their existing knowledge and experience" (Barkley, 2010, p. 17).	Students come together in teams to discuss their ideas formed through reflection; collectively discuss, defend, and agree on a group response; and report to the class.
Engaged learning: Learning that "foster[s] complexity in students' thinking, feeling, relating, and acting . . . as well as create[s] connections between students' learning experiences and with social contexts and communities" (Swaner, 2012, p. 80), and that "results from the synergistic interaction of motivation and active learning" (Barkley, 2010, p. 8).	Student teams use the tools or processes they have been working with in class to engage in action research with community clients, analyze the client data they collect through their research, construct a narrative to document the process and outcome, and present their findings.

teaching philosophy or learning style theory. In that book, Zull mapped what was known at that time about the brain and learning to the stages of the *experiential learning cycle* defined by Kolb (1984) in his cornerstone book *Experiential Learning: Experience as the Source of Learning and Development*. (More of the neuroscience that supports these activities is detailed in Chapters 2, 3, and 10.) Because experiential learning has multiple meanings and each has its own particularly focused research and emphasis in the literature (as well as relevance to the design and implementation of my capstone course), it is important to consider the three prominent meanings as framed in the writings of Houle (1980), Brookfield (1984), and Kolb (1984).

Houle (1980) focused on experiential learning in the context of learning that happens in individuals simply from the experiences of daily life, while Brookfield (1984) placed it in terms of students learning from applying what they know and using the skills they have acquired in a relevant context. In *Experiential Learning*, Kolb (1984) presented a conceptualization of experiential learning based on a continuous spiral of deep learning that involves concrete experiences, reflective observations, abstract hypotheses, and active testing. The cycle Kolb described is essentially instantaneous, with individuals experiencing multiple overlapping and/or parallel learning spirals at a time. Each of these descriptions can be traced back to much earlier foundational theories presented by Dewey, Piaget, and Jung, among others, who all wrote about the role of experience in learning. The connection to neuroscience is basic, as Zull (2011) explained in his later work that the purpose of the brain is to produce behavior. Zull argued, "Gathering sensory information and/or processing that information is of little value without action" (p. 28). In essence, Kolb knew that action must take place—it's the purpose of the brain. While the brain can engage in rather mindless action, the purpose of education is to reduce the randomness of that action to foster mindful or conscious choices and, in keeping with the purpose of this book, hopefully choices that will lead to creative problem solving, higher-order thinking, and possibly compassion and peace.

When I examine the learning my students experience in *capstone*, I find each of these definitions relevant. Aligning with Houle's definition, the *capstone experience* extends well beyond the classroom and is considered disruptive to the lives of most students in the class. Students have reported spending more time with their capstone teammates during the semester than with their families and friends. Capstone essentially becomes a life experience around which everything else is scheduled. Aligning with Brookfield's definition, each student team applies what its members have learned to help a community client determine the most significant challenges it is facing and to recommend solutions the client firm can implement to achieve greater success (whether measured in terms of profit or service). The relevance the context of working with a community client provides varies from student to student, ranging from simply providing a way to meet the course requirement, to providing an opportunity for future employment. Finally, the process framework capstone students use to complete their semester-long client projects can easily be aligned with Kolb's (1984) cycle of deep learning. Teams of students do the following:

- Experience learning in the classroom, in fieldwork (primary research), and through document review (secondary research).

- Deconstruct and reflect on the observations made and the knowledge and insights gained.
- Conceptualize and synthesize the facts and concepts learned into alternatives for the firm's consideration.
- Experiment with and test findings among themselves and with the instructor and client.

Do I believe Kolb intended his theory to be used this way? Not really. What this mapping exercise does, however, is provide insights into the benefits of looking at Kolb's cycle of learning from the perspective of how it can be applied to the intentional design of an entire course construct and, thus, to the intentional purpose of education: to reduce the randomness in human behavior by providing a well-designed experiential learning opportunity.

Drawing on his experience as a biologist, Zull (2002) mapped each step in Kolb's experiential learning cycle to the area of the brain in which it occurs to produce deep learning—learning that physically changes the brain. Later, Zull (2011) updated his research to illustrate additional findings in neuroscience and to highlight gaps in his 2002 work—gaps he knew existed and gaps that may still exist. Nonetheless, in very simple terms, we understand that two parts of the brain have to be involved for learning to be transformative. The emotional part of the brain (see details about the limbic system in Chapters 1–3) is integral in students sensing, feeling, storing, and recalling memories. Yet it must work in partnership with the front part of the brain (see details about the prefrontal cortex in Chapters 1–3), where reasoning, problem solving, and choice making reside. Zull (2011) described the place where students receive information, reflect on what to do with the information, and then consciously choose an action as the place where transformation can occur; this is the place or process where dynamic connections between the prefrontal cortex and limbic system communicate with each other. Zull went on to note that if the cycle is broken after reflection and there is no idea generation or action (owning and acting), learning is incomplete and deep understanding cannot be achieved. The student is just a passive learner, merely memorizing (2002). When the cycle is complete from back to front, deep learning occurs and the brain physically changes, thus changing the learner. This is particularly important if we are to ask the student to integrate what is being learned with what is happening in her real life (Zull, 2011). When the learner begins to view her self (see Chapter 4 for more details) and her place in the world differently, that learning becomes transformative (Zull, 2002, 2011).

I have referred to transformative learning and learning that transforms throughout this chapter. It is this level of learning that changes a person's view of her self and her place in the world. While transformative learning theory in adult education dates back to Jack Mezirow's (2000) writings in 1975, it is still considered even by Mezirow to be a complex, evolving, and maturing theory. It makes sense that I can find meaning in what I experienced in Ernie's way of teaching in the transformative learning theory presented by Mezirow, as Mezirow's theory has constructivist underpinnings (Taylor & Cranton, 2012). Some of the key elements of Mezirow's theory that I have experienced and observed in my students include experiencing disorientation, engaging in reflection, expressing discontent to others, creating a new action plan, gaining knowledge and skills to pursue a new plan, experimenting with new roles, building confidence in new ways, and reintegrating new ways of thinking and perceiving the world (Mezirow, 2000). In *Learning as Transformation: Critical Perspectives on a Theory in Progress* (2000), Wiessner and Mezirow examined many studies to determine elements needed to foster transformative learning and identified that "much time, intensity of experience, risk, and personal exploration are required of both students and teachers" (p. 315). They also pointed out that "much more research is needed to understand how adult educators establish these conditions within classes that meet a few hours a week" (p. 315).

In what promises to be a seminal book on the fundamental challenges of higher education, *Transforming Undergraduate Education: Theory That Compels and Practices That Succeed* (2012), Harward called transformative learning both "desirable and achievable" (p. 29). However, he also noted, "It is lamentable that national surveys indicate that few students report having transformational experiences during their undergraduate years" (p. 29). In "The Disorienting Dilemma: The Senior Capstone as a Transformative Experience" (2009), Sill, Harward, and Cooper noted, "Preparing students to move from college to the world beyond is both a significant part of baccalaureate education and an underlying rationale for creating transformative experiences in senior capstones" (p. 50). Students who studied senior capstone with me and participated in my sabbatical research in 2012 and 2013 provide insights that begin to answer some of these concerns and certainly contribute to this ongoing conversation.

Learning From Students

In the previous sections, I shared insights from my lived experiences as a doctoral student and professor, from the intersection of my lived experiences with Ernie Stringer's lived experiences, and from my review of others' research and writings. In what follows, I share insights from my own research—from reflections of former students on their lived experiences as reported to me.

Quotes without specific references all come from students who have studied with me over the past 10 years and participated in my study.

The best source for insights into the essential elements of the CSUMB College of Business experiential capstone course is from the students who have experienced it. The qualitative study I began in 2012 certainly provides insights worth sharing about student success and the kind of experiential learning that changes lives. It is important to point out that I am not using the typical institutional definition of *student success*, which is framed in terms of student retention and graduation. In the narrative that follows, the voices shared are all from students who have successfully completed their college degrees and have shared views of their own personal and career success and transformation. The evidence presented through the voices of the alumni reveals that they learned and developed as individuals in their capstone course experience in ways that contributed to their success after college. I have drawn my own conclusions from that evidence.

From what CSUMB College of Business alumni have reported about their experiential senior capstone course, the most succinct conclusions I can provide are that the experience does the following:

- It incorporates motivational elements that encourage students to stay engaged.
- It supports a developmental approach to learning.
- It facilitates deep understanding that leads to transformative learning as an achievable outcome.

Considering the Importance of Motivation

When I reflect on the students who have participated in the experiential senior capstone course with me over the past 10 years, I am first and foremost compelled to comment on the level of motivation I have observed. Other faculty members in the College of Business have frequently told me that students taking capstone seemed more motivated to excel in that course than in their other courses—even to the extent of skipping other classes, trying to rearrange test schedules in other classes, and sacrificing good grades in other courses to spend more time on their capstone projects. Consider the following comments from alumni about their motivation to do well in capstone:

- "I felt like the project and presentation were going to be a representation of everything I learned in all my classes, not just one."
- "I felt the most responsibility to others and myself by far in capstone."

- "This was the pinnacle of our college education; we weren't about to let each other down."
- "I knew my group and [the instructor] were counting on me. I was not going to let them down."
- "I knew that this presentation would be a reflection to the business I worked with about the skill set level of students from CSUMB, and I wanted that reflection to be a good one."

To understand these comments and the many more related to what motivated the students to stay engaged and to achieve success in capstone, I found a useful framework for analyzing the students' words in Daniel Pink's (2009) *Drive: The Surprising Truth About What Motivates Us*. In his book, Pink reviews volumes of research related to the science of motivation and reveals that the three greatest contributors to motivation are autonomy, mastery, and purpose (rather than grades or pay).

Pink (2009) defines *autonomy* as being self-directed and "acting with choice—which means we can be both autonomous and happily interdependent with others" (p. 88). He discusses how important it is to give people autonomy (control) over their tasks, in terms of what they will do; their time, in terms of when they will do it; their technique, in terms of how they will do it; and their team, in terms of with whom they choose to work. In the business capstone program, students self-select their teammates (who) and their project clients (what), and they set their individual and team schedules (when). Faculty provide the process framework to model how the pieces of prior learning in courses in the major are integrated in capstone and to guide the techniques used by teams of students to conduct the strategic analysis for their client firm. Students then adapt these to fit the circumstances of their client firm's operations. Alumni comment that the level of autonomy they have in capstone is significant:

- "Ninety percent of our work was conducted outside of the classroom and at our own pace. We were accountable for staying on track and creating something we could be proud of."
- "We experienced a level of autonomy unmatched to any other course prior to capstone. This freedom, at times, became difficult to deal with because it forced us to thoroughly search for the intended requirement and decide what course to take to meet it."
- "It always came down to me to choose the path and make any and all decisions along the way. If [the instructors] had held my hand the whole way it wouldn't be anywhere near as meaningful."

- "Our groups were given the base guidelines and we were allowed the freedom to deliver the information in any manner falling within the base guidelines."

Pink (2009) defines *mastery* as "the desire to get better and better at something that matters" (p. 109) and acknowledges that it develops over time—months, years, decades, or a lifetime. Science cited and discussed by Pink reveals that "mastery is a mindset" (p. 119) (also discussed in the introduction of this book) that values the incremental nature of mastery, learning goals over performance, and effort as a way to improve at something that matters. Pink also draws on the work of Anders Ericsson in describing mastery as a pain that is "difficult" and requires "all-consuming effort over a long time" (p. 122). In essence, attention, emotion, and cognitive regulation strengthen neural pathways of the brain, and that strengthening doesn't occur without concerted effort (see Chapters 3, 6, and 10 for more details). Finally, Pink describes mastery as governed by asymptote—it can never really be achieved but is totally worth the struggle. Along with general comments made by alumni about mastery, such as "I learned perfection may not be totally possible, but excellence most definitely is—don't give up," and "It challenged me to continue striving toward a standard of excellence," specific comments about mastery focused on two areas: skills development and instructor expectations. Skills development comments clustered around the following.

- "Capstone gave me the *writing skills* needed to work in a business profession."
- "I have become more confident in my *speaking ability* after this capstone class and I believe that it will aid me as I work on [my] MBA."
- "Developing recommendations fostered *critical thinking* in a way no other class did."
- "It made me a master of *time management.*"
- "I credit that course for teaching me how to work as part of a *team* and how to manage expectations and outcomes." (Emphases added.)

While comments made by alumni about skills development primarily focused on core competencies like writing, speaking, and critical thinking, it is clear that the high instructor expectations motivated many students to achieve in those areas and in the course:

- "The most significant contributor to my success was the high standards the professors had on the students and on the capstone project."

- "Looking back six years later, I fully appreciate the no-nonsense approach by the course faculty because it was as close to the 'real world' as could be."
- "[The instructor's] relentless drive to demand excellence absolutely raised the level of my work."
- "The professors . . . pushed me to achieve better than I thought I ever could."
- "[The instructor's] passion for achieving excellence was contagious and constantly made me want to do better."

Additionally, alumni frequently commented on the "pressure and weight that capstone enforces," including the following:

- "The requirements in capstone were more challenging than I expected."
- "I would feel overwhelmed if I didn't have a class in college help prepare me for a heavy workload."
- "The end results of our capstone project made all of the hard work worth doing."
- "I started to believe more in my ability to . . . work long hard hours into the wee hours of the morning to get things done."
- "There were countless hours of hard work, stress, and frustration that culminated in one outstanding final product."

According to Pink (2009), *purpose* is best defined as working for a cause larger than oneself. He describes purpose in terms of goals, placing purpose above profit; words, focusing on why something is done as opposed to how it is done; and policies, creating work environments that support autonomy, mastery, and purpose and, thereby, are motivating. When students practice specific attention, emotion, and cognitive regulation training techniques, their ability to identify their life's purpose emerges (see Chapters 3, 4, and 10 for details). Former capstone students who participated in the study reported deriving a sense of purpose from two primary sources: the responsibility they felt to their teammates and the responsibility they felt to their capstone clients. Almost unanimously, alumni reported they were motivated to do well because they did not want to disappoint their teammates:

- "You realize that as an individual you have a responsibility to your team to know what [you're] talking about, work hard, and perform."

- "In other courses teamwork was just teamwork, but in capstone we spent so much time together and worked so hard as a team that it was important for all of us to be responsible to one another equally."
- "It's a team and you have to do more than show up. There is a high level of responsibility to others."

In terms of the responsibility they felt to their client firms, the following are representative of the many comments made by alumni:

- "My 'aha' moment came from learning that business, in a global sense, can have a larger impact on society and one's self when viewed/practiced from a lens other than mere capital gain."
- "Capstone provided a real hands-on opportunity, and it felt like our recommendations had real potential to benefit our client."
- "The recommendations that my team made will allow a business that was weeks from shutting down have the ability to dominate [its] niche market. That is a powerful feeling to know how impactful we were."
- "I felt far more responsible to produce quality material than I ever had before, knowing the client was genuinely waiting for our recommendation and suggestions."
- "I loved knowing I was giving real-time advice and trying to help a company succeed to its highest potential."
- "The project seemed more important because it was an important grade for us and important to our capstone business."
- "It was meaningful to me because we worked with a real client and helped . . . launch a new product line."
- "It helped me realize that business isn't a figure or group of buildings; it is a community working together to support each other."
- "In the end, I wanted our capstone to be perfect because I wanted our team to succeed, our professor to be proud, and for our community partner to use our recommendations."

Supporting Developmental Approaches to Learning

I view my intentional design of support of experiential student development and learning to be one of my primary responsibilities as an instructor. Specific statements reflecting the value alumni place on the support they received from peers as well as their instructor in capstone can be summarized in the words of one former student: "[This course] allows those students, who truly want to succeed, to walk on a high wire with the assurance of a safety net underneath." As illustrated in the following statements, alumni specifically valued peer and faculty feedback, as well as the team process required in the course:

- "Having constant feedback on our progress was stressful but at the same time helped immensely."
- "Having other students not in your group critique our work was essential."
- "Because I have completed a task where high-level thinking was required and received (endless) feedback on improving that process, I have confidence that I can apply the same things in my professional career."
- "Learning how to compromise, when to fight for something, and how to pick your battles was a big learning experience."
- "Our group learned to maximize individual strengths to reach a common goal."
- "[I] learned the importance of valuing the experience of others. This was hard for me as I like to have control."

Achieving Personal Transformation

If transformative learning is achieved when a person's view of her self and her place in the world changes, there is no doubt that the CSUMB College of Business senior capstone experiential course is transformative for many students. How did the former students' views of their selves and their place in the world and workplace change based on their experiences in capstone? Let the words of our alumni speak for themselves:

- "As odd as this may sound, [the] project was the first time I realized that I was smart."
- "Everything about the way in which I viewed my academic capabilities changed during that semester."
- "It was a turning point in my career. . . . The lessons learned changed the way I approached almost every day in my career."
- "The biggest aha moment I had was turning in the final draft of the report. From then on I had confidence in myself that I was capable of producing top-level, deep analysis, thoughtful work—something that I didn't always have being a mid-2.0 GPA student. Capstone raised my confidence in academics and that has translated to my professional career."

- "When you can push yourself further than expected, the confidence to face the future becomes embedded in you when facing new challenges ahead in the job market and life in general."
- "I walked away from this class feeling confident about my abilities to overcome nearly any professional obstacle."
- "Capstone did give me the confidence to apply for various jobs knowing that I would succeed."
- "No other class at CSUMB prepared me for the workplace more than capstone. Capstone basically transformed me from a student to a professional."
- "I went to college because I wanted to be a manager in the field I chose. After completing capstone I have new confidence and I now expect to be a director, vice president, or executive in my field."
- "Upon completion of capstone I was ready to take on the world."

Summarizing Essential Elements

When the words of my former students are aligned with my own transformative learning experience with Ernie, my prior research on the capstone experience across the CSUMB campus, and the key findings from the science of learning and the science of motivation presented in this chapter and throughout this book, definite patterns emerge that contribute to our understanding of what it means for high-impact practices to be done well. The patterns can be summarized as the essential elements that inform the intentional design of high-impact experiential learning (Table 5.2). This alignment reveals that any faculty member who wants to design high-impact experiential learning should follow the guiding principles of providing developmental support to students and incorporating motivational elements in course design.

Through the structure, process, and emphases of the experiential capstone program described in this chapter, students achieved learning outcomes and competencies, and their views of their selves and their futures changed. However, when I started teaching capstone a decade ago, I never intentionally designed learning experiences to support transformative learning. My goal had always been for my students to achieve deep understanding and to leave the university knowing they are capable of achieving success in their chosen careers. Based on what I learned in my sabbatical research from my former students, as well as from the science of motivation, the science of learning, and the theories of teaching and learning I examined, I began to intentionally design every course I teach by applying the framework outlined in Table 5.2. I believe that applying that

TABLE 5.2
Essential Elements of High-Impact Experiential Learning

Guiding Principle	*Essential Elements*	*Examples*
Provide developmental support.	Provide cycles of feedback and continuous support.	Instructor feedback Peer feedback Student/team response to feedback Class-time interactions Office hours Team consultations
	Support mastery of core competencies relevant to future careers.	Written communication Oral communication Critical thinking Information literacy Quantitative reasoning Time management Teamwork
	Give purposeful assignments to support achievement of deep learning.	Readings/lectures to acquire new knowledge and skills (passive learning) Reflective time to relate to prior learning and assess new learning (reflective learning) Practice time to conceptualize how to apply learning (active learning) Test time to experiment and apply learning (engaged learning)
	Structure the course to support student success.	Importance of early grades Expectation of continuous improvement Adequate preparation for the rigor of the course Adequate communication with students
Incorporate motivational elements.	Hold high expectations of learners.	Intensity of effort Commitment of time Level of achievement Respect for deadlines Professionalism of work Expectation of excellence

	Provide options for autonomy.	Selection of teammates (who)
		Schedule of work (when)
		Client/community project or case to pursue (what)
		Location of work (where)
		Modality of work (face-to-face, technology based, blended)
	Incentivize responsibility to others.	Classmates
		Teammates
		Instructor
		Real-world client
		University community
		Surrounding community
	Create a community of learners.	Long-term/semester-long teamwork
		Flexible seating
		Bonding experiences
		Storytelling and sharing times

framework gives students every opportunity I can conceivably give them to experience deep understanding—understanding that can significantly impact their lives and their futures. In every encounter I have with a student, I intentionally maintain an ever-watchful heart for the potential that lies within that student.

Editor's Summary Points and Questions to Consider

1. Learning and development must be intentionally designed. Students must experience learning (passive learning), reflect on observations (reflective learning), conceptualize alternatives (active learning), and experiment with and test findings (engaged learning). How does your institution's intentional design for holistic learning and development encompass these components?
2. Simply engaging students in high-impact educational practices, such as a culminating senior experience like capstone, does not necessarily result in students achieving learning outcomes or deep

understanding. How has your institution assessed student learning and transformation in high-impact educational practices?

3. A great deal of research, including the research presented in this chapter, has illustrated that experiential capstone courses can have a significant impact on student success. Where in your institution could you design and implement an experiential learning course or out-of-classroom experience similar to the one described in this chapter?

4. While the essential elements of high-impact experiential course design outlined in this chapter can be applied in any course, instructors who teach via technology or who teach large-enrollment classes must determine for themselves how to adapt the elements to fit their circumstances. How can the design elements outlined in this chapter be adapted at your institution for large-enrollment and/or technology-based courses?

5. Intentional design of high-impact experiential learning include the following essential elements in the course design that provide development support to students and motivate learners: (a) provide cycles of feedback, (b) support mastery of core competencies, (c) give purposeful assignments, (d) structure the course to support student success, (e) create a community of learners, (f) hold high expectations of learners, (g) provide options for autonomy, and (h) incentivize responsibility to others. Where might you be able to implement these elements in an integrated curricular and cocurricular design at your college or university?

References

Aquinas, St. Thomas (1866). Prayer for all virtues to a Christian man. In *The path to heaven, a collection of all the devotions in general use* (p. 67). Oxford University.

Bain, K., & Bass, R. (2012). Threshold concepts of teaching and learning that transform faculty practice (and the limits of individual change). In D. W. Harward (Ed.), *Transforming undergraduate education: Theory that compels and practices that succeed* (pp. 189–207). Lanham, MD: Rowman & Littlefield.

Barkley, E. (2010). *Student engagement techniques: A handbook for college faculty.* San Francisco, CA: Jossey-Bass.

Barr, R., & Tagg, J. (1995). From teaching to learning: A new paradigm for undergraduate education. *Change, 27*(6), 12–25.

Bass, R. (2012). Disrupting ourselves: The problem of learning in higher education. *EDUCAUSE Review, 47*(2), 22–21.

Bean, J. (2011). *Engaging ideas: The professor's guide to integrating writing, critical thinking, and active learning in the classroom.* San Francisco, CA: Jossey-Bass.

Brookfield, S. (1984). *Adult learning, adult education and the community.* Milton Keynes, UK: Open University Press.

Brownell, J., & Swaner, L. (2010). Five high-impact practices: Research on learning outcomes, completion, and quality. *Peer Review, 14*(3), 29.

Harward, D. W. (2012). *Transforming undergraduate education: Theory that compels and practices that succeed.* Lanham, MD: Rowman & Littlefield.

Houle, C. (1980). *Continuing learning in the professions.* San Francisco, CA: Jossey-Bass.

Johnson, D. W., Johnson, R. T., & Smith, K. A. (1991). *Cooperative learning: Increasing college faculty instructional productivity.* Washington, DC: School of Education and Human Development, George Washington University.

Kolb, D. A. (1984). *Experiential learning: Experience as the source of learning and development.* Englewood Cliffs, NJ: Prentice Hall.

Kuh, G. D. (2008). *High-impact educational practices: What they are, who has access to them, and why they matter.* Washington, DC: Association of American Colleges and Universities.

Mezirow, J. (2000). *Learning as transformation: Critical perspectives on a theory in progress.* San Francisco, CA: Jossey Bass.

Petrie, N. (2013). *Vertical leadership development, part 1: Developing leaders for a complex world.* Paper presented at the Center for Creative Leadership in San Diego, CA.

Pink, D. (2009). *Drive: The surprising truth about what motivates us.* New York, NY: Penguin.

Sill, D., Harward, B. M., & Cooper, I. (2009). The disorienting dilemma: The senior capstone as a transformative experience. *Liberal Education, 95*(3), 50–56.

Stringer, E., Agnello, M., Baldwin, S., Christensen, L., Henry, D., Henry, K. . . Tinsely-Batson, P. (1997). *Community-based ethnography: Breaking traditional boundaries of research, teaching, and learning.* Mahwah, NJ: Lawrence Erlbaum Associates.

Swaner, L. E. (2012). The theories, contexts, and multiple pedagogies of engaged learning: What succeeds and why? In D. W. Harward (Ed.), *Transforming undergraduate education: Theory that compels and practices that succeed* (pp. 73–89). Lanham, MD: Rowman & Littlefield.

Tagg, J. (2003). *The learning paradigm college.* Bolton, MA: Anker.

Taylor, E. W., & Cranton, P. (2012). *The handbook of transformative learning: Theory, research, and practice.* Hoboken, NJ: Wiley.

Tinsley McGill, P. (2012). Understanding the capstone experience through the voices of students. *Journal of General Education, 61*(4), 488–504.

Wiessner, C. A., & Mezirow, J. (2000). Theory building and the search for common ground. In J. Mezirow (Ed.), *Learning as transformation: Critical perspectives on a theory in progress* (pp. 329–358). San Francisco, CA: Jossey-Bass.

Zull, J. E. (2002). *The art of changing the brain: Enriching the practice of teaching by exploring the biology of learning.* Sterling, VA: Stylus.

Zull, J. E. (2011). *From brain to mind: Using neuroscience to guide change in education.* Sterling, VA: Stylus.

ENHANCING WELL-BEING AND RESILIENCE

Christine L. Hoey

It is about being fully awake in our lives. It is about perceiving the exquisite vividness of each moment. We also gain immediate access to our own powerful inner resources for insight, transformation, and healing.

—Jon Kabat-Zinn ("Mindfulness-Based Interventions in Context," 2003, p. 144)

Through my many years of experience as a healthcare clinician and educator, as I have cared for people I have been privileged to witness firsthand how resilience, compassion, and well-being skills have transformed those who are going through life-changing events. Our contemporary society is filled with complex and challenging events, the pace and occurrence of which serve to magnify levels of stress in ways not typically a part of an individual's experience in higher education. The rapidity and multiplicity of those events place heavy demands on our attention and at times test our ability to cope. The spectrum of stressful events can range from the inconvenience of misplaced car keys to major life events such as the loss of a beloved pet, a course or major test failure, or even a job loss or cancer diagnosis. Globally, events such as natural disasters, disease epidemics, terrorism, and war pose threats to our well-being and resilience, especially if we are personally affected. Stress, whether chronic or acute, can have significant detrimental physical and psychological implications. Yet in all the complexity we experience, how we respond to stress can determine whether we flounder and fail or triumph and flourish.

College and university student resilience and well-being have gained steady ascendance as important concerns of higher education faculty and administrators. As national attention has focused on the high proportion of increasingly diverse students who, for one reason or another, leave the institution and never graduate, it is apparent that those concerns are not unfounded. Academic and social integration as reasons for student failure to thrive and subsequently drop out have been explored elsewhere in the literature (Tinto, 1982, 1993). What have not been as well explored are students' mental landscapes as they encounter the expectations of academia. In this chapter, we explore student stress and the development of resilience and well-being through countervailing strategies such as focused training—strategies that aim to address the manifold forms of stress students experience and enable them to thrive.

As part of the university culture, students are expected to negotiate social, academic, and personal experiences—a set of endeavors that may usher in levels and varieties of stress for which they may not be prepared (Pierceall & Keim, 2007; Towbes & Cohen, 1996). In 2015, a national survey of college students showed 30% reported stress as the largest factor negatively impacting academic performance in the last 12 months. In addition, rates of depression (34.5%), anxiety (56.9%), and feeling overwhelmed (85.6%) also impacted student performance (American College Health Association [ACHA], 2015, pp. 13–14). One out of four first-year students who felt overwhelmed (23%) was less likely to report his or her emotional health as "above average" (Pryor et al., 2012, p. 15). According to the 2014 "Stress in America" survey, results showed teen stress rivaled that of adults. Even more alarming is that teens underestimate the potential impact of stress on their physical and mental health. Furthermore, stress can lead to negative health behaviors such as tobacco use, alcohol or drug abuse, eating disorders, insomnia, and social withdrawal (American Psychological Association, 2014).

To undergird in the relevant literature the ways in which students can deal with stress and flourish in their academic careers, this chapter provides an overview of current research as it relates to resilience and well-being as well as the role compassion plays in enhancing social connections, resilience, and well-being. The concepts of psychological well-being, resilience, and focused attention are explored along with evidence-based methodologies that can serve to enhance positive behaviors and skills contributing to well-being and emotional intelligence. The chapter concludes with a discussion on how these methodologies and best practices can be integrated into a higher education setting.

Our Body on Stress

As you have read in this book, our knowledge of how the brain functions has expanded tremendously over the last 20 years and continues with new discoveries. Understanding how the brain operates under stress is essential to developing skills to manage stress; cultivate resilience; increase well-being; and, thus, promote student success. To begin our understanding, we journey back to a more primal point in time. Our brain's capacity to negotiate stressful events can be traced back to evolutionary origins of brain development and survival. A defining characteristic of brain evolution is its ability to adapt and change to environmental demands, often referred to as "brain plasticity" or "neuroplasticity" (Giedd, 2012). Neuroplasticity can further be described as the process of how the brain creates new neurons (nerve cells) and connections, reorganizing and changing brain structure in response to experiences and environmental changes as well as to thoughts and purposeful thinking. These structural changes can modify the function of brain regions by increasing or decreasing neural networks and brain circuit activity and by regulating the brain's chemical messengers (Pascual-Leone et al., 2011).

Stressful events have been shown to influence neuroplasticity in specific brain regions. Applying Darwin's brain evolution theory, neuroscientist Paul Maclean's model divided the brain into three parts: the reptilian complex, the mammalian brain, and the neocortex. A description of several concepts of brain evolution (e.g., Kolb & Whishaw, 2014; Striedter, 2004) provides background. Located in the lower brain or "old mammalian brain" is a small structure called the amygdala, which is part of the limbic system. It is our automatic "fight-or-flight" response to danger as well as the center for emotions, attention, and social function. Two other important structures of the limbic system are the hippocampus, responsible for recording short- and long-term memories, and the thalamus, our switchboard for sending sensory and motor signals to the higher brain—otherwise called the cerebral cortex (our "thinking" brain). Through nervous system pathways in the brain, the limbic system immediately alerts the cortex to act. In other words, the amygdala sounds the alarm, the hippocampus remembers if the stimulus is safe or dangerous, and the thalamus sends the message to the cortex, which then precipitates our decision on how to respond—either fight, flee, or "rest and digest."

If the cortex decides to "flee," it communicates with the hypothalamus, which then alerts the pituitary and adrenal glands (HPA axis), which together initiate a hormone stress response cascade to release cortisol and other neuroendocrine hormones. (Refer to Chapter 2 for a refresher on the electrical and chemical communication processes of the brain.) The body responds to cortisol by diverting glucose to the critical organs (the heart and brain) necessary for the challenge at hand, which falls under control of the *sympathetic system* (speeds systems up—the so-called fight-or-flight response). Once the stress has resolved, the brain turns off the HPA axis and

Figure 6.1 The limbic lobe.

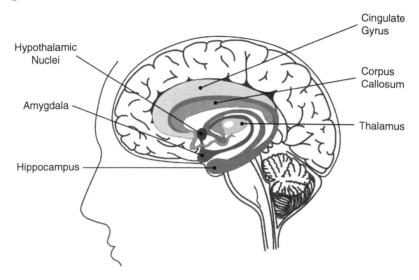

the body returns to homeostasis under control of the *parasympathetic system* (slows systems down—the so-called rest-and-digest system). This set of relationships among brain functions is illustrated in Figure 6.1.

Over time in our evolutionary history, the cortex gradually increased in size and the area behind the forehead called the prefrontal cortex became responsible for executive functions such as complex decision making, emotion regulation, social behavior, planning, working memory, and impulse control. Furthering our modern understanding of brain development, neuroscientists have made significant discoveries about the function and architecture of the brain through the use of magnetic resonance imaging (MRI). Before these imaging studies became available, most scientists believed the brain was completely developed by age 12. Now with this advanced ability to peer inside the brain, research over the last 25 years has provided evidence that the prefrontal cortex is the last to reach maturity. According to studies by National Institute of Mental Health, development may not finalize until our mid-20s (Giedd, 2012; Johnson, Blum, & Giedd, 2010; Sowell, Thompson, & Toga, 2004). From a neurobiological basis, implications of an immature prefrontal cortex provide insight as to why adolescents are more prone to act impulsively and make poor decisions (Giedd, 2012). This finding emphasizes the need to provide attention, emotion, and cognitive regulation training in the college years; more about this type of training is discussed in Chapter 10 (also recall neuroscience research introduced in Chapter 3).

In modern-day society, rarely do we encounter truly life-threatening events to trigger an acute stress response (Do I defeat it, or does it eat me?). However, day-to-day events and even lifestyles can induce chronic forms of stress that over time can affect the way the body and brain age. Chronic stress and elevated cortisol levels have been shown to alter brain structure and neural connectivity among the prefrontal cortex, hippocampus, and amygdala, which may play a role in memory, learning difficulties, cognition, anxiety, and depression (Chetty et al., 2014; Lucassen, Oomen, Naninck, Fitzsimons, van Dam, Czeh, & Korosi, 2015).

Sometimes a stressful event triggers an extreme emotional response where the amygdala overrides the prefrontal cortex in an instant if threatened—for example, as seen in "road rage." Daniel Goleman (1995), in his classic work *Emotional Intelligences* coined the term *amygdala hijack*, where the emotional response (limbic system) literally takes over the rest of the brain and interrupts the ability of the prefrontal cortex to respond to a stressful stimulus in a reasoned manner. Three signs of an amygdala hijack are strong emotional reaction; sudden onset of the emotional reaction; and, later, reflecting and realizing the reaction was inappropriate (Goleman, 1995).

Detrimental effects of repeated, chronic stress are seen in areas of behavior such as self-control and self-regulation (referred to in Chapter 3 as attention, emotion, and cognitive regulation); flexible thinking; memory; and physiologic responses to immune function, inflammatory processes, heart disease, and autoimmune disease (Cohen, Janicki-Deverts, & Miller, 2007; Hölzel et al., 2010; McEwen, 2009; Shors, 2006). Furthermore, the state of being stressed can result in sleep deprivation (four hours or less per night), which has been associated with obesity, cognitive impairment, and unhealthy lifestyle behaviors (McEwen, 2006). Neuroimaging studies have confirmed stress-induced brain alterations trigger an enlargement of the amygdala (our emotion center) and a reduced size of the hippocampus (memory), as well as a reduced size of the brain's chief executive officer—the prefrontal cortex (Davidson & McEwen, 2012). Chronic psychosocial stress appears to target the prefrontal cortex in particular, thereby reducing attention control and function (Liston, McEwen, & Casey, 2009). The question arises as to whether or not these brain changes are reversible. The good news in many ways is that they are. Liston and colleagues (2009) demonstrated stress-induced plasticity can be reversed in as little as one month of reduced psychosocial stress. New discoveries in neuroscience research confirm that through neuroplasticity, cognitive and psychobehavioral interventions can promote new brain/neuro pathways to strengthen emotion regulation and well-being (Davidson & McEwen, 2012).

Well-Being

Humanity has pondered happiness and well-being since the time of Aristotle (Ryan & Deci, 2001). Martin Seligman, Ernst, Gillham, Reivich, and Linkins (2009) noted, "More well-being is synergistic with better learning" (p. 294). What is well-being? The World Health Organization (WHO) includes well-being as a component of health—"a state of complete physical, mental and social well-being, and not merely the absence of disease or infirmity" (WHO, 1946, p. 1315). Confusion arises when the term *well-being* is used interchangeably with the term *wellness*. One can be physically well without having arrived at what we might term *well-being*. The latter term is more inclusive and multidimensional; it connotes not only positive physical conditions but also positive psychological and social states, including empathy and compassion. The objective value of well-being cannot be overstated. According to psychologists Ed Diener and Martin Seligman, a high degree of well-being correlates with higher incomes, better social relationships, and rewarding marriages, and it confers improved health and longevity (Diener & Seligman, 2004; Konrath, Fuhrel-Forbis, Lou, & Brown, 2012).

Among science and humanities disciplines, *well-being* has been distilled down to two juxtaposed viewpoints: eudemonia and hedonia (Deci & Ryan, 2008). Early Greek philosophers used the term *eudemonia* to describe happiness as the process of living well or actualizing one's human potential. Modern psychology describes eudemonia well-being as the development of self, personal growth, and purposeful engagement resulting in happiness. One who lives an engaged life can achieve a state of "flow," where one is so deeply immersed and engaged with the task at hand that time seems to stop—in other words, flow facilitates learning (Seligman et al., 2009). According to psychiatrist Daniel Siegel (2012), "A life of eudemonia is filled with a sense of connection, purpose, and equanimity" (pp. 40–42). Psychologists Carol Ryff and Corey Lee Keys (1995) further divided psychological well-being into six dimensions: autonomy, environmental mastery, self-acceptance, positive relationships with others, personal growth, and purpose in life. Their research suggested that higher levels of well-being contribute to positive health by enhancing biological systems, reducing disease, or enhancing rapid recovery from illness or adversity (Ryff & Keyes, 1995; Ryff, Singer, & Love, 2004).

Barbara Fredrickson's (2001) theory of "broaden and build" (p. 220) posited that positive emotions of joy, interest, contentment, and love "broaden" one's attention to see the big picture, which in turn enhances well-being. Findings from her 20 years of research have facilitated an understanding that positive emotions can increase well-being and enhance resilience, which in turn facilitates greater well-being in an upward spiral fashion. Negative emotions are minimized in this state, and there is an expanded ability to cope with challenging events. A broad range of positive emotions exists, including gratitude, serenity, interest, hope, pride, amusement, joy, inspiration, awe, tranquility, and love (Fredrickson, 2001; Fredrickson & Joiner, 2002). Laughter and humor are also positive emotions linked to health and well-being (Bachorowski & Owren, 2001; Tugade & Fredrickson, 2004). Rod Martin's (2007) book *The Psychology of Humor: An Integrative Approach* describes humor as a universal aspect of human experience that has psychological and social benefits including its use as a vehicle to relieve tension, regulate emotion, provide perspective, and cope with stress. Furthermore, research suggests humor acts as a natural stress and pain reliever while enhancing the cardiovascular, immune, and endocrine systems (Bennet & Lengacher, 2009; Berk et al., 1989; Fredrickson & Levenson, 1998), while neuroimaging studies demonstrate that humor engages the reward center of the brain (Mobbs, Greicius, Abdel-Azim, Menon, & Reiss, 2003). Psychologist William James so aptly pointed out, "We don't laugh because we're happy; we're happy because we laugh" (Roeckelein, 2006, p. 325).

In contrast to eudemonia, the hedonic approach is based on a subjective view that increased pleasure and decreased pain leads to happiness and well-being (Kahneman, Diener, & Schwarz, 1999). The well-known psychiatrist Ed Diener coined the term *subjective well-being* to further define hedonic characteristics of happiness, or how people evaluate their lives vis-à-vis positive emotions, the absence of negative emotions, life satisfaction, optimism, and positive functioning (Diener, 2009). Definitions of *well-being* centered on the concept either of eudemonia or hedonia continue to be debated, but there exists general agreement that well-being is dynamic and multidimensional, and includes social, psychological, and physical states. The distinction between the two philosophies may be whether one thinks of well-being as a destination (hedonic view) or a journey (eudemonic view).

From Fredrickson's research (Fredrickson, 2001; Fredrickson & Joiner, 2002), we know that positive emotions as a whole contribute to well-being, but to what degree is compassion in particular associated with well-being? As further discussed in Chapter 8, compassion can be thought of as the emotional response to perceived suffering (empathy) with a genuine desire to help (altruism). The research supports a connection between compassion and well-being. It appears the act of giving provides meaningful connections with others and improves our mental and physical health, as well as accelerates healing from illness (Diener & Seligman, 2004). Furthermore, brain-imaging studies confirm activation in the brain's pleasure center, such as when an individual is instructed to give money to others versus himself or herself (Moll et al., 2006). Another study reported that participants trained in compassion demonstrated improved stress-related immune responses and personal well-being (Pace et al., 2009).

Compassion can also be directed to oneself when life events occur beyond one's control or personal failures occur. According to psychologist Kristin Neff (Neff, 2011; Neff, Hsich, & Dejitterat, 2005), the three components of self-compassion include self-kindness, feelings of common humanity, and *mindfulness* defined as "the clear seeing and nonjudgmental acceptance of what's occurring in the present moment" (Neff, 2011, p. 80). In Neff's study on self-compassion among college undergraduate students, she found self-compassion facilitated the learning process, reduced self-criticism in the face of failure, and facilitated self-kindness and emotional balance. Self-compassion was also associated with lower anxiety levels and was more likely to enable individuals to tap into positive coping strategies of acceptance and positive reinterpretation in the face of failure (Neff et al., 2005).

Physical well-being, an important facet of the overall well-being picture, is an area of growing research examining the relationship between exercise and well-being. There already exists a large body of work documenting the benefits of physical activity on depression and anxiety. We know, for example, that exercise triggers the release of endorphins from the brain, also known as our "feel-good" neurotransmitters (think of a "runner's high") while lowering the stress hormones cortisol and adrenaline. According to psychiatrist John Ratey, there is a "biological relationship between the body, the brain, and the mind" (Ratey & Hagerman, 2008, p. 3). Engaging in regular exercise has also been shown to increase one's self-confidence and resilience. Longitudinal and randomized controlled trials with diverse populations and age-groups demonstrate that exercise and physical activity are associated with improved mood states and better quality of life and physical health outcomes (Penedo & Dahn, 2005). Furthermore, individuals engaging in higher levels of physical activity reported higher levels of optimism (Pavey, Burton, & Brown, 2015) and a reduced risk for heart disease, diabetes, and cancer while controlling weight and enhancing brain health and longevity (Centers for Disease Control and Prevention, 2011). Recent research suggests that positive emotions can improve present and future physical health at the cellular level, further contributing to evidence for the importance of physical well-being (Cohen, Alper, Doyle, Treanor, & Turner, 2006; Fredrickson et al., 2013).

Resilience

Whether we consider well-being a journey or a destination, it is closely related to the concept of resilience. Interest and research in resilience began

50 years ago and has seen an accelerated expansion over the past 20 years (Goldstein & Brooks, 2013). As our society becomes more technologically complex, there is a need to understand risk factors, protective mechanisms, and interventions to promote positive outcomes in shaping individual and community resilience. The concept of resilience has been embraced throughout a number of sciences, and an in-depth review of the research literature is beyond the scope of this chapter. Instead, resilience concepts presented here focus on research from the psychosocial and neuroscience disciplines.

Resilience is defined as the ability to "bounce back" after stressful events and trauma while preserving normal physical and psychological equilibrium (Bonanno, 2004; Lazarus, 1993; Zautra, Hall, & Murray, 2010). Resilient individuals are able to overcome challenges and misfortune; learn from these challenges; and reach out for new experiences, allowing them to adapt to change in a healthy way, which in turn enhances well-being (Block & Kremen, 1996; Zautra et al., 2010). No one is immune to life's trauma and the negative effects of stress; however, the difference between well-being and psychological illness can be determined by the degree of effective coping and adaptation abilities one possesses to build resilience (Tugade & Fredrickson, 2004). The brain can be considered the primary organ of resilience because it regulates the biologic feedback systems that respond and adapt to stress (Karatsoreos & McEwen, 2011). Resilient skills are therefore intrinsic traits that everyone possesses in varying degrees and are considered a normal part of human adaptation and development (Masten, 2001). Evidence shows that resilience is not only beneficial to those already displaying resilient traits, but also learned, modified, and improved (Coutu, 2002). In the last decade, psychologists, sociologists, and neuroscientists have uncovered evidence that the degree of an individual's resiliency can depend on such factors as genetics, epigenetics (chemical reactions that switch genes off or on in response to the environment), and psychosocial networks, as well as developmental, neurochemical, or neural circuitry factors (Southwick & Charney, 2012; Wu et al., 2013). Genetic variations can influence the fight-or-flight sympathetic nervous system, triggering greater increases in norepinephrine or amygdala activation in response to stressful situations that result in higher levels of anxiety. Evidence of this can be seen in people who have "panic attacks" or other anxiety disorders (Neumeister et al., 2005; Zhou et al., 2008). Furthermore, traumatic early life events can not only have a negative effect on brain development and neural pathways but also impair the immune response, leading to increased illness and difficulty in coping with hardship and misfortune as an adult (Davidson & McEwen, 2012; Wu et al., 2013).

Research in the emerging field of epigenetics suggests diet, stress, behavior, toxins, and other factors can modify gene expressions, which can be passed on from parents to offspring (Gaydos, Wang, & Strome, 2014; Mathews & Janusek, 2012). From a broad perspective, not all stress is bad—it can strengthen us or create a "steeling" effect, seen when a child acquires adaptive skills to successfully cope with and master small doses of stress or adversity. For example, children who experienced happy separations (sleepovers, staying with grandparents) were better able to cope with the stress of a hospital admission; that is, they had cultivated resilience through happy separations to later unhappy separations (Stacey, Dearden, Rill, & Robinson, 1970). Or in the case of economic family adversity, an adolescent takes on more responsibility, leading to psychological strengths and enhanced resilience as an adult (Rutter, 2012; Southwick & Charney, 2012).

Qualities that promote resilience include optimism, flexible thinking, positive problem solving, and a spirited approach to life—traits that also build and contribute to sustainable flourishing communities (Fredrickson & Branigan, 2005; Tugade & Fredrickson, 2004). Steven Southwick identified other resilient qualities through in-depth interviews with highly resilient people and was able to establish common coping strategies that were crucial and even lifesaving to individuals when confronted with adversity. He developed a list of 10 "resilient factors" as recurrent themes, some of which overlap with the previously mentioned qualities: realistic optimism, facing fear, moral compass, religion and spirituality, social support, resilient role models, physical fitness, brain fitness, cognitive and emotional flexibility, and meaning and purpose (Southwick, Vythilingam, & Charney, 2005). Furthermore, Southwick's research found that resilient individuals who engaged in physical and mental behaviors to enhance health and well-being were active problem solvers and used their experiences as a springboard for growth.

According to psychologists Brooks and Goldstein (2004), resilient individuals possess a particular mind-set in addition to skills that help them cope more productively to life's challenges. They further describe strategies for consciously developing a "resilient mind-set" through self-awareness and self-acceptance, becoming "stress hardy" by focusing on situations within one's control, and employing empathy and compassion with self and others.

Emotional intelligence plays a significant role in resilience. Conscious attention and self-awareness of how one reacts to a stressful event allows an individual to gain greater control over one's reactions. Daniel Goleman (1995), author of *Emotional Intelligence*, delineated the five components of emotional intelligence into self-awareness, self-regulation, motivation, social skills, and empathy. He maintained that an emotionally intelligent individual

Figure 6.2 Well-being and resilience traits.

appears confident and is good at working toward goals. Such individuals are also adaptable, flexible, and resilient. Goleman (2011) maintained that resilience could be accomplished through retraining the brain and employing both an optimistic attitude and outlook. In addition to the traits mentioned previously, highly resilient people use humor, optimistic thinking, and relaxation training as strategies to nurture positive emotions to cope with stress. As author Stephen Covey (1998) noted, "Between stimulus and response there is a space. In that space is our power to choose our response. In our response lies our growth and our happiness" (p. 27). To summarize our discussion on well-being and resilience, I offer a visual representation in Figure 6.2 of the various facets of our mental landscape included under the general concept of well-being and resilience: good physical health, spirituality, purpose and life satisfaction, self-awareness and flexible thinking, positive social relationships, optimism and humor, and empathy and compassion. Furthermore, it appears that through neuroplasticity these facets of well-being and resilience are all trainable and therefore achievable. Having provided an in-depth discussion of the specific facets of well-being and emphasized the important role of resilience, I turn now to techniques through which well-being and resilience may be developed across three general domains: the physical domain, the social domain, and the cognitive and emotional processes domain.

Building Resilience and Well-Being

Building one's well-being and resilience involves developing insight and the desire to create a conducive environment in a compassionate, purposeful way across a number of domains (Lyke, 2009; Siegel, 2012). Our environment, the manner in which we experience it, and how we relate to it all constantly change. Making purposeful changes and choosing the most appropriate tools to enhance resilience and well-being begin with a basic focus on physical well-being and encompasse a larger consideration of social as well as cognitive and emotional processes in well-being.

First, we consider the physical domain. No matter an individual's socioeconomic status, it is common knowledge that physical exercise is good for us. As mentioned earlier, and also emphasized in Chapter 10, the benefits of physical exercise have been well documented, including improving mental health; reducing chronic diseases such as heart disease, obesity, and diabetes (Penedo & Dahn, 2005; Warburton Nicol, & Bredin, 2006); and improving physical symptoms of Parkinson's disease and dementia (Matta Mello, Portugal et al., 2013). Furthermore, exercise has been shown to reduce stress, slow aging (Puterman et al., 2010), increase levels of the brain chemical gamma-Aminobutyric acid (GABA) associated with improved mood and decreased anxiety (Streeter et al., 2010), boost cognition, enhance neuroplasticity, and build self-esteem (Cotman & Berchtold, 2007; Ratey et al., 2008). Current exercise recommendations include 150 minutes per week engaged in aerobic activities (including brisk walking, running, yoga, and other exercises that increase heart rate) and two or more days per week engaged in muscle-strengthening activities (Centers for Disease Control and Prevention, 2015a).

As beneficial as physical exercise is, diet also merits consideration. "You are what you eat," the old adage goes. Combined with our busy lifestyles that promote a diet of convenience, we have seen profound changes in what and how we eat. Fruits, vegetables, and nutritious foods have been largely displaced by processed food products high in salt, sugar, and fat. Because these foods appeal to the brain's pleasure center (McGonigal, 2012), it's hard "to eat just one," thereby contributing to weight gain and reduced well-being. Obesity rates in America are at an all-time high of 35%. There also are implications of increased heart disease, type 2 diabetes, high blood pressure, poor mental health, and certain types of cancer (Ogden, Cornell, Kit, & Flegal, 2014). States with the highest rates of obesity also have the lowest life expectancies, particularly in the southeast region of the United States (Centers for Disease Control and Prevention, 2015b). Neuroscience research has found obesity and poor health decrease cognitive function, requiring more effort for an individual to finish a complex decision-making task (Verstynen et al., 2012). Changing poor dietary habits and eating foods rich in omega-3 fatty acids; curcumin; vitamins B, C, D, and E; and the minerals calcium, zinc, and selenium (all found in vegetables, fruit, dairy, and fish) promote cognitive function as well as improve the negative health consequences leading to chronic disease (Gómez-Pinilla, 2008).

Second, we consider the social domain. Building resilience and well-being extends to the web of relationships we create. Humans are social in nature and are dependent on interactions with others and a sense of a group membership. The ability to foster reciprocal caring relationships is necessary for resilience, well-being, and physiological health (Seppala, Rossomando, & Doty, 2013). Poor social support and isolation can contribute to loneliness, depression, illness, and a shortened life span. Purposefully strengthening caring relationships with close friends and family promotes self-esteem, reduces stress levels, and facilitates a quicker recovery from adverse events. According to Tom Rath and James Harter (2010), authors of *Wellbeing: The Five Essential Elements*, data suggest that we need six hours of social time to have a thriving day. Meditation training with a focus on compassion (more on this in Chapter 8) has also been shown to increase a sense of social connection to others along with more empathy and a desire to help others. In the secondary educational context, compassion and mindfulness training for at-risk schoolchildren has been shown to facilitate positive social connections and less bullying behaviors (Reddy et al., 2013).

Third, we consider the cognitive and emotional processes domain. The neuroscience supporting the necessity of purposeful, focused effort to build one's well-being and resilience has both validated contemplative tools and techniques such as mindfulness and expanded our knowledge and understanding of how thoughts can change brain neuroplasticity (see Chapter 2 for details). In particular, there is a growing interest in activities that reduce stress and enhance positivity, such as mindfulness and contemplative practices. Referring to our previous discussion of brain functioning, we know that when mindfulness meditation (see Chapter 3) and cognitive behavioral therapy (reframing negative events in a more positive light—see Chapter 10) are combined, increased activation is seen in the prefrontal cortex during functional MRI (fMRI, a way to measure brain activity by looking at changes in blood flow) and electroencephalogram (EEG) scans tracking electrical brain activity (Davidson & McEwen, 2012; Southwick & Charney, 2012). According to Richard Davidson, resilience increases activation in the left prefrontal cortex (rational planning), inhibits the amygdala (anxiety, fear-based emotions), facilitates the hippocampus's response to stress, and enhances immune function.

Meditation originated from the Buddhist and Vedic traditions and has been practiced since 500 BCE as a spiritual exercise. More recently, these meditative practices have been integrated into Western healthcare as a secular form of mental training to promote relaxation and enhance well-being (Lutz, Slagter, Dunner, & Davidson, 2008). As we continue to emphasize throughout this book, brain-imaging studies examining the effects of positive mental training practices (mindfulness and meditation) on brain anatomy showed a moderate effect in increases in gray matter in the prefrontal cortex, right anterior insula, and hippocampus, while decreases were noted in the amygdala. This suggests these training practices are associated with emotion regulation and response control as well as enhanced positive emotions, self-regulation, and memory consolidation (Fox et al., 2014; Hölzel et al., 2010; Hölzel, Lazar, et al., 2011; Lazar et al., 2005; Luders, Togar, Lepore, & Gaser, 2009). In another comprehensive meta-analysis looking at the psychological effects of meditation, the authors concluded that meditation does have positive effects on cognitive and emotional processes (Sedlmeier et al., 2012).

Table 6.1 provides a summary of types of purposeful skill development within the general domains of resilience and well-being discussed in this section, and the many benefits associated with each type of purposeful skill development. There is one more aspect that needs to be discussed in order

TABLE 6.1
Domains and Purposeful Skill Development That Build Well-Being and Resilience

Domain	Purposeful Skill Development	Well-Being/Resilience Benefits
Physical	Good sleep habits, regular exercise, balanced diet, scheduled relaxation, mindful living	Enhances mood, neuroplasticity, self-esteem, resilience to stress, sleep, and well-being
Social	Involvement with social-interest groups, community volunteer programs, compassion meditation training	Promotes strong social networks via perspective taking; improves academic performance, self-esteem, optimism, compassion, empathy, and altruism
Cognitive, emotional	Mindfulness meditation, cognitive reappraisal, daily positive emotion journaling, emotional intelligence training	Enhances learning, problem solving, and cognitive flexibility; reduces stress and anxiety; improves positive emotions and psychological resilience

for the skill development in Table 6.1 to truly seed itself: the practice of focused attention. (Refer to Chapters 3 and 10 for foundational reading.) I now turn our discussion to an in-depth consideration of the practical aspects of focused attention training that are associated with increased well-being and resilience, the types of contemplative practices normally used, and the neuroscience that supports their efficacy.

Focused Attention: Key Practices in Well-Being and Resilience Skill Development

In Daniel Goleman and Peter Senge's (2014) book *The Triple Focus*, the authors state, "Attention is the essential skill for learning" (p. 22). We can assume the same for skill development. Accomplishing everyday tasks at work, home, or school, particularly when learning new well-being practices, is dependent on an individual's ability to focus attention. Focusing attention is also essential to regulating emotions—one's ability to increase positive emotions and decrease negative affect. Attention can be trained through practice, and it appears that meditation not only acts as "the biceps curl for the brain" (Harris, 2014) but also facilitates healthy thoughts and reduced mind wandering and is an effective methodology in enhancing emotional well-being (Brewer et al., 2011; Chambers, Gullone, & Allen, 2009).

As discussed in Chapter 3, focused attention training or meditation practice does not require a religious stance. The practice of meditation is more about focus, concentration, and the art of paying attention. Meditation practices can be divided into two styles: focused attention, which involves voluntarily focusing attention on a chosen object, and open monitoring meditation, which entails nonreactive monitoring of the moment-to-moment content of experience (Cahn & Polich, 2006; Lutz, Slagter, et al., 2008b). For example, concentrative meditation or focused meditation uses an object (e.g., the breath) to maintain focus, while bringing back attention to the breath whenever the mind wanders (Hasenkamp, Wilson-Mendenhall, Duncan, & Barsalou, 2012; Lutz, Slagter, et al., 2008). Choosing an object to focus on and maintaining attention on that object requires cognitive control or regulation, and it is central to the brain's prefrontal cortex, an area of increased activity seen during meditation practice. In Figure 6.3, I have diagrammed how this process functions, using the breath as an example. By continually (re)focusing on the breath, we build strength of attention. When the mind wanders from the object of attention, we become aware of that lapse in focus, acknowledge it simply as wandering of attention, and gently refocus our attention on the breath.

Figure 6.3 Focused attention practice.

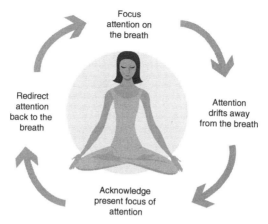

Focus
attention on
the breath

Attention
drifts away
from the breath

Acknowledge
present focus of
attention

Redirect
attention
back to the
breath

Other types of meditative practices, such as mindfulness and compassion meditation (CM), involve a process of training mental states, which, as noted in this chapter's discussion of neuroplasticity, has demonstrated positive brain changes associated with attention (Davidson et al., 2003; Lazar et al., 2005). One of the most researched meditation practices is mindfulness-based stress reduction (MBSR), developed by Jon Kabat-Zinn, which uses a combination of focused attention and the open-monitoring technique (Goldin & Gross, 2010; Hölzel et al., 2010; Lutz, Slagter, et al., 2008). Kabat-Zinn (2003) defined *mindfulness* as "the awareness that emerges through paying attention on purpose, in the present moment, and nonjudgmentally, to the unfolding of experience in the present moment" (p. 145), and is also know as the open-monitoring technique (Kabat-Zinn, 2003; Lutz, Slagter, et al., 2008). The MBSR program is structured as an eight-week course to train mindfulness through focused breathing attention, body awareness exercises (body scan), open monitoring of observing the present moment, sitting and walking meditation, eating meditation, and hatha yoga (Kabat-Zinn, 2013). The program has been shown to reduce stress and anxiety symptoms, and it has also demonstrated improvement in well-being and reduced symptoms of depression, anger, and repetitive tendencies to focus on symptoms of distress or rumination (Chiesa & Serretti, 2009; Goldin & Gross, 2010; Hoge et al., 2013; Hölzel, Lazar, et al., 2011, Kabat-Zinn et al., 1992).

Individuals practicing MBSR utilize a problem-solving approach to stress rather than problem avoidance. Furthermore, in as little as eight weeks of mindfulness training, measurable changes in brain fMRI scans confirm decreases in gray matter in the amygdala and increases in gray matter in the prefrontal cortex, right anterior insula, and hippocampus—all areas involved with learning, memory, emotion regulation, and perspective taking (Hölzel,

Carmody, et al., 2011). Mindfulness practices incorporated with cognitive-based therapy are proving to be an effective treatment to prevent depression relapse (Geschwind, Peeters, Drukker, van Os, & Wichers, 2011; Ma & Teasdale, 2004) and anxiety disorders (Evans et al., 2008; Hofmann, Sawyer, Witt, & Oh, 2010). This combination is called *mindfulness-based cognitive therapy* (MBCT), and participants report life-changing attitudes, awareness of self-devaluative thoughts, increased sense of control over depression, and increased acceptance of self (Allen, Bromley, Kuyken, & Sonnenberg, 2009).

In addition to MBSR, two other meditation practices using focused attention to regulate emotions are CM and loving-kindness meditation (LKM). Both meditative practices cultivate an emotional state of positive feelings, unconditional love, compassion, and empathy toward self and others (Hofmann, Grossman, & Hinton, 2011; Neff, 2011; Salzberg, 1995). Other studies have demonstrated improved personal well-being and immune responses to stress with compassion training (Pace et al., 2009; Pace et al., 2010). Brain-imaging studies of LKM practitioners showed increased gray matter in the insula and anterior cingulate cortices of the brain associated with empathy and empathy responses and amygdala activation in response to negative sounds, supporting the connection between the limbic system and emotions (Leung et al., 2013; Lutz, Brefczynski-Lewis, Johnston, & Davidson, 2008). Enhanced vagal tone (nervous system marker for homeostasis in the body) is seen in LKM, suggesting positive emotions serve as "nutrients for the human body," boosting social connections and health (Kok et al., 2013, p. 1131). Even in brief sessions of LKM, inexperienced participants showed increased positive social connections (Hutcherson, Seppala, & Gross, 2008). Stanford University's Compassion Cultivation Training (CCT) (described in Chapter 8) consists of a nine-week training program composed of weekly two-hour classes and daily compassion-focused meditation practice. Program participants demonstrated improved emotional well-being and the ability to be more compassionate to self and others. Furthermore, additional benefits included increased mindfulness and happiness and less worry—important factors in well-being and resilience (Jazaieri et al., 2013; Jazaieri et al., 2014).

Cognitively based compassion training (CBCT), created at Emory University by Lobsang Tenzin Negi, uses a systematic practice to train the mind in compassion. The eight-week CBCT program utilizes focused attention training to cultivate thoughts and behaviors centered on others while overcoming self-centered thinking. Two published studies evaluating CM and depression among undergraduates showed CBCT reduced depression and neuroendocrine, inflammatory, and behavioral responses to psychosocial stress (Pace et al., 2009; Pace et al., 2010). Emory is currently conducting further studies using CBCT for youth in foster care in Kosovo to heal war trauma and facilitate optimization of physiological responses to psychosocial stress.

Another popular technique, *mental imagery*, or seeing with the mind's eye, is a mind-body approach used to direct attention to influence physical and emotional states. It is defined as an experience that "resembles perceptual experience, but occurs in the absence of the appropriate external stimuli" (Thomas, 2014). In *The Case for Mental Imagery*, the authors suggest mental imagery is important in memory, problem solving, creativity, emotional intelligence, and comprehending language (Kosslyn, Thompson, & Ganis, 2006). One neuroimaging study compared visual imagery and visual perception neural processes and found they engage similar areas of the prefrontal cortex and parietal regions—areas of cognitive control processes (Ganis, Thompson, & Kosslyn, 2004). Also called visualization or mental rehearsal, mental imagery can be used to reduce stress, promote relaxation, improve mental imagery athletic and artistic performance, instill positive thinking, achieve goals, or influence outcomes. The body scan exercise used in MBSR or similar progressive muscle relaxation techniques are an example of focusing attention on areas of body discomfort or tension and visually releasing that tension.

Maharishi Mahesh Yogi introduced transcendental meditation (TM) to India in the 1950s and brought TM to America a decade later. TM is a twice-daily 20-minute meditation practice using a *mantra*—a word (or words) or sound silently repeated as a way to focus attention inward through quieter levels of thought to experience a peaceful level of awareness. Research has documented the TM technique reduces anxiety (Orme-Johnson & Barnes, 2014); reduces blood pressure (Anderson, Liu, & Kryscio, 2007); reduces psychological distress, depression, and work burnout (Elder, Nidich, Moriarty, & Nidich, 2014); and reverses the effects of chronic stress (MacLean et al., 1997). TM practice was shown to increase academic achievement and reduce psychological stress in urban students, accounting for 15% higher graduation rates from high school (Colbert & Nidich, 2013). Another randomized controlled study of college students instructed in TM demonstrated significant reduction in stress and sleepiness and an increase in positive brain wave patterns associated with relaxation during finals week (Travis et al., 2009). A small study evaluating the effects of TM training in veterans with post-traumatic stress disorder (PTSD) showed a 50% reduction in their symptoms of stress and depression and measured improvement of quality of life (Rosenthal, Grosswald, Ross, & Rosenthal, 2011). To further evaluate the effect of TM on veterans, the Department of Defense is providing a $2.4 million grant in partnership with the Maharishi University of Management Research to study TM at the San Diego VA Hospital (Maharishi University of Management, 2012).

It would seem most of the neuroscience research on neuroplasticity is focused on meditation. However, there have been some studies comparing meditation with contemplative prayer, which involves repetition of a word, prayer, or phrase as a focus of attention. Benson and Klipper's (2000) research on the relaxation response found that participants employing repetitive prayer (i.e., rosary-type prayer, centering prayer, davening-type prayer) experience a similar physiological relaxation response to that seen in TM. Furthermore, contemplative practices in religions (Christian and non-Christian) that focus on concepts of love, joy, optimism, and hope seem to demonstrate similar positive brain changes and health benefits as seen in mindfulness meditation (Newberg & Waldman, 2010).

According to Jon Kabat-Zinn (2013), activity combined with mindfulness can be a form of meditation. The exercise component of the MBSR is hatha yoga, a secular form of yoga which combines breathing, bodily postures, and meditation. A practice with ancient roots in India, *yoga* is a Sanskrit term meaning "to unite" the body, breath, mind, and heart to attain physical and mental health. Originating in China, qigong and tai chi are closely choreographed movement exercises that incorporate similar principles to those used in yoga. These three exercises, often called "meditative movement" practices, facilitate training attention that is focused on body movements synchronized with the breath. Therapeutic health benefits of yoga include decreased anxiety and stress and increased feelings of emotional and social well-being (Larkey, Jahnke, Etnier, & Gonzalez, 2009; Ross & Thomas, 2010). Furthermore, tai chi and qigong demonstrated increases in self-efficacy, physical health, and immune function, while significant decreases were seen in anxiety and depression (Jahnke, Larkey, Rogers, Etnier, & Lin, 2010).

Table 6.2 is a summary of the different research-based meditative practices that have demonstrated a positive effect on attention, well-being, and resilience; how the methods work to regulate attention; and the outcomes observed in the research to date on each method.

Implementing Well-Being and Resilience Practice Into Higher Education

In this chapter, current research and evidence from the last two decades are presented in support of practices that engage the mind and body, and the relative positive impact of those practices on well-being and resilience were explored. As noted earlier, college students are expected to master the developmental task of managing excess stress while actively engaging in healthy challenges that promote growth. Yet in reality, few students enter college with the

TABLE 6.2

Contemplative Practices That Enhance Attention

Method	Type	How It Regulates Attention	Outcome
Mindfulness-based stress reduction (MBSR)	Open monitoring and focused attention meditation that includes yoga practice	Present moment focusing and awareness of the mind and body without judgment	Increases self-esteem, self-insight, self-regulation, compassion, and well-being
Mindfulness-based cognitive therapy (MBCT)	Open monitoring meditation and cognitive-based therapy	Focused attention on changing thoughts/feelings that lead to depression and anxiety	Prevents depression relapse and reduces anxiety
Concentrative meditation	Focused attention meditation	Sustained attention on an object or the breath	Enhances perception and object concentration
Loving-kindness meditation (LKM)	Focused attention and compassion meditation	Positive thoughts directed at self and others	Reduces anxiety and negative affect, increases compassion and self-compassion
Compassion cultivation training (CCT)	Focused attention and compassion meditation	Five-step practice of awareness/feelings of compassion for self, others, and all things	Improves positive emotional state, compassion, and altruistic behavior
Cognitively based compassion training (CBCT)	Compassion meditation combined with cognitive reappraisal	Eight sequential steps training the mind in compassion and altruism	Reduces depression and inflammatory and behavior responses to stress, increases compassion
Transcendental meditation (TM) and contemplative prayer	Focused attention mantra meditation or prayer repetition	Focused attention on a mantra or sacred word that is repeated	Reduces stress, anxiety, and depression; increases well-being
Mental visualization (MV)	Imagery meditation using focused attention	Desired positive traits in the present moment visualized, active muscle relaxation	Strengthens emotional and physical well-being
Hatha yoga, tai chi, and qigong	Focused attention, meditative movement	Focused attention on body movement	Strengthens mind–body connection, increases flexibility

necessary skills to smoothly adapt to the stress of campus life. A recent meta-analysis of 24 studies addressing interventions to reduce university students' stress provided strong support for the effectiveness of behavioral, cognitive, and mindfulness interventions in reducing anxiety, depression, and cortisol response (Regehr, Glancy, & Pitts, 2013). Behavioral techniques included focused breathing and muscle relaxation to regulate physical stress reactions, while cognitive interventions facilitated the ability to identify and modify dysfunctional beliefs and subsequent psychological and physiological responses to stress. Interventions using a combination of behavioral and cognitive behavioral therapy (relaxation, education, and imagery) were found to be beneficial in reducing stress (Regehr et al., 2013). Another recent study surveying belief structures underlying the decision to meditate among university students, faculty, and staff found participants felt positive about meditating but felt lack of time, quiet space, support, and knowing how to meditate were barriers (Lederer & Middlestadt, 2014). These findings on salient beliefs show how campuses can institute environmental changes more conducive to meditation.

With these and other results in mind, college campuses on a national level are taking a hard look at student/faculty well-being and are beginning to implement programs that focus on training skills to reduce stress while making positive choices to enhance well-being and resilience. At the policy level, Healthy Campus 2020 (adapted from the "Healthy People 2020" guidelines) calls for health professionals to assist with reducing student, faculty, and staff stress and promoting healthy lifestyle behaviors (American College Health Foundation, 2012). A number of colleges and universities including Florida State University, New York University, University of Oregon, and University of South Carolina have adapted and implemented these guidelines through on-campus programs.

Faculty professional development programs to facilitate student well-being and resilience skill building are another major intervention in use. These interventions are based on the premise that if faculty don't understand the underlying principles, then it is highly unlikely that students will. Examples of promising practices are included here to demonstrate the substantial activities already under way, point the way forward for others, and provide encouragement. Wake Forest University, for example, is implementing a new well-being initiative called Thrive that specifically focuses on the well-being of students, faculty, and staff. Thrive is a voluntary online program with tips and resources to address the eight dimensions of well-being: emotional, environmental, financial, intellectual, occupational, physical, social, and spiritual. Furthermore, Wake Forest University is providing more flexible space on campus for fitness programs and gatherings with plans to conduct longitudinal research on student and alumni well-being. Saint Louis University

Medical Center conducted a study on medical student well-being and developed an innovative model to address the pressures of medical school. It evaluated the root causes of medical student stress within the school's curriculum and implemented integrated curriculum changes, including a required resilience/mindfulness class for students. The study results demonstrated that first-year students' depression rates dropped by half and anxiety rates dropped by a third. Students also felt more socially connected to each other as a group, their board scores went up, and student performance improved. According to study authors Slavin, Schindler, and Chibnall (2014), the lessons learned from the curriculum changes can be applied in a variety of environments from high schools to the most competitive law firms.

The University of Southern California's Mindful USC is a new campus interdisciplinary initiative using mindfulness to promote the mental and physical health of students, faculty, and staff. The free five-week workshops facilitate developing personal mindfulness practices, self-compassion, stress reduction, workplace happiness, and innovative creative learning. Additional universities offering mindfulness programs include Carnegie Mellon, Princeton University, and University of Oregon.

Lessons being learned at Wake Forest University, Saint Louis University Medical Center, and USC can and are being applied elsewhere (more practices are introduced in Chapters 11 and 12). The trend will continue to gather support as more and more institutions discover the positive impact of mindfulness-based practices on student well-being, resilience, student success, and ultimately college outcomes. Longer term, the prognosis is also positive. More K–12 schools across the country are integrating mindfulness and compassion-based programs such as Headstand, MindUp, Kindness Curriculum and SEL (social and emotional learning). A unique research project in progress by University of Wisconsin–Madison called the Kindness Curriculum is teaching MBSR principles to kindergarten-aged students in the Madison school district. Preliminary results show students are able to demonstrate improved attention, prosocial behavior, and emotion regulation when compared with a controlled group (Flook, Goldberg, Pinger, & Davidson, 2014). Therefore, a future generation of students will be entering college with higher levels of resilience and well-being to meet the demands of higher education. It has been shown classroom teachers also benefit from training in mindfulness-based techniques, resulting in reduced burnout and emotional exhaustion while seeing increased self-compassion and improved classroom organization (Flook, Goldberg, Pinger, Bonus, & Davidson, 2013).

In this chapter, we explored affirming traits and behaviors that make up the landscape of well-being and resilience—qualities that affect psychosocial and physiological homeostasis. Evidence was presented on how well-being and resilience can be cultivated and strengthened through training in mindfulness-based practices and positive health behaviors. The research and neuroscience behind these practices over the past two decades offer support for the understanding that various mindfulness practices can increase attention and emotional intelligence, promote neuroplasticity, regulate emotions, and optimize the stress response to one's circumstances. Furthermore, individuals possess better problem-solving skills, can reframe challenging events more positively, and demonstrate cognitive flexibility—all skills necessary for resilience. Mindfulness practices have been shown to strengthen inner peace, self-compassion, and compassion/empathy toward others, which contributes to community resilience.

To reaffirm our focus on improving student success in college, this chapter culminated in a discussion of how these economically accessible methodologies and best practices can be integrated into a higher education setting and provided examples of institutions that are in the vanguard of promising practice to enable our students to thrive in the midst of the complexity they experience through understanding the nature and effects of stress; having research-validated practices available to them; and being trained in those mindfulness techniques that enable compassion, calmness, and focus even in the eye of the storm. Malcolm Gladwell (2000) pointed out, "If you want to bring a fundamental change in people's belief and behavior . . . you need to create a community around them, where those new beliefs can be practiced and expressed and nurtured" (p. 173). We have a wealth of techniques and opportunities to nurture well-being, resilience, and compassion.

Editor's Summary Points and Questions to Consider

1. Chronic and acute stress can have a negative impact on well-being and resilience. What are sources of chronic and acute stress for your students, faculty, and administrators? How might you be able to use the research presented in this book thus far to address those sources of chronic and acute stress?

2. We have a wealth of research on what domains contribute to enhancing well-being, resilience, and compassion (revisit Figure 6.2 and Tables 6.1 and 6.2). How many of these practices can you identify in your daily life and within your organizational structure? How many can you easily implement in and out of the classroom?

3. We can educate students, faculty, and administrators on how to use research-proven strategies to enhance their overall well-being

and resilience (see Tables 6.1 and 6.2). How many of these strategies are embedded in your daily lives and organizational structures? What kinds of resources or conversations would you need in order to foster more well-being practices in your and your students' daily lives?

References

Allen, M., Bromley, A., Kuyken, W., & Sonnenberg, S. (2009). Participants' experiences of mindfulness-based cognitive therapy: "It changed me in just about every way possible." *Behavioural and Cognitive Psychotherapy, 37*(4), 413–430.

American College Health Association. (2015). *American College Health Association-National College Health Assessment. Reference Group Executive Summary, Spring 2015*. Retrieved from www.acha-ncha.org/reports_acha-nchaii.html

American College Health Foundation. (2012). *Healthy Campus 2020*. Retrieved from www.acha.org/HealthyCampus/index.cfm

American Psychological Association. (2014). *Stress in America: Are teens adopting adults' stress habits?* Retrieved from www.apa.org/news/press/releases/stress/2013/stress-report.pdf

Anderson, J., Liu, C., & Kryscio, R. (2007). Blood pressure response to transcendental meditation: A meta-analysis. *American Journal of Hypertension, 21*(3), 310–316.

Bachorowski, J., & Owren, M. (2001). Not all laughs are alike: Voiced but not unvoiced laughter readily elicits positive affect. *Psychological Science, 12*(3), 252–257.

Bennet, M. P., & Lengacher. C. (2009). Humor and laughter may influence health IV. Humor and immune function. *Evidence Based Complementary Alternative Medicine, 6*(2), 159–164.

Benson, H., & Klipper, M. (2000). *The relaxation response*. New York, NY: HarperTorch.

Berk, L. S., Tan, S. A., Fry, W. F., Napier, B. J., Lee, J. W., Hubbard, R. W., . . . Eby, W. C. (1989). Neuroendocrine and stress hormone changes during mirthful laughter. *American Journal of the Medical Sciences, 298*(6), 390–396.

Block, J., & Fremen, A. (1996). IQ and ego-resiliency: Conceptual and empirical connections and separateness. *Journal of Personality and Social Psychology, 70*(2), 349–361.

Bonanno, G. A. (2004). Loss, trauma, and human resilience: Have we underestimated the human capacity to thrive after extremely aversive events? *American Psychologist, 59*(1), 20–28.

Brewer, J. A., Worhunsky, P. D., Gray, J. R., Tang, Y. Y., Weber, J., & Kober, H. (2011). Meditation experience is associated with differences in default mode network activity and connectivity. *Proceedings of the National Academy of Sciences of the United States of America, 108*(50), 20254–20259.

Brooks, R., & Goldstein, S. (2004). *The power of resilience: Achieving balance, confidence, and personal strength in your life.* New York, NY: McGraw-Hill.

Cahn, B. R., & Polich, J. (2006). Meditation states and traits: EEG, ERP, and neuroimaging studies. *Psychological Bulletin, 132*(2), 180–211.

Centers for Disease Control and Prevention. (2015a). *How much physical activity do adults need?* Retrieved from www.cdc.gov/physicalactivity/basics/adults/index.html

Centers for Disease Control and Prevention. (2015b). *Division of nutrition, physical activity and obesity.* Retrieved from www.cdc.gov/nccdphp/DNPAO/index.html

Chambers, R., Gullone, E., & Allen, N. (2009). Mindful emotion regulation: An integrative review. *Clinical Psychology Review, 29*(6), 560–572.

Chetty, S., Friedman, A. R., Taravosh-Lahn, K., Kirby, E. D., Mirescu, C., Guo, F., . . . Kaufer, D. (2014). Stress and glucocorticoids promote oligodendrogenesis in the adult hippocampus. *Molecular Psychiatry, 19*(12), 1275–1283.

Chiesa, A., & Serretti, A. (2009). Mindfulness-based stress reduction for stress management in healthy people: A review and meta-analysis. *Journal of Alternative and Complementary Medicine, 15*(5), 593–600.

Cohen, S., Alper, C. M., Doyle, W. J., Treanor, J. J., & Turner, R. B. (2006). Positive emotional style predicts resistance to illness after experimental exposure to rhinovirus or influenza a virus. *Psychosomatic Medicine, 68*(6), 809–815.

Cohen, S., Janicki-Deverts, D., & Miller, G. (2007). Psychological stress and disease. *Journal of the American Medical Association, 298*(14), 1685–1687.

Colbert, R. D., & Nidich, S. (2013). Effect of the transcendental meditation program on graduation, college acceptance and dropout rates for students attending an urban public high school. *Education, 133*(4), 495–501.

Cotman, C. W., Berchtold, N. C., & Christie, L. A. (2007). Exercise builds brain health: Key roles of growth factor cascades and inflammation. *Trends in Neurosciences, 30*(9), 464–472.

Coutu, D. (2002). How resilience works. *Harvard Business Review, 80*(5), 46–55.

Covey, S. R. (1998). *The 7 habits of highly effective families.* New York, NY: Golden Books.

Davidson, R. J., Kabat-Zinn, J., Schumacher, J., Rosenkranz, M., Muller, D., Santorelli, S. F., . . . Sheridan, J. F. (2003). Alterations in brain and immune function produced by mindfulness meditation. *Psychosomatic Medicine, 65*(4), 564–570.

Davidson, R. J., & McEwen, B. S. (2012). Social influences on neuroplasticity: Stress and interventions to promote well-being. *Nature Neuroscience, 15*(5), 689–695.

Deci, E. L., & Ryan, R. M. (2008). Hedonia, eudaimonia, and well-being: An introduction. *Journal of Happiness Studies, 9*(1), 1–11.

Diener, E. (2009). Subjective well-being. In E. Diener (Ed.), *The science of well-being* (pp. 11–58). New York, NY: Springer.

Diener, E., & Seligman, M. E. (2004). Beyond money toward an economy of well-being. *Psychological Science in the Public Interest, 5*(1), 1–31.

Elder, C., Nidich, S., Moriarty, F., & Nidich, R. (2014). Effect of Transcendental Meditation on employee stress, depression, and burnout: A randomized controlled study. *Permanente Journal, 18*(1), 19–23.

Evans, S., Ferrando, S., Findler, M., Stowell, C., Smart, C., & Haglin, D. (2008). Mindfulness-based cognitive therapy for generalized anxiety disorder. *Journal of Anxiety Disorders, 22*(4), 716–721.

Flook, L., Goldberg, S. B., Pinger, L. J., Bonus, K., & Davidson, R. J. (2013). Mindfulness for teachers: A pilot study to assess effects on stress, burnout, and teaching efficacy. *Mind, Brain, and Education, 7*(3), 182–195.

Flook, L., Goldberg, S. B., Pinger, L. J., & Davidson, R. J. (2014). Promoting prosocial behavior and self-regulatory skills in preschool children through a mindfulness-based kindness curriculum. *Developmental Psychology, 51*(1), 44–51.

Fox, K., Nijeboer, S., Dixon, M., Floman, J., Ellamil, M., Rumack, S. P., . . . Christoff, K. (2014). Is meditation associated with altered brain structure? A systematic review and meta-analysis of morphometric neuroimaging in meditation practitioners. *Neuroscience and Biobehavioral Reviews, 43*, 48–73.

Fredrickson, B. L. (2001). The role of positive emotions in positive psychology: The broaden-and-build theory of positive emotions. *American Psychologist, 56*(3), 218–226.

Fredrickson, B. L., & Branigan, C. (2005). Positive emotions broaden the scope of attention and thought-action repertoires. *Cognition & Emotion, 19*(3), 313–332.

Fredrickson, B. L., Grewen, K., Coffey, K., Algoe, S., Firestine, A., Arevalo, J., . . . Cole, S. W. (2013). A functional genomic perspective on human well-being. *Proceedings of the National Academy of Sciences of the United States of America, 110*(33), 13684–13689.

Fredrickson, B. L., & Joiner, T. (2002). Positive emotions trigger upward spirals toward emotional well-being. *Psychological Science, 13*(2), 172–175.

Fredrickson, B. L., & Levenson, R. W. (1998). Positive emotions speed recovery from the cardiovascular sequelae of negative emotions. *Cognition & Emotion, 12*(2), 191–220.

Ganis, G., Thompson, W., & Kosslyn, S. (2004). Brain areas underlying visual mental imagery and visual perception: An fMRI study. *ScienceDirect, 20*(2), 226–241.

Gaydos, L. J., Wang, W., & Strome, S. (2014). H3K27me and PRC2 transmit a memory of repression across generations and during development. *Science, 345*(6203), 1515–1518.

Geschwind, N., Peeters, F., Drukker, M., van Os, J., & Wichers, M. (2011). Mindfulness training increases momentary positive emotions and reward experience in adults vulnerable to depression: A randomized controlled trial. *Journal of Consulting and Clinical Psychology, 79*(5), 618–628.

Giedd, J. (2012). The digital revolution and adolescent brain evolution. *Journal of Adolescent Health, 51*(2), 101–105.

Gladwell, M. (2000). *The tipping point: How little things can make a big difference.* New York, NY: Little, Brown and Company.

Goldin, P. R., & Gross, J. J. (2010). Effect of mindfulness-based stress reduction (MBSR) on emotion regulation in social anxiety disorder. *Emotion, 10*(1), 83–91.

Goldstein, S., & Brooks, R. (2013). Why study resilience? In S. Goldstein & R. B. Brooks (Eds.), *Handbook of resilience in children* (2nd ed., pp. 3–14). New York, NY: Springer.

Goleman, D. (1995). *Emotional intelligence: Why it can matter more than IQ.* New York, NY: Bantam Books.

Goleman, D. (2011, April 25). *Resilience for the rest of us.* Retrieved from blogs.hbr .org/2011/04/resilience-for-the-rest-of-us/

Goleman, D., & Senge, P. (2014). *The triple focus: A new approach to education.* Florence, MA: More Than Sound.

Gómez-Pinilla, F. (2008). Brain foods: The effects of nutrients on brain function. *Nature Reviews Neuroscience, 9*(7), 568–578.

Harris, D. (2014). *10% Happier: How I tamed the voice in my head, reduced stress without losing my edge, and found self-help that actually works—a true story.* New York, NY: HarperCollins.

Hasenkamp, W., Wilson-Mendenhall, C., Duncan, E., & Barsalou, L. (2012). Mind wandering and attention during focused meditation: A fine-grained temporal analysis of fluctuating cognitive states. *NeuroImage, 59*(1), 750–760.

Hofmann, S., Grossman, P., & Hinton, D. (2011). Loving-kindness and compassion meditation: Potential for psychological interventions. *Clinical Psychology Review, 31*(7), 1126–1132.

Hofmann, S. G., Sawyer, A. T., Witt, A. A., & Oh, D. (2010). The effect of mindfulness-based therapy on anxiety and depression: A meta-analytic review. *Journal of Consulting and Clinical Psychology, 78*(2), 169–183.

Hoge, E. A., Bui, E., Marques, L., Metcalf, C. A., Morris, L. K., Robinaugh, D. J., . . . Simon, N. M. (2013). Randomized controlled trial of mindfulness meditation for generalized anxiety disorder: Effects on anxiety and stress reactivity. *Journal of Clinical Psychiatry, 74*(8), 786–792.

Hölzel, B. K., Carmody, J., Evans, K. C., Hoge, E. A., Dusek, J. A., Morgan, L., . . . Lazar, S. W. (2010). Stress reduction correlates with structural changes in the amygdala. *Social Cognitive and Affective Neuroscience, 5*(1), 11–17.

Hölzel, B. K., Carmody, J., Vangel, M., Congleton, C., Yerramsetti, S. M., Gard, T., & Lazar, S. W. (2011). Mindfulness practice leads to increases in regional brain gray matter density. *Neuroimaging, 191*(1), 36–43.

Hölzel, B. K., Lazar, S. W., Gard, T., Schuman-Oliver, Z., Vago, D. R., & Ott, U. (2011). How does mindfulness meditation work? Proposing mechanisms of action from a conceptual and neural perspective. *Perspectives on Psychological Science, 6*(6), 537–559.

Hutcherson, C., Seppala, E., & Gross, J. (2008). Loving-kindness meditation increases social connectedness. *Emotion, 8*(5), 720–724.

Jahnke, R., Larkey, L., Rogers, C., Etnier, J., & Lin, F. (2010). A comprehensive review of health benefits of qigong and tai chi. *American Journal of Health Promotion, 24*(6), e1–e25.

Jazaieri, H., Jinpa, G., McGonigal, K., Rosenberg, E., Finkelstein, J., Simon-Thomas, E., . . . Golding, P. R. (2013). Enhancing compassion: A randomized controlled trial of a compassion cultivation training program. *Journal of Happiness Studies, 14*(4), 1113–1126.

Jazaieri, H., McGonigal, K., Jinpa, T., Doty, J. R., Gross, J. J., & Goldin, P. R. (2014). A randomized controlled trial of compassion cultivation training: Effects on mindfulness, affect, and emotion regulation. *Motivation and Emotion, 38*(1), 23–35.

Johnson, S., Blum, R., & Giedd, J. (2010). Adolescent maturity and the brain: The promise and pitfalls of neuroscience research in adolescent health policy. *Journal of Adolescent Health, 45*(3), 216–221.

Kabat-Zinn, J. (2003). Mindfulness-based interventions in context: Past, present, and future. *Clinical Psychology: Science and Practice, 10*(2), 144–156.

Kabat-Zinn, J. (2013). *Full catastrophe living: Using the wisdom of your body and mind to face stress, pain, and illness* (Rev. ed.). New York, NY: Bantam Books.

Kabat-Zinn, J., Massion, A. O., Kristeller, J., Peterson, L. G., Fletcher, K. E., Pbert, L., . . . Santorelli, S. F. (1992) Effectiveness of a meditation-based stress reduction program in the treatment of anxiety disorders. *American Journal of Psychiatry, 149*(7), 936–943.

Kahneman, D., Diener, E., & Schwarz, N. (1999). *Well-being: The foundations of hedonic psychology*. New York, NY: Russell Sage Foundation.

Karatsoreos, I., & McEwen, B. (2011). Psychobiological allostasis: Resistance, resilience and vulnerability. *Trends in Cognitive Sciences, 15*(12), 576–584.

Kok, B. E., Coffey, K. A., Cohn, M. A., Catalino, L. I., Vacharkulksemsuk, T., Algoe, S. B., . . . Frederickson, B. L. (2013). How positive emotions build physical health: Perceived positive social connections account for the upward spiral between positive emotions and vagal tone. *Psychological Science, 24*(7), 1123–1132.

Kolb, B., & Whishaw, I. (2014). *An introduction to brain and behavior*. New York, NY: Worth.

Konrath, S., Fuhrel-Forbis, A., Lou, A., & Brown, S. (2012). Motives for volunteering are associated with mortality risk in older adults. *Health Psychology, 31*(1), 87–96.

Kosslyn, S., Thompson, W., & Ganis, G. (2006). *The case for mental imagery*. New York, NY: Oxford University Press.

Larkey, L., Jahnke, R., Etnier, J., & Gonzalez, J. (2009). Meditative movement as a category of exercise: Implications for research. *Journal of Physical Activity and Health, 6*(2), 230–238.

Lazar, S. W., Kerr, C. E., Wasserman, R. H., Gray, J. R., Greve, D. N., Treadway, M. T., . . . Fischl, B. (2005). Meditation experience is associated with increased cortical thickness. *NeuroReport, 16*(17), 1893–1897.

Lazarus, R. (1993). From psychological stress to the emotions: A history of changing outlooks. *Annual Review of Psychology, 44*(1), 1–21.

Lederer, A. M., & Middlestadt, S. E. (2014). Beliefs about meditating among university students, faculty, and staff: A theory-based salient belief elicitation. *Journal of American College Health, 62*(6), 360–369.

Leung, M. K., Chan, C. C., Yin, J., Lee, C. F., So, K., F., & Lee, T. M. C. et al. (2013). Increased gray matter volume in the right angular and posterior parahippocampal gyri in loving-kindness meditators. *Social Cognitive & Affective Neuroscience, 8*(1), 34–39.

Liston, C., McEwen, B. S., & Casey, B. J. (2009). Psychosocial stress reversibly disrupts prefrontal processing and attentional control. *Proceedings of the National Academy of Sciences of the United States of America, 106*(3), 912–917.

Lucassen, P. J., Oomen, C. A., Naninck, E. F., Fitzsimons, C. P., van Dam, A. M., Czeh, B., & Korosi, A. (2015). Regulation of adult neurogenesis and plasticity by (early) stress, glucocorticoids, and inflammation. *Cold Spring Harbor Perspectives in Biology, 7*(9), 1–16.

Luders, E., Toga, A. W., Lepore, N., & Gaser, C. (2009). The underlying anatomical correlates of long-term meditation: Larger hippocampal and frontal volumes of gray matter. *NeuroImage, 45*(3), 672–678.

Lutz, A., Brefczynski-Lewis, J., Johnstone, T., & Davidson, R. (2008). Regulation of the neural circuitry of emotion by compassion meditation: Effects of meditative expertise. *PLOS ONE, 3*(3), e1897–e1899.

Lutz, A., Slagter, H. A., Dunne, J. D., & Davidson, R. J. (2008). Attention regulation and monitoring in meditation. *Trends in Cognitive Sciences, 12*(4), 163–169.

Lyke, J. (2009). Insight, but not self-reflection, is related to subjective well-being. *Personality and Individual Differences, 46*(1), 66–70.

Ma, S. H., & Teasdale, J. D. (2004). Mindfulness-based cognitive therapy for depression: Replication and exploration of differential relapse prevention effects. *Journal of Consulting and Clinical Psychology, 72*(1), 31–40.

MacLean, C. R., Walton, K. G., Wenneberg, S. R., Levitsky, D. K., Mandarino, J. P., Waziri, R., . . . Schneider, R. H. (1997). Effects of the transcendental meditation program on adaptive mechanisms: Changes in hormone levels and responses to stress after 4 months of practice. *Psychoneuroendocrinology, 22*(4), 227–295.

Maharishi University of Management. (2012, December 2). *$2.4 million grant to study the Transcendental Meditation program and PTSD in veterans.* Retrieved from mum .edu/Customized/uploads/about/publications/achievements/2012_12_02.html

Martin, R. A. (2007). *The psychology of humor: An integrative approach.* Burlington, MA: Academic Press.

Masten, A. S. (2001). Ordinary magic: Resilience processes in development. *American Psychologist, 56*(3), 227–238.

Mathews, H., & Janusek, L. (2012). Epigenetics and psychoneuroimmunology: Mechanisms and models. *Brain Behavior Immunology, 25*(1), 25–39.

Matta Mello Portugal, E., Cevada, T., Sobral Monteiro-Junior, R., Teixeira Guimarães, T., da Cruz Rubini, E., Lattari, E., . . . Camaz Deslandes, A. (2013). Neuroscience of exercise: From neurobiology mechanisms to mental health. *Neuropsychobiology, 68*(1), 1–14.

McEwen, B. (2006). Protective and damaging effects of stress mediators: Central role of the brain. *Dialogues in Clinical Neuroscience, 8*(4), 367–381.

McEwen, B. (2009). The brain is the central organ of stress and adaptation. *NeuroImage, 47*(3), 911–913.

McGonigal, K. (2012). *The willpower instinct: How self-control works, why it matters, and what you can do to get more of it.* New York, NY: Penguin.

Mobbs, D., Greicius, M. D., Abdel-Azim, E., Menon, V., & Reiss, A. L. (2003). Humor modulates the mesolimbic reward centers. *Neuron, 40*(5), 1041–1048.

Moll, J., Krueger, F., Zahn, R., Pardini, M., de Oliveira-Souza, R., & Grafman, J. (2006). Human fronto-mesolimbic networks guide decisions about charitable donation. *Proceedings of the National Academy of Sciences of the United States of America, 103*(42), 15623–15628.

Neff, K. (2011). *Self-compassion: The proven power of being kind to yourself.* New York, NY: HarperCollins.

Neff, K. D., Hsieh, Y. P., & Dejitterat, K. (2005). Self-compassion, achievement goals, and coping with academic failure. *Self and Identity, 4*(3), 263–287.

Neumeister, A., Charney, D. S., Belfer, I., Geraci, M., Holmes, C., Sharabi, Y., . . . Goldstein, D. S. (2005). Sympathoneural and adrenomedullary functional effects of alpha 2C-adrenoreceptor gene polymorphism in healthy humans. *Pharmacogenetics and Genomics, 15*(3), 143–149.

Newberg, A., & Waldman, M. R. (2010). *How God changes your brain: Breakthrough findings from a leading neuroscientist.* New York, NY: Ballantine Books.

Ogden, C. L., Carroll, M. D., Kit, B. K., & Flegal, K. M. (2014). Prevalence of childhood and adult obesity in the United States, 2011–2012. *Journal of the American Medical Association, 311*(8), 806–814.

Orme-Johnson, D. W., & Barnes, V. A. (2014). Effects of the transcendental meditation technique on trait anxiety: A meta-analysis of randomized controlled trials. *Journal of Alternative and Complementary Medicine, 20*(5), 330–341.

Pace, T. W., Negi, L. T., Adame, D. D., Cole, S. P., Sivilli, T. I., Brown, T. D., . . . Raison, C. L. (2009). Effect of compassion meditation on neuroendocrine, innate immune and behavioral responses to psychosocial stress. *Psychoneuroendocrinology, 34*(1), 87–98.

Pace, T. W., Negi, L. T., Sivilli, T. I., Issa, M. J., Cole, S. P., Adame, D. D., & Raison, C. L. (2010). Innate immune, neuroendocrine and behavioral responses to psychosocial stress do not predict subsequent compassion meditation practice time. *Psychoneuroendocrinology, 35*(2), 310–315.

Pascual-Leone, A., Freitas, C., Oberman, L., Horvath, J. C., Halko, M., Eldaief, M., Bashir, S., Rotenberg, A. (2011). Characterizing brain cortical plasticity and network dynamics across the age-span in health and disease with TMS-EEG and TMS-fMRI. *Brain Topography, 24*(3–4), 302–315.

Pavey, T. G., Burton, N. W. & Brown, W. J. (2014). Prospective relationships between physical activity and optimism in young and mid-aged women. *Journal of Physical Activity and Health.* doi:http://dx.doi.org/10.1123/jpah.2014-0070

Penedo, F. J., & Dahn, J. R. (2005). Exercise and well-being: A review of mental and physical health benefits associated with physical activity. *Current Opinion in Psychiatry, 18*(2), 189–193.

Pierceall, E. A., & Keim, M. C. (2007). Stress and coping strategies among community college students. *Community College Journal of Research and Practice, 31*(9), 703–712.

Pryor, J. H., Eagan, K., Palucki Blake, L., Hurtado, S., Berdan, J., & Case, M. H. (2012). *The American freshman: National norms fall 2012.* Los Angeles, CA: Higher Education Research Institute, UCLA.

Puterman, E., Lin, J., Blackburn, E., O'Donovan, A., Adler, N., & Epel, E. (2010). The power of exercise: Buffering the effect of chronic stress on telomere length. *PLOS ONE, 5*(5), e10837.

Ratey, J. J., & Hagerman, E. (2008). *Spark: The revolutionary new science of exercise and the brain.* New York, NY: Little, Brown and Company.

Rath, T., & Harter, J. K. (2010). *Wellbeing: The five essential elements.* New York, NY: Gallup Press.

Reddy, S. D., Negi, L. T., Dodson-Lavelle, B., Ozawa-de Silva, B., Pace, T. W., Cole, S. P., . . . Craighead, L. W. (2013). Cognitive-based compassion training: A promising prevention strategy for at-risk adolescents. *Journal of Child Family Studies, 22*(2), 219–230.

Regehr, C., Glancy, D., & Pitts, A. (2013). Interventions to reduce stress in university students: A review and meta-analysis. *Journal of Affective Disorders, 148*(1), 1–11.

Roeckelein, J. E. (Ed.). (2006). *Elsevier's dictionary of psychological theories.* New York, NY: Elsevier.

Rosenthal, J. Z., Grosswald, S., Ross, R., & Rosenthal, N. (2011). Effects of Transcendental Meditation in veterans of Operation Enduring Freedom and Operation Iraqi Freedom with posttraumatic stress disorder: A pilot study. *Military Medicine, 176*(6), 626–630.

Ross, A., & Thomas, S. (2010). The health benefits of yoga and exercise: A review of comparison studies. *Journal of Alternative and Complementary Medicine, 16*(1), 3–12.

Rutter, M. (2012). Resilience as a dynamic concept. *Developmental Psychopathology, 24*(2), 335–344.

Ryan, R., & Deci, E. (2001). On happiness and human potentials: A review of research on hedonic and eudemonic well-being. *Annual Review of Psychology, 52*(1), 141–166.

Ryff, C. D., & Keyes, C. L. M. (1995). The structure of psychological well-being revisited. *Journal of Personality and Social Psychology, 69*(4), 719–727.

Ryff, C. D., Singer, B. H., & Love, G. D. (2004). Positive health: Connecting well-being with biology. *Philosophical Transactions of the Royal Society B: Biological Sciences, 359*(1449), 1383–1394.

Salzberg, S. (1995). *Loving kindness: The revolutionary art of happiness.* Boston, MA: Shambhala.

Sedlmeier, P., Eberth, J., Schwarz, M., Zimmerman, D., Haarig, F., Jaeger, S., & Kunz, S. (2012). The psychological effects of meditation: A meta-analysis. *Psychological Bulletin, 138*(6), 1139–1171.

Seligman, M. E., Ernst, R. M., Gillham, J., Reivich, K., & Linkins, M. (2009). Positive education: Positive psychology and classroom interventions. *Oxford Review of Education, 35*(3), 293–311.

Seppala, E., Rossomando, T., & Doty, J. (2013). Social connection and compassion: Important predictors of health and well-being. *Social Research, 80*(2), 411–430.

Shors, T. (2006). Stressful experience and learning across the lifespan. *Annual Review of Psychology, 57*, 55–85.

Siegel, D. J. (2012). The meaning of well-being. In A. Schore & D. J. Siegel (Eds.), *Pocket guide to interpersonal neurobiology* (pp. 40–42). New York, NY: W. W. Norton.

Slavin, S. J., Schindler, D. L., & Chibnall, J. T. (2014). Medical student mental health 3.0: Improving student wellness through curricular changes. *Academic Medicine, 89*(4), 573–577.

Southwick, S., & Charney, D. (2012). The science of resilience: Implications for the prevention and treatment of depression. *Science, 338*(6103), 79–82.

Southwick, S., Vythilingam, M., & Charney, D. (2005). The psychobiology of depression and resilience to stress: Implications for prevention and treatment. *Annual Review of Clinical Psychology, 1*(1), 255–291.

Sowell, E. R., Thompson, P. M., & Toga, A. W. (2004). Mapping changes in the human cortex throughout the span of life. *Neuroscientist, 10*(4), 372–392.

Stacey, M., Dearden, R., Rill, R., & Robinson, D. (1970). *Hospitals, children and their families: The report of a pilot study.* London UK: Routledge & Kegan Paul.

Streeter, C. C., Whitfield, T. H., Owen, L., Rein, T., Karri, S. K., Yakhkind, A., . . . Jensen, J. E. (2010). Effects of yoga versus walking on mood, anxiety, and brain GABA levels: A randomized controlled MRS study. *Journal of Alternative and Complementary Medicine, 16*(11), 1145–1152.

Striedter, G. (2004). *Principles of brain evolution.* Sunderland, MA: Sinauer Associates.

Thomas, N. (2014). *Mental imagery.* Retrieved from plato.stanford.edu/entries/mental-imagery/.

Tinto, V. (1982). Defining dropout: A matter of perspective. In E. T. Pascarella (Ed.), *Studying student attrition* (pp. 3–16). San Francisco, CA: Jossey-Bass.

Tinto, V. (1993). *Leaving college: Rethinking the causes and cures of student attrition.* Chicago, IL: University of Chicago Press.

Towbes, L. C., & Cohen, L. H. (1996). Chronic stress in the lives of college students: Scale development and prospective prediction of distress. *Journal of Youth and Adolescence, 25*(2), 199–217.

Travis, F., Haaga, D. A., Hagelin, J., Tanner, M., Nidich, S., Gaylord King, C., . . . Schneider, R. H. (2009). Effects of Transcendental Meditation practice on brain function and stress reactivity in college students. *International Journal of Psychophysiology, 71*(2), 170–176.

Tugade, M. M., & Fredrickson, B. L. (2004). Resilient individuals use positive emotions to bounce back from negative emotional experiences. *Journal of Personality and Social Psychology, 86*(2), 320–333.

Verstynen, T. D., Weinstein, A. M., Schneider, W. W., Jakicic, J. M., Rofey, D. L., & Erickson, K. I. (2012). Increased body mass index is associated with a global and distributed decrease in white matter microstructural integrity. *Psychosomatic Medicine, 74*(7), 682–690.

Warburton, D. E., Nicol, C. W., & Bredin, S. S. (2006). Health benefits of physical activity: The evidence. *Canadian Medical Association Journal, 174*(6), 801–809.

WHO. Constitution of the World Health Organization. (1946). *American Journal of Public Health and the Nations Health, 36*(11), 1315–1323.

Wu, G., Feder, A., Cohen, H., Kim, J. J., Calderon, S., Charney, D. S., & Mathe, A. A. (2013). Understanding resilience. *Frontiers in Behavioral Neuroscience, 7*(10), 1–15.

Zautra, A., Hall, J., & Murray, K. (2010). Resilience: A new definition of health for people and communities. In J. R. Reich, A. J. Zautra, & J. S. Hall (Eds.), *Handbook of adult resilience* (pp. 3–30). New York, NY: Guilford.

Zhou, Z., Zhu, G., Hariri, A. R., Enoch, M. A., Scott, D., Sinha, R., . . . Goldman, D. (2008). Genetic variation in human NPY expression affects stress response and emotion. *Nature, 452*(7190), 997–1001.

7

ENHANCING CREATIVITY

Shaila Mulholland

All children are artists. The problem is how to remain an artist once he grows up.

—Pablo Picasso (www.brainyquote.com/quotes/quotes/p/pablopicas169744.html)

We may have watched a musician becoming one with her instrument, been moved by the words of a writer or poet, or felt goose bumps from listening to a singer as we share in the emotions of that moment. In higher education, we see creative people in everyday experiences, in a meeting or in the classroom, with perhaps the emergence of a new or innovative idea, or just a simple insight. It can be an exciting and moving experience to see creative individuals practice their art; their craft; and, very often, their passion.

I found my space for self-expression in the arts, primarily with the piano. From the beginning, playing the piano was something that brought me great joy and held the attention of my curious mind. I remember the first time I tried to learn how to play a song on my own. I was five years old and heard a friend play a piece. I studied the spacing of the black notes and matched them to my fingers on the keyboard until I could play the tune with both hands. A few years later, I began formal lessons. I am very thankful that throughout my youth I had teachers who encouraged my imagination to grow and flow. Based on the stories and memories I have listened to from those who also tried piano lessons but didn't stay with it for very long, I'm guessing that the environments in which they learned (and also possibly the teaching practices) weren't conducive to students' desire for self-expression through music making. While it is certainly possible that piano

177

just wasn't for them anyway, when I reflect on my experiences as a teacher, a researcher, and a musician, I hypothesize that had they experienced an environment and teaching approaches that allowed for more creativity and self-expression, their younger selves would have continued music lessons into adulthood.

I share this story and these reflections as a way to illustrate some of the challenges facing higher education. That is, while a college education offers students experiences for learning and development, as well as preparations for a range of careers and vocations, various barriers to student success exist within the academic environment. There is a similar myth out there that perhaps college "just wasn't for them anyway," when it's possible that these barriers (e.g., social, financial, and many others) may have a profound impact on students' higher education experiences. Instead of being encouraged to develop in a holistic and authentic manner, students (as well as their faculty and administrators) are often faced with negative messages from being situated within hierarchical institutions (Liu, 2014) and a dominant culture (Kuh & Whitt, 1988; Sonn, Bishop, & Humphries, 2000; Winkle-Wagner, 2009).

This chapter focuses on understanding postsecondary education faculty and administrators' role in supporting and nurturing the development of creativity. Using the neuroscience lens highlighted in Chapters 2, 3, and 6, I explore and discuss educational practices to enhance creativity. Specific strategies for developing creativity for both individuals and organizations are addressed, with attention to creating educational environments that nurture creativity and enhance well-being. Ultimately, by developing opportunities to inspire and encourage individuals' creative skills, these strategies also seek to enhance peace, compassion, and critical thinking.

The Value of Creativity

The concept and value of creativity have increasingly gained the attention of employers and educators. As you have already read in this book, employees understand that knowledge acquisition alone does not suffice in addressing current and future problems facing society. The IBM Global Student Study (2012) sought to understand areas where undergraduate and graduate students (more than 3,400 students worldwide) felt unprepared by education. The study also found from interviews with 1,709 CEOs that leaders of organizations increasingly emphasized the importance of greater connectivity, openness, and transparency to help stimulate creativity, innovation, and growth. Both students and CEOs surveyed were asked about personal characteristics for success in the workforce, and four of the same qualities rose to the top of the list for both groups. These four characteristics for success were communication, collaboration, flexibility, and creativity—all characteristics that this book posits can be fostered if we change how we design and deliver higher education. And in this chapter, we focus on enhancing creativity.

Economists have increasingly viewed creativity as a form of capital; ideas can be turned into valuable products and services (McWilliam & Dawson, 2008, p. 625). According to another policy report in the United Kingdom, employers are seeking multicompetent graduates; creativity is one valued competency. Similarly, a 2007 report from the National Center on Education and the Economy posited, "The best employers the world over will be looking for the most competent, most creative, and most innovative people. . . . Those countries that can produce the most important new products and services can capture a premium in world markets that will enable them to pay high wages to their citizens" (p. 7).

The report advocated that if we do not change our approaches to teaching, learning, and training in higher education, we will remain stuck in an older era. "Too often, our testing system rewards students who will be good at routine work, while not providing opportunities for students to display creative and innovative thinking and analysis" (National Center on Education and the Economy, 2007, p. 9). Kaufman and Sternberg (2007) advised that "although one cannot directly teach creativity, one can teach for creativity" (p. 58) by moving away from outdated assessments, such as standardized tests, to rewarding creative behavior when it occurs. It is even possible, Kaufman and Sternberg argued, to integrate creativity into large-scale assessments and admissions.

Finally, along with updating our assessments, the efficient and effective use of technology, including social media, has also been found to be an important consideration for how organizations can prepare to build and communicate with customers (IBM Global Student Study, 2012). This echoes similar findings by Livingston (2010), who suggested that we make more room for creativity in higher education by "turning the technological expertise of our students into a greater asset" (p. 59). Social media have provided a means for students to have more awareness of the world, give students a more powerful voice in society, and help increase students' engagement in local and global concerns. Thus, where and how students learn has extended beyond the classroom and campus. Organizational leaders will be looking to these students to help prepare for future changes and to be more creative, innovative, and responsive to society's needs and challenges.

Defining *Creativity*

Before delving any deeper into understanding how we can enhance creativity in higher education, let's begin by providing a definition for *creativity* as a construct. A definition is helpful since creativity research has been approached from various angles and disciplines, including psychology, sociology, business, education, economics, literature, and neuroscience (Kandiko, 2012; Kaufman & Sternberg, 2007). Not surprisingly, and as Plucker and Makel (2010) noted, we might think of similar and synonymous terms for *creativity* such as *imagination, innovation, talent,* or *originality* (and the ways in which these terms can be defined may vary to a large degree).

Kaufman and Sternberg (2007) outlined the components of creative ideas and explained that creative ideas are

- representative of something different, new, or innovative;
- of high quality; and
- appropriate to the task at hand.

Therefore, "a creative response to a problem is new, good, and relevant" (Kaufman & Sternberg, 2007, p. 55). In this example, the concept of creativity is applied to an idea; however, the authors also clearly explained that creativity can refer to an environment or a product (e.g., a piece of music or artwork). With this in mind, the authors suggested the use of the four-Ps model as a tool for organizing research on creativity. The model is useful for distinguishing among the four Ps: the creative (a) person, (b) product, (c) process, and (d) press/environment. Studies on the creative person, for example, could explore the personality or motivation of the individual (referred to earlier in this book), while others might be more interested in understanding the experience of being creative as it is happening and/or observing the setting or environment of the creative process or activity.

Understanding the process and the press/environment, the last two components of the four-Ps model, are also important factors to consider in the higher education context. Although most definitions of *creativity* note that a product or an outcome results from creative activity, from a developmental perspective, let's consider the benefits that come along with the creative process. From my experience in higher education at both the undergraduate and graduate levels (most likely reflective of your experiences as well), we can see how students engaged in research might not necessarily end up with the result they had hoped for and thought they would have, but the learning that occurred during the research process helps to make the overall experience worthwhile for the student.

Despite the numerous examples of creativity that do exist, Plucker, Beghetto, and Dow (2004) found that a low percentage of creativity researchers actually explicitly outlined their understanding of the construct of creativity in their articles. The authors posited that the lack of a common definition for *creativity* was a possible cause for the confusing research on creativity.

They also noted the importance of considering the social context as a way to acknowledge that a creative idea may be more useful in one context than another. In addition, and in line with questions related to context, social and cultural factors have an influence on creativity (Plucker & Zabelina, 2009).

Origins on the Discourse of Creativity

Most scholars agree that it was a presidential address by J. P. Guilford to the American Psychological Association that initiated interest in the field of creativity (Haring-Smith, 2006). In its early years of development, research on creativity was dominated by trait-based theories and continued in that vein in the decades that followed. Both laypersons and scholars believed that creativity was a product of individual talents and traits, and, as a result, researchers focused more on identifying personality traits that enhanced creativity or sought to measure creativity in the same way intelligence was measured with an IQ test (Haring-Smith, 2006). Although this research helped develop an interest in creativity, "it did little to encourage educators to attend to creativity research since it emphasized nature rather than nurture" (Haring-Smith, 2006, p. 24). According to Amabile and Pillemer (2012), in the 1950s, 1960s, and early 1970s, "the predominant impression that a reader of the literature would glean was something like this: creativity is a quality of the person; most people lack that quality; people who possess the quality—geniuses—are different from everyone else, in talent and personality; we must identify, nurture, appreciate, and protect the creative among us—but, aside from that, there isn't much we can do" (p. 3). Now creativity researchers recognize that creativity is not a "fixed, trait-like quality of individuals, but, rather, a skill that might be taught, learned, practiced, and improved" (Amabile & Pillemer, 2012, p. 4). In the field of psychology, creativity was originally closely aligned with conceptions of intelligence and genius; however, the genius myth has been largely discredited and now we understand that there is only a loose correlation between creativity and intelligence (Kandiko, 2012).

Approaches to measuring creativity have also changed. Most creativity assessments used pencil-and-paper tests; however, new assessment techniques emerged in the 1980s (e.g., Amabile, 1982). Creativity researchers have also gone beyond the laboratory to understand the social-environmental factors that affect creativity, and they have investigated aspects of personality as well as sought to understand creativity's relationship to various factors that shape an individual's effectiveness and efficiency in an organizational setting (Collard & Looney, 2014). For example, one study by Zhou (2003) reported an interesting finding: Of the participants in the study, those who had higher scores on the creative personality scale were less impacted by social-environmental factors than participants with lower scores on the creativity scale. Thus, there is good evidence to suggest that there are strengths associated with facilitating creativity in both individuals and organizations.

Attention to the constructs that are related or linked to creativity have received noticeably more attention over the past decade. Florida (2004) described a dawn of the creative age composed of a new class of workers:

> At its core are the scientists, engineers, architects, designers, educators, artists, musicians, and entertainers, whose economic function is to create new ideas, new technology, or new content. Also included are the creative professions of business and finance, law, health care, and related fields, in which knowledge workers engage in complex problem solving that involves a great deal of independent judgment. . . . Indeed, the United States has now entered what I call the Creative Age. (p. 122)

According to Florida (2004), the roots of this creative age can be traced to the years surrounding World War II, when federal funding for basic research jumped considerably. As early as the 1930s, the United States welcomed "a stream of scientific, intellectual, cultural, and entrepreneurial talent" (p. 124). During the years following the end of World War II, it is possible to see how creativity could emerge as an important value for higher education. Citing the development of the National Defense Education Act (NDEA) and the Sputnik war, scholars have suggested that at that time the need for innovation in the United States was catalyzed and increasing access to higher education was an important philosophy because of the realization that higher education could simultaneously enrich individuals' lives and society as a whole (Thelin, 2004; Urban, 2010). Technology has continued to be an important component in providing individuals with additional tools for both work and education.

More recently, creativity research has explored whether creative skills are domain general or domain specific (Baer, 2012). This is a good question for leaders in higher education to consider. As an organization, postsecondary institutions are intended to serve the diverse interests and career/occupational goals of their students. Another way of understanding this question is through the concept of transfer across domains (i.e., a field of study, discipline, or activity). Is it possible for individuals to transfer learning in diverse situations, or are the skills only applicable in their respective domains? Baer (2012) explained that if creativity were domain general, then any creativity-relevant skills gained through education or training should positively influence creative performance in all domains. On the other hand, domain specificity refers to the idea that "creativity in one domain is not predictive (either positively or negatively) of creativity in other domains" (Baer, 2012, p. 21). To pose this domain question another way, if a student develops creative abilities in one area, will he or she show creative abilities in another area?

Scholars have answered this question differently, but most (e.g., Baer, 1998; Plucker, 2005) have suggested that creativity is domain specific. As Baer (1998) explained, "Domain-specific theories of creativity limit the range of creations and creative processes that are presumed to have some underlying unity" (p. 26). At one point, it was thought that creative talents and skills carry over across various domains and activities, but a lack of theoretical evidence exists to support this idea. While this might seem like bad news for higher education leaders working to find ways to enhance creative skills, it only means that we will need to spend more time thinking about how creativity works in various domains (i.e., science, arts, business, life). If we redesign higher education away from segmented courses, we may just find that creativity isn't as domain specific as we thought. For now, faculty and student affairs professionals, for example, may want to consider how to introduce students to various domains and disciplines through various discussions and activities that take place throughout the course or the cocurricular experience, which will encourage students to think across differing contexts and situations. Instead of using examples from only the education sector or the discipline for which they are educating, faculty might also consider ways to teach course content through alternative perspectives and/or examine similar issues in domains or fields outside their particular discipline. High-impact practices introduced earlier in this book, along with self-authorship and a movement toward holistic education, may provide the solutions to fostering creativity.

Utilizing knowledge about domain specificity, Kaufman, Beghetto, Baer, and Ivcevic (2010) asked a related question: How are some individuals creative in multiple domains? To explore this question, they noted several important considerations for understanding how creativity is developed across various areas. Some of these factors include motivation and ability. A student at a given time, for example, might have a narrow interest in one subject and feel less likely to explore creative endeavors in another area. Another factor noted by Kaufman and colleagues (2010) as a key determinant of creative success is ability. In the context of education, it is also important to keep in mind there might be entrance requirements based on student ability before the student can even begin a creative experience. Or there might be barriers to students' participation in creative activities based on the resources available (i.e., the availability of art and music programs in public schools), which, as a result, impacts students' abilities. Worse, students might lose interest and/or motivation to participate in a creative endeavor if they perceive the environment to be too stifling or strict, which conflicts with their desire for self-expression. All of these possibilities are supported by earlier student success research discussed in this book.

Enhancing Creativity in Higher Education

Faculty and teachers working within institutions of higher education have the opportunity to create environments where students can learn and prepare to work across multiple domains (Collard & Looney, 2014). We often see creative artists in visual arts exploring the uses of technology to enhance their work. And it's also more common to find collaborations among scientists and artists working together to advance understanding and appreciation in both areas. In 2008, a movement emerged to transform science, technology, engineering, and math (STEM) to STEAM by adding art (A) to STEM (Madea, 2013).

One example that integrated science and art is an exhibit I once saw at the San Diego airport that featured microscopic research and illustrations of cells. While this work was helping to further knowledge and work to advance both science and art, what I also found so refreshing and excellent about this art display was that it challenged common notions and beliefs that science and the arts are mutually exclusive. As Andreasen (2014) noted, "The arts and the sciences are seen as separate tracks, and students are encouraged to specialize in one or the other. If we wish to nurture creative students, [segmenting the arts and the sciences or focusing on one in detriment to the other] may be a serious error" (p. 75). Faculty, staff, and others working within colleges and universities can model new ways of thinking that will be more productive and aligned with expectations for today, rather than for an older era of education.

Kaufman and colleagues (2010) suggested that students be afforded opportunities to learn about the domains that are of interest to them, while encouraging and nurturing students' engagement in special interests and/or talents that may fall outside of the traditional curriculum. They provide an interesting and helpful perspective on developing multicreative individuals:

> Joni Mitchell thought music would remain a hobby, playing second fiddle to her serious work as a painter. . . . Alan Greenspan pursued being a saxophone player before 'falling back' on economics. Benjamin Franklin surely could not have known which of his many talents would become most important to him later in life. So it is with our students. What we can offer them is the chance to develop any, and all, of their creative talents. (p. 387)

One useful framework for better understanding the previous example and often cited in the literature is the four-C model of creativity (Kaufman et al., 2010). These four Cs include big-C creators (e.g., Albert Einstein, Duke Ellington) and little-c learning (i.e., everyday activities and experiences in which anyone can participate). Added later to the model, mini-c and pro-C are two other important aspects of the model that inform practice in higher education. Mini-c creativity, while similar to little-c learning, places even greater emphasis on the importance of subjective judgment and meaningfulness (Beghetto & Kaufman, 2007). Rather than relying on external judgment, mini-c insights may not go beyond the creator but can serve as a sign of creative potential. It may be possible that mini-c insights are fostered when students begin to engage in mindfulness methodology.

As teachers, we have the opportunity to provide spaces and learning opportunities where students may gain mini-c insights through class activities and assignments. We can do this by asking questions that help students make connections between the course content and the issues pertinent to students' professional work. I strive to provide course assignments that will develop in students the various skills that are important for navigating issues and problems in the profession and emphasize the importance of forming strategies that will address or remedy these issues and problems. Mini-c creativity offers a helpful way to understand how an individual "combines new and personally meaningful insights and interpretations across different disciplines or domains" (Kaufman et al., 2010, p. 382). For instance, a student who learns the value of using multiple sources of evidence in research could apply mini-c insights by incorporating similar concepts and knowledge into assessment and evaluation strategies. Moreover, individuals are able to build upon mini-c experiences with future creative experiences; therefore, mini-c insights can lead to greater creative contributions.

Pro-C creativity refers to professional-level creators who have not yet reached legendary status (Kaufman et al., 2010). Kaufmann and colleagues suggest that it is more likely for a teacher to encounter pro-C or mini-c creators in the classroom (in other words, it is more common for individuals to spend time in multiple everyday creative activities at any given time, such as cooking, photography, or writing poetry). Thus, if teachers combine the concepts of pro-C and little-c, there are tremendous opportunities for higher education to enhance creativity for various individuals. Again, integration across learning is needed in order to provide these types of creativity-enhancing opportunities for students.

How can we intentionally encourage and nurture creativity in higher education? What can educational leaders do to support environments that provide students with opportunities to participate in creative activities across multiple domains, disciplines, and majors? Higher education institutions are in an excellent position to offer students the chance to learn about a wide range of domains that may be of interest to them. Of all the suggestions provided in the literature, the key might lie in understanding the close relationship between critical and creative thinking. Kaufman and Baer (2006) have provided us with excellent insight into how we develop and pursue the goals for student learning both in and out of the class-room by explaining, "One needs to have appropriate knowledge and well-developed critical thinking skills, and yet one also needs to retain a naïve, spontaneous, and perhaps even childlike imagination. Imagination, skills, and knowledge are all essential to adult creativity" (p. 135). In other words, students in higher education will benefit when they are encouraged to think *creatically* (creatively and critically—a completely made-up term to get your attention and hopefully helpful in remembering this concept). The impor-tant point for educational practice from the research literature is not to separate critical thinking from creative thinking. For example, incorporat-ing case study into a class is an effective way students can practice criti-cal thinking skills and creativity skills. I often assign small groups to work together in analyzing a case, which also offers a way to develop collabora-tive skills. Moreover, case studies are a great in-class or out-of-class course activity because students are able to build and strengthen problem-solving skills, which has been documented in the literature as one important way to increase students' creative skills (Brodin & Frick, 2011). The way students resolve case studies can also be a dynamic way to assess their *creatic thinking* (creative and critical thinking).

I have also come to realize that one insight from music making and piano playing that is helpful from both a teaching and learning perspective is the concept of *flow*, or the feelings and sensations that occur when an individual is intensely engaged in a creative activity (Csikszentmihalyi, 1996; Kaufman & Sternberg, 2007). The creative activities associated with flow are broad in scope, according to Csikszentmihalyi (1975)—in other words, a range of creative individuals from artists to athletes can experience flow. The work on flow has largely been done by Csikszentmihalyi, an influential scholar who interviewed individuals about their experiences of being intensely engaged in creative activity. One way to envision the concept of flow is to think of a per-son becoming lost in thought through an activity. I can picture my brother, who is incredibly creative when it comes to building bicycles, as well as many other things. By having the interest and concentration, as well as the skills (Csikszentmihalyi, 1990) required, he is able to carry out the creative task at hand; in this case, building a bike.

A study by Shernoff, Csikszentmihalyi, Schneider, and Shernoff (2003) provided further insight into the importance of the balance between an individual's skill level and the task or activity and applied the theory of flow to explore student engagement in the high school classroom setting:

> Flow theory is based on a symbiotic relationship between challenges and skills needed to meet those challenges. The flow experience is believed to occur when one's skills are neither overmatched nor underutilized to meet a given challenge. This balance of challenge and skill is fragile; when disrupted, apathy (i.e., low challenges, low skills), anxiety (i.e., high challenges, low skills), or relaxation (i.e., low challenges, high skills) are likely to be experienced. . . . The experience of anxiety or relaxation may prompt an instructor to change the level of challenge, and also prompt the student to increase his or her skill level in order to reenter flow. Issuing appropriate challenges and providing opportunities to enhance skills (e.g., providing immediate feedback and incrementally teaching more complex skills that build upon previously learned skills) may be one of the most ideal ways of engaging students. (p. 160)

Thus, Shernoff and colleagues (2003) explored how flow shapes student engagement. By using a sample of 526 high school students across the United States, the researchers were able to understand the conditions under which students reported being engaged. From this study, the following two key factors not only were found to increase engagement but also were applicable to the higher education setting:

1. The perceived challenge of the task and the individual's skills were high and in balance.
2. The instruction was considered relevant to the student.

Group discussions, for example, were (not surprisingly) found to be more effective at increasing student engagement than listening to traditional lectures, viewing videos, or taking tests. Although the study focused on high school students, the findings from this study provide some helpful insights for teaching in higher education specifically related to how faculty and instructors can vary and effectively set the level of academic challenge, intensity, and concentration required of students in the classroom to maximize learning. Activities and tasks, such as watching a film, may not require sufficient concentration and energy to facilitate learning. But once again, it is also important to consider the context. For example, I find that films and video can be useful ways to introduce sensitive topics for classroom discussion. As I strive to encourage creative and critical thinking among students I teach, I can observe the classroom setting for evidence of flow, for example, by looking for students engaged in deep conversation or for signs of nonverbal communication (e.g., heads nodding, eyes making contact).

One of the challenges to enhancing creativity in higher education is the degree of specialization that is often expected and/or required among college students or in graduate degree programs. The demands of completing an educational degree or program within a certain time frame and with specific knowledge of the subject area may not allow a person to simultaneously pursue interests outside of the degree (Kaufman et al., 2010). Adult learners, students who are employed while in college, and/or students who are specializing in degrees that are already tightly packed with professional accreditation course requirements might have additional challenges to finding the available time for pursuing interests outside their academic majors. Therefore, the opportunities to develop creative skills either in their own disciplines or in other areas can be limited. It will be beneficial to maximize exposure to cocurricular experiences, opportunities for service-learning and other high-impact practices, and activities in the curriculum that encourage students' creative interests, develop students' creative skills, and allow students' natural creative talents and skills to be shared within the academic community.

As a college student, I remember having a key realization. I was a first-year student in a large public state university, and I selected biology as my major. It was a good choice given my interests in health and science, but I spent much of my time in the previous years playing piano at a competitive level, and I also enjoyed playing percussion for the jazz, concert, and marching bands. When I arrived at college, it felt as if all of a sudden, these activities were all gone. I realized I would at the very least need to find some way to continue studying and learning the piano. Although I loved being able to play for leisure in the lounge of my residence hall, I still wanted to learn more and didn't mind the practice time that it would require. For the first year or two of school, I was able to enroll in lessons; however, during my junior year the university added an additional fee, and I had to stop taking lessons. At that time, I decided to enroll in two semesters of art history (originally, I thought I would take only one class). One of the downsides of taking these courses outside my major was that it would extend the time to reach graduation. With that in mind, I changed my degree from a bachelor of science (BS) to a bachelor of arts (BA) so I would not delay my graduation. Making this change did result in limitations for applying for certain jobs/positions in the field of biological sciences that required a BS degree, but I do not regret the decision because those courses allowed me combine my academic and creative interests to find a career as a research professor in higher education. Nonetheless, what would my universe have looked like had I been able to continue to pursue both the sciences and the arts wholeheartedly? How would my career trajectory have been influenced? What would it look like if we intentionally integrated these opportunities back into higher education so students are not forced to choose between the two?

A Final Consideration With Examples

Instead of leaving creative activities for the weekend or special events for students, it is exciting to imagine the positive outcomes that we might see if we encouraged creativity on a more daily basis. Livingston (2010) stated:

> Each human being has a unique way of looking at the universe. As well, each has a distinctive imagination, the seedbed from which true originality grows. If the academy wishes to center its mission on honing creativity, it can best do so by pedagogies that maximize opportunities for students to practice being inventive. Although it is a normal form of human behavior, creativity is also a technique, a skill that can be developed and refined over time. (p. 60)

Integrating creativity into our campus environment will very likely require that the curriculum change; that we move away from a segmented approach to teaching and develop the whole student. But first, we can reflect on our common thinking about teaching and learning. As Livingston (2010) further explained, "The classroom lecture format is, by nature, not a natural laboratory for interaction and collaboration," and he suggested that the curriculum be focused around interpersonal exchange, which opens the learning experience "for every student to express, share, and test his or her creative instincts" (p. 60). Classroom discussions, the incorporation of creative tasks and activities, and encouraging experiential activities are just a few ways we can help develop the whole student. And at the same time, as students gain new knowledge and skills, we can also attend to the training of sensations, emotions, and feelings, and engaging the emotion and cognitive regulation processes to integrate those sensations into action.

As a way to provide a space for individual interests, strengths, and natural gifts to further emerge, I incorporate a creative component into at least one of the assignments in each of my courses. Group projects lend themselves well to practicing creative skills. For example, in each of the courses I teach, students are asked to work in small groups (four students per group) and research a current issue/problem facing postsecondary education. The project requires that each group include an interactive and creative activity within the presentation and that the entire class participate in the activity (while the group members serve as facilitators). This format enables the class to move beyond a lecture format and provides an opportunity for students to share, integrate, and develop creative skills. A curriculum designed around projects and seminars for students to develop skills in collaboration and creativity is also greatly beneficial for preparing individuals for future employer demands.

I also strive to provide examples and demonstrate creative teaching. I have adapted Deborah Stone's (1997) chocolate cake exercise from her book *Policy Paradox* as a way to discuss the topics of perspective and values in a course I teach (Educational Leadership in a Diverse Society at San Diego State University). In my demonstration, instead of using a chocolate cake, I use a pizza. I arrive to class with pizzas (usually a surprise) for the students. But when I open the first box of pizza, I "discover" that the pizza has not yet been cut (the students do not realize that all the other pizzas are cut into slices; it's only this first pizza that someone "forgot" to slice). From that point, I ask the students how we should cut the pizzas. The simplest answer, which I usually hear early on in the discussion of how to cut the pizzas, is, "Cut it evenly so everyone gets one slice." And sometimes, there is one student who has not yet arrived to class. This is often when I ask students to consider if any late students should be allowed to have a slice and to think about what would be fair to the class. As we get more into the exercise, I hint at some of the insights that I hope the students gain from the demonstration: What is a policy and what is policy making? How do individuals determine what is fair or equal? What is the role of individuals' perspectives and values in policy making? As we debate these various questions, with a focus on how we define *fairness* and *equity*, I encourage students to think of some of the other ways these concepts could be defined. Together we propose various questions to consider as we strive to understand fairness and equity: Should second-year students get larger slices than the first-year students? Should the professor have one pizza for herself and the students share what is left? Should we save a slice of pizza for the student arriving later to class? Should we save any slices of pizza for the students who couldn't attend class because they were sick? Should the students who haven't eaten that day get an extra slice of pizza? With an open discussion in this activity that emphasizes creative thinking and problem solving, students are able to generate a number of different ideas. Furthermore, in the process, students learn about significant concepts (perspective and values) and learn more about one another.

Creating and maximizing the opportunities available for students to use their imaginations, share ideas, and be creative is what we can and should strive for within higher education. As Livingston (2010) stated, "The ultimate question, then, is not how to teach creativity, but rather how to understand, harvest, and build up the very creativity that every student already possesses and uses" (p. 61).

Editor's Summary Points and Questions to Consider

1. While we are not certain about the neurocorrelates that are specifically mapped to creative behavior, we are fairly certain that

there is an association between training attention to sensations, emotions, and feelings and engaging the emotion and cognitive regulation processes to integrate those sensations into action. How could the strategies introduced in this chapter be implemented in your college or university inside or outside of the classroom?

2. Flow theory suggests that when students are offered challenges that match with their skill sets and interests, they may be intrinsically motivated to engage in creative problem solving. How could you engage students (inside and outside the classroom) in self-exploration to identify their interests and guide them to where their skill sets and challenges are motivating them toward creativity?

3. Fostering creativity within students at this point does not seem to occur without a domain context. How could your college or university faculty and staff find ways to foster students' creativity within and across domains?

References

Amabile, T. M. (1982). Social psychology of creativity: A consensual assessment technique. *Journal of Personality and Social Psychology, 43*(1), 997–1013.

Amabile, T. M., & Pillemer, J. (2012). Perspectives on the social psychology of creativity. *The Journal of Creativity, 46*(1), 3–15.

Andreasen, N. C. (2014 , July/August). Secrets of the creative brain. *Atlantic*, 62–75.

Baer, J. (1998). The case for domain specificity of creativity. *Creativity Research Journal, 11*, 173–177.

Baer, J. (2012). Domain specificity and the limits of creativity theory. *Journal of Creative Behavior, 46*(1), 16–29.

Beghetto, R. A., & Kaufman, J. C. (2007). Toward a broader conception of creativity: A case for mini-c creativity. *Psychology of Aesthetics, Creativity, and the Arts, 1*, 73–79.

Brodin, E. M., & Frick, L. (2011). Conceptualizing and encouraging critical creativity in doctoral education. *International Journal for Researcher Development, 2*(2), 133–151.

Collard, P., & Looney, J. (2014). Nurturing creativity in education. *European Journal of Education, 49*(3), 348–364.

Csikszentmihalyi, M. (1975). *Beyond boredom and anxiety*. San Francisco, CA: Jossey-Bass.

Csikszentmihalyi, M. (1990). *Flow: The psychology of optimal experience*. New York, NY: Harper & Row.

Csikszentmihalyi, M. (1996). *Creativity: Flow and the psychology of discovery and invention*. London, UK: HarperCollins.

Florida, R. (2004). America's looming creativity crisis. *Harvard Business Review, 82*(10), 122–136.

Haring-Smith, T. (2006). Creativity research review: Some lessons for higher education. *Peer Review, 8*(2), 23–25.

IBM Global Student Study. (2012). *Connected generation: Perspectives from tomorrow's leaders in a digital world.* Retrieved from http://www-935.ibm.com/services/us/en/c-suite/ceostudy2012/

Kandiko, C. B. (2012). Leadership and creativity in higher education: The role of interdisciplinarity. *London Review of Education, 10*(2), 191–200.

Kaufman, J. C., Beghetto, R. A., Baer, J., & Ivcevic, Z. (2010). Creativity polymathy: What Benjamin Franklin can teach your kindergartener. *Learning and Individual Differences, 20*(4), 380–387.

Kaufman, J. C., & Sternberg, R. J. (2007). Resource review: Creativity. *Change, 39,* 55–58.

Kuh, G. D., & Whitt, E. J. (1988). *The invisible tapestry: Culture in American colleges and universities.* ASHE-ERIC Higher Education, Report No. 1. Washington, DC: Association for the Study of Higher Education

Liu, J. (2014). Alternative voice and local youth identity in Chinese local-language rap music. *East Asia Cultures Critique, 22*(1), 263–292.

Livingston, L. (2010). Teaching creativity in higher education. *Arts Education Policy Review, 111*(2), 59–62.

Maeda, J., (2013). STEM + Art = STEAM. *The STEAM Journal, 1*(1). doi: 10.5642/steam.201301.34

McWilliam, E., & Dawson, S. (2008). Teaching for creativity: Towards sustainable and replicable pedagogical practice, *Higher Education, 56*(1), 633–643.

National Center on Education and the Economy. (2007). *Tough choices or tough times: The report of the new commission on the skills of the American workforce.* San Francisco, CA: Jossey-Bass.

Plucker, J. A. (2005). The (relatively) generalist view of creativity. In J. C. Kaufman & J. Baer (Eds.), *Creativity across domains: Faces of the muse* (pp. 307–312). Mahwah, NJ: Erlbaum.

Plucker, J. A., Beghetto, R. A., & Dow, G. T. (2004). Why isn't creativity more important to educational psychologists? Potential, pitfalls, and future directions in creativity research. *Educational Psychologists, 39*(2), 83–96.

Plucker, J. A., & Makel, M. C. (2010). Assessment of creativity. In J. C. Kaufman & R. J. Sternberg (Eds.), *Cambridge handbook of creativity* (pp. 48–73). New York, NY: Cambridge University Press.

Plucker, J. A., & Zabelina, D. (2009). Creativity and interdisciplinarity: One creativity or many creativities? *Mathematics Education, 41*(1), 5–11.

Shernoff, D. J., Csikszentmihalyi, M., Schneider, B., & Shernoff, E. S. (2003). Student engagement in high school classrooms from the perspective of flow theory. *School Psychology Quarterly, 18*(2), 158–176.

Sonn, C., Bishop, B., & Humphries, R. (2000). Encounters with the dominant culture: Voices of indigenous students in mainstream higher education. *Australian Psychologist, 35*(2), 128–135.

Stone, D. A. (1997). *Policy paradox: The art of political decision making.* New York, NY: W.W. Norton.

Thelin, J. R. (2004). *A history of american higher education.* Baltimore, MD: John Hopkins University Press.

Urban, W.J. (2010). *More than science and Sputnik: The National Defense Act of 1958.* Tuscaloosa, AL: University of Alabama Press.

Winkle-Wagner, R. (2009). *The unchosen me: Race, gender, and identity among black women in college.* Baltimore, MD: Johns Hopkins University Press.

Zhou, J. (2003). When the presence of creative coworkers is related to creativity: Role of supervisor close monitoring, developmental feedback, and creative personality. *Journal of Applied Psychology, 88*(1), 413–422.

8

ENHANCING COMPASSION AND EMPATHY

Sara Schairer

If you want others to be happy, practice compassion.
If you want to be happy, practice compassion.

—Dalai Lama (*The Art of Happiness*, Dalai Lama and Cutler, 1998, p. 20)

Meet 22-year-old Jessica, or Jess for short. Her sun-bleached hair, lip ring, trucker hat, fraying denim shorts, flannel shirt, and skateboard invite a pretty obvious first impression. Jess is a California girl through and through. When you chat with Jess, you learn that she's as bright as they come, and she's been a go-getter her entire life. In high school, she was class president, an athlete, and a straight-A student. Currently, she's entering her final semester at San Diego State University and will soon graduate with a double major in business and philosophy. She's involved with the entrepreneur society on campus, volunteers for a start-up nonprofit organization, works as a waitress, and also works at a surf shop. Jess hopes to someday start her own action sports company, and she is motivated to learn as much as possible so that her business ideas will thrive.

It's not uncommon for Jess to attend class all day, go to work in the evening, and then spend the night at a café drinking coffee and studying. When she sleeps, she doesn't sleep well. She worries. She feels as if she's overcommitting herself, but she doesn't want to give up anything. Jessica, like most of us, has been coached to try hard and persevere when she faces challenges. She's heard "no pain, no gain" throughout her life. When she becomes overwhelmed by the burdens of her busy life, she doesn't take time to notice her suffering and tend to it. Jess keeps pushing.

A lot of students just keep pushing when they encounter difficulties. It is a severe understatement to write that being an undergraduate student is not easy. In 2010, researchers from UCLA surveyed more than 200,000 students from 279 baccalaureate colleges and universities and found that "self-rated emotional health for incoming first-year students is at the lowest point since we first asked the question 25 years ago in 1985" ("The American Freshman: National Norms Fall 2010," 2011). The pressure of attending classes, studying, and performing well on exams is tough enough. Combine that with new surroundings, new relationships, new financial concerns, and continuing family obligations and we have more than enough ingredients for an overflowing dose of stress and anxiety.

Of course, as mentioned in the introduction to this book, it's important that our college students learn how to communicate effectively, think strategically, and master skills that will help them after graduation. We want to prepare them for the real world, and we want them to succeed. Yet how can a person be successful when she is suffering from anxiety, insomnia, depression, or some combination of these challenging states?

As I explain in this chapter, research over the past decade indicates that introducing the concepts of self-compassion and compassion to our undergraduates could be vital to their emotional well-being, overall health, academic success (Cohn & Frederickson, 2010; Cohn, Frederickson, Stephanie, Mikels, & Conway, 2009; Hoffman, Grossman, & Hinton, 2011; Neff, Kirkpatrick, & Rude, 2007; Neff, Rude, and Kirkpatrick, 2007). Practicing self-compassion and compassion can benefit the psychological and physical well-being of students, and I believe it can do something even more important: Compassion can inspire our college students to create meaningful lives. (See Chapter 4 on self-authorship for more information on the importance of meaning making and learning and development.) Instead of seeking careers that merely reward them financially, students will seek out fulfilling work that benefits others. If we introduce compassion in higher education, perhaps Jessica and other students will spend their time and energy creating solutions to our world's social problems.

Compassion It

As the founder of the nonprofit organization COMPASSION IT (www .compassionit.com), I get the opportunity to spread the message of compassion to people around the world. I'm a certified teacher of Stanford

University's Compassion Cultivation Training course, and I spend my time teaching, speaking, writing, and sharing the benefits of compassion. I love my job.

I became obsessed with compassion in 2008 after seeing self-help author and motivational speaker Wayne Dyer featured on the daytime talk show *Ellen*. Dyer said that compassion was the most important lesson to teach our children. Dyer posited that if we could teach a younger generation to put themselves in another's shoes, we could solve every social problem on the planet. Civil unrest, poverty, oppression, and other global social issues would vanish if we could create a worldwide culture of compassion.

I couldn't stop thinking about compassion and its power; that evening, the word *compassionate* became two words in my brain—*compassion it*. That made a lot of sense to me. *Compassion* is now a verb. It's like Nike's "Just Do It" or "Google it." The phrase *compassion it* is a simple concept, and it was life changing for me. From that day forward, I began trying on this new "compassion it" way of living.

I "compassioned it" on the freeway and assumed that the person who cut me off was in a hurry as opposed to a reckless jerk. I "compassioned it" with my boss and assumed that he was snippy because he was going through something at home instead of believing he was an unreasonable and ineffective manager. I "compassioned it" with my barista and cut her some slack when she seemed grumpy and made the incorrect drink. I didn't think to myself, "She's an incompetent human!" Even while suffering through a painful and unwanted divorce, I noticed that when I "compassioned it" and tried on my ex-husband's perspective, I had the best outcomes. (I'm not saying I always "compassioned it" with him, but it seemed to work wonders when I did!) In all the situations where I would have previously judged unskilled behavior unfairly, I kept in mind that everyone is human and might be suffering in some way.

A few years after watching that *Ellen* episode and "compassioning it," I founded the nonprofit COMPASSION IT. The best part of my job is teaching, leading workshops, and speaking about compassion. Yes, compassion is a trainable skill.

Compassion in a Nutshell

When I kick off a workshop or speaking engagement, I try my best to connect the audiences with the physical feelings of compassion. Engaging in those feelings gives us a better understanding of why compassion is so powerful. Right now, I'd like to engage you in a similar way, so I'm inviting you to participate in a visualization exercise.

Take a moment and think back to a time when you either gave or received compassion. In other words, think of a time when you noticed suffering and helped alleviate it, or think of a time when you were suffering and someone came to your aid. After you read these instructions, close your eyes and put yourself in that situation. I invite you to keep your eyes closed in this visualization for a minute or two, and pay close attention to how your body feels. (You can set a timer on your phone if you are concerned about taking too much time for this exercise.) After you open your eyes, I'd like you to consider this question: What does compassion feel like?

Often, during that brief visualization, the participants' faces brighten with smiles. When I ask everyone to open their eyes, they look at me with warmth in their eyes. I invite people to share what compassion feels like, and they often tell me (via direct first-person evidence of the experience) that compassion feels warm, light, and peaceful. Whether you're on the giving end or the receiving end, compassion feels good.

Now that you've experienced the feeling of compassion, let's look at its definition. *Merriam-Webster* (www.merriam-webster.com/dictionary/com passion) defines *compassion* as a "sympathetic consciousness of others' distress together with a desire to alleviate it." In other words, you are engaging in the practice of compassion when you witness someone suffering and you want to help. Its Latin roots mean "cosuffering" or "to suffer with." When we are compassionate, we don't run away from suffering or try to block it out. We are able to stay present with suffering without getting overwhelmed.

Stanford University's Center for Compassion and Altruism Research and Education (ccare.stanford.edu) created an eight-week course called Compassion Cultivation Training (CCT). During the course, students learn that compassion has the following four key components:

1. Awareness of suffering.
2. Sympathetic concern related to being emotionally moved by suffering (i.e., empathy).
3. Wish to see the relief of that suffering.
4. Responsiveness or readiness to help relieve that suffering (Jazaieri et al., 2013; Jazaieri et al., 2014; Jinpa, 2010).

Some people have the idea that *compassion* is a fluffy, angel-winged, hippie word. Perhaps you feel that way as well. My hope is to convince you otherwise. Practicing compassion is not a walk in the park; it takes courage, and it takes practice. In order to practice compassion, you must first notice suffering. Compassion and suffering go hand in hand, and this seems to trip people up a little bit. When I challenge students to try to show compassion for everyone they meet, they remark, "But not everyone is suffering!"

I disagree; I think it's safe to say that nearly every single person on the planet is suffering in some way. We may not see it on the outside, but most people are worried or anxious about something. Therefore, each person we meet can be a candidate for our compassion. Don't fret. It's not necessary to show elaborate acts of compassion at every moment. A kind greeting or bright smile might suffice in relieving suffering.

One of the most important lessons we teach in Stanford's CCT course is "Embracing Common Humanity," which is the idea that everyone is "just like me." This lesson reminds participants that when it comes down to it, every person on the planet is a human being. All humans (apart from some who are diagnosed with particular pathologies) have feelings; they desire happiness and freedom from suffering. If we can carry out our lives with this idea in the back (or even the front) of our minds, we can't help but act with compassion.

It's important to note that compassion includes action. That is what separates compassion from empathy. If we feel the distress of others or use our imaginations to put ourselves in others' shoes, we're experiencing empathy. If you've ever teared up or felt upset when you've seen a friend in pain, you know what empathy feels like.

If we are motivated to act, we're experiencing compassion. When you notice someone slip and fall, and you help him to his feet, you are being compassionate. But first you must experience empathy—you must feel the pain or put yourself in the shoes of the person you saw slip and fall. Have you ever seen someone in pain, perhaps even felt his pain, yet not taken any action? Or maybe you have seen someone in pain, not felt his pain, and therefore not taken any action. Compassion requires empathy and action.

On a micro level, engaging in compassion can benefit the individual. Research from many highly regarded institutions, such as Stanford University, University of North Carolina at Chapel Hill, and University of Texas at Austin, indicates that compassion makes us happier, less stressed, and healthier. It helps us feel more connected to others and enriches our interpersonal relationships (Jazaieri et al., 2013; Jazaieri et al., 2014; Neff, Kirkpatrick, & Rude, 2007). When we zoom out and look at compassion's benefits on a macro level, it can get overwhelming (in a good way). What would happen in the world's most violent regions if our fellow global citizens practiced compassion? Mahatma Gandhi, Martin Luther King Jr., Mother Teresa, Desmond Tutu, and the Dalai Lama agree: Compassion is the antidote to violence and can bring peace to our world.

So, we have evidence that compassion benefits us and our society. Yet what do we know about how to create compassion when it may be lacking? Are we born as compassionate beings, or do we need to learn how to be compassionate? To answer these questions, we begin by looking at neuroscience.

The Neuroscience of Compassion

When you read the name Charles Darwin, what one main theory comes to mind? I'm guessing you think of natural selection or survival of the fittest. A basic example of this theory is that strong and fast lions survive while weak and slow lions die. When thinking of our ancestors and which ones survived and passed along genes, you may think of their strength, power, speed, and intelligence. Personally, I picture Fred Flintstone–like brutes yielding large sticks, grunting, and figuring out how to make fire. Needless to say, compassion doesn't really go along with that picture.

It is a little known fact that Darwin believed that compassion is a key ingredient for survival, and he focused a good amount of his work on compassion (although he refers to it as "sympathy"). In his book *The Descent of Man*, Darwin (1871) wrote, "Sympathy will have been increased through natural selection; for those communities which included the greatest number of the most sympathetic members would flourish best, and rear the greatest number of offspring" (p. 130). It makes sense, doesn't it? When mothers care for their newborns, the newborns survive. When people in communities help each other, they thrive.

Thanks to these genes that have been passed along to us by our ancestors, it appears that we may be hardwired for empathy and compassion (Keltner, 2004). However, it may not be instinctual to have compassion for everyone. We can easily offer compassion to those similar to us, but it is much more difficult to feel empathy and then to act compassionately toward someone to whom we don't relate or to someone who has caused harm (Hall & Woods, 2006).

Think of Jessica; she will go out of her way to help one of her friends or a family member in need. But will she help the homeless woman who rides the bus alongside her? Does Jessica even notice her? Does she believe the woman is "just like me"? Let's delve into what's happening in our brains and bodies to better understand how we are wired as empathetic and compassionate beings. (A neuroscientist I am *not*, so bear with me as I try my best to explain this.)

First, let's rewind and review. Do you remember what needs to happen before we can act with compassion? If you said, "Empathy," you're right. Points for you! We can define *empathy* as "the intellectual identification with or vicarious experiencing of the feelings, thoughts, or attitudes of another" (dictionary.reference.com/browse/empathy). Empathy is when you feel another's pain, emotion, or sensation as if it is your own (Stotland, Mathews, Sherman, Hansson, & Richardson, 1978). Empathy and the emotions that arise as we empathize can occur when we use our minds to imagine being in another person's shoes. Empathy can emerge without our even thinking about it or intending for it to happen. How do we know this?

Thanks to an accidental discovery by some Italian neuroscientists in the early 1990s, we believe that our brains have mirror neurons that enable empathy (Rizzolatti & Craighero, 2004). So, when you see someone else engage in an action that you may associate with pain, the areas activated in his or her brain may also be activated in your brain (Iacoboni, 2009). While we are not clear whether this means you have a neural network that allows you to experience the pain firsthand, there is something going on that allows a human being to—at least sometimes—experience empathy for another through the cognitive process of understanding what it may feel like to do the same as another or to be in the same situation as another (Caramazza, Anzellotti, Strnad, & Lingnau, 2014).

Let's see if you can experience your mirror neurons at work. Imagine that your friend walks into the room barefoot. As she closes the door behind her, the bottom of the door scrapes across her big toe and tears off her toenail. (Ouch!) Does any part of you recoil at that thought? Does your own big toe hurt? If so, you just felt empathy. Some fascinating studies highlight how we may be able to feel empathy for some people but not others.

German scientists Bernhardt and Singer collected brain-imaging empathy studies from the past several years and summarized them in a paper published in the 2012 *Annual Review of Neuroscience*. They explained that the a few main parts of the brain are consistently activated when we experience both pain and empathy—mainly the anterior insula (AI) and dorsal-anterior/anterior-midcingulate cortex (dACC/aMCC), which are shown in Figure 8.1. In essence, the AI and dACC/aMCC seem to activate when we feel another's pain in our own body. What is also important to note in this image is that there are other parts of the brain that deal with cognition. These parts of the brain are indicating that an understanding, and perhaps even cognitive reappraisal training, may be helpful to identify that the pain being felt in your body (that may belong to another) is not yours. Findings similar to Bernhardt and Singer (2012) were also affirmed by Eisenberger (2012).

To further unpack what I am describing, I'll share an example. One empathy study enrolled females and their romantic partners (Singer et al., 2006). They asked each woman to lie down in a brain scanner with her romantic partner sitting by her side. The woman's hand was then painfully shocked.

Figure 8.1 Regions of the brain activated during pain and empathy.

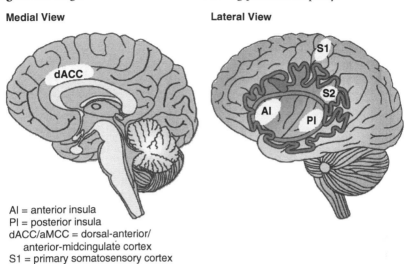

Medial View   Lateral View

AI = anterior insula
PI = posterior insula
dACC/aMCC = dorsal-anterior/
    anterior-midcingulate cortex
S1 = primary somatosensory cortex
S2 = secondary somatosensory cortex

While still inside the brain scanner, researchers shocked the hand of her part-ner while the woman watched. Sure enough, the same areas of the brain were activated when the women felt the pain as when they watched their partners get shocked. Sometimes our mirror neurons do not kick in, however. One study (Singer et al., 2006) found that men, in particular, are less likely to have empathy for someone who behaved unfairly. In fact, the areas of the brain activated for these men indicated a desire for revenge instead of empathy.

Let's bring Jess back to illustrate this key point. Sometimes Jess sits near homeless men and women while she's on the bus. They could use a shower. Sometimes they incoherently mumble to themselves, and they're likely hun-gry and thirsty. Clearly they could use help, but Jess and her fellow passengers don't offer any assistance. Why doesn't Jess feel moved to help them? Recent brain-imaging studies point out that we don't feel empathy for people in our outgroup or outside of our "inner circle." We are more likely to experience empathy for people who are similar to us or people who we believe are worthy of our empathy (Batson, Van Lange, Ahmad, & Lishner, 2007; Decety & Ickes, 2009). Princeton researcher Susan Fiske and colleagues (Fiske, Taylor, Etcoff, & Laufer, 1979) delved more into this concept of empathy toward an ingroup versus an outgroup. In later work, she and colleagues discovered that sometimes people don't experience empathic joy if they don't think another should be happy. In other words, if I see someone happy but don't believe he should be happy, I may not feel happiness (Cikara & Fiske, 2011). Harris and Fiske (2006) explain that in order to feel empathy for another—whether it is for positive or negative experiences—we have to recognize that the other is fully human (Batson & Ahmad, 2009; Chiao & Mathur, 2010; Cikara & Fiske, 2011; Stephan & Finlay, 1999). That seems obvious, right? Shouldn't we recognize *all* humans as humans?

Surprisingly, however, not all humans recognize all other human beings as human. Brain-imaging studies show that we often do not feel empathy for poor people, homeless people, and drug addicts. We don't recognize them as humans with bodies, brains, minds, and feelings—we dehumanize them. Depending on who we are, we may objectify people who fall into certain stereotypes (Chiao & Mathur, 2010). Wealthy people, entrepreneurial Asians, and even "nontraditional women" (women who are professionals, lesbians, feminists, or seductresses) can be seen as objects. When people become objects in the human mind, the empathy area of the brain does not appear to activate (Saarela et al., 2007; Stephen & Finley, 1999). When people envy another, the empathy area of the brain doesn't appear to activate (Takahashi et al., 2009). When the empathy area of the brain is not activated, it's tough to offer compassion.

Take a moment and consider whether or not you feel empathy for the homeless. Perhaps you do, and perhaps you don't. If you've never experienced homelessness and haven't had experiences interacting with the homeless population, your brain may recognize the homeless as outgroup members. Again, I'll point out that we are more likely to feel empathy when we can relate to the person or understand the person's situation (Caramazza et al., 2014). Therefore, if you have ever been homeless (or nearly homeless) or can in some way relate to or identify with being homeless, you are more likely able to be empathetic for that population. Thus, in order to enhance empathy, we must train a person to be able to relate to or identify with others.

When I teach the "Embracing Common Humanity" lesson (a lesson where I guide students in a practice of discovering the commonalities of the human experience) to my CCT students, I share this fascinating study from the University of Bologna. Researchers (Avenanti, Sirigu, & Aglioti, 2010) measured empathic responses to pain by studying the brain activity of participants who watched hands being poked with needles. When Caucasian subjects observed images of hands being poked with needles, the subjects responded with empathy. But they only presented empathic responses when they saw Caucasian hands being poked and did not have empathic responses when they saw African hands being poked. The African subjects, too, responded with empathy toward the African hands but not toward the Caucasian hands. There was an interesting twist on this study. Guess what happens when the subjects observed a purple hand being poked? Believe it or not, both the African and Caucasian subjects experienced empathy. What could this mean? Do we all relate to Smurf-like individuals? The Italian researchers concluded that we are born empathetic for all people but learn racial biases over time.

Let's consider what these studies imply; we make split-second judgments about people and either feel or do not feel empathetic toward them without even realizing it. This is how we condition our brains to work. This is why the "just like me" concept is so powerful (a concept where students discover that another is human, with a mind and a body, "just like me"). If we can train our minds to notice the commonalities we share with everyone, we can then feel empathetic and offer compassion. Think of what this could mean for creating peace within higher education and the world.

Now that we somewhat understand what may be happening in our brains when we experience empathy, let's examine the brain on compassion. Researchers are still not entirely clear about the neuroscience of compassion, because it is truly in its infancy. However, neuroscientists out of Emory University found that our brains' reward systems seem to be activated when we help others, which motivates altruistic behavior (Rilling et al., 2002). It feels good when we offer compassion.

Another important aspect of compassion is the body's physiological response, which we can attribute to our autonomic nervous system (ANS). The ANS has two main divisions, namely the sympathetic nervous system and the parasympathetic nervous system (see Chapter 6 for a refresher of the details). To illustrate what the ANS does, consider the following: Have you ever been afraid, nervous, or startled and felt your heart thumping as if it would bust out of your chest? (I know what you're thinking . . . "You bet my ANS I have!") You can thank your ANS for that. The ANS, which receives signals from our central nervous system (CNS), controls our blood flow and breathing. The sympathetic nervous system, which is a subsystem of the ANS, is responsible for the fight-or-flight reaction when we feel threatened.

The ANS subsystem also includes the parasympathetic nervous system, which allows our bodies to experience a completely different reaction when compassion kicks in. Instead of an increased heart rate and the "get me outta here!" feeling, we experience a decreased heart rate and an urge to approach and offer compassion (Keltner, 2004). You may have experienced this biological response when you visualized compassion earlier. It feels calming, warm, and light. It's the opposite of fight or flight.

Berkeley's Greater Good Science Center has been intently studying a specific part of the ANS known as the vagus nerve, which Berkeley researcher Dacher Keltner (2012) describes as the "caretaking nerve." *Vagus* is Latin for "wandering," and it's an appropriate label for this bundle of nerves that begins at the top of our spinal cords and runs throughout our bodies (Porges, Doussard-Roosevelt, & Maiti, 1994).

Only found in mammals, the vagus nerve attaches to neck muscles that allow us to turn our attention and orient our gazes toward others. It also helps us vocalize empathetic sounds, regulates the relationship between our heart rates and breath, and controls some of our digestive processes (Porges, 2011). These days, the vagus nerve is a hot topic in the world of compassion, because people with strong vagal tone are more apt to stay calm and offer compassion when faced with suffering (Van Kleef et al., 2008).

Training Self-Compassion

If we need empathy before we can offer compassion, the research we highlighted earlier seems discouraging. How can we ever offer compassion for everyone if we automatically, even unconciously, stereotype people and feel or don't feel empathetic? Is it possible to cultivate compassion for people in our outgroups or for people with whom we don't identify? How could we teach students like Jessica to see all people as people? Is it even possible to train our minds to see everyone as "just like me"?

I'm happy to report that it appears to be possible to cultivate (in essence, train) compassion for everyone. But first, you need to start practicing compassion for the most important person—yourself. As we discussed, compassion is something we feel for others. When someone we know is suffering, we can feel that person's pain and we have a desire to alleviate that pain. What about if we are suffering? How should we react toward ourselves?

I believe one of the most important skills a college student can learn is how to practice self-compassion. Think of Jessica. Does she take the time to notice when she's overwhelmed? Does she take time to care for herself? No. She pushes on through her own suffering and it manifests in overwhelmedness, illness, and exhaustion. Self-compassion is a hot topic for psychology researchers, and more and more evidence indicates numerous benefits of self-compassion.

A study out of Duke University (Terry, Leary, & Mehta, 2012) showed that students entering college with high self-compassion levels experienced less difficulty with their transitions to college than those with low levels of self-compassion. These students who rated high in self-compassion experienced less homesickness, less depression, and higher satisfaction with their collegiate experiences.

Kristen Neff, a pioneer of self-compassion research and associate professor of human development, culture, and learning sciences at the University of Texas at Austin, has been researching self-compassion for several years. She (Neff, 2003a, 2003b) subdivides self-compassion into three components. The first is self-kindness; self-compassionate people are kind to themselves and accept their faults and failures without judgment. In Jessica's case, she might take a moment to breathe deeply and say kind words to herself instead of resorting to her usual negative self-talk.

Second is common humanity; self-compassionate people understand that no one is perfect and that everyone on the planet has faults and experiences suffering (Neff, 2003b, 2011b). Jessica could take time to remind herself that there are thousands of college students around the world who are working, taking classes, and feeling overwhelmed. This may comfort Jessica and remind her that she is not alone.

Third is mindfulness; self-compassionate people take an observatory and nonjudgmental approach to their thoughts instead of ruminating and obsessing over them. They also notice when they are suffering instead of blindly living through each day without noticing their own thoughts and feelings. Jessica would observe her physical and mental state of being and notice when she is feeling overwhelmed. Instead of pushing through that pain, she would be able to offer kindness to herself.

It's important to note that self-compassion differs from self-esteem. Research indicates that people with high self-compassion generally avoid narcissistic tendencies, whereas high self-esteem can positively correlate with narcissistic tendencies (Neff, 2011a). Let's take a step back and consider the self-esteem phenomenon. We can't really blame college students for having high self-esteem, can we? Parents have been taught to cultivate high self-esteem within their children. If you search "self-esteem and parenting" online, you'll get article upon article about how parents can develop their children's self-esteem. But there may be a problem with that; high self-esteem often creates an "I'm-better-than-you" attitude and can even foster aggression (Papps & O'Carroll, 1998).

Sure, high self-esteem may help Jessica feel confident and capable. It seemed great when she was student body president in high school and a straight-A student. But when Jessica started college and wasn't at the top of her class, her self-worth tumbled. She felt discouraged. She beat herself up about it. Jessica believed she was a failure.

Researchers from Duke, Wake Forest, and Louisiana State University (Leary, Tater, Adams, Allen, & Hancock, 2007) designed five different studies to learn more about the relationship between self-compassion and self-esteem, and they wanted to evaluate how self-compassionate people would react to unpleasant situations. For each study, undergraduates first took Kristen Neff's (2003a) Self-Compassion Scale, which determined whether or not the participant had high or low levels of self-compassion. For some of the studies, participants also took the Self-Esteem Inventory and/or Narcissistic Personality Inventory to evaluate their levels of self-esteem and/or narcissism.

In the first study, participants kept a log of the best or worst things that happened throughout their weeks. They rated how bad the events were and logged their reactions to the events. The second study looked at narcissism, self-esteem, and self-compassion levels to compare participants' reactions to the following hypothetical situations: (a) getting a bad grade; (b) not performing well at an athletic event and causing his or her team to lose; and (c) forgetting a line while performing on stage, bringing the entire show to a halt.

The third study asked students to introduce themselves into a video camera. Students were told that their introductions were going to be evaluated by someone in another room. Students were then handed the feedback in an envelope, which was randomly assigned as either positive or neutral. Students rated their feelings after they received the feedback. For the fourth study, participants had to finish the story, "Once upon a time there was a little bear . . . " Their stories were videotaped, and then the participants either rated their own videos or rated another's. Researchers wanted to see if levels of self-compassion affected how people rated themselves and others.

For all of those studies, the findings were consistent. No matter whether or not they had high self-esteem, people with self-compassion displayed more stable reactions to both positive and negative circumstances. They didn't harshly judge themselves. They took ownership for their mistakes and did not beat themselves up about them.

For the fifth and final study, researchers wanted to see if they could manipulate people into having self-compassion. They divided participants into four groups, and asked participants to write about negative events in their lives that involved failure, humiliation, and rejection. Researchers gave a self-compassion intervention to the participants in the first group by prompting them to list ways that others have experienced a similar event (which highlights their shared common humanity). Then they asked participants in group one to write kind paragraphs to themselves (an example of self-kindness or self-mentoring). Researchers induced the second group's participants experience with self-esteem by prompting them to write out all of their positive attributes and describe why the negative events were not their faults. The third group simply wrote out their feelings, and participants of the fourth group wrote about their negative events. At the end, researchers asked all participants to fill out surveys that rated their emotions, and they were asked to indicate whether or not they took ownership of the negative event.

The findings revealed that the students conditioned with self-compassion reported less negative feelings than the ones who did not receive the self-compassion intervention reported, even if they took responsibility for the failure. What I found most interesting and encouraging from this study was that the self-compassion intervention greatly affected those who had been rated with low self-compassion prior to the study. This shows that a very simple exercise can create major changes.

When I teach self-compassion in my classes and workshops, a common concern arises with my students. They believe that if they don't beat themselves up for failures, they won't learn from their mistakes and will be unproductive or unmotivated to perform. Research, however, indicates quite the opposite. One study (Sirois, 2013) found that self-compassion was negatively associated with procrastination. In other words, low levels of self-compassion correlated to more procrastination, and high levels of self-compassion correlated to less procrastination.

I hypothesize Jessica's college experience would have been much smoother and less turbulent if she had learned how to develop self-compassion during her freshman year. She would have felt comfort in knowing that she was surrounded by fellow students who were going through stressful experiences. Jessica would have noticed when she was feeling tired or anxious, and she could have countered those feelings with self-compassion. Jessica would have procrastinated less and would have been more productive.

Research shows that simple self-compassion interventions can positively impact our lives, but what about widening our circle to include acts of compassion for others? How can we cultivate compassion so that it extends to everyone around us?

Training Compassion

"Compassion is a muscle that gets stronger with use" is a quote generally attributed to Mahatma Gandhi. We have research to back up Gandhi's claim. European researchers (Klimecki, Leiberg, Lamm, & Singer, 2013) were curious to see if compassion training can, indeed, cultivate compassion. They conducted a study using two groups of women (about 30 in each group) who received two different types of rigorous brain training. One of the groups attended a daylong loving-kindness meditation (LKM) course. The researchers called that the "compassion training group." The other group took a daylong memory-training course, and they were called the "memory control group."

The researchers created a new kind of measure, a socio-affective video task, to find out if patients in either group had an increase or decrease in empathy, positive feelings, and negative feelings. The subjects watched two types of emotion-evoking videos before their brain-training courses. One set of videos showed people that were in distressing situations (considered high emotion), and the other set of videos depicted people doing mundane, everyday tasks (considered low emotion). After watching the videos, the participants were asked to rate their empathy, positive feelings, and negative feelings on a scale. Subjects watched the videos before their brain-training sessions and also following their brain training. The researchers then collected the data from the self-reports and also conducted functional magnetic resonance images (fMRI) to observe what was happening in their brains. Participants who received compassion training had significant increases in positive feelings for both high- and low-emotion videos, and they had increased empathy for the low-emotion videos. The memory control group did not show the same results.

The researchers uncovered something else that indicates that even short and simple compassion training works. To validate their measure, they performed brain scans on someone who has been practicing LKM more than 35 years. Their research indicated that the longtime practitioner had similar brain activity as the participants in the compassion-training group, who had only learned LKM over one day. (See www.contemplativemind.org/practices/tree/loving-kindness for an example of the LKM practice.) This tells me that a little bit of training can go a long way.

It seems as if it's possible to train our minds to be more compassionate. But why should we? If I'm Jessica, I might say, "Sure, compassion seems awesome. It's nice to help other people. But what's in it for me?" A 2008 study by University of North Carolina at Chapel Hill researcher Barbara Fredrickson and colleagues looked at the benefits of directing LKM toward self and others over a nine-week period (Fredrickson, Cohn, Coffey, Pek, & Finkel, 2008). She was interested to see if LKM would affect their levels of positive emotions.

Frederickson's subjects were professionals at an IT services company. One hundred and two professionals received an LKM intervention that consisted of six separate group sessions lasting an hour each. They also received CDs with guided meditations and were instructed to follow them five times per week. One hundred other participants were put in a wait-list control group. The subjects who received the LKM intervention had greater experiences of positive emotions like love, joy, contentment, gratitude, pride, hope, interest, amusement, and awe. Even two weeks after the conclusion of the study, subjects experienced the same positive-emotion results. Imagine working at a company where employees often felt joy, love, hope, and gratitude. LKM sounds like the formula for high retention rates and highly motivated employees.

Compassion can also be linked to improved health. Most of us have experienced the negative effects of stress: sleepless nights, fatigue, muscle tension, headaches, and depression (Mayo Clinic, 2013). Compassion seems to buffer the effects of stress. Researchers evaluating stress levels of their subjects often measure cortisol, the hormone released in response to stress. Increased cortisol levels contribute to a myriad of health problems from weight gain to bone loss, and research shows that compassion meditations can be linked to a reduction in cortisol levels (Pace et al., 2008).

Speaking of stress, many of my students sign up to take my CCT course because they experience "compassion fatigue" (Boscarino, Figley, & Adams, 2004). They are surrounded by suffering, whether at work or at home. These demands create overwhelmedness and burnout, and it happens across several professions, including education (Adams, Boscarino, & Figley, 2006). It's important to realize that from a neuroscience perspective, this experience is actually more akin to "empathy fatigue" (Stebnicki, 2008). As you've read in this chapter, compassion fuels us. It can make us happier and healthier. Empathy, however, is known to drain us (MacKenzie, Poulin, & Seidman-Carlson, 2006). If we are only allowing ourselves to feel the pain of others (empathy), we become depleted of energy, and we feel overwhelmed (Goodman & Schorling, 2012). This is another reason why self-compassion and compassion training can benefit you and your students. It can help you avoid empathy fatigue.

University at Buffalo researcher Michael J. Poulin was curious about the associations among helping others, stress, and mortality rates. He and his team asked 846 subjects in the Detroit, Michigan, area if they had experienced a stressful event in the past year and if they had helped others or "provided tangible assistance to friends or family members." Poulin kept track of whether or not subjects died over the following five years through monitoring obituaries and state death records. The results of this study blow my mind. Stressful events did not predict mortality. I repeat, stressful events did not predict mortality. What *did* predict mortality was whether or not the subject helped others (engaging in altruism). Those who had assisted friends or family members had reduced mortality rates, whether they had experienced stressful events or not (Poulin, Brown, Dillard, & Smith, 2013).

What does this mean for Jessica? By practicing compassion for others, she could go through stressful life events without suffering as much. Consider this question: What do you think will impact Jessica's health and longevity more: (a) understanding college-level math, or (b) knowing how to make altruism and compassion a part of her everyday life?

Hopefully, I've sold you by now on the benefits of compassion toward self and others. To review, you've learned the following:

- The definition of *compassion* and how it feels
- The concept of "just like me"
- The relationship between empathy and compassion
- That mirror neurons contribute to our ability to feel empathy

- That our brains sometimes stereotype and prevent us from feeling empathetic toward outgroup members
- The definition and benefits of *self-compassion*
- That we can train self-compassion and compassion
- The physical and psychological benefits of practicing compassion

Now it's time to get practical. When all is said and done, it doesn't matter if I've convinced you of the power of compassion. I believe the most important part of compassion is *action*. Therefore, the most important part of the compassion chapter of this book is . . . you guessed it: *action*.

Putting the Neuroscience of Compassion Into Action

Here are eight practical ways you can put the neuroscience of compassion into action in your daily work.

Lead by Example

Practice self-compassion and compassion for others. Start by paying attention to how you speak to yourself. Are you hard on yourself, or do you have an "I'm human and therefore make mistakes" type of approach? Notice how you feel and how you react to those feelings. Perhaps try speaking to yourself as if you are speaking to a friend. I highly recommend a self-compassion letter-writing exercise, which employs Neff's (2003a, 2003b) three components of self-compassion.

Check your example and presentation by asking yourself a series of questions. Are you showing your students that you care? Do you offer them compassion? Do you offer your fellow educators compassion? What about your community members? Are you viewing the world around you with a "just like me" attitude?

A fun compassion-prompting exercise you can try is to pick one compassionate act you will extend every day for one week. Your act can be compassionate (nonjudgmental) listening. Or perhaps you will put a $5 bill in your pocket and give it to the first person who might benefit from it. Or maybe you'll smile to everyone who comes within five feet of you. Be creative, and notice what happens when you start incorporating compassion into your daily life.

Foster a Compassionate Environment in Your Classroom

I teach compassion to students of all ages, and I spend most of my first class creating a safe and compassionate environment in my classroom. By fostering a compassionate atmosphere from the beginning, the students feel connected, safe, and ready to engage each time they enter my classroom. How do we do this? As a class, we discuss our class rules. I divide the class into groups of three or four and ask them to come up with rules that they think are important for creating a compassionate, comfortable, and safe learning environment. Some examples of the rules that we establish include the following:

- Confidentiality: Remember that this classroom is like Vegas (without the drinking and gambling). In other words: What happens here, stays here.
- Compassionate listening (also referred to as mindful listening): This means we listen without interrupting and without succumbing to the need that may arise to respond back. Believe it or not, many students, colleagues, and parents simply want to know that you hear them. They don't need us to always respond.
- Authenticity and honesty: I encourage my students to be themselves no matter what. I've found that compassion emerges when we are vulnerable to each other.

Incorporate Compassion Into Your Area of Expertise

Do you teach history? Can you include a lesson about how compassion curbed violence during a certain historical event? Do you teach science? Can you incorporate work from University of California, Berkeley's Greater Good Science Center or Stanford's Center for Compassion and Altruism Research and Education? Are you a professor of business? Can you introduce a case study of a social enterprise that succeeds financially and altruistically, helping our fellow man and/or our planet? Do students write papers for your class or cocurricular program? Can you assign papers that ask students to highlight compassion? How can you incorporate the previously mentioned strategies into your classroom and cocurricular activities or staff meetings?

If you assign books for your students or recommend titles for your colleagues to read, I highly recommend *Tattoos on the Heart: The Power of Boundless Compassion*, by Gregory Boyle (2010). Boyle worked as a pastor in one of the most violent and gang-ridden areas of Los Angeles. I guarantee that the stories of compassion that he shares in his book will profoundly impact you, your students, and anyone with whom you share it.

Bring a Compassion Cultivation Course to Your Campus

Stanford University's Center for Compassion and Altruism Research and Education has developed a meditation-based compassion cultivation program, and its benefits include increased mindfulness and happiness and decreased worry and emotional suppression (Jazaieri et al., 2013).

Stanford University's CCT is

> [an] eight-week course designed to develop the qualities of compassion, empathy, and kindness for oneself and others. The course, developed by a team of contemplative scholars, clinical psychologists, and researchers at Stanford University, combines traditional contemplative practices with contemporary psychology and scientific research on compassion. The training includes: mindfulness; daily meditation, visualization, and breathing practices to develop loving-kindness, empathy, and compassion; coursework; two-hour weekly classes that include lecture, discussion, and in-class listening and communication exercises with partners and small groups; assignments and real-world homework to help you practice compassionate thought and action. (Stanford School of Medicine, 2014)

Stanford CCT teachers are scattered around the world, and you can reach out to an instructor near you to see if it's possible to bring CCT to your campus. Visit ccare.stanford.edu/education/cct-staff/ for a directory of teachers.

Introduce COMPASSION IT Wristbands

You can make compassion front of mind by using reversible COMPASSION IT wristbands as a tool for introducing compassion and self-compassion in an easy-to-understand and tangible way. (Think Livestrong with a twist.) Start the day with the one side out and flip it to the other side once you "compassion it." Marilee J. Bresciani Ludvik gives her students COMPASSION IT wristbands upon conclusion of the compassionate part of her integrative inquiry course. People have self-reported how wearing the wristbands—even in student affairs department meetings or faculty department meetings— reminds them to rethink and select compassionate responses when feelings of anger and frustration arise. They employ compassionate self-talk when they feel they are not performing at their best at work or in their family lives. Students and faculty can join the COMPASSION IT movement and can begin incorporating compassion and self-compassion into their daily lives. COMPASSION IT also plans to create online educational modules and compassion curriculum for teachers to lead with their students (www .compassionit.com).

Lead Guided Compassion Exercises

As an instructor of any higher education course or a professional development activity, you, yourself, can lead simple exercises that can help your students view the world through compassionate lenses. Refer to Chapter 10 of this book to find out how to skillfully fold these practices and ideas into your curriculum.

Encourage Volunteerism or Service-Learning

Most universities provide opportunities for students to give back to their communities and world through volunteering, fund-raising, or service-learning courses. As was mentioned in the introduction, engagement in service-learning is a high-impact activity. Find out how you and your students can get involved. You can also create ways to incorporate compassion into your class or staff development by coordinating field trips to local homeless shelters, retirement homes, or neighborhoods that could use some tender, loving care. Often, we believe that we need to travel abroad to see true suffering and make a great impact. This is not the case. We can find people who are suffering and need our help in our own backyards.

Sign the Charter for Compassion

The Charter for Compassion is a pledge to live and behave compassionately, and it is a call to action that has been signed by more than 100,000 people around the world. Visit www.charterforcompassion.org if you are interested.

Consider Jess, our motivated, overachieving, hardworking, over-stressed San Diego State senior. Will she enter the workplace upon graduation equipped with skills to help her navigate the turbulence of life? Will she be kind to herself when she faces adversity? Will she seek out opportunities to help others? Will she take time to be mindful of her surroundings and notice the suffering of others?

Because Jessica is a volunteer for COMPASSION IT, I hope that I can help her hone these skills over the next few months. I doubt that she has learned these skills from her classroom or cocurricular experiences, so I'll gladly and gratefully take on this responsibility.

I invite you to take a moment and imagine what could happen if we infused our global society with college graduates who believed each person was "just like me." Jess and other students who learn how to practice self-compassion and compassion for others will not only be primed for the real world; they will *change* our real world.

Editor's Summary Points and Questions to Consider

1. Neuroscience research indicates that our brains contain mirror neurons that allow every human being to understand another's

pain and suffering as well as joy and happiness. How might you refine the way you educate (either in the classroom or through the cocurricular) students, faculty, administrators, or community members to increase the awareness of these neuroscience findings?

2. Neuroscience research shows us that the presence of mirror neurons means that we can all (apart from those with particular diagnoses) practice empathy and compassion. The practice of compassion can allow every educator and student to feel another's pain and suffering while avoiding burnout. How might you refine the way you educate and train students, faculty, administrators, or community members to increase the awareness of these neuroscience findings?

3. We can train/cultivate both self-compassion and compassion. Compassion training can be incorporated into classroom, out-of-classroom, and staff professional environments. How might you add or refine compassion training for students, faculty, administrators, or community members?

4. Engaging in compassion may reduce stereotyping and increase openness to diverse peoples and ideas. How might you add or refine compassion training for students, faculty, administrators, or community members?

References

Adams, R., Boscarino, J., & Figley, C. (2006). Compassion fatigue and psychological distress among social workers: A validation study. *American Journal of Orthopsychiatry, 76*(1), 103–108.

The American freshman: National norms fall 2010. (2011, January). Retrieved from www.heri.ucla.edu/PDFs/pubs/briefs/HERI_ResearchBrief_Norms2010.pdf

Avenanti, A., Sirigu, A., & Aglioti, S. (2010). Racial bias reduces empathic sensorimotor resonance with other-race pain. *Current Biology, 20*(11), 1018–1022.

Batson, C., & Ahmad, N. (2009). Using empathy to improve intergroup attitudes and relations. *Social Issues and Policy Review, 3*(1), 141–177.

Batson, C., Van Lange, P., Ahmad, N., & Lishner, D. (2007). Altruism and helping behavior. In M. Hogg & J. Cooper (Eds.), *The SAGE handbook of social psychology: Concise student edition* (pp. 241–259). London, UK: Sage.

Bernhardt, B., & Singer, T. (2012). The neural basis of empathy. *Annual Review of Neuroscience, 35*(1), 1–23.

Boscarino, J. A., Figley, C. R., & Adams, R. E. (2004). Compassion fatigue following the September 11 terrorist attacks: A study of secondary trauma among New

York City social workers. *International Journal of Emergency Mental Health, 6*(2), 57–66.

Boyle, (2010). *Tattoos on the heart: The power of boundless compassion.* New York, NY: Free Press.

Caramazza, A., Anzellotti, S., Strnad, L., & Lingnau, A. (2014). Embodied cognition and mirror neurons: A critical assessment. *Annual Review of Neuroscience, 37,* 1–15.

Chiao, J., & Mathur, V. (2010). Intergroup empathy: How does race affect empathic neural responses? *Current Biology, 20*(11), R478–R480.

Cikara, M., & Fiske, S. (2011). Bounded empathy: Neural responses to outgroup targets' (mis)fortunes. *Journal of Cognitive Neuroscience, 23*(12), 3791–3803.

Cohn, M. A., & Frederickson, B. L. (2010). In search of durable positive psychology interventions: Predictors and consequences of long-term positive behavior change. *Journal of Positive Psychology, 5*(5), 355–366.

Cohn, M. A., Frederickson, B. L., Stephanie, L., Mikels, J. A., & Conway, A.M. (2009). Happiness unpacked: Positive emotions increase life satisfaction by building resilience. *Emotion, 9*(3), 361–368.

Dalai Lama, & Cutler, H. C. (1998). *The art of happiness: A handbook for living.* New York, NY: Riverhead Books.

Darwin, C. (1871). *The descent of man, and selection in relation to sex.* Princeton, NJ: Princeton University Press.

Decety, J., & Ickes, W. (2009). *The social neuroscience of empathy.* Cambridge, MA: MIT Press.

Eisenberger, N. I. (2012). The pain of social disconnection: Examining the shared neural underpinnings of physical and social pain. *Nature Reviews Neuroscience, 13,* 421–434.

Fiske, S., Taylor, S., Etcoff, N., & Laufer, J. (1979). Imaging, empathy, and causal attribution. *Journal of Experimental Social Psychology, 15*(4), 356–377.

Fredrickson, B., Cohn, M., Coffey, K., Pek, J., & Finkel, S. (2008). Open hearts build lives: Positive emotions, induced through loving-kindness meditation, build consequential personal resources. *Journal of Personality and Social Psychology, 95*(5), 1045–1062.

Goodman, M., & Schorling, J. (2012). A mindfulness course decreases burnout and improves well-being among healthcare providers. *International Journal of Psychiatry in Medicine, 43*(2), 119–128.

Hall, L., & Woods, S. (2006). *The importance of similarity in empathic interaction.* Retrieved from www.irma-international.org/viewtitle/13138/

Harris, L., & Fiske, S. (2006). Dehumanizing the lowest of the low: Neuroimaging responses to extreme out-groups. *Psychological Science, 17*(10), 847–853.

Hoffman, S. G., Grossman, P., & Hinton, D. E. (2011). Loving-kindness and compassion meditation: Potential for psychological interventions. *Clinical Psychology Review, 31*(7), 1126–1132.

Iacoboni, M. (2009). Imitation, empathy, and mirror neurons. *Annual Review of Psychology, 60*(1), 653–670.

Jazaieri, H., Jinpa, G., McGonigal, K., Rosenberg, E., Finkelstein, J., Simon-Thomas, E., . . . Goldin, P. R. (2013). Enhancing compassion: A randomized controlled trial of a compassion cultivation training program. *Journal of Happiness Studies, 14*(4), 1113–1126.

Jazaieri, H., McGonigal, K., Jinpa, T., Doty, J., Gross, J., & Goldin, P. R. (2014). A randomized controlled trial of compassion cultivation training: Effects on mindfulness, affect, and emotion regulation. *Motivation and Emotion, 38*(1), 23–35.

Jinpa, G. T. (2010). *Compassion Cultivation Training Program (CCT Program): Instructor's manual.* Unpublished manuscript.

Keltner, D. (2004, March 1). *The compassionate instinct.* Retrieved from greatergood .berkeley.edu/article/item/the_compassionate_instinct

Keltner, D. (2012, July 31). *The compassionate species.* Retrieved from greatergood .berkeley.edu/article/item/the_compassionate_species

Klimecki, O., Leiberg, S., Lamm, C., & Singer, T. (2013). Functional neural plasticity and associated changes in positive affect after compassion training. *Cerebral Cortex, 23*(7), 1552–1561.

Leary, M., Tate, E., Adams, C., Allen, A., & Hancock, J. (2007). Self-compassion and reactions to unpleasant self-relevant events: The implications of treating oneself kindly. *Journal of Personality and Social Psychology, 92*(5), 887–904.

Mackenzie, C., Poulin, P., & Seidman-Carlson, R. (2006). A brief mindfulness-based stress reduction intervention for nurses and nurse aides. *Applied Nursing Research, 19*(2), 105–109.

Mayo Clinic. (2013, June 19). *Stress symptoms: Effects on your body and behavior.* Retrieved from www.mayoclinic.org/healthy-living/stress-management/in-depth/ stress-symptoms/art-20050987

Neff, K. (2003a). The development and validation of a scale to measure self-compassion. *Self and Identity, 2*(3), 223–250.

Neff, K. (2003b). Self-compassion: An alternative conceptualization of a healthy attitude toward oneself. *Self and Identity, 2*(2), 85–101.

Neff, K. (2011a). Self-compassion, self-esteem, and well-being. *Social and Personality Psychology Compass, 5*(1), 1–12.

Neff, K. (2011b). *Self-compassion: The proven power of being kind to yourself.* New York, NY: HarperCollins.

Neff, K., Kirkpatrick, K., & Rude, S. (2007). Self-compassion and adaptive psychological functioning. *Journal of Research in Personality, 41*(1), 139–154.

Neff, K., Rude, S., & Kirkpatrick, K. (2007). An examination of self-compassion in relation to positive psychological functioning and personality traits. *Journal of Research in Personality, 41*(4), 908–916.

Pace, T. W., Negi, L., Adame, D., Cole, S., Sivilli, T., Brown, T., . . . & Raison, C. (2008). Effect of compassion meditation on neuroendocrine, innate immune and behavioral responses to psychosocial stress. *Psychoneuroendocrinology, 34*(1), 87–98.

Papps, B., & O'Carroll, R. (1998). Extremes of self-esteem and narcissism and the experience and expression of anger and aggression. *Aggressive Behavior, 24*(6), 421–438.

Porges, S., Doussard-Roosevelt, J., & Maiti, A. (1994). Vagal tone and the physiological regulation of emotion. *Monographs of the Society for Research in Child Development, 59*(2/3), 167–186.

Porges, S. W. (2011). *The polyvagal theory: Neurophysiological foundations of emotions, attachment, communication, and self-regulation* (The Norton Series on Interpersonal Neurobiology). New York, NY: W. W. Norton.

Poulin, M., Brown, S., Dillard, A., & Smith, D. (2013). Giving to others and the association between stress and mortality. *American Journal of Public Health, 103*(9), 1649–1655.

Rilling, J., Gutman, D., Zeh, T., Pagnoni, G., Berns, G., & Kilts, C. D. (2002). A neural basis for social cooperation. *Neuron, 35*(2), 395–405.

Rizzolatti, G., & Craighero, L. (2004). The mirror-neuron system. *Annual Review of Neuroscience, 27*(1), 169–192.

Saarela, M., Hlushchuk, Y., Williams, A., Schürmann, M., Kalso, E., & Hari, R. (2007). The compassionate brain: Humans detect intensity of pain from another's face. *Cerebral Cortex, 17*(1), 230–237.

Singer T., Seymour, B., O'Doherty, J. P., Stephan, K. E., Dolan, R. J., & Frith, C. D. (2006). Empathic neural responses are modulated by the perceived fairness of others. *Nature, 439*(7075), 466–469.

Sirois, F. (2013). Procrastination and stress: Exploring the role of self-compassion. *Self and Identity, 13*(2), 128–145.

Stanford School of Medicine. (2014). *Compassion Cultivation Training (CCT)*. Retrieved from ccare.stanford.edu/cct-details

Stebnicki, M. (2008). *Empathy fatigue healing the mind, body, and spirit of professional counselors*. New York, NY: Springer.

Stephan, W., & Finlay, K. (1999). The role of empathy in improving intergroup relations. *Journal of Social Issues, 55*(4), 729–743.

Stotland, E., Mathews, K. E., Sherman, S. E., Hansson, R. O., & Richardson, B. Z. (1978). *Empathy, fantasy and helping*. Beverly Hills, CA: Sage.

Takahashi, H., Kato, M., Matsuura, M., Mobbs, D., Suhara, T., & Okubo, Y. (2009). When your gain is my pain and your pain is my gain: Neural correlates of envy and schadenfreude. *Science, 323*(5916), 937–939.

Terry, M., Leary, M., & Mehta, S. (2012). Self-compassion as a buffer against homesickness, depression, and dissatisfaction in the transition to college. *Self and Identity, 12*(3), 278–290.

Van Kleef, G., Oveis, C., van der Löwe, I., LuoKogan, A., Goetz, J., & Keltner, D. (2008). Power, distress, and compassion: Turning a blind eye to the suffering of others. *Psychological Science, 19*(12), 1315–1322.

BALANCE BEGETS INTEGRATION

Exploring the Importance of Sleep, Movement, and Nature

Bruce Bekkar

We need balance. We need to balance our inner life with our outer life. Nature is always sitting there waiting to help us, but we have to do the work. Nature is probably the greatest teacher that we'll ever have . . . the Earth and nature.

—Dave Davies (www.brainyquote.com/search_results.html)

I received an e-mail containing my physician's work schedule for August while sitting in my office one late Friday afternoon in June 2005. To my dismay, it contained four overnight assignments. Three of them consisted of duty in the hospital covering the obstetrics service from 6 p.m. to 8 a.m the following morning after a full day in the office. I had asked for no such shifts, having learned over several years that 24-hour shifts ruined my sleep for at least three days and made me anxious, irritable, and less productive. It was often possible to trade assignments with other doctors in my department, but there was never a guarantee; four night calls were going to be tough to get rid of. I felt myself tensing up, thinking about the coming work month.

Insomniac Doc

I first learned of my insomnia 10 years prior, around my fortieth birthday. In the early stages, troubled sleep was only occasional, and I fell back into a normal pattern with little difficulty. However, for many years, despite strictly adhering to all the sleep hygiene recommendations (i.e., avoiding late-night caffeine and alcohol, having regular sleep times, keeping my bedroom cool and dark) and even taking sleep medications, I rarely slept through the night. It was common for me to lie awake for hours many times a week and arrive at work already exhausted. The problem steadily worsened and ballooned into a major focus of my life.

It might have been smarter for me to avoid a specialty like obstetrics that involved lots of night work, given my father's history of sleep problems. It also didn't help that my choice of specialty required lots of critical decision making at all hours. However, until the problem began, I tolerated my work schedule with no more difficulty than anyone else in my group. I had no idea what was on the horizon.

I wanted to know more as my insomnia worsened. I discovered that millions of Americans had the same problem. There were some identifiable causes—certain medications, dietary habits, anxiety, depression—but most cases were simply the result of inherently fragile sleep patterns. I learned of research showing the health effects of chronic sleep difficulties— major problems like obesity, heart disease, and diabetes (Harding & Feldman, 2008). I now had reason to attack the problem from all angles. One promising approach to both reduce the severity of my insomnia and to help deal with its impacts was to improve the "balance" in my life.

Living a balanced life is a foreign concept to many physicians. Our personal expectations and work demands often create the opposite lifestyle—one consistently overloaded with work and pressure to perform, and lacking in personal or family time. We trade the gratitude of our patients and society and some financial reward for a large negative impact on our well-being and physical health. Evidence for this is seen in numerous studies documenting physician stress, burnout, and unhappiness—despite the fact that virtually all of us feel very fortunate to practice medicine.

Imbalance is certainly not unique to doctors. It applies to many busy professionals; those caring for children or loved ones; and, in the context of this book, overloaded college and university students, professors, and administrative personnel. We all run the risks of prolonged stress: more serious health problems, personal relationships in crisis, premature aging, and worsening of conditions like insomnia. I discovered that I was just another in a (very) long list of people suffering from chronic off-balance living.

So, how does one balance a life? In general terms, the idea essentially boils down to treating ourselves like human beings with not only an intellectual/academic/work life but also a physical body and emotional/interpersonal needs. There are as many definitions and recommendations as there are therapists, coaches, and other practitioners in the burgeoning world of work–life balance.

The approach I took included, at the recommendation of my own doctor, a visit with a sleep medicine specialist. After concluding that I had already done all I could to maximize my sleep, he proceeded to immediately stop my night-shift work. It was both difficult to accept and a huge relief. I had limits, and he explained that it made no sense to continue ignoring them after 10 years. Changing my work hours improved what sleep I did get and created time for more regular exercise and creative outlets. I felt a huge weight lift off my shoulders, and my energy, relationships, and overall mood rebounded.

Moving toward this way of living was clearly paying off, but it also left the doctor in me with questions. What does balance mean in the body? If my body craved balance, did my brain as well? For example, does sitting most of the day in front of a computer or staring at a mobile device's screen use the brain in an optimal way? As important, is balance of either the brain or body, or both, the ultimate goal? Could there be a more optimal relationship between them? Perhaps there was a different way to look at this.

Although the definitive answers to most questions about the brain aren't yet determined, recent studies begin to paint a picture. My own search for understanding goes back—way back—to our collective beginnings as a species.

Evolution and the Brain

We discussed some key evolutionary brain details in Chapter 6 of this book; I share reminders here in order to shape the conversation of our search for balance. Around 200 million years ago, early mammals first developed a cerebral cortex, an outer layer of the brain that enabled the creation, remembering, and sharing of new behaviors—a tremendous survival advantage (Carter, 2014; Kaku, 2014; Kurzweil, 2012; Newberg & Waldman, 2009; Siegel, 2012). The next major leap occurred 66 million years ago with the Cretaceous extinction event, in which an estimated 75% of all animal and plant life on Earth disappeared. This opened up opportunities for the surviving mammals to rapidly evolve, (Carter, 2014; Jablonski & Chaloner, 1994), a club we're fortunate our predecessors successfully joined.

Our early bipedal human ancestors first began to use stone tools about two million years ago (Pollan, 2013). This coincided with a period of rapid growth of the cortex and the appearance of what we know as a forehead, to accommodate the increasing size of the brain. The brain grew in structural complexity as well, with particular areas like the temporal lobes and the neocortex outpacing others (Figure 9.1) (see en.wikipedia.org/wiki/Human_evolution; see also Carter, 2014; Kaku, 2014; Siegel, 2012). This

Figure 9.1 Reptilian, limbic, and neocortex portions of the brain in comparison to regions of the brain.

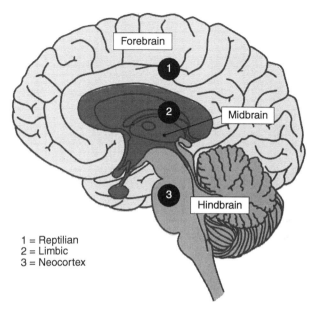

1 = Reptilian
2 = Limbic
3 = Neocortex

disproportionate growth enabled the development of language and complex decision-making abilities perhaps needed by individuals in newly emerging societies (see en.wikipedia.org/wiki/Human_evolution; see also Carter, 2014; Kaku, 2014; Siegel, 2012).

It is probably not coincidental that the control of fire and development of cooking happened in this same narrow slice of geological time, greatly reducing the time our ancestors required to absorb calories from food (Pollan, 2013). It has been estimated that primates devoted half their waking hours—and therefore lots of their energy—to the simple act of chewing prior to the use of fire (Pollan, 2013). Notably, later species like *Homo erectus*, in comparison, had smaller jaws, smaller teeth, smaller guts, and much larger brains (Pollan, 2013, pp. 81–82; Wrangham, 2009).

Cooked food, then, seems to have met the high caloric demands of that bigger brain. Brains are voracious eaters, consuming 20% of our energy at rest, despite constituting only 2.5% of our total weight. One theory suggests that cooked food, with its more easily "digestible energy, unleashed the brain's potential. Cooking, in other words ennobled us, putting us on the path to philosophy and music" (Pollan, 2013, p. 129).

Our brains, however, are not defined—structurally or otherwise—by the cerebral cortex alone (refer to Chapter 1 for a refresher on brain parts and

Figure 9.2 Hindbrain and its components.

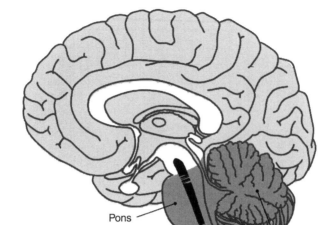

functions). This organ's evolutionary process has been somewhat simplistically conceptualized as occurring in three stages: the primitive hindbrain emerged first, followed by the midbrain, and then crowned by the neocortex or forebrain. Our adaptive abilities, from feeding ourselves to dealing with progressively complex social interactions, to imagining and thus preparing for future situations, took a quantum leap forward as each successive layer was added. Structures within the primitive hindbrain are illustrated in Figure 9.2.

The brain's development began with the brain stem and cerebellum. The oldest part of our central nervous system (which dates back 500 million years) controls basic necessities like breathing and the beating of our heart. This portion of the hindbrain also enables behaviors like mating, fighting, and territoriality, required for the survival of our reptilian, relatively asocial predecessors (Carter, 2014; Kaku, 2014). Further neural growth and evolution led to the appearance of additional structures atop this root complex over succeeding millennia.

A portion of the limbic system resides in the midbrain (see Figure 9.3). The limbic system includes the hippocampus, amygdala, and thalamus (Carter, 2014). These specialized neuronal structures and others within the midbrain took over various physiologic maintenance functions like controlling body temperature and circadian rhythm. They also gave rise to an

Figure 9.3 The limbic system.

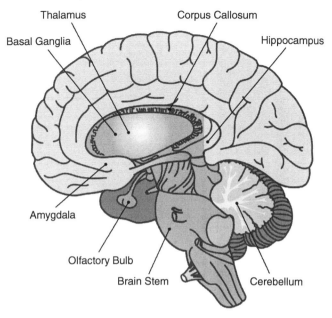

amazing sense-ability for interpreting and interacting with others that we term *emotions*. The hippocampus is also where long-term memories are formed—another key for successful social interaction and therefore survival (Carter, 2014). Note the midbrain structures (thalamus, hippocampus, amygdala) above the hindbrain when examining Figure 9.3.

Finally, the forebrain (also known as the cap or cortex) developed and grew, bringing with it improvements in sensory processing and a great enhancement in cognitive abilities. The convoluted cortex, though only a few millimeters thick, has so much surface area that it makes up 80% of the brain's mass and contains roughly 20% of the brain's nearly 90 billion neurons (Herculano-Houzel, 2013; Kaku, 2014).

Two concepts are crucial to fully understand the human brain. First, as evolution crafted new regions, it also improved those parts that preceded it, leading to a functionally smarter combination. This is similar to remodeling a home, where the existing structure is updated at the same time a second story is added; the result is better on all levels.

Second, all areas of the brain are vastly interconnected and interdependent, working cooperatively in the name of survival (Kaku, 2014). For example, when confronted by a bear, our brain harnesses the shortest path to a response. We react emotionally, from our midbrain, because that gut reaction gets us out of there faster than conscious reasoning (cortical processing).

Think of how well our species would have bested mortal threats if we stopped to think twice!

Evolution's optimization of function can also be appreciated in how our conscious awareness is kept free of extraneous information. This was evident one summer Sunday while I rode a beach cruiser along the boardwalk in Venice Beach, California. My brain harnessed lots of complex pathways so I could simultaneously balance the bike; negotiate the twisty, uneven path; and avoid the sea of other riders—all with minimal intrusion on my conscious awareness. It's a good thing too, because the bizarre variety of humans who inhabit that location is pretty distracting.

This all suggests that the brain evolved as a complex, integrated organ where all inputs, and thus all structures, have purpose. How, then does this discussion of the brain's evolution relate to the concept of balance? More simply, do we use this magical instrument (the brain) in the way it was intended?

It's a Question of Blood Flow

We have learned much about how we use our brains from contemporary imaging technologies that follow the flow of blood. The functional magnetic resonance image (fMRI) (described in Chapter 1) revolutionized our understanding in the 1990s as it followed blood-borne oxygen moving through the brain—a good surrogate of neural activity (Kaku, 2014).

Other imaging modalities, as mentioned in Chapter 1, have been developed, and although none are perfect, a picture of the brain in action is emerging. We learned previously that the prefrontal cortex is the region that processes most rational thought and imagines and plans for the future. These new imaging data show that thoughts do not just involve the prefrontal cortex but travel across the brain in complex ways. The theory of embodied cognition even suggests that thoughts live beyond our minds, involving our bodies and the surrounding environment (Aschwanden, 2013; Glenberg, 2010). However, the growing understanding about these neural complexities doesn't change the basic concept that is primarily anchored in the prefrontal cortex (Kaku, 2014; Siegel, 2012; Zull, 2011).

When we examine our modern way of work—which also describes the daily activities of many students, faculty, and administrators—the complex, dynamic process of thinking, of creativity, learning, and problem solving, is currently organized to occur in a most sedentary way. We try to extract the best from our brains while immobile, sitting still for hours at a time except for some measured finger movements on a keyboard. We are largely indoors and isolated. Zull's (2011) and Carey's (2014) recent compilations of research told us that this is not the best way the brain learns. There is much more to uncover here.

We can look back 250,000 years to the emergence of *Homo sapiens* for a historical context and contrast of human activity. Our predecessors lived as as hunter-gatherers from then until the advent of modern agriculture. They spent most of each day engaged in gathering edible plants and capturing prey—a very active, physical way of living. It wasn't until about 10,000 years ago that modern agriculture became widespread and replaced the need for much of this hunting-gathering (Kaku, 2014; Pollan, 2013). Furthermore, it's true that growing domesticated crops and raising livestock also involved lots of daily physical work. So-called subsistence agriculture—farming for our own consumption—was how food ended up on the table until well into the twentieth century. Stopping at the local grocery store for premade lasagna came much later.

It appears that from 250,000 years ago until about 10,000 years ago, we solved our most pressing daily problem—feeding ourselves—while on our feet. It's likely that much of our creativity was needed for this task as well. This means that for at least 96% of our time on Earth, we humans didn't sit much until we were done—physically and mentally—for the day. It's not a big leap, then, to propose that natural selection favored individuals who were wired to think on their feet. Those whose brains worked best while their bodies were in motion simply had more to eat and were therefore more likely to pass on their genes (Pollan, 2013). (See Chapter 7 for more about fostering creativity.)

Modern life couldn't stray much further from the learned wisdom of our collective history; today's worker/professor/student is often an inactive body propping up a partially used mind. In a cruel twist, "progress" brought us so-called fast food—a cheap, dense source of calories (which evolution programed us to crave) so we both move less and ingest too much (Pollan, 2013). Our days relegated to a chair, too many of us have taken on its shape and resulting immobility. No wonder we feel such a strong urge to find balance.

So, if most of the time we are sedentary, almost exclusively using our prefrontal cortex, perhaps we're ignoring much of the sophisticated neural integration hard-won by evolution. Certainly, our bodies suffer health consequences when we mistreat them (Chapter 6 addresses much of this). Are we prone to an overuse injury of various groups of neurons—a carpal tunnel of the cortex? It's not difficult to imagine that, at a minimum, some synaptic fatigue could result if we were persistently trying to extract a function not intended by the mind's form.

McGonigal (2013) attested in her book that indeed when it comes to the synapses and neurotransmitters involved in exerting willpower we can exhaust ourselves in applying the use of willpower. We later discover, in our exhaustion, that we have engaged in behavior that contradicts what our will-power was intending to create. So it is possible that we could exhaust our thinking neurons as well. The Mayo Clinic (2013) certainly thinks so.

How is it that we believe we think differently and perhaps better when we move around and use more of our minds? Does movement or engagement in a creative or pleasurable outlet reduce the stress that too much thinking can cause, as argued by the National Institute on Aging (2012) and others (Chaput, Drapeau, Poirier, Teasdale, & Tremblay, 2008; Jabr, 2012; Olson, 2007)? Or is lots of thinking energizing, rather than exhausting, only if it is pleasurable (Chambers, Bridge, & Jones, 2009)?

As mentioned in Carey's (2014) compilation of research that suggests students move around in order to learn best, MRIs would certainly show that brain blood flow—and thus neural activity—changes when we're no longer sitting still. Maybe the answer is just that simple. I confess to being more a lumper than a splitter; that is, I look for one answer to several questions. In this case, there are a number of seemingly unrelated lines of evidence that point, at least, in the same direction. Let's look at some case studies to gain clarity.

Why Google Has Ping-Pong Tables in Its Headquarters

It is well known that tech companies, from giants like Google to small start-ups, have play areas in the midst of their offices. Aside from being appealing to job applicants, there seems to be a belief that shooting some hoops, playing video games, or going a few rounds of Ping-Pong doesn't harm worker productivity, it actually promotes it.

In his 2008 TED talk, Stuart Brown, a psychiatrist and founder of the Institute for Play in Carmel Valley, California, reported research showing that using our hands for play or fixing things is directly related to problem-solving ability. Employers like the California Institute of Technology's Jet Propulsion Lab (JLP) and the National Aeronatuics and Space Administration (NASA) and NASA specifically hire people with this trait. Brown added that play deprivation in animal models correlates with a reduction in brain development, while engaging in play increases inquiry in babies and pre-schoolers (Butler & Markman, 2012; Cook, Goodman, & Schulz, 2011; Gopnik, 2012; Schulz, 2012).

Exercise also changes blood flow in the brain. Stanford researchers examined whether exercise impacts creativity and found that even a brief period of treadmill walking had a positive effect on a subject's ability to come up with novel ideas. This benefit also lingered after the walk was over. The study concluded that the effect is acute and not due to permanent changes in brain activity or structure. The cause, however, is unknown (Oppezzo & Schwartz,

2014). Other researchers have also found positive correlations with regular exercise and improved executive functions (Best, 2010; Godman, 2014; Ratey & Hagerman, 2008).

Tony Schwartz (2013), an author and a business consultant, wrote recently in the *New York Times* about research on renewal during the workday. Addressing the chronic fatigue and burnout common in today's eat-at-your-desk workplace, he referenced studies showing that workers who took more vacations, increased their sleep hours, or took daytime naps showed improved performance in measures like memory, reaction time, and job performance. Neuroscientist Daniel Levitin (2014), director of the Laboratory for Music Perception, Cognition and Expertise at McGill University, in a similar finding, reported recently that work breaks like taking a walk in nature or listening to music can hit the reset button on our brains, increasing our ability to refocus on demand and helping foster creativity. He also reported that taking naps was even better, demonstrating improved cognitive function and a reduction in fatigue (Meek, 2014; Thompson, 2012).

Another area of active research focuses on a practice known as mindfulness training, which begins with nonjudgmental awareness of emotions, sensations, and thoughts in the moment (Kerr, Sacchet, Lazar, Moore, & Jones, 2013). A recent review looked at the impact of mindfulness practice on people suffering from mental or physical problems and reported that chronically depressed patients had reduced rumination and better attention control. Social anxiety patients also showed decreased amygdala (emotional) responses, and those with chronic pain had increased attentional freedom (they weren't as constantly focused on their pain).

Recall that the brain has two dominant modes of attention (Chapters 2 and 3): one in which we are engaged in focused attention on one particular activity, called *the task-positive network*, and another, in which we experience no focused attention and the mind is wandering. This daydreaming mode is called the *task-negative network*. These two attentional networks operate like a seesaw in the brain: When one is active, the other is not.

So, a wide range of activities such as playing Ping-Pong (Croce & Horvat, 1992; Heber, 2005; Padnani, 2012; Pozen, 2012; Tarkan, 2012), walking in nature (Baer, 2014; Burkeman, 2013; Williams, 2012), taking a nap (Levitin, 2014), listening to music (Ciotti, 2014), or engaging in mindfulness practice all seem to enhance brain function, specifically in areas useful to learning like problem solving, creativity, attention, and memory (Konnikova, 2012). These shared varied activities seem to give the focused part of the prefrontal cortex some "downtime"—and beneficial effects accrue.

Many of us have experienced the benefits of this cortex downtime when we got a great idea, solved a problem, or remembered something important only *after* we stopped working. It might have happened to you while on a walk, or waking up from sleep, as Levitin's (2014) research shows; all may be effective practices for giving our prefrontal cortex a break. I notice this phenomenon often when I'm running. I live at the beach, and my runs (balance and spatial awareness courtesy of my hindbrain) frequently trigger pleasant memories (hippocampus and amygdala in the midbrain), my senses are flooded with beautiful sights and sounds in nature (sensory cortex), and I forget about work. Before I know it, an answer I wasn't trying to find comes to me. The only problem I have with this happy occurrence is creating a mnemonic good enough to remember my idea(s) once I get home. Also, coming up with that mnemonic is rather prefrontal, so I have to be careful not to trip over my feet.

How to Get More out of Our Brains Within Higher Education

It appears from this discussion that one idea to consider when applying neuroscience to the teaching–learning paradigm is that we can improve results by working with—rather than imposing some model on—the evolutionary wisdom of our bodies and brains. Specifically, as I have previously illustrated (see also Chapter 6), our physical selves benefit from consistent, whole-body workouts, and it's likely that our minds do too.

Just as important, we must appreciate that the mind and body grew up together, being used in concert—so we're seeking ways to mimic that idea. This approach sounds less like balance, where we are guessing how much of our day we should be engaged in focused attention and how much we could allow ourselves to reset through play, and more like integration. Integration of the whole body with the whole mind is likely to lead us to healthier ways of living and thus improved ways of using our minds. There is already work being done in this direction.

The notion of a flipped classroom (refer to the introduction to this volume) turns the typical passive information-sharing teaching experience into one of more integrated, active learning. Students help each other learn and use the class content (consumed before class) to solve problems and do practical work. This approach reinforces learning in a way that seems more in keeping with how the brain works. But what if we integrated even more of what we understand about the brain into higher education?

Learning is more than just retaining information to pass an exam a few days later. In a recent interview, Benedict Carey (2014), author of *How We Learn: The Surprising Truth About When, Where, and Why It Happens* and a science writer for the *New York Times*, suggested that varying studying locations is helpful. Instead of cramming for hours in the library or at the kitchen table, moving to a different locale from time to time helps the brain make stronger associations with the material and improves retention. The brain wants variation. It wants to move; it wants to take periodic breaks (Parker-Pope, 2014).

Tony Schwartz, a business consultant, advocates a radically different schedule for a workday that might be applicable to learning. Three focused 90-minute work segments (from research by Professor K. A. Ericsson and colleagues at Florida State University) with 30 to 90 minutes for renewal between—a total of only four and a half hours per day—can significantly increase productivity. Schwartz (2013) argued that perhaps the best way to get more done just may be to spend more time doing less. Where was this guy when I was in medical school?

What to do with those renewal breaks also deserves mention. A wide range of activities may be helpful in stimulating the brain functions we want in learning, as we have seen from the research presented in this chapter. Regularly making time for yoga, meditation, exercise, a walk around campus, or just taking a nap can reasonably be seen not as a distraction but an important part of a holistic experience that maximizes our capacity to learn and ultimately recall classroom lessons long after exams are over.

Ideas about how to employ the concept of whole body–mind learning are worthy of investigating, and much remains to be worked out. What if students were required to enroll in courses that invited them to incorporate prefrontal cortex downtime as described in this chapter? Within the education community, many different parties must interact from students to professors to various support staff. Although their roles differ, the rules for optimizing brain function remain the same. This means that professors and administrators, in their leadership roles, have an opportunity to model better learning behavior and help expand the teaching environment for the benefit of all. What would it look like if they were required to engage in prefrontal cortex downtime? Why not replace conference tables with Ping-Pong tables? How about requiring one-on-one meetings to include walks outdoors (weather and accessibility permitting of course)? What about simply requiring that all offices and conference rooms have windows and natural lighting to provide us with a brief nature holiday?

This chapter began with a personal story about a women's health doctor with a wicked case of insomnia. I wrote this chapter because my career has evolved from caring for patients to helping care for our planet; in particular, I'm seeking ways to remind people of how we are integrated into the whole of life on Earth. I believe we are too focused on our species and its recent history—as if the last 100 years were the entirety of our existence and all that matters. Clearly, that's not the case. We must learn to integrate our minds with our bodies to solve the global environmental crisis of today. Making better use of our entire brain and allowing more prefrontal cortex downtime might be part of the answer.

We are unlikely to make peace with one another and ourselves until we reconnect with our place as just one part of the living world. My bond with nature, particularly the ocean outside my door, reminds me of this every day; how to best share that with others is the challenge of my new career. I have a feeling that the answer will come to me one of these days while I'm on a run.

Or maybe I'll just sleep on it.

Editor's Summary Points and Questions to Consider

1. The evolution of our brain illustrates the complexities of how our brain was developed and how it best functions. What are some key ways you could incorporate that understanding in the design and delivery of in-class and out-of-class learning and development opportunities?
2. An "unbalanced" or unintegrated life is common to those in business, medical, and higher education professions. How might you, as a role model, improve your own life's structure and habits to benefit yourself and others?
3. This chapter discussed how providing "prefrontal cortex downtime" might benefit the outcomes for which we strive in higher education. How might your teaching, out-of-classroom programming, assessment of student learning and development, and other student interactions implement this research and suggested ideas?
4. How can your institution become a leader in applying a more integrated mind–body learning approach to the entire student experience in the classroom and out of the classroom?

References

Aschwanden, C. (2013, May 20). *Where do thoughts occur?* Retrieved from discover magazine.com/2013/june/12–where-do-thoughts-occur

Baer, D. (2014, August 10). *6 surprising ways nature improves your memory and productivity.* Retrieved from www.businessinsider.com/surprising-ways-nature-improves-your-memory-and-productivity-2014-8

Best, J. (2010). Effects of physical activity on children's executive function: Contributions of experimental research on aerobic exercise. *Developmental Review, 30*(4), 331–351.

Brown, S. (2008, May). *Play is more than just fun*. Retrieved from www.ted.com/talks/stuart_brown_says_play_is_more_than_fun_it_s_vital?language=en

Burkeman, O. (2013, March 17). *Even short engagements with nature boost productivity*. Retrieved from www.businessinsider.com/nature-boosts-productivity-2013-3

Butler, L. P., & Markman, E. M. (2012). Preschoolers use intentional and pedagogical cues to guide inductive inferences and exploration. *Child Development, 83*, 1416–1428.

Carey, B. (2014). *How we learn: The surprising truth about when, where, and why it happens*. New York, NY: Random House.

Carter, R. (2014). *The human brain book*. New York, NY: DK Publishing.

Chambers, E., Bridge, M., & Jones, D. (2009). Carbohydrate sensing in the human mouth: Effects on exercise performance and brain activity. *Journal of Physiology, 587*(8), 1779–1794.

Chaput, J., Drapeau, V., Poirier, P., Teasdale, N., & Tremblay, A. (2008). Glycemic instability and spontaneous energy intake: Association with knowledge-based work. *Psychosomatic Medicine, 70*(7), 797–804.

Ciotti, G. (2014, July 11). *How music affects your productivity: You might be rocking headphones while you read this—but does what's playing make you better at your job?* Retrieved from www.fastcompany.com/3032868/work-smart/how-music-affects-your-productivity

Cook, C., Goodman, N., & Schulz, L. E. (2011). Where science starts: Spontaneous experiments in preschoolers' exploratory play. *Cognition, 120*(3), 341–349.

Croce, R., & Horvat, M. (1992). Effects of reinforcement based exercise on fitness and work productivity in adults with mental retardation. *Adapted Physical Activity Quarterly, 9*(2), 148–178.

Glenberg, A. M. (2010). Embodiment as a unifying perspective for psychology. *Wiley Interdisciplinary Reviews: Cognitive Science, 1*(4), 586–596.

Godman, H. (2014, April 9). *Regular exercise changes the brain to improve memory, thinking skills*. Harvard Health Blog. Retrieved from www.health.harvard.edu/blog/regular-exercise-changes-brain-improve-memory-thinking-skills-201404097110

Gopnik, A. (2012). Scientific thinking in young children: Theoretical advances, empirical research and policy implications. *Science, 337*(6102), 1623–1627.

Harding, K., & Feldman, M. (2008). Sleep disorders and sleep deprivation: An unmet public health problem. *Journal of the American Academy of Child & Adolescent Psychiatry, 47*(4), 473–474.

Heber, D. (2005). *Health options: How nutrition and exercise can increase productivity and lower health care costs*. Retrieved from www.uclahealth.org/workfiles/documents/insights/UCLA_LOS_1005.pdf

Herculano-Houzel, S. (2013). *What is so special about the human brain?* TED Talks transcript. Retrieved from http://www.ted.com/talks/suzana_herculano_houzel_what_is_so_special_about_the_human_brain?language=en

Jablonski, D., & Chaloner, W. G. (1994). Extinctions in the fossil record (and discussion). *Philosophical Transactions of the Royal Society B: Biological Sciences,*

344(1307), 11–17. Retrieved from https://en.wikipedia.org/wiki/Cretaceous%E2%80%93Paleogene_extinction_event

Jabr, F. (2012, July 18). *Does thinking really hard burn more calories?* Retrieved from www.scientificamerican.com/article/thinking-hard-calories/

Kaku, M. (2014). *The future of the mind: The scientific quest to understand, enhance, and empower the mind.* New York, NY: Doubleday.

Kerr, C., Sacchet, M., Lazar, S., Moore, C., & Jones, S. (2013). Mindfulness starts with the body: Somatosensory attention and top-down modulation of cortical alpha rhythms in mindfulness meditation. *Frontiers in Human Neuroscience, 7,* 12–26.

Konnikova, M. (2012, December 15). *The power of concentration.* Retrieved from www.nytimes.com/2012/12/16/opinion/sunday/the-power-of-concentration.html?pagewanted=2&_r=0

Kurzweil, R. (2012). *How to create a mind: The secret of human thought revealed.* New York, NY: Penguin.

Levitin, D. J. (2014, August 9). Hit the reset button in your brain. *New York Times.* Retrieved from http://www.nytimes.com/2014/08/10/opinion/sunday/hit-the-reset-button-in-your-brain.html?_r=0

Mayo Clinic. (2013, February 27). *Symptoms fatigue.* Retrieved from www.mayoclinic.org/symptoms/fatigue/basics/definition/sym-20050894

McGonigal, K. (2013). *The willpower instinct: How self-control works, why it matters, and what you can do to get more of it.* New York, NY: Penguin.

Meek, T. (2014, June 5). *To be more productive at work, take a vacation—or a nap.* Retrieved from www.forbes.com/sites/delta/2014/06/05/to-be-more-productive-at-work-take-a-vacation-or-a-nap/

National Institute Aging. (2012). *Fatigue: More than being tired.* Retrieved from www.nia.nih.gov/health/publication/fatigue

Newberg, A., & Waldman, M. R. (2009). *How God changes your brain: Breakthrough findings from a leading neuroscientist.* New York, NY: Ballantine Books.

Olson, K. (2007). A new way of thinking about fatigue: A reconceptualization. *Oncology Nursing Forum, 34*(1), 93–99.

Oppezzo, M., & Schwartz, D. (2014). Give your ideas some legs: The positive effect of walking on creative thinking. *Journal of Experimental Psychology: Learning, Memory, and Cognition, 40*(4), 1142–1152.

Padnani, A. (2012, August 11). The power of music, tapped in a cubicle. *New York Times.* Retrieved from www.nytimes.com/2012/08/12/jobs/how-music-can-improve-worker-productivity-workstation.html?_r=1&

Parker-Pope, T. (2014, October 6). Better ways to learn. *New York Times.* Retrieved from http://well.blogs.nytimes.com/2014/10/06/better-ways-to-learn/

Pollan, M. (2013). *Cooked: A natural history of transformation.* New York, NY: Penguin.

Pozen, R. (2012, October 23). Exercise increases productivity. *Huffington Post.* Retrieved from www.huffingtonpost.com/robert-pozen/exercise-productivity_b_2005463.html

Ratey, J., & Hagerman, E. (2008). *Spark: The revolutionary new science of exercise and the brain.* New York: Little, Brown and Company.

Schulz, L. (2012). The origins of inquiry: Inductive inference and exploration in early childhood. *Trends in Cognitive Sciences, 16*(7), 382–389.

Schwartz, T. (2013, February 9). Relax! You'll be more productive. *New York Times.* Retrieved from www.nytimes.com/2013/02/10/opinion/sunday/relax-youll-be-more-productive.html?_r=0

Siegel, D. J. (2012). *Pocket guide to interpersonal neurobiology: An integrative handbook of the mind.* New York, NY: W. W. Norton.

Tarkan, L. (2012, September 15). *Work hard, play harder: Fun at work boosts creativity, productivity.* Retrieved from www.foxnews.com/health/2012/09/13/work-hard-play-harder-fun-at-work-boosts-creativity-productivity

Thompson, D. (2012, August 6). The case for vacation: Why science says breaks are good for productivity. *Atlantic.* Retrieved from www.theatlantic.com/business/archive/2012/08/the-case-for-vacation-why-science-says-breaks-are-good-for-productivity/260747/

Williams, F. (2012, November 28). *Take two hours of pine forest and call me in the morning.* Retrieved from www.outsideonline.com/fitness/wellness/Take-Two-Hours-of-Pine-Forest-and-Call-Me-in-the-Morning.html

Wrangham, R. (2009). *Catching fire: How cooking made us human.* New York, NY: Basic Books.

Zull, J. E. (2011). *From brain to mind: Using neuroscience to guide change in education.* Sterling, VA: Stylus.

IO

ENHANCING AND EVALUATING CRITICAL THINKING DISPOSITIONS AND HOLISTIC STUDENT LEARNING AND DEVELOPMENT THROUGH INTEGRATIVE INQUIRY

Marilee J. Bresciani Ludvik, Philippe Goldin, Matthew R. Evrard,
J. Luke Wood, Wendy Bracken, Charles Iyoho, and Mark Tucker

The faculty of voluntarily bringing back a wandering attention, over and over again is the very root of judgment, character, and will . . . An education which should improve this faculty would be the education par excellence.

—William James (psychclassics.asu.edu/James/Principles/prin11.htm)

I (Marilee J. Bresciani Ludvik) once resisted anything that had to do with stillness. Because focused breathing required one to be still, I didn't want to have anything to do with it. Even when my sister, Elizabeth, and my dear friend, Jan, shared with me the health benefits of engaging in focused breathing, I still didn't want anything to do with it. From time to time I would appease their invitations to "just try it" and agree to attempt sitting "still." I think it would be about five seconds after arriving into the room and settling into my seat before I hatched my escape plan. Somewhere around one to two minutes later, just about when I was ready to scream aloud and pull my hair out, I would leave.

As their invitations to attend meditation (i.e., focused breathing) classes continued, I reminded them that I managed my stress just fine through rigorous exercise. I would run about five miles every day and lift weights every other day. In addition, I would hike, rock climb, ski, and do whatever I could to stay active. Given my active lifestyle, Jan thought yoga (focused movement with breath) might be a better option than meditation. When I finally agreed to attend a class, pretty much the same thing happened. The instructors would start with stillness and an invitation to focus on the breath. While I usually stayed in the room a few minutes longer than I would for just the focused breathing class, the extended stay was largely due to the need to devise a more complicated plan to exit the room without stepping on anyone.

I just didn't see any value in stillness. As far as I was concerned, nothing got "done" when people sat still. And what was the point of focusing on the breath? Everyone alive breathes—even though some people need technology to aid them in breathing or perhaps medication. Why focus on it? How unproductive and uninteresting is that?

Oddly, I didn't have any interest in exploring the science behind the practice Jan and Elizabeth were promoting. The technology to measure what was happening in the brain was only just emerging and so you really couldn't *see* what was happening in the brain at the time—at least, not like we can today. While I didn't go as far as believing that if you can't see it and measure it, it doesn't exist, I did adopt the belief that if you can't see it and measure it, why give it any of your time and attention? That, after all, would be highly unproductive. My interest in the science that explained or sought to explain that which is unseen and still all changed rather dramatically however.

In August 2005, I became ill. At first, I was just really tired and I thought that my sister and Jan were just . . . well . . . right. I thought that the chronic stress I had been experiencing in my personal and professional life was taking its toll. However, the illness progressed. Over the course of four months, I lost feeling in my legs; it was as if they had fallen asleep. And just as in various stages of limb sleepiness, you cannot feel your limbs at all until something hits them, and then it is really painful. Or just like when your limbs fall asleep, you are not really sure of how to move them or where to place them, but you can move them and place them, albeit rather clumsily.

With the onset of the disease, of course I became interested in the science of the unseen. Several neurologists later, we finally landed with a firm diagnosis of transverse myelitis (TM) and a pending diagnosis of multiple sclerosis (MS). The good news was that my disease wasn't terminal; the bad news was that out of the five doctors I had seen, none of them knew what to do for the disease, apart from prescribing pain and other typical MS medications, which were designed to slow the progression of the potentially but not assuredly debilitating disease—a disease for which the cause remained unidentifiable while the resulting neurological damage was quite measurable. Due to uncertainty about my future, along with the inability to keep up with my workload, my stress was growing, but I was no longer able to run. I finally took Jan up on her offer to learn how to focus on my breathing. As soon as my sister, Elizabeth, discovered I was practicing focused breathing, she started sending books. The learning journey into the unseen began.

Over a decade later, thanks to my coach, Robert, and several other amazing people, I can run for up to 20 minutes at a time before my feet or portions of my legs begin to fall asleep. (I want to make sure I don't offer false hope. I am limited in the physical activity I can do, but I can do it.) I practice focused breathing daily and yoga (focused movement with breath) four to five days a week. I also hike, swim, and cycle. I credit the unseen, unidentifiable, and seemingly unmeasurable at its origin for giving me my legs back, along with so much more.

I share this personal story first to encourage you—just in case you are as skeptical as I was or as resistant to engaging or inviting others to engage in mindfulness methodology and mindful inquiry. Second, I share this story because it was the gift of this illness, this experience that motivated me to study just how regenerative neural connections can be. And, finally, as I studied this physical regeneration process from a perspective fueled by a desire to run again, I felt a great deal of conviction as an educator.

Measuring what we can see is important and we must continue to do this. However, to this day, I can't craft a rubric to measure the effectiveness of my practice in the alternative methods that I believe led to my recovery. Furthermore, crafting a rubric to measure such a practice must by definition take the student outside of the inner experience as she looks to our description to see if she is doing it "right." That would indeed be counterproductive. For the first time in my life, I was beginning to notice how trying to measure something could actually inhibit the innately designed process from working.

For example, we couldn't see what healing was occurring as I engaged in the practices. I couldn't really even describe my experience of engaging in the practices. However, I was coached into staying with the practices and with whatever my experiences were as I practiced—just simply noticing, breathing, acknowledging, suspending judgment, accepting, and choosing. With six-month intervals of magnetic resonance imaging (MRI) evidence, we could see how much the spinal cord had healed. We could see the evidence that the lesions in the brain were still there but no new lesions had developed, and the ones that are present have not grown larger. We have no evidence as to the effectiveness of my engagement in the methodology for which I credit the spinal cord healing and the stability of the brain lesions. And, we understand that one third of the patients diagnosed with TM do, over time, recover the use of that which was lost. But I wanted to know whether we could intentionally change the neurology. As such, I remain a subject in a study that explores such alternative healing methodologies.

It all begs the question: If we do embed what we know to be true about the neuroscience of learning and development into a truly integrative approach to learning and development, how much do we measure and how much do we leave unmeasured? Unpacking this question, we also ask: How much of the learning and development experience do we intentionally design? How much learning and development do we simply hypothesize will occur over time if we engage students in and intentionally guide them along certain types of unstructured learning and development experiences that neuroscience supports? If we intentionally provide unstructured, unmeasurable learning and development opportunities, how do we justify this in a climate of accountability?

In this book, we share neuroscience, psychology, and student success research, as well as learning and development theory. In this chapter, it is our intention to weave all these components together in a manner that hopefully creates additional questions in your mind (whatever the mind is anyway) and moves you to experiment with what we are discovering with an intention to improve holistic student learning and development.

Overview

If you have read the previous chapters, you have begun to gather several ideas of how the research in neuroscience can be used to enhance student learning and development. For example, we have illustrated how neuroscience and psychology data show that specific types of prolonged training for attention regulation (AR), emotion regulation (ER), and cognitive regulation (CR) may foster awareness, focus, compassion, overall well-being, engagement, creativity, critical thinking, conscious decision making, and many other outcomes (Baer, Smith, & Allen, 2004; Beilock, 2010; Bergen-Cico, Possemato, & Cheong, 2013; Bravers, Reynolds, & Donaldson, 2003; Brown & Ryan, 2003; Buchheld, Grossman, & Walach, 2001; Chadwick et al., 2008; Chiesa, Calati, & Serretti, 2011; Cotman & Berchtold, 2002; Cotman, Berchtold, & Christie, 2007; Dmasio & Carvalho, 2013; Damasio, Damasio, & Tranel, 2013; Dove, Pollmann, Schubert, Wiggons, & von Cramon, 2000; Garland, Gaylord, & Park, 2009; Gilbert & Shallice, 2002; Goldin, Hakimi, Manber,

Canli, & Gross, 2009; Goldin, Manber-Ball, Werner, Heimberg, & Gross, 2009; Goldin, Ramel, & Gross, 2009; Goleman, 2001; Hayes & Feldman, 2004; Hutcherson, Goldin, Ramel, McRae, & Gross, 2008) demanded by employers (AAC&U, 2013; Arum & Roksa, 2011; Kavat-Zinn, 2013; Langer, 1989; Lesch, 2007; Levy, 2007; Mahone, Bruch, & Heimberg, 1993; Mitcheson, Yeatman, Rao, Holmes, & Green , 2008; Orthner, Jones, Sanpei, & Williamson, 2004; Philippi et al., 2012; Salovey, Mayer, Goldman, Turvey, & Palfai, 1995; Smith et al., 2008; Strong et al., 2005; Stroop, 1935; Swainson et al., 2003; Taras, 2005). In this chapter, we draw on all the training methodologies we discussed in the previous chapters and integrate them into a single training methodology that we call integrative inquiry (INIQ). INIQ was originally designed as a 16-week hybrid AR/ER/CR training program for undergraduate and graduate students. In Chapter 3, we highlighted the specific methodology used in INIQ and the portions of the brain that are known to be associated with these training methodologies. In this chapter, we present the assessment results we have gathered on the efficacy of INIQ after having piloted INIQ in various modalities. In addition, we discuss the various assessment strategies used in evaluating the effectiveness of INIQ.

As the introduction to this book indicates, there is an urgency to resolve the precipitous decline of higher education outcomes. Moreover, with learning environments changing significantly, higher levels of stress and anxiety have been associated with students' experiences of earning degrees and completing courses (Ashcraft, 2002; Hembree, 1990; Mallow, 2006; Tobias, 1993). Yet, despite this increased stress, there are indications that employers are not satisfied with the preparedness level of students who complete any degree. The Employment Outlook (2010) report from the Organisation for Economic Co-operation and Development (OECD) suggests that analytical and problem-solving skills are among the most important sets of skills that graduates could demonstrate. To corroborate the disconnect, the Collegiate Learning Assessment (CLA) reports that 45% of students made no statistically significant increases in critical thinking, complex reasoning, and writing skills during their college years. If you add these data to the most recent OECD data, we have a growing urgency to improve higher education (Blumenstyk, 2014; Bok, 2013; Mettler, 2014).

Considering the presumed stagnant and, in some cases, declining levels of critical thinking, innovative solutions are needed. Thus, one effective solution to promote access, enrollment, and degree completion in undergraduate and graduate students may be to reduce the perceived stress and anxiety that impedes the decision to enroll, persist in, and complete degrees, while also increasing the activation of neural correlates associated with awareness and executive functions. In addition to hypothesized benefits, in this chapter we present research that will hopefully further the theoretical understanding of the limiting effects of stress and anxiety on student enrollment and performance. In addition, this research provides a look at the development of critical thinking dispositions within the context of concepts already discussed in this book. We hope that this information will guide the efforts of current educators and researchers in their own practices. Note that we are not positing that INIQ is *the* solution to our problems in higher education; we are simply offering it as one way in which to combine the aforementioned wisdom and research contained in this book to enhance the learning and development outcomes we need evident in our graduates.

While we have maintained from the beginning of this book that we need to rethink our design of higher education, we found that we had to design a training program within the context of how higher education is currently organized so that we could test the efficacy of the proposed neuroscience of which we have been writing. That is, we had to design a training program that could be delivered within a 16-week semester and embedded into either a course or delivered apart from a course, such as in a leadership training program or in a resident situation within a sorority. Nonetheless, we invite you to read this chapter keeping in mind that this training program has been unpacked and implemented in a variety of modalities and settings, so as to accomplish the primary goal for which it was developed—the integration of the students' intellectual self, feeling or sensing self, and the student's ability to navigate the unknown.

Using AR, ER, and CR as theoretical undergirding (see Chapter 3 for a reminder of the details), Bresciani Ludvik used the research highlighted in this book and many of the training methods featured in the book *Search Inside Yourself* (C. M. Tan, 2012) as a foundation for designing a training program called integrative inquiry or INIQ. INIQ is the process of integrating the knowledge gained from research, course learning, and book learning with the wisdom gained from intuition, sensing, and the mindful experiencing of emotions *with* the ability to embrace the unknown. With the ability to integrate multiple sources of information through generative questions and other training methodologies, participants of the INIQ curriculum are able to manage stress and creatively problem solve while experiencing ambiguity. This is intended to lead to the promotion of peace and compassion through conscious choice making.

In consultation with Philippe Goldin, one of the original designers of Google's Search Inside Yourself professional development program, along with many others (including adapting training from the Search Inside Yourself Leadership Institute at www.siyli.org, Jon Kabat-Zinn, Saki Santorelli, Baron Baptiste Power Yoga Institute, Rick Hanson, and the Chopra Center for Well-Being), INIQ was piloted as a 16-week online or hybrid training program that met two hours a week for undergraduate students, one day a month for doctoral students, and about 15–45 minutes a week for master's students. (While there are other versions of INIQ available—8 weeks and 10 weeks—the efficacy of those versions has not yet been fully researched.) Pilots of INIQ, which have included a small sample of STEM undergraduate students, a larger sample of master's students, and a large sample of doctoral students have reported significant effectiveness in decreasing stress and anxiety, while also increasing AR, ER, and CR.

Students experience INIQ as a novel and innovative approach in that it changes commonly held perceptions about situations that engender stress and anxiety. It accomplishes this change by promoting attention, inquiry, and an individual's ability to embrace ambiguity through cognitive reappraisal, but only with engagement in the practice of mindfulness. In other words, CR runs the danger of looking a lot like suppression or avoidance if the students have not allowed themselves to fully experience the emotion that is arising or has arisen, reflected upon their experience of the emotion, practiced inquiry into the experience, and then made an intentional choice of how to be with the experience in relationship to who they are, what they want, and their life purpose.

INIQ facilitates change in current teaching and learning environments by engaging in practices that literally change the structure and function of the brain, so that the amygdala (where fight and flight is activated) becomes downregulated on demand while the insula and portions of the prefrontal and medial cortices—where executive functions and sensory-motor processors reside—become upregulated on demand. Using this methodology, the researchers expect that participation in INIQ will increase persistence in and completion of degrees and improve the overall quality of learning and development.

The Neuroscience and the Numbers

Chapters 1 through 3 provide in-depth information about how we understand the brain to function and how we understand the brain can change through specific training methodologies. This research was used in the design of the INIQ training program. For example, if students' stress and anxiety decrease, students are likely to increase their executive functions. In essence, as we have mentioned several times in this book, neuroscience illustrates that when participants engage in specific types of training methodology, their amygdala—the emotional center of the brain and the key activator of fight-or-flight-reactivity—will be downregulated (Hölzel, Carmody, et al., 2011; Luders, Toga, Lepore, & Gaser, 2009).

We also understand from neuroscience that engaging in these same practices strengthens the neural connections in the insula and prefrontal and medialfrontal cortices (Hölzel, Carmody, et al., 2011; Hölzel, Lazar, et al., 2011; Luders et al., 2009). Such strengthening of the prefrontal and medial frontal cortex can lead to increases in critical thinking, analytical reasoning, creative problem solving, ability to prioritize, and effective communication (Hölzel, Carmody, et al., 2011; Hölzel, Lazar, et al., 2011; Luders et al., 2009). A more detailed description of other attainable learning and development outcomes can be found in the preceding chapters.

In an early pilot assessment of INIQ (analysis of later INIQ cohorts has been completed and is being submitted for publication in refereed journals; this assessment evidence of pilot programs is being shared to emphasize the connection of the research to the design and selection of assessment instruments), students who participated in online and hybrid modalities saw a significant increase in attention, emotion, and cognitive regulation skills. Additionally, one aspect of critical thinking—that of confidence in reasoning measured by the California Critical Thinking Dispositions Inventory (CCTDI)—significantly increased.

Results from the Perceived Stress Scale indicated that there was a significant decrease between the pretest (M = 16.27, SD = 6.76) and the posttest scores: M = 11.93, SD = 4.35; $t(14)$ = 2.053; $p < .05$. This difference indicates that perceived stress declined following INIQ. The effect size for the decrease in perceived stress was medium at .53.

There was also a significant difference in the scores for the pre-Beck Anxiety Index (BAI) (M = 34.4, SD = 9.89) and post-BAI (M = 29.1, SD = 4.36); $t(14)$ = 2.32, $p < .05$. This indicates that participants' anxiety decreased following INIQ. The difference represented a medium effect size at .60.

There was a significant increase in the confidence in reasoning scores of the CCTDI before the test (M = 44.72, SD = 6.75) and after the test (M = 47.13, SD = 6.87), $t(14)$ = −1.904, $p < .05$. The effect size for this increase was approaching medium at .49.

Finally, there also was a significant difference for all of the pre– and post–Five-Factor Model Questionnaire (FFMQ) scores for each of the five factors: observing prescore (M = 24.0, SD = 3.12) and observing postscore (M = 27.87, SD = 4.78); $t(14)$ = −3.45, $p < .001$; describing prescore (M = 27.27, SD = 6.23) and describing postscore (M = 30.80, SD = 6.30); $t(14)$ = −3.2, $p < .01$; acting with awareness prescore (M = 25.00, SD = 5.55) and acting with awareness postscore (M = 28.67, SD = 6.09); $t(14)$ = −2.41, $p < .05$; nonjudging of inner experience with awareness prescore (M = 25.67, SD = 6.52) and nonjudging of inner experience postscore (M = 29.47, SD = 4.87);

$t(14) = -2.29$, $p < .05$; and nonreactivity to inner experience prescore ($M = 20.40$, $SD = 3.99$) and nonreactivity to inner experience postscore ($M = 23.93$, $SD = 3.94$); $t(14) = -3.04$, $p < .01$.

Several of the effect sizes were or approached large. This included effect sizes for observing (.89), describing (.83), and nonreactivity (.78). The effect sizes for acting and nonjudging were moderate (.62 and .59, respectively). These results are extremely compelling as the findings were consistent across undergraduate- and graduate-level participants.

Additional assessment of later cohorts of INIQ participants revealed compelling results for resilience, as measured by the Brief Resilience Scale (BRS); compassion, as measured by Neff's Self-Compassion Scale (Neff); and overall critical thinking dispositions, as measured by the Postsecondary Education Critical Thinking Dispositions Inventory (PECTDI). The details of these findings are under review by specific refereed journals and so are intentionally excluded from this chapter. For the purposes of this chapter, note that INIQ has shown evidence of achieving the learning and development outcomes derived from qualitative analysis of direct learning artifacts listed in Table 10.1. Specific student quotes, collected from reflective journal writing prompts throughout the term, are shared to illustrate what achievement of the outcome may look like.

The Design Informed by Theory

The design of INIQ includes reading assignments, online mini lectures, reflective questions, interactions with nature, mindfulness methodology assignments, creative expression assignments, and journal assignments. Many of these activities can be formatively assessed using adaptions of the AAC&U rubrics (see www.aacu.org/value). Participants who engage fully in the course involve themselves through focused breathing, focused movement, didactic exercises, presentations, compassion exercises, expressive exercises, and community service projects.

As previously mentioned, the primary theories that inform the design of INIQ include AR, ER, and CR. These theories are discussed in more detail in Chapter 3. We briefly revisit these theories used in the design of INIQ in the following narrative. Included in the narrative are more illustrative descriptions of the mindfulness methodology and the mindful inquiry process for developing AR, ER, and CR, so that the reader can gain an understanding of how these theories form the basis of the design of INIQ. The researchers also relate these theories and the training tools used to explain the relationship to increased critical thinking dispositions, well-being and resilience, decreased

TABLE 10.1
Qualitative Evidence of Specific INIQ Learning and Development Outcomes

Learning and Development Outcome	Direct Artifact Analyzed	Example Student Quote
Critical thinking	Observation from an exercise Reflective journal entry	"I almost did not want to raise my hand because I thought for sure everyone is going to think that I am crazy for not being able to differentiate a thought [from] a feeling. After talking through an extremely difficult issue I struggle with (taking on too much and bearing the brunt of responsibility even if I am not responsible), I understood. . . . I was thankful that we could walk outside the class after that [exercise] because I needed an extra second to collect myself. . . . I am glad I could work through something that clearly. I have always associated the thought of guilt with many feelings that I have internalized. Taking on too much has always been an issue for me and I may have to unload before things fester and build up in the form of indigestion." —African American male
Decreased stress and anxiety	Observation from an exercise Reflective journal entry	"I feel calmer, even though I have so many things going on. It's like I'm aware of all of these responsibilities and tasks that I have to do, but I am seeing them with a different lens. I don't feel they are all coming at me at once. They are separate things I have to take care of." —Latina female
Flexibility in thought	Observation from an exercise Reflective journal entry	"My mental pathway for success was originally constructed such that success equals perfection, being the best or at least, better than the rest. This is not the definition of *success* I want for myself anymore. It does not lend to good mental health or positive emotions, nor does it model these things for others. Instead I want to redefine my definition of *success* as realizing my potential (whatever that may be) and committing to myself that I try my best (whatever that may be) for anything that I attempt to accomplish." —Caucasian male
Improved relationships	360 evaluation observation Reflective journal entry	"All of a sudden, I noticed I was not reacting to this employee like I had in the past. She was stunned as well. . . . For the first time, we found a new solution for her to try in a situation where she and I had been repeatedly frustrated." —African American male.
Increased resilience	Reflective journal entry	"I am remembering statements from my parents growing up about how I have to set an example for my sisters, since I am the oldest female. Whatever I do, they will do. So I have grown up always being careful about the choices I have made. Looking back at my life, I am grateful to a certain extent, because it helped me get through my young adult years, safely (this is the word that comes to mind). I also am feeling a bit resentful about not being able to take as many risks. . . perhaps this contributes to my feeling nervous when public speaking. . . . I am speaking out now and others are noticing. . . . I feel empowered." —Latina female

(*Continues*)

TABLE 10.1 (Continued)

Learning and Development Outcome	Direct Artifact Analyzed	Example Student Quote
Suspended judgment	Reflective journal entry	"I can be a little, or at times very, stubborn. I am extremely harsh or at least I have been in the past whenever people hurt me intentionally. Whenever people hurt me, I draw an invisible line that I do not cross nor will I allow the person who hurt me to cross. I guess I put up my walls as a way to protect myself. . . . I now notice when I am doing this and I realize I have the choice to choose differently in the next moment." —African American male
Improved focus	Reflective journal entry	"First and foremost I love that it helps me focus on what I need to do and how it can help me become more efficient with all the various things happening in my life professionally and personally: writing center coordinator, new full-time faculty member, faculty training institute program, EdD program's three classes, teaching four English classes, teaching one RWS class, teaching one tutor training class, being on the academic skills committee, being on the basic skills committee, raising the sweetest little boy in the world, flourishing in a marriage, and honoring a commitment to self-care which included surfing, walking, yoga, and meditation. That's a lot, but it's not. When I think about it, it brings stress. When I think about where I am, at this moment, the now, the chair I am sitting in, my fingers tapping the keys of the keyboard, my breath in and out, slowly, I can find that emptiness." —Mixed-race, ethnically underrepresented male
Improved well-being	360 evaluation observation Reflective journal entry	"I have been practicing religiously. Whenever I feel stressed, I stop myself to breathe and practice mindfulness meditation even more. I feel so much better mentally and physically. While I know I feel great, it's even more interesting to me that other people (five people in the last week—one a chemistry professor) have told me that I look great. I only mention this because now I want to share this practice with the people around me." —Caucasian female

stress, and increased persistence in all types of undergraduate and graduate students.

For a refresher of the training methodology and how it maps to specific regions of the brain, refer to Table 3.1. What we attempt to do here and in Table 10.2 is place INIQ into a context to simplify its replication by your faculty, staff, and students. In Table 10.2, the column that is labeled "Category" is to help guide your use of the table. You will also note that we list the goals for each practice, some of the practices we use to achieve the outcomes intended, the outcomes themselves, and the correlating expected learning and development outcomes adapted from the AAC&U rubrics. In addition, we include the means used to evaluate whether the outcomes have been met.

Attention Training

We first train students' ability to direct their attention on demand and without attachment to their judgment of their experience. We also train students to notice *when their attention has wandered away* from what they desire and invite them to return it to the desired object of their attention without attachment to their judgment and to do so on demand. We have discovered that the mindfulness methodology (discussed throughout this book as meditation or focused breathing, yoga or focused movement, body scan, etc.) used in attention training is an effective way to train AR as well as ER.

We use various forms of focused breathing exercises (concentration meditation) to train student's focused attention (i.e., the ability to remain focused on one object of their attention), open attention (i.e., the ability to move from attention to one object to attention in the open environment where the object resides and then back to the object of attention), and meta-attention (i.e., the ability to recognize/become aware of where the attention has been placed). While administering the training methodology, we literally use our own senses, including observation, to ascertain the extent to which students are engaged in these exercises.

Before proceeding, let's clarify an important point. Technology such as functional MRI, electroencephalograms, or physiological markers are considered invasive processes for collecting evidence of student learning and development in the classroom. Thus, inviting students to train their attention to their breath and measuring their success is rather "messy." To make our point quite clear, we don't have a rubric to evaluate their focusing ability. As mentioned, we have tried to create one. For example, the first rubric

TABLE 10.2
INIQ Methodology and Related Outcomes

Category	Goals	Practices	Outcomes	Correlating Critical Thinking Learning Outcomes (Adapted From AAC&U Rubrics)	Assessment Measures/Tools
Attention regulation	Attention management/ awareness; awareness of awareness	Focused breathing; meta-attention; open attention; mindful meditation; mindful listening	Increased attention regulation	Able to focus and direct attention on demand; able to follow and give directions, whether written or oral; states problem/issue to be considered critically clearly; describes problem/issue comprehensively, delivering all relevant information necessary for full understanding	FFMQ; MAAS; observation; sensing; journaling
Attention regulation; emotion regulation	Attention management/ awareness; emotional awareness; compassion	Focused breathing; meta-attention; open attention; mindful meditation; mindful listening; empathic listening; focused movement; body scan; movement in nature; journaling	Increased emotion regulation	Aware of emotions in the body; aware of emotions as physiological expressions and thoughts as intellectual expressions; compares and evaluates opposing arguments or ideas	FFMQ; MAAS; observation; sensing; journaling; Beck; PSS

Cognitive regulation	Attention management/ awareness; emotional awareness; self-awareness; compassion; conscious choice making	Naming emotions; cognitive reappraisal; task switching; just like me; unwelcomed emotions meditation; loving-kindness meditation; generating goodness meditation	Increased cognitive regulation	Provides reasoned support for beliefs or ideas; recognizes and analyzes arguments that support theories and perspectives other than their own; distinguishes between fact and opinion; evaluates creative process and product using domain-appropriate criteria; information is taken from source(s) with enough interpretation/evaluation to develop a comprehensive analysis or synthesis Questions viewpoints of experts thoroughly; extends a novel or unique idea, question, format, or product to create new knowledge or knowledge that crosses boundaries; integrates alternate, divergent, or contradictory perspectives or ideas fully; thoroughly (systematically and methodically) analyzes own and others' assumptions and carefully evaluates the relevance of contexts when presenting a position	FFMQ; MAAS; observation; sensing; journaling; Beck; PSS; PECTDI; Stroop color word task; problem-solving case study analysis; action planning; communication planning
Self-regulation; leadership abilities	Attention management/ awareness; emotional awareness; self-awareness; conscious choice making; adaptable leadership	Journaling; dyad dialogue; group discussion; alignment of experience with personal and professional goals and values; insight meditation; creative expression; nature encounters; nutrition encounters; well-being exploration	Increased self-regulation	Identifies a problem and outlines or describes a realistic approach to solving the problem; draws conclusions based on the outcomes; analyzes content, discovers meaning or significance, draws conclusions, and makes an assessment; navigates complexity and ambiguity with self-awareness, agility, adaptability, and creativity; actively seeks out and follows through on untested and potentially risky directions or approaches to the assignment in the final product; specific position (perspective, thesis/hypothesis) is imaginative, taking into account the complexities of an issue Acknowledges limits of position (perspective, thesis/ hypothesis)	Observation; sensing; journaling; Beck; PSS; 360 evaluation observation; portfolio; brief resilience scale; problem-solving case study analysis; action planning; communication planning; strategic planning; change planning; professional development planning; vision statement

(Continues)

TABLE 10.2 (Continued)

Category	Goals	Practices	Outcomes	Correlating Critical Thinking Learning Outcomes (Adapted From AAC&U Rubrics)	Assessment Measures/Tools
				Synthesizes other's points of view within position (perspective, thesis/hypothesis); comes to conclusions and related outcomes (consequences and implications) that are logical and reflect student's informed evaluation and ability to place evidence and perspectives discussed in priority order; engages in thinking within a network, spanning boundaries, and recognizing the opportunities for cocreation; promotes others' engagement with diversity; tailors communication strategies to effectively express, listen, and adapt to others to establish relationships to further the well-being of the organization and its members; develops a logical, consistent plan to solve problem, recognizes consequences of solution, and articulates reason for choosing solution.	
Compassion	Attention management/ awareness; emotional awareness; self-awareness; kindness in relationship building; conscious choice making	Just like me; loving-kindness; common humanity; self-compassion letter writing; cognitive re-appraisal; compassion nonverbal; empathic listening	Increased compassion	Transforms ideas or solutions into entirely new forms; engages in empathic communication; engages in compassionate practice.	Observation; sensing; journaling; Neff SCS; Jazaieri compassion scale; 360 evaluation observation; portfolio; brief resilience scale; problem-solving case study analysis; action planning; communication planning

Note. Beck = Anxiety Inventory; FFMQ = Five-Factor Model Questionairre; MAAS = Mindful Attention Awareness Scale; Neff SCS = Neff Self-Compassion Scale; PECTIDI = Postsecondary Education Critical Thinking Dispositions Inventory ; PSS = Percieved Stress scale we created was applied to observation of students' appearance of nonverbal body language concentration. However, we quickly found that even students who "look like" they are focused on their breathing may later self-report they were focused on planning what they were going to do next or worrying about engaging in the exercise correctly. Apart from observing the students who were falling asleep (head bobbing), clearly looked pained (scrunched eyebrows, frowns, and other facial expressions and bodily movement indicating discomfort), or continued to open their eyes repeatedly to look at the clock, the nonverbal cues were generally unhelpful in ascertaining the level of engagement with the exercise. Furthermore, when we had a working rubric, we noticed that students focused on the criteria for "getting the exercise right," rather than paying attention to the inner experience. The very inner attention and awareness that we were intending to train was undermined by the instrument created to measure its effectiveness. Thus, without equipment to test for neurological and physiological changes, the reliance on self-reported data is incredibly important. And our reliance on our senses, including observation, to guide us in how to lead students in their attention training is necessary.

Many researchers have shared their perspective that self-reported data are invalid reporting tools (Brener, Billy & Grady, 2003; Catania, Gibson, Chitwood, & Coates, 1990; Del Boca & Noll, 2000; Herzog & Bowman, 2011). And yet accurate self-reporting ability is exactly what we are training—(a) awareness of what is actually happening in the body (sensations and emotion) and (b) awareness within the entity that notices awareness (mind)—as one experiences the learning and development journey. We are training students' awareness of where their attention is residing and whether they are regulating their emotions as they engage in complex issues that may challenge their personal values and beliefs or who they are (in regard to their identity).

To further complicate this challenge, no one actually knows what each individual student is experiencing in her own learning and development process, except for the individual student herself. With an increased number of students enrolled in classes, increased use of online technologies to deliver knowledge, and increased uncertainty in our world, training students to regulate their own attention, emotions, and decisions is of primary importance if we are to advance holistic learning and development.

All of this conversation simply invites in the importance of bringing back to higher education the type of self-reported data that involve first-person reporting of the *experience or process* of learning and development. But we can't really do this confidently unless we train students to develop their own awareness. What we understand from the research presented in Chapter 3 is that training for awareness all begins with training attention (Posner & Fan, 2004; C.M. Tan, 2012).

When students self-report they are ready to try another practice and we sense (reaffirming the messy notion of using senses to train others in their awareness of their senses) that students have begun to consistently pay attention to their breath when asked to do so, we move to training attention to their bodies. As an aside, for many undergraduates, we flip this practice and we begin with training attention to their bodies in motion—then move to training their attention to the breath—and then back to training attention toward emotions within the body. For many undergraduates (as well as some administrators), starting with training attention to a body in motion is a much more accessible way to begin attention training.

Emotion Training

In training students' attention to their bodies and awareness of that attention, students begin to experience their emotions and thoughts as physical sensations. They feel a burning in the chest or a churning in the stomach. They feel a tightening in their shoulders or in their lower backs. As we invite students to direct attention to the sensations in their bodies, we also invite them to become aware of the ebb and flow of the intensity of the sensation. In essence, students begin to discover for themselves that whatever they are experiencing in their body comes and goes. Some experience chronic pain in portions of their body; in time, they become aware that even their chronic pain has varying levels of intensity. For students who have lost a great deal of sensing capability in their body due to a spinal cord injury or other reason, they can feel the ebb and flow of sensation in their breath. These data are gathered via self-report or first-person experience. We also use our own senses to guide the practice and process of what to do next.

If you feel skeptical about the self-report data, we invite you to remember what the neuroscience research states: What you pay attention to and focus on will change the structure and function of your brain. We remind participants of this fact regularly. The point is that if students are making something up in their "minds," then that indeed may be exactly what they are experiencing. We don't know; what we do understand is that without training awareness of attention and emotion, students won't be able to discern, for themselves, what is true for them and what may be true for another. They won't be able to distinguish fact from interpretation.

Thus, once we sense that students can consistently direct their attention to their breath (they have awareness of the placement of their attention) and self-report awareness of bodily sensations without judgment when invited to do so, we move to the CR training part of the program.

Cognitive Training

In CR training (further detailed in Chapter 3), we intend for students to recruit their prefrontal cortexes for discerning what is real and what is not real for them in any given moment (Campbell-Sills & Barlow, 2007; Goldin & Gross, 2010; Ochsner & Gross, 2005). This process includes a series of exercises where students are invited to name emotions and thoughts as they arise. Later, we move them into imagining themselves in specific daily scenarios (nothing traumatic), experiencing the emotions and thoughts that arise in those scenarios, and then moving beyond naming through a specific process where they begin to practice inquiry into their emotions and thoughts. We introduce task switching, cognitive reappraisal, and metacognitive practices, among many other practices.

The intention of these sets of exercises is to invite students' awareness that what they may be experiencing as emotions and thoughts and sensations in their body may not be what another is experiencing. Thus, what may be true for them in a given moment may not be true for another. Using mindful inquiry, we guide students in discerning fact from interpretation and exploring their relationship (based on who they are, what they want, what their life purposes are, and for what they are grateful) to whatever it is they are experiencing in each moment. This portion of the course is where we have experienced the most profound feedback from students, their supervisors, their family members, and sometimes their supervisees.

Once students use inquiry to become aware of the relationship between their emotions and thoughts in certain situations, they can transfer this practice of inquiry to their work and the work they do with others. Students begin to see possibilities for solutions where they didn't before because they have become skilled in suspending their judgments, realizing that what may be true for them may not be true for others. This momentary suspension of judgment allows them to remain in inquiry for just a moment longer than they used to practice. In this place of inquiry, they may see something "new" and, as a result, experience a previously not thought of possibility. In essence, students self-report realizations that when they can discern their own experience of something as potentially different from the way another is experiencing something, they can stay in inquiry longer, see possibilities that perhaps their judgment would not previously allow them to see, and access creative thinking and expression. They report being less reactive. Instead, they feel more empowered to make a thoughtful choice.

In our study of stress-inducing thoughts, acute stress may arise from particular traumatic experiences such as those mentioned in Chapters 6 through 9. And other acute stress may arise from the thoughts that linger after a traumatic event, thus becoming chronic stress (Baum, 1990; Baum, Cohen & Hall, 1993; Compas, Connor-Smith, Saltzman, Thomsen, & Wadsworth, 2001). Other acute stress may result from an inability to see something differently, considering "it" to always be the same, even when another doesn't feel that to be true or even when "it" isn't always the same.

While acute and chronic stress are complex research topics, we simply want to provide a context for how we integrate attention, emotion, and cognitive regulation practices into daily student life. A simple example is when a student fails a math test. The fact is, the student failed the math test. Upon recieving the failed math test, the student may feel bodily sensations such as a hot flush throughout her body, dizziness, a feeling of loss of energy, or as if she will pass out. If the student has not gone through INIQ, she may be unaware that this physiological state that she just experienced will pass (it feels real and true now but won't always feel real and true). It is as temporary as the physiological state of feeling butterflies in the stomach and a different type of light-headedness than what she experienced just moments earlier when she spotted a person she loves, or is merely temporarily infatuated with—who knows? We are not judging.

If this student hasn't gone through INIQ training, she won't know the best next steps. She would be unable to acknowledge and then regulate her physiological state through focused breathing (downregulating her limbic system, particularly her amygdala, which just sent her into fight-or-flight mode and of course stabilizing all the neurochemical transmissions that resulted from the ignition of the fight and flight). She may not be able to recruit her prefrontal cortex to gain access to higher order thinking of prioritizing what to do next. She may simply be lost in the fight-or-flight response and then move to blame others for her failure (interpretation or fact remains inconclusive in fight-or-flight state) or think she is a failure (definitely interpretation, not fact) and drop out of college altogether (reactive and therefore likely an unconscious choice).

With INIQ training, she would have been trained to downregulate her activated amygdala with the breath and then move into the cognitive processing of what is true for her in this moment. For example, is it true that she failed that test? Yes. Is it true that she is a failure? No. What is true? She failed the test. What can she do about it? Well, she can examine, without judgment, her steps that led up to her failing the test. She may recall that she chose to visit and tend to her sick grandmother instead of studying. INIQ training would invite her to see that as a choice with potential consequences.

Was she aware of the potential consequence of failing the test when she made that choice? If she was an INIQ-trained student, we would hope the answer would be yes. She set her priorities, she made her choice, and she accepts the consequences and the sets of choices that must follow. Being in that space without self-judgment allows her to recruit the executive reasoning portions of her brain to now focus on solutions and next steps. This same practice works in meetings, when receiving a "no go" decision on what you thought was a great idea, and in many other circumstances, which all contribute to enhancing resilience.

There are two other parts of the training that are embedded in the training for AR, ER, and CR. (We realize it is difficult to discuss this nonlinear training in a linear way, so forgive this rather clunky transition.) Embedded in the training is deep self-inquiry (self-awareness which leads to self-regulation). The intention of the self-inquiry is to invite students to engage in the scientific method with themselves as the subject of their investigation. Several exercises are included in this portion of the course and they involve values clarification exercises (attributed to Search Inside Yourself Leadership Institute [SIYLI]); envisioning their future possibilities (attributed to SIYLI); explorations into having difficult conversations (attributed to Stone & Patton, 1999); examining the way they relate to others in communication (attributed to Rosenburg, 2003; SIYLI); and consistently questioning "who they are, what they want, what their life purpose is, how they can serve, and for what they are grateful" (attributed to the Chopra Center for Well-Being Primordial Sound Meditation Practice). In this portion of the training, students delve into how they make meaning out of all they experience, whether they are experiencing emotions that arise as they read a journal article and relating it to what they value or the emotions that arise as they engage in a service-learning project and relate it to their expressed life's purpose.

Compassion Training

Compassion training is an important component of the process. Many of the practices introduced in Chapter 8 are used in the course along with a few more (attributed to Stanford University's Compassion Cultivation Training [CCT] and SIYLI). The intention in adding this component may not seem as obvious. What does compassion have to do with enhancing critical thinking? Our answer is that it may have nothing to do with critical thinking but it may have a lot to do with building trusting relationships; demonstrating care and concern for yourself, peers, and others; being able to work collaboratively while solving problems; and it just may be related to many other inter- and intrasocial skills documented in Chapter 8. In essence, how can we really expect to resolve the world's wicked problems without working with others in a manner that empowers them to show up as their best selves?

This line of logic is why we added compassion training as another primary component of INIQ; not just because it may enhance personal well-being but because we intend to educate students who think beyond themselves when they solve problems. We intend for INIQ to foster the 2011 Expected Emerging Leadership Outcomes generated from the Center for Creative Leadership (CCL) research. CCL reports expectations from Fortune 500 companies that believe that future leaders must be able to navigate complexity and ambiguity; be agile, adaptable, and boundary spanning; as well as be creative, able to engage in network thinking, self-aware, and able to cocreate.

To do this, we take the concept of "just like me" (introduced in Chapter 8) and change it to "just as me," as we embed this concept into an actual practice (C. M. Tan, 2012) that is a part of the self-inquiry section of the course. However, we do this after we have gauged students' ability to effectively train their own attention and emotional awareness. We also embed the loving-kindness practices found in C. M. Tan's (2012) book (and also referred to in Chapter 8) so that students can practice compassion toward themselves as well as others, thus contributing to their own personal resilience.

The previous chapters are filled with evidence of how well-being can influence holistic learning and development. If a student is not practicing compassion toward himself, he may not engage in well-being practices. A simple example of a self-compassion practice is to sleep. We understand from neuroscientists (Rasch & Born, 2013) that the waking brain is optimized for encoding memories (an important part of the learning process). However, the sleeping brain is important to learning and development as well. We understand that when the brain sleeps, there is an offline consolidation of memory that is principle to long-term memory formation (Rasch & Born, 2013). This research caused us to muse about how our students would feel if we put sleeping tasks in their research course syllabi.

Assessing an Integrative Design

Before we delve into comparable quantifiable measures, we want to emphasize the integrative approach to designing holistic student learning and development that we have been espousing in this book all along. We have plenty of examples in our world history where passionate, sensing human beings did not think critically and therefore took their own lives or the lives of others. We have other examples where someone may have resolved a problem only to find out she harmed many others in the process. By introducing INIQ, we don't wish to mislead anyone into thinking that we feel a solution to addressing our problems in higher education (or the world) is to return only to our sensing selves. We believe a solution in higher education is to return to intentionally developing our sensing selves and integrating our sensing selves with our intellectual selves. There is no "or" in this proposal. It is about the "and."

How do we design higher education that allows students, faculty, and administrators to play, enjoy nature, sleep, eat well, and think critically? How do we design higher education that allows students, faculty, and administrators to express themselves creatively and write an algorithm that will resolve a complicated problem? How do we design higher education that will embrace the feeling and sensing aspects of a student while he sequences genomes? It is in the "and." If we remove the emphasis on the course or perhaps integrate the emphasis on knowledge acquisition with the practices discussed in this chapter and the chapters that preceded it, we believe we will be returning to a holistic way of designing and delivering student learning and development.

Figure 10.1 illustrates our integrated model by showing the possibility of focusing on the whole human being by fueling the intellect, body, emotions, and senses, and then allowing students to delve into the ambiguity and uncertainty of "real-life" problem solving. When we take time to train students' AR, ER, and CR, our data illustrate that students can better handle the messiness of uncertainty and the ambiguity of the unknown while resolving problems in compassionate ways. We understand that in the unknown creativity and insight abound, and undetermined solutions to problems not yet identified can be resolved (O. Tan, 2009).

How do we assess all this? As we mentioned, the process of evaluating the depth of students' ability to pay attention to their breath and other bodily sensations is a process that involves using our own senses as we guide them through training their senses. It also involves their becoming more aware of what awareness is and how they can recognize it. All "that" is intended to lead to greater awareness and validation of self-report processes. Nonetheless, because we really do like to "measure what we can see," we have measured INIQ's efficacy with a pretest and posttest design.

Assessment of INIQ's Efficacy

In the introduction, we highlighted some assessment of student learning and development challenges that exist in higher education and how the use of a

Figure 10.1 Integrative inquiry.

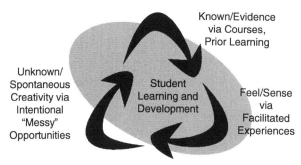

Note. Created and copyright by Bresciani Ludvik (2016).

reflective student learning and development portfolio can address those challenges. Because INIQ develops students' AR, ER, and CR, implementing INIQ or similar training programs early on in students' academic journeys could lead to trustworthy (self-aware and integrated) student reflections integral to reflective student learning portfolios. Such reflections would aid educators in guiding students through their learning and development processes, providing more evidence for intentionally fostering the kinds of outcomes employers demand. For now, we simply discuss how we have determined the effectiveness of INIQ's design. Refer to Table 10.2 to note specific outcomes and measures.

Students who fully participated in INIQ would do the following:

- Reduce levels of stress and anxiety as measured by pre- and post-BAI and Perceived Stress Scale.
- Increase their resilience levels as measured by pre- and post-BRI.
- Increase their critical thinking dispositions and ability to task switch as measured by pre- and post-CCDTI) and PECTDI.
- Increase AR, ER, and CR ability as measured by pre- and post-FFMQ, MAAS, and the Stroop Color Word Task.
- Increase compassion and self-compassion as measured by the Jazaieri Compassion Scale and the Neff Self-Compassion Scale.

Table 10.3 outlines the alignment of key performance indicators (or impact factors) with INIQ expected learning and development outcomes. It also includes the evidence that is used to measure whether the outcome has been achieved.

TABLE 10.3
INIQ Impact: Pre- and Postdesign of Outcomes Measurement

Performance Indicators/ Impact	Learning and Development Outcomes (Students Who Complete Entire Course)	Assessment Measures/ Evidence
Reduced perceived stress and anxiety	Students will experience reduced perceived stress and anxiety.	Pre- and posttest Beck Anxiety Index and Perceived Stress Scale
Increased resilience	Students will experience increased resilience in their ability to bounce back from a perceived negative event (e.g., bad grade).	Pre- and posttest Brief Resilience Scale; reflective journal content analysis; focus groups
Increased critical thinking dispositions	Students will experience increased critical thinking dispositions as indicated by increased truth seeking, open-mindedness, analyticity, systematicity, confidence in reasoning, inquisitiveness, and maturity of judgment. Further, they will improve in their ability to task switch.	Pre- and posttest CCTDI or PECTDI; Stroop Color Word Task; reflective journal content analysis; problem-solving case study analysis
Increased attention, emotion, and cognitive regulation	Students will experience increased attention, emotion, and cognitive regulation.	Pre- and posttest FFMQ and MAAS; Stroop Color Word Task
Increased persistence and completion of degree programs	Students will experience an increase in persistence and degree completion.	Reports from institutional enrollment offices
Increased compassion and self-compassion	Students will experience increased compassion for self and for others.	Pre- and posttest Jazaieri Compassion Scale and Neff Self-Compassion Scale (NSCS)
Improved leadership	Students will demonstrate improved compassionate and effective leadership practices.	360 degree evaluations; action plans; strategic plans; communication plans

Broader Impacts/Benefits of Implementing INIQ

If institutional leaders can adopt and adapt INIQ for their purposes, either as an online, mobile-friendly, out-of-classroom application (see pollinate .life/discovery for details); a classroom application; or a stand-alone course/ training program, then we may see students demonstrate the increased attention and focus necessary for complex reasoning. In addition, if INIQ proves effective in a variety of settings and modalities, then we may see decreased anxiety toward specific subjects and, as a result, be able to identify an increase in access for the number of women, persons with disabilities, and other underrepresented populations entering higher education. An affordable solution to managing AR, ER, and CR could prove impactful in resolving access to and persistence and completion of all students while also increasing the quality of learning and development.

In Table 10.4, we summarize desired higher education accountability objectives as they relate to creating broader impacts and immediate benefits for all students.

INIQ Implications for Holistic Assessment of Student Learning and Development

In the introduction, we discussed the compelling reasons to rethink how we design, deliver, and evaluate higher education. In the preceding chapters, you have gained a perspective on various methods and ideas to enhance holistic learning and development within your institutions. We have touched on some assessment methodology along the way as well. Before we close this chapter, we want to provide you with more detail of how to connect the evaluation methodology with holistic learning and development.

We have always had great respect for the practical and theoretical application of Astin's (1993) I-E-O (input-environment-output) model. Using Astin's methodology, where organizations are invited to assess who their

TABLE 10.4
INIQ Broader Impacts

Higher Education Accountability Objectives	Broader Impacts	Benefits
Application of translational neuroscience and student success research to the improvement of holistic student learning and development Affordable and accessible training methodology to improve learning and development outcomes	Increased persistence and degree completion for all students Increased access in the number of women, persons with disabilities, and other underrepresented populations entering and completing higher education degrees Increased evidence of desired learning and development outcomes	Decreased stress and anxiety Increased AR, ER, CR, and critical thinking dispositions Increased compassion, resilience, and overall well-being Improved leadership

students are, what they are able to do, and where they need the most support prior to entering their postsecondary education learning and development journey (this equates to inputs assessment, the "I" of the model), an organization could theoretically design a holistic learning and development experience that is meaningful for every student. The organization could then evaluate the effectiveness of that experience (E) as the students journey through their postsecondary experience, regardless of how many years that takes. The organization can then evaluate the outcomes for each particular student (O). However, for several reasons, many of which are included in the challenges we discussed in the introduction and in other areas of this book, most institutions have not been able to practice the I-E-O methodology for all of their students.

As such, we used pre- and posttests to determine the effectiveness of specific courses or other intentionally designed interventions or training programs. Using quasi-experimental design, we can even compare the outcomes for particular educational treatments (courses, training programs, interventions). While this practice is much more accessible to many of us in higher education, it also may be moving us further away from the holistic learning and development conversation. We used a pre-/postdesign to assess the effectiveness of INIQ largely because that is often the measure required to gain funding to support further investigation into the specifics of identifying the process of learning. These further investigations then more precisely inform the effective design, delivery, and evaluation of higher education. We used many other measures that are not reported in this chapter and that were not included in the pre-/postdesign, such as the way we evaluated students' creative expressions where they wrote music and poetry; performed their music, poetry, and dance; and shared their artwork, photographs, garden designs, nature experiences, and so on. We remain committed to being with the messiness of the unseen and the ambiguity of guiding students in holistic learning and development. We also remain committed to gathering data using quasi-experimental design methodology as well as randomized controlled trials. We seek to embody what we are teaching, namely an integrated approach to designing, delivering, and evaluating the student experience.

Designing holistic learning and development is much more than behavioral intervention. Experiencing the unknown with our students and using our own senses to guide students on their holistic learning and development journeys meant not assessing everything we designed and delivered. Yes, that was "weird" when we started out, but now we are embracing it; the final self-report experience of our students, their supervisors, and their family members has been nothing short of compelling (details of which hopefully will be shared in refereed journal publications under review). Our intention is to return to a higher education design where the student engages fully in the content of what she is studying; monitors her own AR and ER; and engages CR to discern how to prioritize what information has been gathered, how to use it, and what she needs to do next to expand on the learning. We intend to continue focusing on the process of learning and development as we incrementally dip into the students' journey to monitor how they are progressing, continually adjusting what we offer and how we offer it to ensure success. If we can educate students to engage in their learning and development journey with awareness and ability to regulate their own attention, emotion, and cognition, we can free our resources to guide them through their experiences.

After three years of piloting INIQ and gathering assessment data, we continue to "experiment" with various versions of INIQ as we gather additional data based on first-person experience, rubrics, 360 evaluations, pre- and posttests, and more. We continue to marvel at the ideas that INIQ participants present to enhance the design of INIQ and how they adopt and adapt it for their own uses in their workplace, community service, and home life. Well-designed reflective student learning and development portfolios allow us to continue to collect the type of data to ascertain when students are making meaning of the content they are experiencing from their courses and how they are making meaning of applying that content out of class. We use rubrics to evaluate the portfolios and invite in external partner evaluation as well.

Given all of this, perhaps we can continue to transform higher education while keeping the course in the driver's seat. We could return to offering development methodology that we know is missing in the context of segmented courses. We could require courses on nutrition and exercise, nature, and creative encounters, among other tips offered in this book, but that would likely increase the time to degree for every student. We don't know "the" solution. What seems to be true is that what we have been doing in the past doesn't seem to be working. So, we invite the reader to consider what we do "know" about neuroscience and its relevance to redesigning and evaluating learning and development opportunities.

Editor's Summary Points and Questions to Consider

1. The design of INIQ in higher education requires use of the research-informed mindfulness methodology and mindful

inquiry. How might you embed this methodology and its practices in your college or university classroom and out-of-classroom experiences?

2. INIQ requires training the students' sensing capabilities and integrating those with the intellect so the student can embrace uncertainty while creating solutions to wicked problems; this process, however, is rather "messy." Where might you most easily be able to intentionally integrate "messy" aspects of fostering learning and development within your college or university?

3. Astin's (1993) I-E-O model is considered by many to be a gold standard for evaluation of holistic student learning and development. Reflective student learning portfolios are offered as a way to meet this model. Where might you be able to implement reflective student learning portfolios at your institution allowing you to collect data that reflect the holistic student learning and development experience?

References

Association of American Colleges & Universities. (2013). *It takes more than a major: Employer priorities for college learning and student success.* Retrieved from www.aacu.org/leap/documents/2013_EmployerSurvey.pdf.

Arum, R., & Roksa, J. (2011). *Academically adrift: Limited learning on college campuses.* Chicago, IL: University of Chicago Press.

Ashcraft, M. H. (2002). Math anxiety: Personal, educational, and cognitive consequences. *Directions in Psychological Science, 11*, 181–185.

Astin, A. (1993). *What matters in college: Four critical years revisited.* San Francisco, CA: Jossey-Bass.

Baer, R. A., Smith, G. T., & Allen, K. B. (2004). Assessment of mindfulness by self-report. The Kentucky inventory of mindfulness skills. *Assessment, 11*(3), 191–206.

Baum, A. (1990). Stress, intrusive imagery, and chronic distress. *Health Psychology, 9*(6), 653–675.

Baum, A., Cohen, L., & Hall, M. (1993). Control and intrusive memories as possible determinants of chronic stress. *Psychosomatic Medicine, 55*(3), 274–286.

Beilock, S. (2010). *Choke: What the secrets of the brain reveal about getting it right when you have to.* New York, NY: Free Press.

Bergen-Cico, D., Possemato, K., & Cheon, S. (2013). Examining the efficacy of a brief mindfulness-based stress reduction (brief MBSR) program on psychological health. *Journal of American College Health, 61*(6), 348–360.

Blumenstyk, G. (2014). *American higher education in crisis: What everyone needs to know.* New York, NY: Oxford University Press.

Bok, D. C. (2013). *Higher education in America*. Princeton, NJ: Princeton University Press.

Bravers, T. S., Reynolds, J. R., & Donaldson, D. I. (2003). Neural mechanisms of transient and sustained cognitive control during task switching. *Neuron, 39*(4), 713–726.

Brener, N., Billy, J., & Grady, W. (2003). Assessment of factors affecting the validity of self-reported health-risk behavior among adolescents: Evidence from the scientific literature. *Journal of Adolescent Health, 33*(6), 436–457.

Brown, K. W., & Ryan, R. M. (2003). The benefits of being present: Mindfulness and its role in psychological well-being. *Journal of Personality and Social Psychology, 84*, 822–848.

Buchheld, N., Grossman, P., & Walach, H. (2001). Measuring mindfulness in insight meditation (Vipassana) and meditation-based psychotherapy: The development of the Freiburg Mindfulness Inventory (FMI). *Journal for Meditation and Meditation Research, 1*(1), 11–34.

Campbell-Sills, L., & Barlow, D. H. (2007). Incorporating emotion regulation into conceptualizations and treatments of anxiety and mood disorders. In J. J. Gross (Ed.), *Handbook of emotion regulation* (pp. 542–559). New York, NY: Guilford Press.

Catania, J., Gibson, D., Chitwood, D., & Coates, T. (1990). Methodological problems in AIDS behavioral research: Influences on measurement error and participation bias in studies of sexual behavior. *Psychological Bulletin, 108*(3), 339–362.

Chadwick, P., Hember, M., Symes, J., Peters, E., Kuipers, E., & Dagnan, D. (2008). Responding mindfully to unpleasant thoughts and images: Reliability and validity of the Southampton mindfulness questionnaire (SMQ). *British Journal of Clinical Psychology, 47*(4), 451–455.

Chiesa, A., Calati, R., & Serretti, A. (2011). Does mindfulness training improve cognitive abilities? A systematic review of neuropsychological findings. *Clinical Psychology Review, 31*(3), 449–464.

Compas, B., Connor-Smith, J., Saltzman, H., Thomsen, A., & Wadsworth, M. (2001). Coping with stress during childhood and adolescence: Problems, progress, and potential in theory and research. *Psychological Bulletin, 127*(1), 87–127.

Cotman, C. W., & Berchtold, N. C. (2002). Exercise builds brain health: Key roles of growth factor cascades and inflammation. *Trends in Neuroscience, 25*(6), 295–301.

Cotman, C. W., Berchtold, N. C., & Christie, L. A. (2007). Exercise: A behavioral intervention to enhance brain health and plasticity. *Trends in Neuroscience, 30*(9), 464–472.

Damasio, A., & Carvalho, G. (2013). The nature of feelings: Evolutionary and neurobiological origins. *Nature Reviews Neuroscience, 14*(2), 143–152.

Damasio, A., Damasio, H., & Tranel, D. (2013). Persistence of feelings and sentience after bilateral damage of the insula. *Cerebral Cortex, 23*(4), 833–846.

Del Boca, F., & Noll, J. (2000). Truth or consequences: The validity of self-report data in health services research on addictions. *Addiction, 95*(Suppl. 3), S347–S360.

Dove, A., Pollmann, S., Schubert, T., Wiggins, C. J., & Yves von Cramon, D. (2000). Prefrontal cortex activation in task switching: An event-related fMRI study. *Cognitive Brain Research, 9*(1), 103–109.

Garland, E., Gaylord, S., & Park, J. (2009). The role of mindfulness in positive reappraisal. *Explore (NY), 5*, 37–44.

Gilbert, S. J., & Shallice, T. (2002). Task switching: A PDP model. *Cognitive Psychology, 44*(3), 297–337.

Goldin, P. R., & Gross, J. J. (2010). Effects of mindfulness-based stress reduction (MBSR) on the emotion regulation in social anxiety disorder. *Emotion, 10*, 83–91.

Goldin, P. R., Hakimi, S., Manber, T., Canli, T., & Gross, J. J. (2009). Neural bases of social anxiety disorder: Emotional reactivity and cognitive regulation during social and physical threat. *Archives of General Psychiatry, 66*, 170–180.

Goldin, P. R., Manber-Ball, T., Werner, K., Heimberg, R., & Gross, J. J. (2009). Neural mechanisms of cognitive reappraisal of negative self-beliefs in social anxiety disorder. *Biological Psychiatry, 66*, 1091–1099.

Goldin, P. R., Ramel, W., & Gross, J. J. (2009). Mindfulness meditation training and self-referential processing in social anxiety disorder: Behavioral and neural effects. *Journal of Cognitive Psychotherapy, 23*, 242–257.

Goleman, D. (2001). *An EI-based theory of performance: The emotionally intelligent workplace: How to select for, measure, and improve emotional intelligence in individuals, groups, and organizations.* San Francisco, CA: Jossey-Bass.

Hayes, A. M., & Feldman, G. (2004). Clarifying the construct of mindfulness in the context of emotion regulation and the process of change in therapy. *Clinical Psychology: Science and Practice, 11*(3), 255–262.

Hembree, R. (1990). The nature, effects, and relief of mathematics anxiety. *Journal for Research in Mathematics Education, 21*, 33–46.

Herzog, S., & Bowman, N. (2011). *Validity and limitations of college student self-report data: New directions for institutional research, number 150.* San Francisco, CA: Jossey-Bass.

Hölzel, B. K., Carmody, J., Vangel, M., Congleton, C., Yerramsetti, S. M., Gard, T., & Lazar, S. W. (2011). Mindfulness practice leads to increases in regional brain gray matter density. *Psychiatry Research: Neuroimaging, 191*(1), 36–43.

Hölzel, B. K., Lazar, S. W., Gard, T., Schuman-Olivier, Z., Vago, D. R., & Ott, U. (2011). How does mindfulness meditation work? Proposing mechanisms of action from a conceptual and neural perspective. *Perspectives on Psychological Science, 6*(6), 537–559.

Hutcherson, C. A., Goldin, P. R., Ramel, W., McRae, K., & Gross, J. J. (2008). Attention and emotion influence the relationship between extraversion and neural response. *Social Cognitive and Affective Neuroscience, 3*, 71–79.

Kabat-Zinn, J. (2013). *Full catastrophe living (revised edition): Using the wisdom of your body and mind to face stress, pain, and illness.* New York, NY: Bantam Books.

Langer, E. (1989). *Mindfulness.* Reading, MA: Da Capo Books.

Lesch, K. P. (2007). Linking emotion to the social brain. *EMBO Reports, 8*(Suppl. 1), S24–S29.

Levy, D. (2007). No time to think: Reflections on information technology and contemplative scholarship. *Ethics and Information Technology, 9*(4), 237–249.

Luders, E., Toga, A. W., Lepore, N., & Gaser, C. (2009). The underlying anatomical correlates of long-term meditation: Larger hippocampal and frontal volumes of gray matter. *NeuroImage, 45*(3), 672–678.

Mahone, E. M., Bruch, M. A., & Heimberg, R. G. (1993). Focus of attention and social anxiety: The role of negative self-thoughts and perceived positive attributes of the other. *Cognitive Therapy and Research, 17*(3), 209–224.

Mallow, J. V. (2006). *Science anxiety: Research and action.* Retrieved from static.nsta .org/files/PB205X-1.pdf

Mettler, S. (2014). *Degrees of inequality: How the politics of higher education sabotaged the American dream.* New York, NY: Basic Books.

Mitcheson, P., Yeatman, E., Rao, G., Holmes, A., & Green, T. (2008). Energy harvesting from human and machine motion for wireless electronic devices. *Proceedings of the IEEE, 56*(9), 1457–1486.

OECD. (2010). Moving beyond the jobs crisis—Supporting material for Chapter 1 of the 2010 OECD employment outlook. Paris, France: OECD Publishing. Retrieved from http://www.oecd.org/employment/emp/48806664.pdf

Ochsner, K. N., & Gross, J. J. (2005). The cognitive control of emotion. *Trends in Cognitive Science, 9*(5), 242–249.

Orthner, D. K., Jones-Sanpei, H., & Williamson, S. (2004). The resilience and strengths of low income families. *Family Relations, 53*(2), 159–167.

Philippi, C., Feinstein, J., Khalsa, S., Damasio, A., Tranel, D., Landini, G, . . . Rudraug, D. (2012). Preserved self-awareness following extensive bilateral brain damage to the insula, anterior cingulate, and medial prefrontal cortices. *PLOS ONE, 7*(8), e38413–e38416.

Posner, M. I., & Fan, J. (2004). *Attention as an organ system: Topics in integrative neuroscience: From cells to cognition.* Cambridge, UK: Cambridge University Press.

Rasch, B., & Born, J. (2013). About sleep's role in memory. *Physiological Reviews, 93*(2). 681–766.

Rosenburg, M. B. (2003). *Nonviolent communication: A language of life.* Encinitas, CA: Puddledancer Press.

Salovey, P., Mayer, J. D., Goldman, S. L., Turvey, C., & Palfai, T. P. (1995). Emotional attention, clarity, and repair: Exploring emotional intelligence using the Trait Meta-Mood Scale. In J. W. Pennebaker (Ed.), *Emotion, disclosure, & health* (pp. 125–154). Washington, DC: American Psychological Association.

Smith, B. W., Dalen, J., Wiggins, K., Tooley, E., Christopher, P., & Bernard, J. (2008). The brief resilience scale: Assessing the ability to bounce back. *International Journal of Behavioral Medicine, 15*(3), 194–200.

Stone, D., & Patton, B. (1999). *Difficult conversations: How to discuss what matters most.* London, UK: Penguin.

Strong, W. B., Malina, R. M., Blimkie, C. J. , Daniels, S. R., Dishman, R. K., Gutin, B., & Trudeau, F. (2005). Evidence based physical activity for school-age youth. *Journal of Pediatrics, 146*(6), 732–737.

Stroop, J. R. (1935). Studies of interference in serial verbal reactions. *Journal of Experimental Psychology, 18*(6), 643.

Swainson, R., Cunnington, R., Jackson, G. M., Rorden, C., Peters, A. M., Morris, P. G., & Jackson, S. R. (2003). Cognitive control mechanisms revealed by ERP and fMRI: Evidence from repeated task-switching. *Journal of Cognitive Neuroscience, 15*(6), 785–799.

Tan, C. M. (2012). *Search inside yourself: The unexpected path to achieving success, happiness (and world peace)*. New York, NY: HarperOne.

Tan, O. (2009). *Developing creative learning environments in problem-based learning*. Retrieved from www.academia.edu/744107/Developing_Creative_Learning_Environments_in_Problem-based_Learning

Taras, H. (2005). Physical activity and student performance at school. *Journal of School Health, 75*(6), 214–218.

Tobias, S. (1993). *Overcoming math anxiety*. New York, NY: W. W. Norton.

MINDFULNESS AT WORK IN HIGHER EDUCATION LEADERSHIP

From Theory to Practice Within the Classroom and Across the University

Les P. Cook and Anne Beffel

Mindfulness is a state of being fully present, aware of oneself and other people, and sensitive to one's reactions to stressful situations. Leaders who are mindful tend to be more effective in understanding and relating to others, and motivating them toward shared goals. Hence, they become more effective in leadership roles.

—William W. George ("Mindfulness Helps You Become a Better Leader," 2012, retrieved from hbr.org/2012/10/mindfulness-helps-you-become)

Mindfulness and contemplative practices have been around for centuries and more recently have become part of both corporate and higher education culture. This chapter examines some of the ways in which these practices are being explored and infused onto college and university campuses. Readers are provided examples of the intersection of mindfulness, social intelligence, and compassion. We also take the reader on a journey that investigates how two very different campuses have introduced the practices. We conclude with considerations for introducing the practices on campus and some common pitfalls that can be avoided.

Located on the northern tip of Michigan on the shores of Lake Superior, Michigan Technological University (Michigan Tech) is surrounded by pristine natural beauty, wilderness areas, and one of the largest bodies of freshwater in the world. The members of our community have, among others, cultural roots in European Judeo-Christian groups; Nordic groups; Mediterranean groups; and the indigenous cultures of the Menominee, Nocquet, Mishinimaki, and Ojibwe tribes. Residents of this region who arrived from elsewhere in the nineteenth century developed industry based on copper mining. Thus, a state-supported college of mines and engineering emerged. Like the rest of American Society, the institution has evolved. At Michigan Tech, our students and faculty are primarily focused on disciplines related to science, technology, engineering, and math (STEM) fields. We are, like much of Western culture, driven by rapid advances in science and technology. Along with this, we are driven to succeed, sometimes at almost any cost with an almost constant "go-go-go" mentality. Even though recent research (Bergen-Cico & Cheon, 2014; Bergen-Cico, Possemato, & Cheon, 2013; Razza, Bergen-Cico, & Raymond, 2013) has found that this type of mentality is associated with higher rates of anxiety and less compassion for self and others, it is challenging to think about slowing down enough to be present or to be in the moment. Similar to our colleagues mentioned throughout the book, we wondered how we too might develop practices that support mindfulness, compassion, and meaning making on our campus without losing our ability to think critically and lead members of our community toward problem solving when crisis erupts.

Mindfulness: More Than an Experience, It's a Commitment

Les's Story

My name is Les P. Cook. I have been in a senior leadership role at Michigan Tech for 11 years. One December, I found myself on the campus of the oldest university in the United States and one of the most well known and respected universities in the world: Harvard. The previous summer, I had spent nearly two weeks on the ivy-lined campus immersed in an intensive leadership development program for college and university administrators. I was attending the December meeting as a follow-up to the summer session to further explore leadership and decision making in higher education. As I sat cross-legged on a yoga mat, I began thinking, "This is a session on mindfulness, contemplative practice, and how to develop focused attention. Around the room are Montessori education leaders, academic department chairs, and other educators. Many of us are well-seasoned professionals." I thought back to my own college campus and wondered, "Shouldn't we be incorporating these types of experiences and practices into what we do with our students, so *they* are not all sitting around when they get to be seasoned midcareer professionals, wondering what really matters? Why, at this age, are we all sitting here trying to determine how to have better focus and make better decisions?" By the end of the training, I knew it was time for me to explore more. I was eager to learn and wanted to consider how these concepts, ideas, and contemplative practices could be infused into my own campus.

Anne's Story

My name is Anne Beffel. I have been interested in creativity as long as I can remember, and I have been schooled in the Bauhaus tradition, modernism, and the "artist as activist" model of the Whitney Museum of American Art Studio Program. In 2008, I began to consciously incorporate my long-standing interests in contemplative practices into my teaching. Prior to arriving at Michigan Tech, I taught at Syracuse University for 13 years. A while ago, upon completing a four-day silent meditation, I was struck once again by the simplicity of the practice of being present. I noticed how simple it was to sense the connectedness between myself and the world of people, places, and things. It was simple—and it was very hard. It has been a matter of continual practice to experience even a full cycle of breath without distraction; to stop striving, pause, and notice a dew drop on a leaf; or to hear the complaint of a colleague, understanding that it is specific to a moment we are sharing, as well as part of shared, human suffering.

As I am new to Michigan Tech and the role of an artist at a STEM-focused university, making myself constantly aware of this experience during silent retreats has been essential. Volumes of e-mail arrive in my inbox, meetings multiply, and course prep rises to the top of the pile. Amid all of this, it is important to remember to pause. When I pause, I notice connectedness. Precisely by spending time listening to seemingly disconnected moments and stories with colleagues and students, I gain insights and find that I have more to offer. For example, I was recently preparing a talk for a conference on contemplative pedagogy. Striving to explain to former student, current friend, and Buddhist filmmaker Yao Xu how the three components of my talk title were related, I turned the question back to her. Out of our conversation grew her inspired reply:

> When my life is in a constant flow of contemplation, I feel grounded and connected to the place I reside in. And that just provides such rich soil and meaning to my work, and the meaningfulness keeps me excited about my art. When I lose the sense that I am connected to my subject, the excitement is vanished right away. All these doubts start to emerge. How can I be creative inside waves of doubt about me, my surroundings, and the work where I put my life? (Xu, personal communication, 2014)

More than just an answer to a writing problem, Yao's comment demonstrates the necessary good of opening up opportunities for mindful, self-reflective education.

Our Story, Your Story

While both of us have been in higher education most of our adult careers, we both grew professionally on somewhat different paths. Les has been a student affairs practitioner, teacher, and administrator, while Anne has been an artist and faculty member deeply involved in teaching, administration, and research. These two stories represent the shared interests as well as the pivotal points that inspired us to bring mindfulness practices to Michigan Tech's campus. We both discovered that we care about being present in our life's experience and actively feeling compassion for self and others. We also discovered that we both strive to find our own way of weaving peace and compassion into our life and work.

This chapter draws on personal experiences and scholarly literature to give pause and consideration to the questions we have pondered. What inherent practices or missed opportunities of mindfulness can we draw from to open perspectives, show benefits, and inspire participation in an integrated set of contemplative practices, compassion, and meaning making? How is it possible to introduce mindfulness in leadership development? What can we do that will allow our campuses to be places where diverse students can find the space they need to recognize themselves and their connectedness to the world they help steward?

The Mindful Paradox

With technology, economic pressures, work, and family, it is hard, if not impossible, to stay on top of everything. As mentioned throughout this book, these pressures upset our natural balance and push us into an overloaded and overwhelmed state, which can lead to anxiety, fear, and depression. While we can't check out of life and avoid responsibility, we can approach things in a gentler way (Vozza, 2014). We know, despite how we may feel at the moment of striving, that slowing down can make us more productive and enable us to connect to our surroundings and one another in more meaningful ways while also helping students, faculty, and staff develop their sense of self the context of the larger world (Langer, 1989; Levy, 2007).

We both work in a high-stress university environment. Les's roles as an administrator, father, husband, involved community member, and engaged contributor in higher education—like that of many others—can be overwhelming. He can feel the pressure of the onslaught of work—ensuring that enrollments are where they need to be at the institution; developing the programs and resources that students need to be successful; making sure that companies are coming to campus and hiring students; providing students with a rich, safe, and positive learning environment; encouraging athletic success; obtaining adequate resources to do what we need to do; and being a decent dad, spouse, and contributor in his family, community, and professional world of higher education. This is all somewhat akin to what Kadison (Kadison & DiGeronimo, 2004) described in his book *College of the Overwhelmed*. This is partially what led Les to Harvard and the Institute on Decision Making and Mindfulness Practice.

After attending the session at Harvard, Les returned to campus with renewed hope and excitement for possibilities that could occur on campus. The impact of the sessions was dramatic and he began noticing how his sense of urgency and frustration was minimized, even with airport personnel when experiencing flight delays and changes. With this new heightened awareness, he began to realize that he didn't necessarily have to worry about or bog his mind down with all of the little decisions that others would like to make anyway. Rather, he began to "know" when to focus on the decisions that matter. Engaged in his mindfulness practice, it became apparent to him that through the practices of mindfulness, meditation, focused attention, and being present in the moment he became a more compassionate, thoughtful, and all more caring human being. Because of this, he could become a better decision maker, leader, and contributor to society.

Anne's role as a practicing artist and professor does not always make it easy or convenient to be fully present in the moment. In 2008, Anne was honored with an academic fellowship from the Center for Contemplative Mind in Society (CCMS). The CCMS fellowship allowed her to explore mindfulness in an academic course and provided support for her to travel to the summer session on contemplative pedagogy at Smith College. She returned from the summer session with much more than a feeling of institutional support for her mindfulness work. She had a better understanding of the nomenclature; a fresh perspective on a variety of practices; and, most important, ideas for how to more consciously integrate those practices into curricula and programs across campus.

We realize that at first the practice can seem both challenging and overwhelming, but it is really quite simple once one has a conceptual understanding of the basic premise. Simply stated, mindfulness is the process of noticing things and the state of being present in the present (Langer, 1989). Accordingly, Jerry Murphy (2011), dean emeritus of the Harvard Graduate School of Education, asserted, "Mindfulness is not aimed at making us feel better, but rather at getting better at noticing our feelings and thoughts" (p. 40). The mindfulness practice also involves letting go of the striving and other urges to effortlessly notice the situation and your surroundings. And all of it can be grounded in the idea of well-being or, put simply, just being.

Intertwined with simply being are daily practices of taking care of oneself (the neuroscience for which has already been outlined in this book) while having compassion for self and compassion for others. For Les, this translates into taking time and seizing opportunities to interact with others in an interested, caring, and personal manner, as well as making space in his daily routine for exercise, yoga practice, or other decompression activity. It's about being in tune with his whole self—mind and body—and with others and able to embrace and enjoy each moment in an appreciative manner. For Anne, daily self-care means practicing yoga or playing tennis, sitting meditation practice, taking time to breathe, reflecting on a certain thought or idea, turning her camera into a tool for knowing her surroundings, or seeing things in a way we often do not afford ourselves. These practices provide the context for the contemplative interactions, which rest at the heart of Anne's public and socially engaged art projects and teaching.

Our experiences have helped us integrate mindfulness into *our* daily practices, but similar to our colleagues mentioned throughout the book, we wondered how we might develop practices that support mindfulness, compassion, and meaning making on our college campus.

Using Mindfulness to Enhance Social Intelligence and Compassion

This book has already shared several issues regarding how we do and don't provide integrated learning and development in higher education. We won't repeat a lot of what you have already read. We do want to emphasize, however, that much of Daniel Goleman's (2011, 2012) work on emotional intelligence points to the disconnect between intelligence quotient (IQ), which recruits certain parts of the brain, and emotional empathy, which recruits other parts of the brain. While this book has illustrated that IQ and emotional intelligence may not be as separate as once believed, simply being smart still isn't going to "cut it."

In their book, *We're Losing Our Minds: Rethinking American Higher Education*, Keeling and Hersh (2012) indicate that while we once thought the brain was fully developed when students reached their adult height and when bone growth stopped, this is no longer the case. As emphasized in Chapters 2 and 6, the brain is capable of change far into adulthood. It is therefore critical that our college and university students are provided experiences that inspire well-being, reflection and introspection, compassion, and meaning making. A repeating theme of Goleman's work is that if you are not emotionally attentive, you can't have empathy; without empathy, you can't have effective relationships or interactions; and without effective relationships or interactions, you are less likely to be effective in your job (Baron & Markman, 2000). Therefore, no matter how smart you are, you are not going to get very far without emotional attentiveness (Goleman, Boyatzis, & McKee, 2013). How much do we foster that awareness in our educational institutions? How could we do so to an even greater extent?

To begin to answer this question, we would like to look at what we do know about social intelligence to determine how we could use mindfulness to enhance student ability to relate to one another and build connections (Gardner, 1983; Goleman, 2006), teach compassion (as referred to in Chapters 7 and 10), and encourage intentional design of high-impact practices (as referred to in the introduction and in Chapter 5). In the early part of the twentieth century, Thorndike coined the term *social intelligence* as the way in which we act wisely in human relations (Thorndike & Stein, 1937). In the past, others have used their own framework for observing and evaluating social intelligence to elaborate on whether we experience wise connections among humans. These early observations and results focused on understanding and managing relationships (between men and women, boys and girls) through social technique and knowledge of social matters. Much of this research was based on family, playground/school, and work relationships. More recently, an emphasis on students demonstrating social intelligence is emerging, perhaps because of the extensive use of technology. We are unsure whether connections via technology are meaningful and wise (Engelberg & Sjogberg, 2004). Goleman (2006) suggests that social intelligence should be at the forefront of understanding, especially as we look at neuroscience and at the brain and its regulation of interpersonal dynamics (see Chapters 3, 5, 6, and 10 for more details). Goleman's emotional intelligence model begins with understanding one's own state (self-awareness) and encompasses broad understanding, empathy, and compassion for others (social awareness and facility).

The recognition of the importance of social intelligence is modeled at Stanford's School of Design (D-school) through its practices of empathetic design (Hass Plattner, 2014). D-school founder David Kelly (Kelly & Kelly, 2013), who worked with Steve Jobs to create the first computer mouse, emphasizes multidisciplinary design teams with students from STEM fields and the arts and humanities. At the core of their education is the notion of empathetic design. The designer must watch and sense how people interact with the product being used to understand how to be a good designer. Attentiveness and empathy (also referred to as attention, emotion, and cognitive regulation [AR, ER, and CR] in this book) are moving into the center of design education, and with them moves the importance of mindfulness practices (Kelly & Kelly, 2013).

Adding to the examples given in Chapters 5 and 10, we see the D-school as a model for teaching social intelligence and compassion. Looking forward, we are hopeful that if we can show how mindfulness (or AR, ER, and CR) benefits enhancement of social intelligence (Gardner, 1983; Goleman, 2006) and creativity, critical thinking, and compassion (as described in Chapters 7–10), we can increase student success in an integrative, holistic, institution-wide manner.

Inviting Contemplation and Mindfulness

As mentioned in Chapter 4, regardless of your vocation—whether you are a university professor who is always engaged in laboratory research, a classroom instructor, an academic adviser, a student activities director, or a vice president for student affairs and enrollment management—you can play a pivotal role in helping students find meaning in their lives, learn how to be present in the moment, and make positive contributions to society. The self-acceptance and compassion that often accompany mindfulness practices (discussed in Chapter 8) are foundational to engaged citizenship (a key educational goal mentioned in the introduction), which challenges individuals to both get along with others and be able to stand alone in integrity when necessary (Shankman & Allen, 2008). In doing this, we have the opportunity to share experiences and ideas and help students shape their lives in ways that will shape who they are and how they interact with and impact others.

Mindful leadership is about paying attention to your emotions, being present in the moment, and being aware of your presence and the ways in which your presence impacts other people (George, 2012). As discussed in Chapter 4, self is not something that one just has; rather self is built, "accomplished through the act of establishing communication between the mind and heart, the mind and experience, that you become an individual, a unique being—a soul" (Deresiewicz, 2014).

What can we do to make our campuses places that invite contemplation, mindfulness, and building of selves? How do we take what might already exist in contemplative pedagogy and mindfulness-based practices and adapt or build on it in order to infuse mindfulness practices into the routine of our students? Amherst, Brown University, Michigan Tech, San Diego State University, Syracuse University, University of California–San Diego, University of Michigan, University of San Diego, University of Southern California, University of Virginia, University of Washington, and other institutions referenced throughout the book are obviously at different stages of cultivating mindfulness practice (or AR, ER, and CR training) into their organizations.

Certainly, all campuses may have pieces in place that could form a foundation for mindfulness practice. In order to aid idea generation around implementation, we share two case studies: one from Syracuse University and one from Michigan Tech.

Syracuse University—Anne's Experience

The artist's "way of seeing" is different from ordinary seeing and requires an ability to make mental shifts by conscious volition . . . this ability to see things differently and to enable insight to rise to conscious level . . . has many uses in life aside from drawing—not the least of which is creative problem solving.

—Betty Edwards, personal communication, October 14, 2013

My experiences as an art professor, public artist, and colleague have encouraged my mindfulness practice. As I work with Les on the Mindfulness Council, I see how what I've come to know through public art practice in urban centers across the United States, my education, and experiences at Syracuse University is highly transferable and applicable to students and colleagues at Michigan Tech. As mentioned earlier, in many ways Syracuse University stands in contrast to Michigan Tech. Syracuse University has a student body that is more heavily female than Michigan Tech's, with many students from the greater metropolitan New York and New Jersey areas. Its curriculum is oriented toward the humanities, art, and design. This is in stark contrast to Michigan Tech's STEM focus, more heavily male student body, and students mostly from rural midwestern areas. I find it compelling that despite these differences, the benefits of mindfulness practices are highly applicable.

When it comes to mindfulness practices, I have witnessed the profound reverberations of simple and small acts of mindfulness. One such reverberation originated in Syracuse in 1971, when graduate student Robert G. Strickland felt a book "grab his heart." Robert spent an entire afternoon engrossed in the book, an original source on Zen Buddhism. In this book, Robert found reflections of himself and a pedagogy that would support his work and life for decades to follow. After his introduction to Zen Buddhism, Robert was inspired to sit with a small group of students interested in meditation at Syracuse University (Robert Strickland, personal communication, 2014).

Although they did not know they were planting the seeds of a contemplative studies minor (established 43 years later), Robert and friends understood the importance of keeping things simple at the start—wisdom that we at Michigan Tech fully appreciate. Robert and friends simply read and sat in meditation together. Their persistence in meditating together eventually inspired the founding of the Zen Center of Syracuse Hoen-ji, under the leadership of Roko Sherry Chayat, Shinge Roshi with Reverend Jikyo Bonnie Shoultz, who plays a fundamental role in the secular contemplative pedagogy movement at Syracuse University and the offering of Buddhist meditation practices at Hendricks Chapel.

As an associate professor in visual arts in 2008, I was only vaguely aware of the Zen Center. I was, however, well aware that I wanted to change the way I taught, shift my presence in the classroom, and improve how students related to not only their work but also one another. That same year, I received an academic fellowship (the one I mentioned earlier in this chapter) from the CCMS, with funding from the Fetzer Institute. My fellowship project drew together my public art practice, the curriculum I developed to teach video, and my interest in social science. Contemplative practice was the lens through which I saw the ways in which these different fields of knowledge were connected. Integrating them into opportunities for integrative student learning was my goal.

The fellowship enabled me to gain a deeper understanding of contemplative pedagogies through travel and study. Along with a few like-minded colleagues from Syracuse University, I attended a conference on contemplative pedagogy. We sought to develop practical ways to integrate our meditation practices into our courses. Many of the concepts my colleagues and I encountered at the weeklong conference would prove to serve us well over time. Conference attendees and leaders explored philosophical and practical questions. As we listened to the conference leaders speak, the link between careful use of language and success with contemplative pedagogies and programming became clear.

The conference was led by Arthur Zajonc, former director of the CCMS, professor emeritus of physics at Amherst College, and current president of the Mind & Life Institute. Zajonc provided examples of how students' learning can deepen through instructors' subtle shifts toward contemplative pedagogies. He brilliantly explained several practices and asked us to test them. These practices have proven useful to faculty teaching in a wide range of disciplines.

Beth Wadham (2008), former program assistant for the CCMS at Amherst College, summarized Zajonc's key concepts:

> Arthur Zajonc observed that general contemplative practices—which include silence, self-observation, and attention to breathing—support learning because they help establish equanimity and the ability to sustain attention. The ability to apply voluntary focus to an object—a painting,

a poem, or an equation—for sustained periods can be cultivated with intention over time and is probably the single quality most important for becoming a successful student. Alternating a quiet, focused attention with what Zajonc calls "open attention" is well known in contemplative traditions as an attitude of "not seeking" that allows one to break free of reactive, associative thinking and allows for subtle and unexpected discoveries.

Inspired and energized by what we learned, my colleagues and I began integrating some of the practices and techniques into our courses. This was initially implemented for students of art and design at Syracuse University who were enrolled in courses I offered. A series of blogs, journals, projects, and critique discussions evidenced the students' increasing awareness of the movement of their minds. Some discovered they could watch their mind's movement or their thoughts without being completely captured by them. Contemplative art courses engaged students in different kinds of meditation: sitting, walking, looking, listening, and practicing yoga with the assistance of taught by a certified yoga instructor. In addition, students focused on gestures involved in making art as objects of attention: a pencil point moving across paper, a video or photograph being recorded, hands carving plaster, a paintbrush loaded with only water used to "paint" a block of wood.

In contemplative arts workshops, high school students from inner-city Syracuse worked alongside their university student neighbors. Despite the trepidation many students initially felt when faced with differences in age and cultural and socioeconomic backgrounds, the students connected and collaborated to create artworks reflective of how they felt, thought about, and viewed their surroundings (Oliveras, 2014).

Being mindful not only helped with art project construction, but also enhanced the process of evaluating the artworks themselves. We evaluated students' progress through a supportive group critique process during which we reviewed students' artworks. With increasing present-ness and openness, students were able to listen deeply (Brady, 2009; Oliveras, 2014) to one another's stories of being highly observant. Students heard and acknowledged for one another how each individual looked at the world. While in a state of mindfulness, students reflected on their sense of wonder with small visual details contained in their artworks: movements, reflections, colors, and textures—all of which they failed to notice when they were hurried. This experience of wonder at the world, combined with sharing more wonder when seeing their artworks more mindfully, correlated with the quickening of relationships among the students.

My studio arts courses enable us to see the results of mindful practices because, in essence, time-based art forms such as video art are practices of attentiveness. In fact, all artists are crafting something that will inspire people to pay attention. Art is about being aware of the audience, their reactions, and their responses to the art. To remind us of what Goleman (2006) said, we repeat it again: If you are going to interact and successfully develop rapport, you need to have empathy; to empathize, you need to be attentive. While some people may think being attentive or sharing our creativity is the domain of artists and designers, it is the domain of all of us. Making art is all about give-and-take. It is about interactions, attentiveness, and empathy—even compassion. Speaking in bigger, broader terms, there is very little we do in the world that isn't about our interactions with other beings, places, memories, and people.

In subject areas in addition to art, Dessa Bergen-Cico and Rachel Razza teach courses on mindfulness and have led research on mindfulness and self-regulation of emotion among college students and young children. Their research found that when mindful yoga was integrated regularly into the school day by the classroom teacher, student self-regulation, measured by attention, executive function, and effortful control significantly increased (see Razza, et al., 2013). In addition, Bergen-Cico's research on college courses that routinely integrated mindfulness-based meditation into course structure found that practicing moment-to-moment attention and open awareness enabled students from many disciplines to approach course content with more dimensionality to their thinking and less self-criticism (Bergen-Cico & Cheon, 2014; Bergen-Cico et al., 2013).

The courses previously described represent one of several areas at Syracuse University where students are able to find opportunities for mindfulness. Academic affairs and volunteer staff offer programming to parallel faculty efforts. Leaders at Hendricks Chapel, including Dean Tiffany Steinwert, host activities including regular sitting meditation sessions. Buddhist chaplain Reverend Jikyo Bonnie Shoultz supports hourlong meditation sessions every day of the week in collaboration with the Student Buddhist Society. Sessions occur at a small chapel at various times of the day, including the lunch hour. They are led by a range of students, staff, faculty, and administrators (details may be found at hendricks.syr.edu/spiritual-life/chaplaincies/buddhist.html). The Syracuse University Counseling Center offers an eight-week course free to students interested in mindfulness-based stress reduction (MBSR). Founded in 1979 by Jon Kabat-Zinn, these stress reduction programs have benefitted people with chronic pain, anxiety, and depression (more information is available at www.umassmed.edu/cfm/stress-reduction/history-of-mbsr/). The MBSR course at Syracuse University has been popular among students for several years (counselingcenter.syr.edu/documents/mbsr_bro chure.pdf#mbsr%20brochure).

The Syracuse University mindfulness activities benefited from a grass-roots organization called the Wellness Group (WG). The WG was facilitated by what I call "mindful leadership in action" (after the SU model of scholarship in action). In order to draw a clearer picture of mindful leadership in action, or the implementation of mindfulness in higher education by an administrator, I detail how Buddhist chaplain Reverend Jikyo Bonnie Shoultz successfully leads the WG to extraordinary levels of cooperation and productivity.

Shoultz, like many of us, is drawn to contemplative practice in response to an extremely active mind. Years of mindfulness practice as a Buddhist nun inform her leadership by way of what she does not do or say. Stated somewhat differently, her influence manifests in the stillness and receptiveness of her presence, which opens up space for others to engage with the group mindfully.

This approach leads Shoultz to share governance of the group with those interested. Shoultz strives to set an example of fair treatment of faculty and staff, regardless of their positions within the university. She achieves this by "[paying] attention to everyone's ideas" (Shoultz, personal communication, October 14, 2013). I have experienced her abilities to listen mindfully and suggest productive collaborations based upon what she knows of each individual. Her expectation that we will all cooperate is palpable and quietly sets a powerful normative standard. As a consequence, the content of the annual WG meetings remains focused upon what members want to accomplish together. At a WG meeting, 10–20 faculty and staff members might share basic foundations and content for courses, programs, or projects. They might talk about the challenges encountered, solutions found, and questions remaining. For example, they might discuss how to conduct research on student outcomes in new areas of mindfulness within university policy. Faculty and staff might consider progress on the remodeling of a classroom to see if a designed space would be flexible enough to store meditation cushions and yoga mats. The conversations are built on mindful practices modeled by Shoultz.

Arthur Zajonc, director of the Mind & Life Institute, visited Syracuse University in the spring of 2013 and further enriched the WG discussions and brought new momentum to our efforts. According to WG leader Shoultz, Zajonc "helped us think of how to establish ourselves more solidly and formally on campus; how to get the word out of what possibilities (for formalizing the ongoing activities of the WG) might be" (personal communication, October 13–15, 2013). Subsequently, the WG met to discuss how to create a more formal campus entity that would have greater visibility and credibility. The goal was for the growing contemplative pedagogy movement to become part of the mainstream programming and curricula, and, as a result, be available to more students, faculty and staff. According to Shoultz, faculty, staff, and students campus-wide offered several important recommendations to advance this intention. Shoultz recalls that establishing an "academic home" within a department that would administer degree programs in contemplative studies was an immediate priority. This academic home could serve other supportive functions in the future, such as hosting visiting speakers. The group also determined that developing a website where the WG could centralize information was critical (Shoultz, personal communication, October 13–15, 2013).

The notion of offering an academic minor in contemplative studies for undergraduate students at Syracuse University particularly resonated with the WG. In an instance of overlapping values, Dean Diane Murphy offered the Falk College of Sport and Human Dynamics as the academic home for academic mindfulness programming. With this critical piece in place, Shoultz invited Daniel Barbezat, director of CCMS and professor of economics at Amherst College, to consult on developing a minor in contemplative studies; a research center that might draw together faculty from disciplines such as education, public health, social work, sciences, the arts, and communication, and additional structures that might formalize the work of the WG to provide greater visibility and regularity of offerings (Shoultz, personal communication, October 13–15, 2013).

Barbezat started his session at SU with a simple breathing meditation. Rather than focusing on the specific steps for creating an academic minor, he thoughtfully guided us back to the central questions that grew from attitudes of curiosity. This working group practiced listening deeply—we practiced what we had been professing. The tone and sharing of ideas was open and reflective. It is no coincidence that the WG members, many of whom have devoted contemplative practices, have great capacities to listen, empathize, and be reflective. Barbezat challenged us to ask how to integrate new people into an existing effort. What ensued was an abundance of questions that would require more than an afternoon to answer. The questions that encouraged us to practice mindful decision making included the following:

- What do you really mean when you speak of mindfulness?
- How do you address the diversity of traditions out of which contemplative pedagogies grow?
- How do you empower students to occupy the center of the contemplative educational experience?

- What is the most important thing you want for your students, faculty, and staff? How do you meet the challenges to reaching those goals?
- How can your leaders draw upon their own contemplative practices? (Barbezat, personal communication, October 15, 2014)

Barbezat focused our discussions on core definitions and values. The key result was that rather than being distracted by institutional policies or competiveness, new relationships were forged among all interested parties, inclusive of newcomers. The movement toward contemplative pedagogy grew in strength. After Barbezat's visit, a small committee worked with faculty across campus and ironed out the basic course structure of the contemplative studies minor. A number of courses and programs already existed and were integrated in a way that reflected interests of faculty, staff, and students (Shoultz, personal communication, October 13–15, 2013).

Shoultz and the WG view the contemplative studies minor as a first step. The possibilities drawn out of the cooperative efforts and mindfulness practices of the faculty, staff, and students are yet to be developed and explored. There has been discussion about a concentration in contemplative studies, a contemplative studies major, and perhaps research opportunities. The birth of the contemplative studies minor has fueled a new wave of faculty enthusiasm for contemplative pedagogy at Syracuse University (Shoultz, personal communication, October 13–15, 2013). The efforts at Syracuse University around mindfulness continue to grow and evolve.

In summary, some of the contemplative activities at SU that supported the rapid approval of the contemplative studies minor included the following:

- Shared foundation of knowledge and nomenclature among early adaptors of contemplative pedagogies, developed at the CCMS Summer Session conference
- Application of core concepts of contemplative pedagogies
- Sitting meditation groups offered daily at the small chapel
- MBSR courses at the counseling center
- Curricula and programming inside and beyond the classroom, which engaged communities and students with contemplative arts
- Visiting speakers, including mindfulness leaders and educators
- Mindful leadership guided by administrators and faculty with established mindfulness practices
- A WG of faculty and staff (including early adopters of mindfulness)
- Grassroots efforts that developed a history of mindfulness practices among members of community organizations, students, faculty, and staff into a contemplative studies minor

Part of what drew me from Syracuse University to Michigan Tech was the appreciation for contemplative arts I saw during my 2012 visit to the area for my "Color of Kindness" community art project and exhibit at Finlandia University's Finnish American Heritage Center. I was compelled to see what mindfulness practices might look like at a STEM-focused university. A year later, I joined the visual and performing arts department at Michigan Tech. In 2014, I had the privilege of attending the annual summer session on contemplative pedagogy at Smith College (now hosted by the Association for Contemplative Mind in Higher Education) with a half-dozen faculty from both Michigan Tech and Syracuse University. I felt honored to have moved from an attendee to a faculty member who helped to lead the conference. Here, I witnessed a Michigan Tech colleague, Mary Muncil, who serves as interim director of Michigan Tech's Rozsa Center for Performing Arts, embrace and remake into her own the questions she gathered in breakout sessions with Barbezat.

In preparing for the summer session, I further articulated the connections among my experiences as a younger student, artist, meditation practitioner, and faculty member. I shared stories of these integrated roles with colleagues. In response, many of them found or rearticulated links among some of their own contemplative practices, research, and creative pursuits. After the summer session, we returned to our home institutions ready to engage in ideas and collaborate with our colleagues. At Michigan Tech we plan to keep it simple, and to remember to be patient. My hope is that our campus culture will grow to become more mindful as an increasing number of individuals practice just being.

Michigan Technological University—Les's Experience

Over the years, Michigan Tech has sought out and brought in speakers on a variety of subjects. When I started at Michigan Tech in the student affairs division more than 10 years ago, we undertook significant efforts to develop a robust professional development program. These efforts have paid off in many ways, including encouraging a culture and mind-set willing to explore new ideas, innovation, and creativity. I had done some of my own self-exploration as had others on my staff, but the pivotal moment for me was my experience at Harvard University (mentioned in the beginning of this chapter).

As I began to consider mindfulness work on campus, I contacted and had follow-up conversations with numerous colleagues, scholars, and mentors who had familiarity and expertise in mindfulness practice, emotional intelligence work, and leadership development. Included among those discussions was Marilee J. Bresciani Ludvik—scholar, professor, author, and editor of this publication. Marilee, in many ways, introduced me to the practice and had recently introduced mindfulness-based courses on her campus. As we embarked on this journey, consulting with Marilee seemed like the right thing to do. I also consulted with Marcy Levy-Shankman, director of Leadership Cleveland, scholar, writer, and consultant on emotionally intelligent leadership. Marcy's work with emotional intelligence and student leadership is compelling. We discussed emotional intelligence, the intersection of mindfulness practices, and how campuses might successfully embrace both. Metta McGarvey, visiting scholar and chair of Harvard University's Inner Strengths of Successful Leaders Program, was also consulted because of her research and involvement with higher education leaders. Metta shared what she had witnessed in her role as chair of the Harvard program and what campuses were doing to cultivate mindfulness discussions and practice. Finally, I had rich conversations with Paul Pyrz (president of the LeaderShape Institute, colleague, and scholar) about mindfulness practices and the importance of exposing student leaders to mindfulness work. Both of us concluded that we were interested in exploring additional ways to incorporate these ideas into leadership curricula. All provided rich opportunities for thinking, energized commitment, and idea generation.

With the aforementioned thoughts and ideas in mind, I began to brainstorm with my own leadership team about how we might be able to introduce the practice to our campus and infuse these types of activities and practices into the culture of our institution. As a way of introducing mindfulness practice, we had a couple of meetings early on where we demonstrated the process by engaging in some mindfulness activities. We discussed the practice's basic simplicity—it's about being present in the moment, about allowing what life brings, entangling the mishaps, and embracing self-compassion as well as compassion for others. Through our conversation and initial discussion, we decided that although developing the space for mindfulness practices on a primarily STEM-focused campus seemed like an audacious move, it was indeed a realistic undertaking.

As previously mentioned, over the past 10 years, we began to build and introduce a culture of creativity, innovation, and progressive thinking. A robust professional development program was in place, and scholars and practitioners had visited campus to speak on a variety of topics including leadership, emotional intelligence, technology, spirituality, legal issues in higher education, generational difference, diversity, assessment, communication, branding, and student success, among many other topics. While students were involved in many of these events, most were designed specifically for staff and faculty. During this time, the university also worked to develop a number of programs and activities to support student success and provide additional opportunities for students to take advantage of the incredible environment they are afforded on our campus. New developments for students included a robust outdoor adventure program, a new fee structure that granted students unlimited access to many of our fitness facilities and arts programming, and initiatives focused on leadership development, community service, and wellness.

While these activities helped to inculcate a mind-set for progressive ideas and embraced professional development, we needed a focused effort to determine how we could bring mindfulness into our day-to-day work. Thus, one of the first endeavors—which helped us move the mindfulness discussion further along—was inviting Marilee to campus in the spring of 2013. Marilee spent a couple of days on campus working with our staff and introducing them to the mindfulness practice, neuroscience, and the art of meditation (i.e., focused breathing and focused movement). It was from this that further discussion ensued and interest developed.

In the fall of 2013, a small group gathered to begin talking about how we move the mindfulness practice along on our campus. Over the course of the year, the members of this small group met and explored different ideas and options, including developing programming to address student requests associated with stress, yoga/meditation, and time management. While these were natural campus considerations, we also looked at how we could expand the conversation and begin to inform the campus of opportunities for mindfulness. An opportunity to plant the seeds of mindfulness practice and further expand the discussion evolved with a webinar that was sponsored by the team at the Search Inside Yourself Leadership Institute (SIYLI) organization (www.siyli.org) born out of the mindfulness program and developed and researched at Google. The webinar, attended by approximately 50 members of the campus community, created awareness of how one organization has taken the practice to a different level by introducing it into the workplace. Follow-up conversation helped the committee consider additional ideas.

During the spring of 2014, I visited the headquarters of SIYLI in the Bay area to discuss the possibility of bringing the program to our campus. One option of the SIYLI program involves a large lecture-type activity that introduces participants to the principles of SIYLI and those of founder Chade-Meng Tan, followed by a two-day intensive training program for upward of 50 participants. SIYLI works in three steps: attention training, self-knowledge and self-mastery, and creating useful mental habits to improve leadership practice. SILYI leaders and Chade-Meng Tan aim to further expand the mindfulness leadership practice and infuse mindful, compassionate, and emotionally intelligent leaders into as many communities as they can, including college and university campuses. Ideally, SILYI would like to expand the program by sharing it with as many people as possible throughout the United States and the world, hoping to "enlighten minds, open hearts, and create world peace," as described by Tan himself (see chademeng .com). The members of our mindfulness planning team feel that this will be a significant launching activity for us to introduce the mindfulness practice in a creative and provocative way to our students, particularly because of the nature of our institution and SIYLI having been born at Google. The SIYLI program will undoubtedly draw a large, diverse, and interested crowd. The groundwork is being laid to bring this program to campus within the next 12 to 18 months.

Along with bringing outside consultants, scholars, and facilitators to campus, the division of student affairs has also sponsored a biannual "professional development day" conference for the entire campus community. In the fall of 2013, the team that organizes the conference decided that "Be smart, be mindful" would serve as the theme for the spring 2014 conference. The team invited Metta McGarvey, Harvard University visiting scholar and chair of the Inner Strengths of Successful Leaders Program, to serve as the keynote lecturer and facilitator for the conference and individual sessions. In addition to those responsibilities Metta also offered morning meditation and an introduction to mindfulness, which the Michigan Tech president attended. Mindfulness, focused attention, and contemplative practice sessions were woven into the program agenda to add yet another simple but perhaps budding seed to the institution.

Planning for the current academic year is well under way. Our wellness team has incorporated a variety of events around mindfulness and compassion, including a large outdoor yoga/meditation activity in the fall. Additionally, two colleagues attended the Association for Contemplative Mind in Higher Education Summer Session at Smith College. One even served as a faculty member. Further discussions are ongoing about classroom opportunities as well as defining experiences and creating space for staff/faculty colleagues to embrace mindfulness practices. Much like Chade-Meng Tan (2012), the mindfulness team understands the value of focused attention, self-mastery, and compassion in the work we do with and for students and as colleagues in higher education.

While striving to do things on our campus and to infuse the mindfulness practice within, we developed a purpose statement to guide our travels. The statement is simple, reminding us that we should focus on being and create opportunities for mindfulness (see www.mtu.edu/student-affairs/administration/mission). It's really quite accessible and something that will continue to evolve as we become more aware, in-tune, and compassionate beings.

While both authors of this chapter come from a higher education background, we have had dramatically different personal and career experiences. The commonalities shared, however, make us more alike than different, as we are both seeking ways to incorporate mindfulness practice into our lives, work, and campus. We also both realize that while the perception of mindfulness and contemplative practice is really quite simple, the practice can be difficult. Finding the space to indulge in practice for oneself can be a challenge; getting others on board to consider the practice and to identify space can often be even more of a challenge.

Introducing and Practicing Mindfulness on Your Campus

As you can see, Michigan Tech and Syracuse University are in different phases of the creation of a mindfulness culture. Each institution has its own experience and history. In this chapter, we have attempted to articulate how a culture of mindfulness has evolved on two different campuses. Your experience will be as unique as you and your colleagues are. Consider the following as you introduce faculty, staff, and students to mindfulness practices:

- Be patient.
- Keep it simple to start.
- Notice what is already there.
- Find the early adopters.
- Tap into internal/external resources.
- Have fun and enjoy the journey.

Pitfalls to avoid include the following:

- Don't expect immediate interest.
- Be careful how you couch it—what does this look/sound like?
- Be mindful of nomenclature—what are you really saying?

The perceptions of contemplative practice vary from individual to individual, community to community, and campus to campus. Outside of the traditional places and practices, there seems to be a renewed emphasis and, some might say, even a proliferation of new interest in mindfulness practices. Some of these new perceptions may be due to the increasing emphasis on mindfulness practices in corporate America as well as in our academic and/or personal communities. We are also far more aware of the malleability of the brain and the impact of mindfulness practice on the brain (see Chapters 2, 7, and 11 for more information). Colleges and universities are paying attention to student success through efforts to ensure students on their campuses are provided opportunities to thrive and be successful. Many of these efforts are supported by mindfulness practice.

It is the case that some types of institutions, because of their curriculum and mission, may provide more readily available opportunities to infuse mindfulness work into their campus. For example, liberal arts institutions or those with some religious affiliation or past may be more likely to offer mindfulness-based practices than institutions that are highly oriented toward science, math, or engineering. The verbiage alone around mindfulness, meditation, and focused attention can be confusing to some. Those campuses with curricula that cultivate the ability to grasp the more ambiguous or abstract concept may provide for more opportunities, at least at first.

We are also now keenly aware that while the practice can seem complex, once understood, it may be widely embraced due to research that has been completed and continues to emerge around neuroplasticity. Several of the chapters in this book provided evidence that substantiates the benefits of mindfulness practice on the brain. While the notion may be complex, the research presented in this book is indicative of its impact and will likely continue to drive much of the discussion as well as the opportunity to introduce the practice on more campuses in the future. Our brains are plastic; we know we can retrain our thinking, learn to be present centered, and live more compassionate, fulfilling lives.

Additionally, we are now more aware of the importance of emotional and social intelligence and their roles in the lives of those in leadership positions. We know that today's world is radically different from that of just a few decades ago due to advances in technology, attitudinal and philosophical differences about work–life balance, and the striving to get ahead. In an ideal world, we seek to infuse and embrace mindfulness practice into our campuses so that students, faculty, and staff are able to create space for focused attention, awareness, practice, compassion for self, and more intentional and meaningful interactions among each other.

Editor's Summary Points and Questions to Consider

1. A definition for *mindfulness* and various ways its methodology could be implemented on campuses has been introduced in this chapter. Which ideas would garner interest on your campus? Who might need to be involved in the conversations to determine the feasibility of implementing these ideas or additional ideas that are generated from this chapter?
2. Social skills, emotional capacity, and intra- and interpersonal relationship skills have been documented as necessary in order to lead effectively. How would key decision makers on your campus receive this research?
3. Key considerations or practices to avoid when implementing mindfulness on your campus have been provided. Which considerations might you want to take into account for any action plan you may design for your particular campus?
4. Several benefits of mindfulness practice have been introduced in this chapter and throughout this book. Which benefits might best motivate key decision makers on your campus as you strive to improve holistic student success?

References

Baron, R., & Markman, G. (2000). Beyond social capital: How social skills can enhance entrepreneurs' success. *Academy of Management Perspectives, 14*(1), 106–116.

Bergen-Cico, D., & Cheon, S. (2014). Mediating role of mindfulness and self-compassion in reducing trait anxiety. *Mindfulness, 5*(5), 505–519.

Bergen-Cico, D, Possemato, K., & Cheon, S. (2013). Examining the efficacy of a brief mindfulness-based stress reduction (brief MBSR) program on psychological health. *Journal of American College Health, 61*(6), 348–360.

Brady, M. (2009). *Right listening.* Langley, WA: Paideia Press.

Deresiewicz, W. (2014, July 21). Don't send your kid to the Ivy League: The nation's top colleges are turning our kids into zombies. *New Republic.* Retrieved from www.newrepublic.com/article/118747/ivy-league-schools-are-overrated-send-your-kids-elsewhere

Engelberg, E., & Sjoberg, L. (2004). Internet use, social skills, and adjustment. *CyberPsychology & Behavior, 7*(1), 41–47.

Gardner, H. (1983). *Frames of mind: The theory of multiple intelligences.* New York, NY: Basic Books.

George, B. (2012, October 26). Mindfulness helps you become a better leader. *Harvard Business Review*. Retrieved from hbr.org/2012/10/mindfulness-helps-you-become

Goleman, D. (2006). *Social intelligence: The revolutionary new science of human relationships*. New York, NY: Bantam.

Goleman, D. (2011). *The brain and emotional health*. New York, NY: More Than Sound.

Goleman, D. (2012). *Emotional intelligence: 10th anniversary edition*. New York, NY: Random House.

Goleman, D., Boyatzis, R., & McKee, A. (2013). *Primal leadership: Unleashing the power of emotional intelligence*. Boston, MA: Harvard Business School Publishing.

Hasso Plattner. (2014). *Our point of view*. Retrieved from dschool.stanford.edu/our-point-of-view/

Kadison, R., & DiGeronimo, T. (2004). *College of the overwhelmed: The campus mental health crisis and what to do about it*. San Francisco, CA: Jossey-Bass.

Keeling, R., & Hersh, R. (2012). *We're losing our minds: Rethinking American higher education*. New York, NY: Palgrave Macmillan.

Kelly, D. M., & Kelly, T. (2013). *Creative confidence*. New York, NY: Random House.

Langer, E. (1989). *Mind-fulness*. Cambridge, MA: Da Capo Press.

Levy, D. (2007). No time to think: Reflections on information technology and contemplative scholarship. *Ethics and Information Technology, 9*(4), 237–249.

Murphy, J. (2011). Dancing in the rain: Tips on thriving as a leader in tough times. *Phi Delta Kappan, 93*(1), 36–41.

Oliveras, P. (2014). *Mission statement: Across boundaries, across abilities*. Retrieved from deeplistening.org/site/content/about

Shankman, M., & Allen, S. (2008). *Emotionally intelligent leadership: A guide for college students*. San Francisco, CA: Jossey-Bass.

Silverthorne, S. (2010, September 7). *Mindful leadership- when east meets west*. Retrieved from http://hbswk.hbs.edu/item/mindful-leadership-when-east-meets-west.

Tan, Chade-meng. (2012). *Search inside yourself: The unexpected path to achieving success, happiness (and world peace)*. New York, NY: HarperCollins.

Tan, Chade-meng. *Meng's Bio*. Retrieved from http://www.chademeng.com/meng_bio.html

Thorndike, R. L., & Stein, S. (1937). An evaluation of the attempts to measure social intelligence. *Psychological Bulletin, 34*(5), 275.

Vozza, S. (2014, February 26). *Why you really need to quiet your mind*. Retrieved from www.fastcompany.com/3026898/work-smart/why-you-really-need-to-quiet-your-mind-and-how-to-do-it

Wadham, B. (2008). *Report on the 2008 summer session on contemplative curriculum development*. Retrieved from www.contemplativemind.org/practices/tree

A MINDFUL APPROACH TO NAVIGATING STRATEGIC CHANGE

Laurie J. Cameron

Whatever you can do or dream you can, begin it. Boldness has genius, power, and magic in it.
—Johann Wolfgang von Goethe (german.about.com/library/blgermyth12.htm)

The ideas about how to transform the way we educate and evaluate learning in American higher education are simultaneously vividly compelling and daunting. The complexity, scope, and attachment to the current methods of education require change strategies and methods led by present, agile, and mindful leaders who can navigate uncertainty across the educational enterprise. In today's complex world, no one person or group can see the whole. What is needed in our methodology and approach to change is cocreation and collaboration with multiple stakeholders, who are able to sense and actualize a new ecosystem of education that allows the highest potential of all players to emerge.

What does it mean to mindfully lead change? How can we rise to the challenge? How do we become better at being agile and adapting, even transforming, to a new vision for how we educate our students and a new way of being as a teacher? How do we do that as individuals, and collectively, with more awareness and intention? And what is required to cocreate a new vision in a large and complex ecosystem such as American higher education? Combining the neuroscience of mindfulness methodology with systemic methods to navigate ecosystem change might provide a path to realizing our hopes for the new vision in how we educate at the university level.

Change is a process of moving from a present state through a transition state to a desired state (Conner, 1992). Our patterns, mind-sets, and behaviors can change. Rick Hanson (Hanson & Mendius, 2009) states that we can use the mind to change the brain to change the mind. As mentioned earlier in this book, neuroplasticity reveals that what we repeatedly think and do can change the structure and function of our brains, which allows us to adopt new ways of seeing, behaving, and interacting with others. We can cultivate and strengthen our own capacities for increasing awareness and self-mastery during change. In this chapter, we integrate strategic change methodology with mindful inquiry methodology, boosting the methods of change journey navigation with the more recent evidence-based skills and mind-sets of being present with open awareness, curiosity, and intention. The sensing capacity from being present involves opening the mind, opening the heart, and opening the will (Scharmer & Kaufer, 2013). This powerful combination might be just what is needed to meet the resistance and challenge we face in transforming the American higher education system.

Earlier in this book we describe the current context and environment in higher education. Professors, administrators, and students today often feel inundated with 24/7 communications, tech-saturated days, fragmented attention, and an explosion of new learning modalities and initiatives. We have an epidemic of overwhelmed and distracted educators, performing in a domain of rapid change and volatility with the rise of innovative tech-enabled teaching platforms and global classrooms. At the same time, we have centuries-old institutions standing on pillars of tradition, ritual, custom, and entrenched cultural patterns that can be like the walls of red bricks under the ivy vines—solid barriers and tangled ways of operating that make mobilizing systemic change quite daunting (Bok, 2013).

Mindfulness practices and skills generated from practice can be integrated into our methodologies for navigating change, thereby amplifying the effectiveness of leading change. Mindful inquiry methods (described earlier in this book) provide leaders in education with a way to increase the awareness of their own reactions, emotions, assumptions, conditioned ways of thinking, and resistance. Mindfulness also increases awareness and empathy of what others are experiencing, and expands our awareness of the connected, relational field, along with an awareness of what is emerging from the future (Goleman, 2013; Tan, 2012). This would suggest that mindfulness capabilities increase the efficacy of change methodologies by allowing educators and change agents to notice their present-moment experience in each phase of change, expand their capacity for generating innovative new approaches, and enhance their ability to connect with others with a nonjudgmental awareness.

I have been working in the field of organizational change for more than two decades and across three continents. While people within countries and industries demonstrate cultural idiosyncrasies, I have nevertheless observed common, basic human reactions to change. Early in my career with Accenture as part of change management, we partnered with Daryl Conner, a deep expert in change, who had made similar observations. Conner observed that these predictable human reactions fall into patterns; these patterns form a structure for understanding and leading change (Conner, 1992). The change methodology we posit here draws on Conner's work, David Cooperrider's appreciative inquiry method of transformational change (Bushe, 2011; Cooperrider, 2008; Cooperrider & Srivastva, 1987), Robert Fritz's (1989) ideas of creative structural tension, and the whole-systems presencing approach of Otto Scharmer's Theory U (Scharmer, 2007; Scharmer & Kaufer, 2013).

Methodologies for navigating strategic change are also evolving with the increased consciousness of human developmental theory and ideas about what drives sustainable change (Benn, Dunphy, & Griffiths, 2014; Newman & Newman, 2007; Shove & Spurling, 2014). The roles that leaders play as the architects of the evolving culture, practices, behaviors, and systems are directly correlated with the success of the change intervention (Bok, 2013; Fullan & Scott, 2009). The same can be true in the complex system of American higher education (Bok, 2008; Ewell, 2006). We require a shift from a deficit-based, problem-solving model to a strengths-based inquiry model. One of the most important underpinnings of appreciative inquiry is the simple premise that "organizations grow in the direction of what they repeatedly ask questions about and focus their attention on" (Mohr & Watkins, 2001). The higher education system is a socially constructed reality. As Cooperrider (2008) states, forms of inquiry are a potent method of initiating change in social systems, compared with using problem-solving methods. Furthermore, we can use a powerful force for change, which involves generating new ideas (Bushe, 2011; Cooperrider & Srivastva, 1987). Conventional action research that looks at what is broken often robs the change process of social innovation, which may be what is required to change a complex system such as higher education.

In addition to the macro, systemic change process, our vision for higher education also considers how we bring mindfulness to the individual. We can now infuse our strategies for leading change with what we know about how attention, emotion, and cognitive regulation (i.e., self-awareness and self-regulation) can increase the effectiveness of leaders at every stage of the change journey. Change leaders, and those experiencing the changes, might be better equipped to notice their present moment experience—their reactions and resistance to change. Mindfulness states and skills allow us to pay attention to relevant aspects of experience in a nonjudgmental way (Ludwig & Kabat-Zinn, 2008). Change makers can cultivate a deep level of attention and listening (Scharmer, 2014), not only to others but also to oneself. This requires "facing yourself" with an open mind and open heart. Scharmer (2014) describes this as "bending the beam of observation" back to yourself. Each change leader can step in to moments of stillness to investigate the deep developmental and change journey that they are experiencing.

We can broaden and expand the change interventions, events, and experiences by moving from one-way telling, communicating, and training to actively enrolling, involving, and cocreating new ideas, solutions, and futures. To design and implement the recommendations for higher education that we have explored in earlier chapters will require fundamental change in both the human components and the environmental infrastructure of our education system (Scharmer, 2009). We need to determine what will change, who is affected by the change, the depth and impact of the change for each stakeholder, the motivation and potential benefits for highly impacted groups, the key challenges and areas of resistance, and the timing in which the changes will begin to be experienced (Conner, 1992). We take into account that once we communicate the desire for change and involve key influencers, we are already initiating the change process. The first inquiry is really to determine what or who starts the movement in the system. That is, even as we begin to hold conversations around defining the vision or getting clear about the current state, shifts in mind-sets and ways of thinking are introduced and begin to take hold (Cooperrider & Whitney, 2001; Mohr & Watkins, 2001). Consider for yourself what is occurring in your own mind while reading this book.

The Heart of the Change

A *change initiative* or *project* can be defined as an individual or collaborative enterprise that is planned to achieve a particular aim . . . to cause to move forward or outward toward a desired result, the next idea or evolving vision (Cooperrider & Whitney, 2001; Mohr & Watkins, 2001). Throughout this book, we have explored the heart of the changes required to bring about a new level of performance in American higher education. We are continually asking the following questions:

- What principles underlie how we design and deliver higher education?
- Are we using the right evaluation tools and criteria for assessing student learning and development?
- What are we actually evaluating?
- Are we organized in a way that can improve student success?
- Are we investing resources that will systematically and fundamentally improve student success?

From the evolution of the university model in the introduction, we saw the origins of the university and how a shift eventually occurred from centering the student and interactive discourse in the learning process to centering the course in how learning is organized. What naturally followed was the development of the entire set of performance indicators, metrics, systems, recognition, and rewards to measure the course, department, or school as the core element to be evaluated (Bok, 2008; Ewell, 2006). We are now generating momentum for a radical shift that will center the process of learning and development at the core of education. We understand that our students are actually in a nonlinear, complex system of learning, and the neuroscience of development illuminates the way the mind works in integrating learning insights across developmental experiences. The mind wants to make meaning at a meta level of all of the developmental insights and leaps—to connect the parts and allow new, integrated maps to emerge. We need to harness our collective energy to implement the research we shared in earlier chapters, research that is already pointing to a rethinking of how we deliver learning in higher education today.

How do we do this? We can embrace mindful inquiry in education from Chapter 10 to enhance the change journey methodology described in this chapter. The change journey methodology has the potential to get us from where we are today to where we are going. Professors, faculty, administration, academic leaders, and students can use mindful inquiry to learn to self-author their own change journey road map and to blaze new trails for their teams, departments, and institutions, and the enterprise as a whole. Mindful inquiry provides a set of steps to help us stop, notice, observe, attune, and reflect on our experience of "letting go" of tried-and-true methods of teaching content and "letting come" developmental, learner-centered modalities (Scharmer, 2007; Tan, 2012).

Structure and the Creative Change Process

As we start to see the change road map and determine where we are now and where we are going, we can utilize a creative process that generates questions that pull us forward toward the vision for higher education that is emerging. Robert Fritz (1989), a creative systems scholar and composer, described the creative process as a way to think structurally to ask better and more useful questions. Rather than asking, "How do I get this current situation to go away?" we can ask, "What structures should we adopt to create the results we want?" When you are creating, Fritz explained, you are taking action to have something come into being: the creation. We get clear on answering the vital question of the creative process: "What do we want to create?" We can generate a path from the concept of what we want to create to its reality. The question allows us to focus our minds and collective energy toward the desired result.

Start With Vision

The best place to begin the creative change process is at the end (Cooperrider & Srivastva, 1987; Fritz, 1989). Where are we heading in American higher education? This allows us to conceive of the result that we want independently from how we will create it. Fritz posits that this is typically the opposite of what we learn in school. Often, it seems that our educational system teaches us how to do things before we have any notion of what we will use the knowledge for, thus giving a sense of purposelessness. As discussed earlier in this book, some of the most effective education relates what the student is learning to what can result from its mastery. Thus, as we go forward on this change journey, we may gain tremendous power from having a visual, cocreated picture for what is possible in regard to the enactment of what we want to see for American higher education (Cooperrider & Whitney, 2001; Fritz, 1989). Decision makers across the system essentially go on a joint journey from seeing the present and the future from their own perspective to seeing and experiencing it from the perspectives of multiple stakeholders, particularly those who are on the edges, or margins, of the change. Scharmer (Scharmer & Kaufer, 2013) describes the goal as being able to cosense, co-inspire, and cocreate an emerging future that values the well-being of all, rather than a few.

Being able to vividly envision what we want the American higher education system to look like creates a strong image in the minds of all who are affected by the change. The vision has great benefits, as it allows us to filter and assimilate the large amounts of research and data available during the design and change process (Cooperrider & Stavros, 2013; Cooperrider & Whitney, 2001; Fritz, 1989). Relationships among the different elements of the new structure that we envision begin to appear—classrooms, learning labs, online platforms, global video hangouts, evaluations, assessments, learning cohorts, self-directed learning, field-based learning experiences, and so on. The picture that begins to form of the vision for American higher education includes shape, contour, design, function, feel, and life, and the clear visionary goal allows us to work from knowledge with alignment, rather than from speculation (Fritz, 1989).

How clear do we need to be in creating the vision? Clear enough that we would recognize it as it emerges. We know that we will design, iterate, improvise, and experiment during the change journey as we reshape our educational institutions and create new ones. A compelling vision creates a pull and alignment among stakeholders and leaves space for iterative design and testing. Recall that a key principle of this book involves reminding ourselves that what we focus on changes the structure and function of our brains. Therefore, if you can't remain focused on the vision, it is challenging to recognize what individual leadership or organizational practices are in alignment with the vision.

What comes after vision? Developing a clear understanding of current reality as it relates to the vision comes after the visioning process (Fritz, 1989). We don't need to capture and understand everything about the existing structures and methods for designing, organizing, implementing, and financing higher education. We just need to have a solid understanding of the dimensions of learning, teaching, organizing, and evaluating within the scope of the vision we are creating. For example, if we are looking at a new vision for evaluation, we need to capture the reality of how we evaluate today.

With the picture of current reality next to the vision of the goal, a structural tension is created. Holding these two pictures in the minds of all key stakeholders produces a need to offset the imbalance—to create a pull (a desire to achieve the vision) toward the new future (Fritz, 2003). Sufficient seeds of dissatisfaction with the status quo are embedded in the current reality that the vision creates sufficient movement to offset the natural resistance that swells in the face of any change. The result created from this movement feeds growth organically. With intention from leadership and mindfulness methodology implemented, movement toward the new future becomes evident in three distinc phases within the body of the organization.

As ideas germinate, groups sense freshness and excitement, which sets creation in motion (Fritz, 2009). This is the ideal time for mobilizing resources and generating action. It is an important stage in the creative change process, but it is not usually sustainable (Fritz, 2009). Thus, we must move from the first stage of *germination* to the second stage of *assimilation*—integrating the ideas into our consciousness (i.e., moment-to-moment awareness), building momentum based on moment-to-moment awareness of what is working and what is not, and designing the new solutions. The third stage is *completion*—bringing plans to fruition and following through on the creation (Fritz, 2009). There is a great deal of creative energy released over these three phases. We create the path that Fritz describes in much of his work, the path of least resistance, which is generated by the structural tension frame of the current reality and the vision of possibility. When the vision is clearly developed and described, and the current reality is assessed and described, there is a gap created in the mind, which creates an emotional and energetic tension that seeks to be resolved. Fritz calls this a *tension-resolution system* and illustrates it with a rubber band. Imagine that the top of the rubber band represents the vision and the bottom of the rubber band represents current reality. As you stretch the rubber band, tension develops. The greater the gap between the vision and reality, the greater the energetic tension; the greater the tension, the stronger the motivation and energy in the system to resolve that tension (Fritz, 1989).

Large-Scale, Strategic Change

The creative change process through the lens of structural tension provides a simple backdrop to approach change methodology, particularly for large-scale change, which is what we are laying the groundwork for in this book. We suggest that American higher education would benefit significantly from integrating and adopting well-researched, evidence-based, and neuroscience-backed pedagogies for putting the learner and the process of learning and development at the center of the experience. Because many evidence-based practices are in place, a first necessary step in change planning, then, may be understanding the scale of this new way of educating.

Large-scale change involves complex systems and organizations with multiple sites, countries, cultures, and stakeholders—all shifting in accordance with their own change over multiple years. The dimensions of what we are trying to change include the attitudes, mind-sets, behaviors, and actions of those leading the change; those designing the new solutions; and the targets of change. In addition to the human side of change, we are also changing the environments, structures, systems, and processes that support the new vision for American higher education. For this, we need the support of stakeholders.

If we were to map out all of the stakeholders in American higher education, what would our stakeholder map look like? The term *stakeholders* here encompasses any individual, group, organization, or entity affected by the change. In the context of what we propose in this book, stakeholders would include professors, administrators, students, alumni, governing board members, employers of graduates, union leadership, vendors, community partners, and teaching and graduate assistants to start. A visual mapping process can be used to capture all stakeholder groups and key individuals, and depict relationships, power, and influence with thick, thin, and dotted lines connecting the groups. The stakeholder map becomes a dynamic source in our change plan, continually being updated throughout the planning, design, and implementation processes. If we can dynamically assess, update, and track where key groups are in the change journey, we can focus our resources and attention on critical and critically placed stakeholders to ensure that awareness, understanding, and ultimately acceptance are developing for creating the change.

Moving Through the Curve

How do we know where people are with respect to understanding, denying, resisting, or accepting the new vision for education? Can we know if some stakeholders are moving into acceptance and others are not on board at all? Is there a way to help groups with differing needs, identities, roles, interests, and positions engage and get involved?

When planning change, we can use proven methodologies that employ interventions designed to move stakeholders through stages of change. We don't see *change* as an event, but define it as a transitional process through a series of stages in a curve with a time dimension. Based on the work of Kübler-Ross (1969), there are different curves with varying labels of individual stages, but they all follow a similar pattern that starts with a precontemplation stage; moves through understanding and motivation; and follows with initiation, acceptance, and adoption of the new ways of being and doing (Connor, 1993).

Within these models, different cognitive and emotional factors become important at different stages, and we match strategies and interventions (mindfulness methodology serving as the foundation for all strategy and intervention) to each stage in a way to move stakeholders from one stage to the next. For example, in a large-scale, two-year strategic change process, the project team responsible for moving key stakeholder groups through the change process developed creative tools using a group-labeled "X" to plot where stakeholder groups were based on assessment instruments. In this company culture, the team adopted a slogan of "get your X in gear," with writing pads showing the stages of change and a movable X. The humor is helpful; it reminds us to hold models lightly since no human development process is purely linear. Indeed, development is quite messy, with individuals and groups moving nonlinearly, and even back and then forward again.

Principles of Navigating Change Resistance

Resistance to change can be evidenced in a host of interactions among the roles, functions, systems, and structures of our institutions (Ringleb & Rock, 2013). Resistance, as both a psychological factor in humans and a physical reality of resource-constrained environments, can reside within not only one category of people but also any group in a system (Ringleb & Rock, 2013). Often, resistance is due to inertia in physical resources, in organization structure, or overall systems' performance structure that causes some people to value their own self-interest over the new vision (Kotter, 2002). In addition, we have a tendency to quickly reach for solutions because we are uncomfortable with feeling difficult emotions. We want to move quickly through emotions such as frustration, uncertainty, fear, or grief and move from instability to stability. With change it is inevitable that difficult emotions arise (Brach, 2004).

Strategies to address resistance to change are best when targeted to the root cause of the resistance (Dent & Goldberg, 1999). However, the following general principles can ease moving through the change curve and support cocreation of an innovative future:

- *Utilize innovation hubs to design and prototype spheres of hands-on innovation* (Scharmer & Kaufer, 2013). Hubs allow creative space for generative conversations and create shared ownership of the change process (Brown, 2009; Scharmer & Kaufer2013). At each stage of change, we can involve participants from all stakeholder groups in designing the vision, assessing current reality, designing solutions, and developing and leading change strategies. Involvement in the change process creates ownership of the change process.
- *Create forums of discussion and dialogue that span schools, colleges, universities, and stakeholder groups.* Using mindfulness methodology, we can teach perspective taking and perspective shifting. The ability to incorporate empathy and compassion for others' views and positions is an enormously valuable skill in our ability to relate to and connect with others (Tan, 2012; Walsh & Shapiro, 2006) and is essential in the change process. Taking alternate perspectives, such as stepping into the shoes of others with a stake in the outcome of the next phase of higher education, can yield innovative solutions and shared ownership for the new way of teaching and learning. At the Massachusetts Institute of Technology's Presencing Institute, Otto Scharmer developed the Theory U model (Scharmer, 2007) to take stakeholder groups through a U-curve (Figure 12.1) by harnessing their collective leadership capacities.

    As Figure 12.1 shows, stakeholders move through the left side of the U, connecting to the world that is outside of the institutional bubble, to the bottom of the U, connecting to the inner world, and up the right side of the U, ultimately cocreatively bringing forth the new world in higher education. Change leaders learn to cultivate *presencing*, an uninhibited openness in the here and now, in view of a fuller and deeper perception of reality that begins with uncovering common intention, and ends with innovating new approaches to challenges that affect the whole system.
- *Use a cocreated vision for change, supported by a clear statement of higher purpose, to provide momentum and a guiding framework* (Ken Blanchard

Figure 12.1 Otto Scharmer's Theory U model.

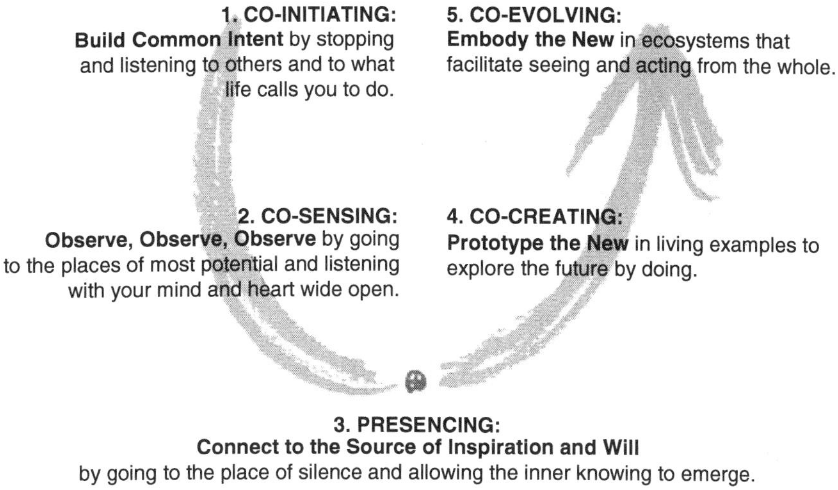

1. CO-INITIATING:
Build Common Intent by stopping and listening to others and to what life calls you to do.

5. CO-EVOLVING:
Embody the New in ecosystems that facilitate seeing and acting from the whole.

2. CO-SENSING:
Observe, Observe, Observe by going to the places of most potential and listening with your mind and heart wide open.

4. CO-CREATING:
Prototype the New in living examples to explore the future by doing.

3. PRESENCING:
Connect to the Source of Inspiration and Will
by going to the place of silence and allowing the inner knowing to emerge.

Companies, 2010). When enthusiasm and energy dip, resistance seems high, debates ensue, or plans get stuck, connecting to a higher purpose—a larger "why" for the vision—can pull stakeholders forward. Purpose creates meaning, and meaning is a core aspect of motivation (Pink, 2011).

- *Create a formal network of key people.* Daryl Connor (1993) terms the individual components of this network *change sponsors, agents, advocates,* and *targets.* These key people can be trained in the mindful inquiry methodology, the change journey methodology, and then take on key roles to build momentum, uncover and address resistance, and sustain the change. A guiding team is critical to begin the change initiative and ensure the vision is established while mobilizing support and resources. What I call a *change network* is an additional structure that creates ownership through involvement. Role assignments for change initiatives rarely follow a formal path in an organizational system, as relationships are highly complex and people play many roles (Conner, 1992). The change network sponsors the selection of agents from key stakeholder institutions that are not necessarily chosen for positional authority, but rather for being recognized as key influencers of opinion and energy in the system. They have personal power and may or may not have positional power. The change network approach has proven to be a successful strategy to create involvement, ownership, and sponsorship in a structured, coordinated way across the change enterprise (Conner, 1992).

- *Create a strategic communication and involvement plan.* This plan should span the lifetime of the change process and continually communicate the "why" of the change (Fritz, 1989). Start high and broad and go narrower and deeper over time. Begin with systems-wide, broad messages of vision and current reality, move to the impacts of change and what will be different, and finish with closer-to-home messages of specific changes and what will be different and new for the stakeholders affected by change.

  An effective communication and involvement plan is a multidirectional tool that uncovers resistance, acknowledges fear and uncertainty, delineates what is unknown from what is known, and utilizes a variety of channels that are relevant for each group involved in the change (Battilana & Casciaro, 2013). Trusting those responsible for designing, prototyping, and developing new ideas for how we educate is critical for effective change, and trust is built by communicating openly, honestly, and transparently (Barrett & Fry, 2005).

- *Aim to alleviate fears about the unknown, the new situation, and one's place within it in order to ease perceived threats to status, control, and identity* (Ken Blanchard Companies, 2010). Hold the intention to attend to fears of participants with empathy and compassion across the entire educational enterprise.

- *Ensure that all stakeholders have the opportunity to develop the knowledge and skills necessary to thrive in the new system* (Carter & Johnson, 1999). For example, how will we teach the best practices in utilizing a flipped classroom model? How do we get students comfortable with engaging in flipped classrooms? What are the latest technologies to support distance and online learning, and how will teachers get the skills they need to shift from today to tomorrow?

- *Constantly scan the overall progress, and continuously iterate and adjust.* Adopt short prototype-iterative-test cycles, and incorporate learning back into the change design team. Plan for evaluation and assessment activities. Acknowledge adjustments along the way to keep the expectations open that change plans are experiments, and we adopt and adjust as we go. Change agents can model the capacity for navigating ambiguity and uncertainty.

- *Begin to institutionalize new models of learning, and place the processes of learning and development at the center* (Carter & Johnson, 1999). Stakeholders in the change will find support and comfort in seeing new structures become stable. Having access to stories, videos, and testimonials of how life (a classroom, a department) looks in the new world will also be reassuring.

- *Cultivate the capacity for mindfulness and emotional resilience for those who have a role in the change process* (Senge, Scharmer, Jaworski & Flowers, 2005). Learning to notice reactions in the moment, downregulate emotions, reduce worry and rumination, direct attention to positive thoughts, and be with and accept difficulty and challenge are keys to tolerating the uncertainty of change (Davis, 2011).

The Quadrant Framework for Strategic Change

When it comes to designing and implementing the set of activities, interventions, and processes to move from our current reality to the new vision while involving all of the stakeholder groups and the ecosystem around them, we can use a systemic, multidimensional framework as a foundation. In the approach we describe in this chapter, strategic change takes into account the inner human landscape and outer cultural ecosystems that are experiencing change. For example, we suggest empathizing with what individual professors are experiencing internally (thoughts, emotions, and body sensations) in each phase of change. In addition, we practice empathy toward what teams and the institution as a whole are experiencing, as well as the larger ecosystem of the United States and even global education trends. In other words, become fully aware of the approaches that focus on individual motivations, university culture and values, and outside rhythms and trends, as well as the forces that are shaping the world at large.

How can mindful inquiry methodology make us more aware and conscious in the strategic planning and execution of the change? As we begin to design strategies and plans for stakeholder involvement, communication, awareness building, and cocreation of the new educational system, mindful inquiry methodology becomes a critical component in increasing the accuracy with which we assess levels of awareness, understanding, resistance, and readiness for change. Moving from visioning to designing new approaches, and then on to education of all those involved has the effect of "making it real" for many people. It is in this stage of change that resistance, which is often based on fear of the unknown or threats to status, control, role autonomy, or fairness (Rock & Cox, 2012), begins to emerge. Mindful inquiry supports the teams charged with making change happen by inviting the change leaders and those who are changing to simply stop, recognize, and observe what is arising in their thoughts and emotions along the way. Leaders learn to be aware of their direct experience in the moment. Change is blocked when resistance goes unrecognized and unaddressed (Rock & Cox, 2012).

A framework for mindful strategic change methodology planning can use a four-quadrant model (Figure 12.2). The holistic lens of Figure 12.2 provides a map for change leaders to navigate from the current reality to the new vision in a way that utilizes mindfulness skills by tuning in to what is happening with oneself, others in the relational field, and the larger environment. The change quadrant model is a holistic, systemic framework for change strategies. The vertical dimension represents stakeholder groups beginning broadly at the societal, enterprise or organizational levels, moving down through institutions, divisions or companies; to functions, teams and units; and, ultimately, to each individual stakeholder who will experience the change. Otto Scharmer (2010) tells the story of a prominent violinist who once said he couldn't just play his violin in the Chartres cathedral—he had to play the entire space, what he called the macro violin. The macro–micro dimension reflects the importance of convening the right set of stakeholders who are affected by the entire value chain (Scharmer, 2010).

The horizontal dimension of the change quadrant model depicts the forces of pushing change out via informing, describing, explaining, telling, and training, to the opposite pole of creating a demand for information, thereby creating a pull. Implementing change interventions from both sides is key, such as using direct social media platforms, e-mail communications, interactive webinars, coaching circles, and training and development programs. Along the horizontal dimension, we are balancing informing messages of present state, transition state, and desired state with

Figure 12.2 Change quadrant model.

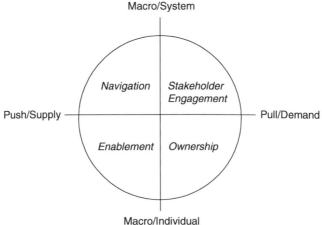

Note. Image provided by Laurie J. Cameron and reprinted with permission.

messages of "why," the pain of the status quo, and the expected benefits of the new world.

The "pull" or "demand" strategies outlined previously also include involvement and ownership activities based on Daryl Connor's (1993) change network concept. The change network, utilizing roles of sponsors, agents, advocates, and targets, is a very effective strategy that maps to the upper- and lower-right-side quadrants—effectively sponsoring the change and building ownership through the involvement of key players in the central aspects of large change: discovering the key inquiry, dreaming the new vision, designing new models and solutions, and fulfilling destiny through delivery and implementation (Cooperrider & Whitney, 2001).

A more recent strategic change process from the lower hemisphere of the quadrant model includes rapid-prototyping processes to test new ideas, seen often in forward-thinking design firms like IDEO (Brown, 2009) and the concept of innovation hubs (Scharmer & Kaufer, 2013). Pilot programs that create labs for experimenting and creating early successes encourage ownership of the new vision, which generates a tension and "pull" or demand toward the new vision. Enablement strategies that involve communicating, educating, and disseminating information are left-side "push" methods that are useful in building awareness and understanding of the vision, benefit, timing, and impact of what will be different and how each group can prepare to succeed in the new world. Both push and pull change interventions at a macro, organizational level and a micro, individual level are necessary to navigate change with a multistakeholder view and allow a shift from debating to cocreating the new (Scharmer, 2010).

The two "macro" quadrants in the top hemisphere represent navigation and stakeholder engagement. We use transparent, inclusion-based principles in these areas to develop strategies for mapping out the change journey over time and navigating interventions, debates, communications, visioning, and design activities in the context of the larger system and society. In the case of higher education, one might consider the school year calendar, major events, and milestones at key universities, along with election cycles and political transitions, as part of the navigation road map. In the "pull" macro quadrant, effective sponsorship is generated by strategic stakeholder engagement. Thoughtful and informed consideration of influential universities and schools is essential for selecting whom to involve early in defining and envisioning the change and who to enroll as sponsors. In addition, stakeholder engagement includes the identification of additional nonuniversity sponsors who can provide guidance, reduce resistance, leverage political influence, remove roadblocks, and provide resources.

Leading Strategic Change in American Higher Education

What does this mean for those leading transformation in education? We can dramatically expand the potential for positive change, influence, resourcefulness, and creativity when we encourage all stakeholders in the change process to be leaders. Deeper than ideas of empowerment, we encourage each person to own his or her leadership change journey. Consistent with the teachings of this book, we invite our readers to take responsibility for understanding what their department's environment is, imagining what it could be, and identifying areas of change in their job and circles of influence that they can guide to achieve their vision. We also invite each person to identify what competencies and skills are needed to thrive in the new environment. This idea is connected to the notion of self-authorship in the learning and development discussions earlier in this book. Self-directed, self-generated change leadership based on an individual being clear on his or her own vision, ideals, beliefs, and values (Kegan, 1994) along with integrating them with the larger change is an effective means of creating ownership for moving toward the new vision (Kouzes & Posner, 2012).

Mindful inquiry practice works to increase both our inner and outer awareness, which together deepen our self-awareness and self-mastery. Trained attention creates a "high-resolution perception" into our own cognitive and emotive processes (Hanson, 2014; Tan, 2012). Over time, mindful inquiry should increase our understanding of the patterns, conditioning systems, beliefs, fears, assumptions, and ways of being that are the underlying operating system for how we show up in the world. Our greater self-awareness allows us to feel our inner state, reflect on our emotions and thoughts, and make them objects of our awareness (Kofman, 2013).

Using mindfulness methodology, we can disidentify with our emotions, noticing that we feel fear as a physiological sensation, but we are not completely fearful (Tan, 2012). There is a part of our self that feels the emotion and the part that is the observer of the emotion. When we start to see and understand our own inner landscape of emotions, we have a more powerful understanding of the choices we make, the responses we have, the actions we take or don't take, and how we impact those around us (Tan, 2012). In using mindfulness methodology, we can create a space within which we can alter those choices and respond in ways that are in alignment with our values and the shared vision that we are moving toward.

Implications

What would it take to create the whole-system-wide change required to implement the findings from neuroscience on learning and development in American higher education? Leaders who are consciously aware of the inner and outer worlds of their present moment experience are likely to be more effective at navigating the uncertainty, complexity, and ambiguity of large-scale change, the relationships, complex interactions, and influences that occur in the space between institutions, organizations, and individuals. Scharmer (2007) calls this "deeper learning from the emerging future *presencing*." The term *presencing* blends the two words *presence*, the now, and *sensing*, the capacity to detect what is to come, and to sense with your heart (or what we have referred to in this book as using the entire brain, which includes the entire neural network of the body). Presencing means to sense an emerging future possibility and then to act from that state of awareness in the now ("sensing and actualizing emerging futures"). At the foundation of presencing is a core capacity of mindful listening. Paying attention with openness and curiosity to oneself, other stakeholders, and the collective is fundamental to moving through the change curve. *Presencing* is an active verb that requires an open mind—a suspension of the inner voices of judgment, criticism, and concern, and an open heart and open will that create conditions for collective cocreation of the future (Scharmer, 2007).

When we can develop the inner resources of stakeholders involved in the change process to be able to open and expand their awareness in the present, we may more readily overcome the challenges to transforming education. Leaders who build the capacity to be present to what is emerging in the field of higher education likely are more easily able to let go of the past and cocreate what can be a new future that integrates the insights from the neuroscience of learning and development to propel our students into new levels of performance.

Editor's Summary Points and Questions to Consider

1. The mindfulness methodology that can be used to enhance student success may also enhance leadership skills. Where does your institution feel it can implement a mindfulness methodology of presence, listening, and inquiry at the administrative and faculty leadership levels?

2. The mindfulness methodology that can be used to enhance student success and leadership practices may also enhance the methodology to implement the change needed to transform American higher education. Where does your institution feel it can begin experimenting with a mindfulness methodology for managing change?

3. Implementation of Otto Scharmer's (2007) Theory U model may also mean experiencing a drop in "productivity" while organizations undergo the steps to transform their learning organizations. How tolerant would your organizational leadership be toward a drop in productivity, whether it includes refereed journal publications from faculty, time to degree, numbers of students provided with specific services, programs offered, or actual attainment of degrees?
4. The change quadrant model provides a framework to consider the balance of push and pull as well as system and individual levels needed to enact widespread organization change. If you were to assess your organization's readiness for change using this model, what might you discover?

References

Battilana, J., & Casciaro, T. (2013). Overcoming resistance to organizational change: Strong ties and affective cooptation. *Management Science, 59*(4), 819–836.

Barrett, F., & Fry, R. (2005). *Appreciative inquiry: A positive approach to building cooperative capacity*. Chagrin Falls, OH: Taos Institute.

Benn, S., Dunphy, D., & Griffiths, A. (2014). *Organizational change for corporate sustainability*. London, UK: Routledge.

Bok, D. (2008). *Our underachieving colleges: A candid look at how much students learn and why they should be learning more*. Princeton, NJ: Princeton University Press.

Bok, D. (2013). *Higher education in America*. Princeton, NJ: Princeton University Press.

Brach, T. (2004). *Radical acceptance: Embracing your life with the heart of a Buddha*. New York, NY: Bantam.

Brown, T. (2009). *Change by design: How design thinking transforms organizations and inspires innovation*. New York, NY: Harper Business.

Bushe, G. R. (2011). Appreciative inquiry: Theory and critique. In D. Boje, B. Burnes, & J. Hassard (Eds.), *The Routledge companion to organizational change* (pp. 87–103). Oxford, UK: Routledge.

Carter, J. D., & Johnson, P. D. (1999). The roundtable project. In C. Elliott (Ed.), *Locating the energy for change: An introduction to appreciative inquiry* (pp. 255–279). Winnipeg, Canada: International Institute for Sustainable Development.

Conner, D. (1992). *Managing at the speed of change*. New York, NY: Random House.

Cooperrider, D., & Srivastva, S. (1987). Appreciative inquiry in organizational life. *Research in Organizational Change and Development, 1*, 129–169.

Cooperrider, D. L., Whitney, D., Stavros, J. M. (2008). *Essentials of appreciative inquiry*. Brunswick, OH: Crown Custom Publishing, Inc.

Cooperrider, D., & Whitney, D. (2001). *Appreciative inquiry handbook: A constructive approach to organization development and change.* Cleveland, OH: Lakeshore Publishers.

Cooperrider, D. L., Whitney, D., Stavros, J. M. (2008). *Essentials of appreciative inquiry.* Brunswick, OH: Crown Custom Publishing, Inc.

Davis, D. (2011). What are the benefits of mindfulness? A practice review of psychotherapy-related research. *Psychotherapy, 48*(2), 198 -208.

Dent, E., & Goldberg, S. (1999). Challenging resistance to change. *Journal of Applied Behavioral Science, 35*(1), 25–41.

Ewell, P. (2006). *Making the grade—how boards can ensure academic quality.* Washington, DC: Association of Governing Boards of Universities and Colleges.

Fritz, R. (1989). *Path of least resistance: Learning to become the creative force in your own life.* New York, NY: Random House.

Fritz, R. (2003). *Your life as art.* Newfane, VT: Newfane Press.

Fullan, M., & Scott, G. (2009). *Turnaround leadership for higher education.* San Francisco, CA: Jossey-Bass.

Goleman, D. (2013). *Focus: The hidden driver of excellence.* New York, NY: Harper.

Hanson, R. (2014). *Hardwiring happiness: The new brain science of contentment, calm, and confidence.* New York, NY: Harmony.

Hanson, R., & Mendius, R. (2009). *Buddha's brain: The practical neuroscience of happiness, love & wisdom.* Oakland, CA: New Harbinger Publications.

Kegan, R. (1994). *In over our heads: The mental demands of modern life.* Cambridge, MA: Harvard University Press.

Kegan, R., & Lahey, L. L. (2009). *Immunity to change: How to overcome it and unlock potential in yourself and your organization.* Boston, MA: Harvard Business Press.

Ken Blanchard Companies. (2010). *Building trust: The critical link to a high-involvement, high-energy workplace begins with a common language.* Retrieved from www.acem.org.au/getmedia/3bba47a4-cb80-47e2-a03a-b27683fc6898/Building_trust_Blanchard.pdf.aspx

Kofman, F. (2013). *Conscious business: How to build value through values.* Boulder, CO: Sounds True.

Kotter, J. (2002). *The heart of change.* Boston, MA: Harvard Business School.

Kouzes, J., & Posner, B. (2012). *The leadership challenge: How to make extraordinary things happen in organizations.* San Francisco, CA: Jossey-Bass.

Kübler-Ross, E. (1969). *On death and dying.* New York, NY: Simon & Schuster.

Ludwig, D., & Kabat-Zinn, J. (2008). Mindfulness in medicine. *Journal of the American Medical Association, 300*(11), 1350–1352.

Mohr, B., & Watkins, J. (2001). *Appreciative inquiry: Change at the speed of imagination.* San Francisco, CA: Jossey-Bass/Pfeiffer.

Newman, B., & Newman, P. (2007). *Theories of human development.* Cresskill, NJ: Psychology Press.

Pink, D. (2011). *Drive: The surprising truth about what motivates us.* New York, NY: Riverhead Books.

Ringleb, A., & Rock, D. (2013). *Handbook of neuroleadership*. Los Angeles, CA: CreateSpace Independent Publishing Platform.

Rock, D., & Cox, C. (2012). SCARF in 2012: Updating the social neuroscience of collaborating with others. *NeuroLeadership Journal, 4*, 1–16.

Scharmer, O. (2007). *Theory U: Leading from the future as it emerges*. San Francisco, CA: Berrett-Koehler.

Scharmer, O. (2010). *The blind spot of institutional leadership: How to create deep innovation through moving from egosystem to ecosystem awareness*. Paper prepared for World Economic Forum, Annual Meeting of the New Champions in Tianjin, People's Republic of China.

Scharmer, O. (2014). Global Presencing Forum [video]. Retrieved from https://www.presencing.com/video-pages/global-forum-2014-video

Scharmer, O., & Kaufer, K. (2013). *Leading from the emerging future*. San Francisco, CA: Berrett-Koehler.

Senge, P., Scharmer, O., Jaworski, J., & Flowers, B. (2005). *Presence: An exploration of profound change in people, organizations, and society*. Cambridge, MA: Crown Business.

Shove, E., & Spurling, N. (2014). *Sustainable practices: Social theory and climate change*. London, UK: Routledge.

Tan, C. (2012). *Search inside yourself: The unexpected path to achieving success, happiness (and world peace)*. New York, NY: Harper One.

Walsh, R., & Shapiro, S. L. (2006). The meeting of meditative disciplines and western psychology: A mutually enriching dialogue. *American Psychologist, 61*(3), 227–239.

AFTERWORD

Adoption, Adaptation, and Transformation

Marilee J. Bresciani Ludvik

We transform organizations by transforming quality of attention and clarity of intention.

—Otto Scharmer (*Theory U*, 2007, p. 166)

We opened this book with the reminder that the same kind of thinking that creates problems is not the kind of thinking that resolves them (a concept usually attributed to Einstein). Thus, it is inherent that we reconsider many aspects of how we design, deliver, and evaluate higher education to impact student success in immediate and lasting ways. We simply can't afford to continue doing business as we have in the past. The redesign of American higher education requires each one of us to participate fully in suspending our judgment of what we "know" to be true and staying in inquiry a little while longer in order to entertain ideas and concepts that we haven't been willing to consider in the past.

This afterword briefly and generally summarizes the detailed findings reported in this book (extracting pieces of some chapters to maintain accuracy). However, if your inclination is to think that this afterword gives you all you need to know of the detailed findings reported in each prior chapter, we strongly encourage you to reconsider that inclination and take time to review each chapter in its entirety. The time you take to review these chapters and ponder their implications for your practice as a faculty member, student affairs professional, academic support services professional, high-level administrator, policymaker, taxpayer, concerned citizen, or student is required. We need everyone contributing to the transformation that is so desperately needed in American higher education. As such, we need everyone *reflecting* in a holistic manner, positing ideas, and suspending judgment in order to stay in inquiry, compassionately working through proposed solutions.

Thus, the remainder of this afterword is dedicated to *some* considerations for higher education faculty, student affairs practitioners, academic support professionals, decision makers, and policymakers. It is our hope that in reading each chapter, you have come away with ideas of how to initially transform your own thinking (or more specifically transform your own attention, emotion, cognitive, and self-regulation systems) prior to attempting to transform others. As Bill O'Brien stated in Otto Scharmer's (2007) book *Theory U*, "The success of an intervention depends on the interior condition of the intervener" (p. 27). Otto Scharmer (2007) went on to explain that this means that we cannot transform the behavior of systems unless we transform the quality of awareness and attention that people apply to their actions within these systems, both individually and collectively. The "people" part begins with me and you—the reader reading these words—long before it translates to our students and our colleagues. This book is full of ideas on how we can do just that.

Brief Summary of Key Neuroscience Findings Drawn From Chapters in This Book

As discussed in the introduction, it is now an accepted fact that our brain is designed for boundary spanning and is highly interconnective (Kaku, 2014). Our brain—which extends beyond the neural networks housed in our cranium to include all of our senses (explained in greater detail in Chapters 2 and 3)—is a dynamic learning machine (Alvarez & Emory, 2006; Chan, Shum, Touloupoulou, & Chen, 2008; Chiesa, Calati & Serretti, 2011; Goldin, & Gross, 2010; Hölzel, Carmody, et al., 2011; Kozasa et al., 2011; Lutz, Slagter, Dunne, & Davidson, 2008; Todd, Cunningham, Anderson, & Thompson, 2012). However, if we don't use our brain in ways that align with its dynamic structural components and functions, it is unlikely we will see evidence of that use in any decision we make or in any learning and development data we collect.

We understand that what we pay attention to literally changes the structure and function of our brain (Alvarez & Emory, 2006; Chan et al., 2008; Chiesa et al., 2011; Goldin & Gross, 2010; Hölzel, Carmody, et al., 2011; Kozasa et al., 2012; Lutz et al., 2008; Todd et al., 2012). For example, if I stay focused on only the problems, I will see only the problems and not be able to see the possibility of solutions a student may be positing. If I stay focused on the possibilities, I will see only the possibilities and may not address the very real challenges being experienced by my students or colleagues.

Another way to illustrate this is with an example that may be familiar to all of us. If our colleagues or supervisors are only focused on one aspect of the problem solving (e.g., getting what they need or think they need for their functional unit or department), then their ability to see or think beyond their unit or department will not be evident. Such problem-solving practices foster conversations around "haves" and "have-nots," or "winners" and "losers" and promote competition for "declining resources," as opposed to creatively and compassionately dialoging solutions that are lasting and positively impactful for many. If we are clear and intentional about what we are creating within our organization, our decision making will follow in alignment with that clarity (Senge, Cambron-McCabe, Lucas, Smith, & Dutton, 2012). We won't be focusing on fighting for scarce resources, because we will be clear on what we are intending to create and realize that the process of its creation and the accompanying resources to support the creation will be ever changing. This realization is not new, yet many of us don't consistently practice this intentional focusing—perhaps because we were unaware of how to practice it or perhaps because we underestimated the neurology involved in intentionally changing our behavior.

And what about our students? If we ask them to focus on their learning and development (assuming they can even manage their attention on demand) one class or cocurricular program intervention at a time, but we fail to create opportunities for them to make cross-course connections to reflect on how they are developing their identity from one cocurricular program to how they are managing stress in another cocurricular program, we are reinforcing students *not* making neural connections that are imperative to their ability to succeed. Where do we facilitate the connection to what they are learning and how they are developing with their reflection about what gives them meaning and purpose so they can gain clarity on what they want to create with their life? Where do we do that for ourselves? Findings indicate that cross-examinations are not happening for the majority of students (OECD, 2013). Thus, we should not be surprised to see that the learning and development we intentionally delivered in a segmented manner is not made evident in data we have collected in a segmented manner. This leads to the critical question of whether the American higher education degree has any value.

As human beings, we can focus on only one thing at a time (Orr & Weissman, 2009; Rubenstein et al., 2001; Weissman, Gopalakrishnan, Hazlett, & Woldorff, 2005; Weissman, Perkins, & Woldorff, 2008). The ability to span our attention successfully rests in our ability to intentionally move our attention from one task to another swiftly and effectively while making connections to the important patterns needed for innovative problem solving or whatever it is we are being asked to do (Carp, Fitzgerald, Taylor, & Weissman, 2012; Weissman & Carp, 2013). However, creative problem solving may be more complex than simply intentionally managing our intention (Kandiko, 2012; Kaufman & Sternberg, 2007; Livingston, 2010; Plucker & Makel, 2010).

Thus, the first apparent step in this entire process appears to be regulating our awareness of where our attention resides (attention regulation, or AR). *AR* refers to processes that modify alerting, orienting, and executive attention

THE NEUROSCIENCE OF LEARNING AND DEVELOPMENT

focusing and processing and does not involve training in reasoning or linguistic processing. Instead, AR involves training in the ability to focus on a selected object, with awareness, while inhibiting irrelevant distracter stimuli. Because attention is the gateway to all other higher-order cognitive abilities and emotional responses, slight modifications in attentional deployment may have large effects on emotion generation (Posner & Fan, 2004) and cognitive abilities.

Goldin and Gross (2010) reported that subjects who engaged in breath-focused attention tasks (AR) actually reduced their amygdala activity (equating to reporting reduced levels of anxiety) and subjects increased the level of activity in other brain areas localized for attention and other executive functions such as analytical reasoning, prioritizing, and decision making (including the insula, other sensory-motor processing areas, anterior cingulate cortex, and prefrontal cortex). Goldin and Gross are not alone in reporting such findings; focused breathing's correlation with abating anxiety and expanding attention or emotions (emotion regulation, or ER) has been validated and extended in various studies (Arch & Craske, 2006; 2010; Batten & Hayes, 2005; Hocking & Koenig, 1995; Mankus, Aldao, Kerns, Mayville, & Mennin, 2013; Roemer, Orsillo, & Salters-Pedneault, 2008). We can postulate that such reported changes in improved attention (AR) and ability to regulate decreased stress and anxiety (ER) would likely increase students' overall well-being and success through awareness of choice (cognitive regulation, or CR).

To further emphasize the importance of AR, ER, and CR in a training model that promotes faculty, administrator, and student success, a wide variety of researchers (Anderson, Goldin, Kurita, & Gross, 2008; Goldin & Gross 2010; Goldin, Hakimi, Manber, Canli, & Gross, 2009; Goldin, Manber-Ball, Werner, Heimberg, & Gross, 2009; Goldin, Ramel, & Gross 2009; Goldin, McRae, Ramel, & Gross, 2008; Hutcherson, Goldin, Ramel, McRae, & Gross, 2008) posited that emotions coordinate a human's experiential, behavioral, and physiological responses to perceived challenges and opportunities. In other words, emotions dictate perception and thus emotions dictate how one responds to events one encounters; emotions can dictate choice. If left untrained, these emotions interfere with our cognitive processing ability (CR) and may lead to students' inability to persist.

Resilience is defined as the ability to bounce back after stressful events and trauma while preserving normal-for-the-individual physical and psychological equilibrium (Bonanno, 2004; Lazarus, 1993; Zautra, Hall, & Murray, 2010). Resilient individuals are able to overcome challenges and misfortune, learn from these challenges, and reach out for new experiences, ultimately allowing them to adapt to change in a healthy way, which in turn enhances well-being (Block & Kremen, 1996; Zautra et al., 2010). No one is immune to life's traumas and the negative effects of stress; however, the difference between well-being and psychological illness can be determined by the degree of effective coping and adaptation abilities one possesses to build resilience (Tugade & Fredrickson, 2004). The brain can be considered the primary organ of resilience because it regulates the biologic feedback systems that respond and adapt to stress (Karatsoreos & McEwen, 2011). The importance of training the brain becomes even more compelling when one considers how the inability to regulate attention, emotion, and cognition can take a student, a faculty member, and an administrator out of their intended life course.

Detrimental effects of repeated chronic stress are seen in areas of behavior such as self-control and self-regulation (e.g., AR, ER, and CR), flexible thinking, memory, physiologic responses to immune function, inflammatory processes, heart disease, and autoimmune disease (Cohen, Janicki-Deverts, & Miller, 2007; Hölzel et al., 2011; McEwen, 2009; Shors, 2006). Furthermore, the state of being "stressed out" can result in sleep deprivation (four hours or less per night), which has been associated with obesity, cognitive impairment, and unhealthy lifestyle behaviors (McEwen, 2006). Neuroimaging studies have confirmed stress-induced brain alterations trigger an enlargement of the amygdala (our emotion center), and a reduced size of the hippocampus (memory), as well as reducing the brain's chief executive officer—the prefrontal cortex (Davidson & McEwen, 2012).

The good news is that the brain is trainable—AR, ER, CR, and self-regulation are all trainable. Hölzel, Carmody, et al.'s (2011) meta-analysis exemplified the effectiveness that specific training interventions can have on cultivating AR, body awareness, ER, and CR. Namely, participants in this study were able to improve their own attention, emotion, and cognitive regulation abilities by engaging in the specific training methodologies provided. Similarly, Hölzel, Lazar, et al.'s (2011) research further confirmed these findings using functional and structural neuroimaging (magnetic resonance imaging [MRI] and functional MRI [fMRI]; see Chapter 1 for a detailed description of these measurement tools). These publications were some of the first to provide empirical evidence that specific attention, emotion, and cognitive regulation training methodologies are associated with neuroplasticity changes in the brain. Markedly, the brain regions affected parallel those in learning and development. A few examples include the anterior cingulate cortex, insula, temporoparietal junction (the division between the temporal lobe and parietal lobe), frontolimbic network, and default mode network (structures within the prefrontal cortex that communicate during resting states). Together with Hölzel and colleagues' work, many publications continue to replicate (and extend) these initial findings, substantially validating the power these training methodologies have on inducing structural and functional changes in the brain (Converse, Ahlers, Travers, & Davidson, 2014; Flook, Goldberg, Pinger, & Davidson, 2015).

Research in clinical psychology and neuroscience reinforces the significance of extrapolating these findings to guide the design, delivery, and evaluation of higher education. For example, clinical psychology research tells us that negative self-thoughts are inversely related to self-efficacy and positively related to stress (Multon, Brown, & Lent, 1991; Schunk, 1985; Zimmerman, 2000). CR, which is the ability to observe, analyze, focus, and reflect into thoughts, allows an individual to choose which thoughts he or she reflects and subsequently acts on. This regulatory strategy has been shown to decrease anxiety (Mahone, Bruch, & Heimberg, 1993) as well enhance overall well-being (Kabat-Zinn, 2013; Segal, Williams, & Teasdale, 2013) through positive choice making.

Because we now understand that we can train this kind of intentional AR, as well as ER and CR, in ourselves and in our students, this book is filled with chapters that detail the intricacies of how we can train such traits. Further, we are confident that when this book goes to press, additional research will continue to emerge to deepen our understanding of the effectiveness of each AR, ER, and CR training practice. For now, suffice it to say that simple, yet not easy, low-cost mind-training methodology that uses focused breathing, focused movement, and other inquiry methods can improve attention (Lutz et al., 2008; Valentine & Sweet, 1999) and reduce mind wandering (Mrazek, Franklin, Phillips, Baird, & Schooler, 2013). These training methods are also known to improve psychological well-being (Brown & Ryan, 2003), reduce levels of stress and anxiety (Astin, 1997; Jain et al., 2007; Rosenzweig, Reibel, Greeson, Brainard, & Hojat, 2009; Shapiro, Schwartz, & Bonner, 1998), and improve cognitive constructs and physiological states (Grossman, Niemann, Schmidt, & Walach, 2004). Use of these training methods has also been known to improve working memory as well as increase performance on standardized tests (Mrazek et al., 2013). Such practices also increase creativity (Capurso, Fabbro, & Crescentini, 2014; Greenberg, Reiner, & Meiran, 2012; Langer, 2005; Ostafin & Kassman, 2012; Ren et al., 2011), problem solving (Murray & Byrne, 2005; Ren et al., 2011), logic thinking (Ostafin & Kassman, 2012; Ren et al., 2011), and executive functions (Heeren, Van Broeck, & Philippot, 2009; Jha, Krompinger, & Baime, 2007; Moore & Malinowski, 2009; Zeidan, Johnson, Diamond, David, & Goolkasian, 2010).

When we add compassion to this list of desired outcomes, we begin to see how we can decrease the negative impact of bias and inhumane treatment (whether overt or covert), which can lead to happier, healthier, and more productive citizens and workforces (Batson & Ahmad, 2009; Chiao & Mathur, 2010; Cikara & Fiske, 2011; Stephan & Finlay, 1999). We also now know that we can train compassion, which is known to create connection to others, thus decreasing bias and bigotry while enriching interpersonal relationships (Jazaieri et al., 2013; Neff, 2007; Singer et al., 2004; Singer et al., 2006).

We understand that fostering student success requires tending to the whole person (Abes, Jones, & McEwen, 2007; Baxter Magolda, 1999; Baxter Magolda, 2001; Evans, Forney, Guido, Patton, & Renn, 2010; Goleman, 2001; Kegan, 1982; Kegan, 1994; Kohlberg, 1969; Pizzolato, 2008; Pizzolato & Ozaki, 2007; Taylor, 2008). In the previous chapters in this book, we detailed very specific ways to foster holistic student success. We know that students take their emotional selves with them everywhere they go and they interact with what is presented to them with their emotions, aware of them or not. We faculty, administrators, and community partners do the same. After all, the business of higher education is a human business. We are an industry that was built to develop human beings—human beings interacting with human beings regardless of how much we use technology to interface or carry out our work. As such, this is a messy business. Our ability to intentionally train our own, let alone our students', attention, emotion, and cognitive regulation in and out of the classroom may be a primary component for students' success as well as the industry of higher education's success.

In this book, we have posited that the holistic learning and development journey is not to be found in the linear course-to-course design, but rather in the process of reflecting on human engagement in and out of the classroom—as messy as that may be. We suggest that the commodity of higher education is not the course-by-course, credit-hour-accumulated degree; rather the commodity of higher education is the human process of learning and development that can be measured through direct evidence gathered in reflective learning portfolios. If we believe this and we have plenty of neuroscience evidence (illustrated throughout this book) to affirm this postulation, then this would require us to design integrative inquiry (INIQ) processes that invite us all to combine (a) the knowledge gained from research, course learning, and book learning with (b) the wisdom gained from intuition, sensing, and the mindful experiencing of emotions with (c) the ability to embrace the unknown, be curious, and inquire into that which we cannot yet see. If we integrate this approach with the ability to join multiple sources of information through generative questions and other training methodologies, participants of this integrative inquiry process are more likely to manage stress and creatively problem solve, while also experiencing ambiguity and compassion. This may just all lead to resolving problems we haven't even identified yet, while promoting peace, equity, access, affordability, resiliency, and wisdom through compassionate, conscious choice making.

In the following sections, we highlight additional considerations posited as questions for key players to use in the engagement of inquiry as they consider just how they will adopt and adapt the many practices outlined in the previous chapters in order to transform the design, delivery, and evaluation of higher education. As these questions are entertained, we invite each reader to practice suspension of judgment just long enough to hold in inquiry a new possibility to dialogue with colleagues and simply try out the new possibility.

After all, what have we got to lose in trying something different than what we are already doing? According to the world, we are statistically significantly below the international average for numeracy, literacy, and problem solving even though we are leading the world in the production of baccalaureate degrees (OECD, 2013). The course-by-course, credit-hour-accumulated degree is not the commodity of higher education, the process of learning and development is. Let's return to modeling, evaluating, and funding that process.

The following considerations—organized into categories for each potential interested reader—are posited with the intent that these questions invite an open dialogue among all those who would have a vested interest in adopting and adapting any or all of the practices outlined in the previous chapters. The research that undergirds each suggested practice is contained within this book. Our recommendation is that you utilize the research to support the request to host open dialogues. It will be up to you in your conversation to determine what evidence you and your collaborators need to see in order to determine whether the pilot project has been worth your investment (whatever that means to you). Keep in mind (whatever the "mind" is, anyway), that as you adopt, adapt, and pilot these practices with the intention to transform the design, delivery, and evaluation of higher education, you must also practice what you are expecting others to practice. If you don't, you will likely miss seeing the very evidence that you are seeking, for your own attention and clarity will not have been trained.

Finally, we encourage you to think broadly about the kinds of evidence you will need for determining whether the pilot is working well. For instance, consider all the research you have read about so far in this book. The process of learning and development is messy for many reasons, and evaluating how well your organization is able to facilitate effective processes will be messy as well for we are, again, human beings fostering other human beings' learning and development. Nonetheless, consider why employers are calling for boundary-spanning thinkers, adaptable and agile self-aware creative problem solvers. It is because we need to create something different than what we currently have. What does that all look like? How will we know when we have achieved our goal? The practices of AR, ER, and CR allow us to remain open to seeing something other than what we have seen before. And maybe, just maybe, we aren't going to know what that looks like until we begin to adopt, adapt, and pilot these practices.

Considerations for Faculty

1. What beliefs do you need to suspend in order to consider adopting and adapting some of the practices in this book? From whom do you need to gain support in order to momentarily suspend those beliefs so that you can consider other options?

2. How willing are you and how well are you prepared to practice some of the methodology suggested in this book, particularly your awareness of your own ability to regulate attention, emotion, and cognitive processes, as well as engage in compassion? From whom do you need to gain support in order to practice?

3. Where do you feel you may want to seek your own training and when in order to share these practices with your students or colleagues? From whom do you need to gain support in order to do so?

4. What current workload do you need to suspend and for how long in order to consider adopting and adapting some of the practices in this book? With whom do you need to speak in order to gain support for the time designated workload suspension?

5. Where in your course or program curriculum would it work well for you to adopt, adapt, and pilot some of these suggested practices?

6. With whom can you partner within the cocurriculum in order to provide facilitation expertise for students' meaning making, ER, and fostering of self-authorship? What support do you need in order to engage in the partnership and from whom can you request that support?

7. Where in your courses and program would it make the most sense to invite students' reflection of their learning and development process?

8. Where in your course or program does it make the most sense to train students in their reflective practice? With whom could you partner to offer this training?

9. Apart from implementing a reflective student learning portfolio process that includes a preassessment component, what other methods might

you use to evaluate the adopted and adapted practices in this book? From whom do you need to gain support in order to implement those evaluative processes?

10. What limitations of our learning and development evaluation methods can you accept in order to embrace the ambiguity of coaching students into some of the AR, ER, and CR processes? Whose support do you need to gain in order to suspend the need to "know" how well a method is working in your course or program?

11. How will the methods you use in your courses calculate into students' grading?

12. What additional assessment and/or research on these methods or similar methods do you want to engage in? With whom do you want to partner in your assessment and/or research?

13. What resources do you need to request and from whom in order to adapt and adopt some of these practices? (Consider that there are free resources available on many websites listed later in this afterword.)

14. What is your own tolerance level for being with the unknown? How can you leverage your ability to embrace the ambiguity required to try out new practices?

15. Would your current process of evaluating courses for teaching effectiveness need to be temporarily suspended or modified in order to allow some of your chosen practices to be adopted, adapted, and piloted? With whom would you need to collaborate in order to ensure no harm comes to you (via course evaluations) while you try out something different?

16. What other conversations would you like to host? With whom? And how can you practice being open to discovering what you do not yet know in order to transform what others may share with you?

Considerations for Student Affairs and Academic Support Professionals

1. What beliefs do you need to suspend in order to consider adopting and adapting some of the practices in this book? From whom do you need to gain support in order to momentarily suspend those beliefs?

2. How willing are you and how well prepared are you to practice some of the methodology suggested in this book, particularly your awareness of your own ability to regulate attention, emotion, and cognitive processes, as well as engage in compassion? From whom do you need to gain support in order to practice?

3. Where do you feel you may want to seek your own training and when in order to share these practices with your students, colleagues, and other constituents that your functional area is designed to serve? From whom do you need to gain support in order to do so?

4. What current workload do you need to suspend and for how long in order to consider adopting and adapting some of the practices in this book? With whom do you need to speak in order to gain support for the time-designated workload suspension?

5. Where in your service provision areas and/or programming curriculum would it work well for you to adopt, adapt, and pilot some of these suggested practices?

6. With whom can you partner within the faculty and other administrative units in order to provide facilitation expertise for students' meaning making, emotion regulation, and fostering of self-authorship? What support do you need in order to engage in these partnerships and from whom can you request that support?

7. Where in your service provision areas and/or programming curriculum would it make the most sense to invite students' reflection of their learning and development process?

8. Where in your service provision areas and/or programming curriculum does it make the most sense to train students in their reflective practice? Could you incorporate this into orientation, summer bridge programming, learning communities, and student success, leadership, organization, and/or activity courses and workshops? With whom could you partner to offer this training?

9. Apart from implementing a reflective student learning portfolio process that includes a preassessment component, what other methods might you use to evaluate the adopted and adapted practices in this book? Would it be possible to place some preassessment information in your required admissions' applicant materials and some postassessment information into withdrawal, transfer, and graduation exit packets? From whom do you need to gain support in order to implement those evaluative processes?

10. What limitations of our learning and development evaluation methods can you accept in order to embrace the ambiguity of coaching students into some of the AR, ER, and CR processes? Whose support do you need to gain in order to suspend the need to "know" how well a method is working in your service provision areas and/or programming curriculum?

11. How can you use some of these suggested training methodologies to enhance your well-being service provision areas and/or programming

curriculum? How about adopting and adapting them into your resilience service provision areas and/or programming curriculum?

12. What additional assessment and/or research on these methods or similar methods do you want to engage in? With whom do you want to partner in your assessment and/or research?

13. What resources do you need to request and from whom in order to adapt and adopt some of these practices? (Consider that there are free resources available on many websites listed later in this afterword.)

14. How do you feel about knowledge and content courses being offered free to students while resources go toward implementing the application of that knowledge and coaching the AR, ER, and CR processes? If this is not something you feel comfortable with, what are your ideas for making higher education more affordable while recognizing the research that has been presented in this book?

15. What is your own tolerance level for being with the unknown? How can you leverage your ability to embrace the ambiguity required to try out new practices?

16. Would your current process of evaluating work performance (including running returns on investments or meeting benchmark performance data) need to be temporarily suspended or modified in order to allow some of your chosen practices to be adopted, adapted, and piloted? With whom would you need to collaborate in order to ensure no harm comes to you (via performance evaluations) while you try out something different?

17. What other conversations would you like to host? With whom? And how can you practice being open to discovering what you do not yet know in order to transform what others may share with you?

Considerations for High-Level Organization Decision Makers

1. What beliefs do you need to suspend in order to consider adopting and adapting some of the practices in this book? From whom do you need to gain support in order to momentarily suspend those beliefs?

2. How willing are you and how well prepared are you to practice some of the methodology suggested in this book, particularly your awareness of your own ability to regulate attention, emotion, and cognitive processes, as well as engage in compassion? From whom do you need to gain support in order to practice?

3. Where do you feel you may want to seek your own training and when in order to share these practices with your colleagues and other constituents

that your organization is designed to serve? From whom do you need to gain support in order to do so?

4. What current workload do you need to suspend and for how long in order to consider adopting and adapting some of the practices in this book? With whom do you need to speak in order to gain support for the time-designated workload suspension?

5. How can you suspend momentarily workload expectations of the staff you supervise or support supervisors whose staff desire to have a lightened workload so that they can pilot some of this methodology in their courses, academic programs, functional areas, and cocurricular programming? With whom do you need to converse with in order to make or meet these requests? What are the expectations that would arise from granting such a request? In other words, what evidence would need to be considered to know how well the practices worked and whether it was worth investing in a suspension of the current workload?

6. Where in your functional areas would it work well for you to adopt, adapt, and pilot some of these suggested practices?

7. With whom can you partner within the faculty and other administrative units in order to provide support for the piloting of practices such as AR, ER, and CR training and/or the integration of play, exercise, nature experiences, walks, and even naps during the work period? What support do you need in order to engage in specific partnerships to pilot these practices and from whom can you request that support? What evidence of these practices' effectiveness would you expect to see as a result of such a pilot? And in what time frame can you reasonably expect to see evidence of effectiveness?

8. Consider how well you know whether your organization is currently learning and developing now; what do you notice? Where in your functional areas would it make the most sense to invite in professionals' or constituents' reflection of their learning and development process?

9. Where in your functional areas does it make the most sense to train staff and faculty in their reflective practice? Could you incorporate this into orientation and ongoing professional development opportunities? With whom could you partner to offer this training?

10. Apart from implementing a reflective professional or organizational learning and development portfolio process that includes a preassessment component, what other methods might you use to evaluate the adopted and adapted practices in this book? Would it be possible to utilize 360 evaluations that ask constituents to address traits characteristic of the

practices you are adopting and adapting? What about using process mind maps? From whom do you need to gain support in order to implement those evaluative processes?

11. What limitations of our learning and development evaluation methods can you accept in order to embrace the ambiguity of coaching professionals into some of the AR, ER, and CR processes? What about for students? Whose support do you need to gain in order to suspend the need to "know" how well a method is working in your functional area and/or academic curriculum?

12. How can you use some of these suggested training methodologies to enhance your well-being service provision areas and/or programming curriculum? How about adopting and adapting them into your resilience service provision areas and/or programming curriculum?

13. What additional assessment and/or research on these methods or similar methods do you want to engage in? With whom do you want to partner in your own assessment and/or research?

14. What resources do you need to request and from whom in order to adapt and adopt some of these practices? (Consider that there are free resources available on many websites listed later in this afterword.)

15. How do you feel about knowledge and content courses being offered free to students while resources go toward implementing the application of that knowledge and coaching the AR, ER, and CR processes? If this is not something you feel comfortable with, what are your ideas for making higher education more affordable while recognizing the research that has been presented in this book?

16. What is your own tolerance level for being with the unknown? How can you leverage your ability to embrace the ambiguity required to try out new practices?

17. Would your current process of evaluating work performance (including running returns on investments or meeting benchmark performance data) need to be temporarily suspended or modified in order to allow some of your chosen practices to be adopted, adapted, and piloted? With whom would you need to collaborate in order to ensure no harm comes to you (via performance evaluations) while you try something different?

18. What political challenges may arise from not knowing how this process may end up working at your institution? How willing are you to be in the "I don't know" space while the new process unfolds? How long will your stakeholders be willing to wait for some evidence of how well this process is "working"? And what can be done to elongate the time frame if it is needed?

19. What kinds of ongoing evidence of student learning and development as well as employee effectiveness will you require while the pilot programs are seeding themselves? What current evaluative processes can you support suspending while new methodology is piloted?

20. What other policies and practices need to be temporarily suspended in order to foster the piloting of some of the chosen methodology? How will you communicate that suspension to your constituents?

21. How will resource allocation and reallocation transform in order to support the chosen methodology? How will you communicate that suspension to your constituents?

22. How do you feel about knowledge and content courses being offered free to students while resources go toward implementing the application of that knowledge and coaching the AR, ER, and CR processes? If this is not something you feel comfortable with, what are your ideas for making higher education more affordable while recognizing the research that has been presented in this book?

23. How comfortable are you with focusing on the process of learning and development as the commodity of higher education, rather than the course-by-course, credit-hour-accumulated degree? Who needs to be involved in the conversations to support such a shift?

24. What else needs to be discussed, by whom, and by when in order for the optimization of these practices to be taken up by your institutional members?

25. What other conversations would you like to host? With whom? And how can you practice being open to discovering what you do not yet know in order to transform what others may share with you?

Considerations for Policymakers

1. What beliefs do you need to suspend in order to consider adopting and adapting some of the practices in this book? From whom do you need to gain support in order to momentarily suspend those beliefs?

2. How willing are you and how well prepared are you to practice some of the methodology suggested in this book, particularly your awareness of your own ability to regulate attention, emotion, and cognitive processes, as well as engage in compassion? From whom do you need to gain support in order to practice?

3. Where do you feel you may want to seek your own training and when in order to share these practices with your colleagues and other constituents

that you and/or your organization are designed to serve? From whom do you need to gain support in order to do so?

4. What current workload do you need to suspend and for how long in order to consider adopting and adapting some of the practices in this book? With whom do you need to speak in order to gain support for the time-regulated workload suspension?

5. How can you temporarily suspend or lighten workload expectations of the staff you supervise or support supervisors whose staff desire to have a lightened workload so that they can pilot some of this methodology? With whom do you need to converse with in order to make or meet those requests? What are the expectations that would arise from granting such a request? In other words, what evidence would need to be considered to know how well the practices worked and whether it was worth investing in a suspension of the current workload?

6. Where in your functional areas would it work well for you to adopt, adapt, and pilot some of these suggested practices?

7. With whom can you partner to provide support for the piloting of practices such as AR, ER, and CR training and/or the integration of play, exercise, nature experiences, walks, and even naps during the work period? What support do you need in order to engage in these partnerships and from whom can you request that support? What evidence of these practices' effectiveness would you expect to see as a result of such a pilot? And in what time frame can you reasonably expect to see evidence of effectiveness?

8. Consider how well you know whether your organization is currently learning and developing now; what do you notice? Where in your functional areas would it make the most sense to invite in professional's or constituents' reflection of their learning and development process?

9. Where in your functional areas does it make the most sense to train staff in their reflective practice? Could you incorporate this into staff orientation and ongoing professional development opportunities? With whom could you partner to offer this training?

10. Apart from implementing a reflective professional or organizational learning and development portfolio process that includes a preassessment component, what other methods might you use to evaluate the adopted and adapted practices in this book? Would it be possible to utilize 360 evaluations that ask constituents to address traits characteristic of the practices you are adopting and adapting? What about using process mind maps? From whom do you need to gain support in order to implement those evaluative processes?

11. What limitations of our learning and development evaluation methods can you accept in order to embrace the ambiguity of coaching professionals into some of the AR, ER, and CR processes? What about for students?

12. What resources do you need to request and from whom in order to adapt and adopt some of these practices? (Consider that there are free resources available on many websites listed later in this afterword.)

13. What is your own tolerance level for being with the unknown? How can you leverage your ability to embrace the ambiguity required to try out new practices?

14. Would your current process of evaluating work performance (including running returns on investments or meeting benchmark performance data) need to be temporarily suspended or modified in order to allow some of your chosen practices to be adopted, adapted, and piloted? With whom would you need to collaborate in order to ensure no harm comes to you (via election results or performance reviews) while you try out something different?

15. What political challenges may arise from not knowing how this process may end up working at your organization or within a higher education institution? How willing are you to be in the "I don't know" space while the new process unfolds? How long will your stakeholders be willing to wait for some evidence of how well this process is "working"? How do you communicate with your stakeholders from the place of "I don't know"?

16. What limitations of our learning and development evaluation methods can you accept in order to embrace the ambiguity of accepting the process of student learning and development as the commodity, rather than the course-by-course, credit-hour-accumulated degree? Whose support do you need to gain in order to suspend the need to "know" how well a method is working in a higher education organization functional area and/or an academic curriculum?

17. What kinds of ongoing evidence of student learning and development as well as employee effectiveness will you require while the pilot programs are seeding themselves? What current evaluative processes can you support suspending while new methodology is piloted?

18. What other policies and performance-based funding practices need to be temporarily suspended in order to foster the piloting of some of the chosen methodology? How will you communicate that suspension to your constituents?

19. How will resource allocation and reallocation transform in order to support an integrated educational model? How will you communicate that transformation to your constituents?

20. How do you feel about knowledge and content courses being offered free to students while resources go toward implementing the application of that knowledge and coaching the AR, ER, and CR processes? If this is not something you feel comfortable with, what are your ideas for making higher education more affordable while recognizing the research that has been presented in this book?

21. How comfortable are you with focusing on the process of learning and development as the commodity of higher education, rather than the course-by-course, credit-hour-accumulated degree? Who needs to be involved in the conversations to support such a shift?

22. What else needs to be discussed, by whom, and by when in order for the optimization of these practices to be taken up by your constituents?

23. What other conversations would you like to host? With whom? And how can you practice being open to discovering what you do not yet know in order to transform what others may share with you?

Final Considerations

We recognize that we are asking a lot of you as a reader of this book. We are asking you to step out into some unknown territory in order for us to collaboratively explore how we can best integrate learning and development, the known and unknown, the sensing and feeling in order for us to succeed at delivering the types of learning and development our constituents are demanding from higher education and do so in an affordable way. This book has given us several ideas of how to do just that. Now we need to adopt and adapt these methodologies through practice, observation, and inquiry. Try them out; have conversations about how well the practices are unfolding; suspend judgment long enough to stay in inquiry to see what is possible.

While this is all simple, it isn't easy. As such, we have provided some additional resources (certainly not all-inclusive and some of which may be more accessible and more plausible than others) for you to consider. We hope that in the near future we will be able to share broadly with others what you have found helpful (and why and how it has been helpful) as well as what you have not found helpful (and why and how it has not been helpful). As such, we invite you to send comments, ideas, pilot results, suggestions, research, and anything else along the lines of this inquiry to rushingtoyoga@gmail.com so we can share it with others to continue the transformation dialogue.

We care about our students and one another learning what we need to know in order to be creative, compassionate citizens. We care about access, equity, and affordability. We care about creating solutions to our world's most challenging unforeseen problems. We care about constructing effective higher learning and development opportunities. And we know that what we currently are doing isn't systematically working. So, we invite you to be bold with us, step out, and stay in inquiry while suspending your judgment for just a moment to see what is possible. And with that, we can transform.

Further Resources for Your Consideration

(Note that inclusion of these resources is not an endorsement of their use; rather, this section is simply a place for you to find additional information that may be helpful to you in this inquiry process.)

1. The references listed in each chapter
2. AR, ER, and CR training apps for iPhone and Androids at Oli Mittermaier—www.pollinate.life
3. Focused movement training at Baptiste Institute—www.baronbaptiste.com
4. Compassion training at Center for Compassion and Altruism Research and Education at Stanford University—ccare.stanford.edu
5. Other pedagogical tools and ideas at Center for Contemplative Mind in Society—www.contemplativemind.org
6. Research on effectiveness of these training methods at Center for Investigating Healthy Minds—www.investigatinghealthyminds.org/cihmDr Davidson.html
7. Focused breathing and other concentration training at Chopra Center for Well-Being—www.chopra.com
8. Compassion training at COMPASSION IT—compassionit.com
9. Free resources for lots of the training methodology as well as course and curriculum construction mentioned in this book at integrative inquiry (INIQ)— www.integrativeinquiry.org/integrative_inquiry_resources.php
10. Research information on mindfulness at Mind and Life Institute—www.mindandlife.org
11. Process mind maps—www.xmind.net/m/dTxX
12. Mindful organizational transformation consulting at Purpose Blue Mindful Leadership—purposeblue.com
13. Reflective Student Learning and Development Portfolio Materials—interwork.sdsu.edu/main/ma_student_affairs/rlp
14. AR, ER, and CR professional development opportunities at Rushing to Yoga Foundation—www.rushingtoyoga.org

15. Mindfulness professional development opportunities at Search Inside Yourself Leadership Institute—www.siyli.org
16. Self-Compassion Research—self-compassion.org
17. 360 degree evaluations—www.leadershipchallenge.com/professionals-section-lpi.aspx
18. The University of California San Diego (UCSD) Center for Mindful ness—health.ucsd.edu/specialties/mindfulness/Pages/default.aspx
19. The University of Massachusetts Center for Mindfulness—www.umass med.edu/cfm/

References

Abes, E. S., Jones, S. R., & McEwen, M. K. (2007). Reconceptualizing the model of multiple dimensions of identity: The role of meaning-making capacity in the construction of multiple identities. *Journal of College Student Development, 48*(1), 1–22.

Alvarez, J., & Emory, E. (2006). Executive function and the frontal lobes: A meta-analytic review. *Neuropsychology Review, 16*(1), 17–42.

Anderson, B., Goldin, P., Kurita, K., & Gross, J. J. (2008). Self-representation in social anxiety disorder: Linguistic analysis of autobiographical narratives. *Behavior Research and Therapy, 46*, 1105–1192.

Arch, J. J., & Craske, M. G. (2006). Mechanisms of mindfulness: Emotion regulation following a focused breathing induction. *Behaviour Research and Therapy, 44*(12), 1849–1858.

Arch, J. J., & Craske, M. G. (2010). Laboratory stressors in clinically anxious and non-anxious individuals: The moderating role of mindfulness. *Behaviour Research and Therapy, 48*(6), 495–505.

Astin, J. (1997). Stress reduction through mindfulness meditation: Effects on psychological symptomatology, sense of control, and spiritual experiences. *Psychotherapy and Psychosomatics, 66*(2), 97–106.

Batson, C., & Ahmad, N. (2009). Using empathy to improve intergroup attitudes and relations. *Social Issues and Policy Review, 3*(1), 141–177.

Batten, S. V., & Hayes, S. C. (2005). Acceptance and commitment therapy in the treatment of comorbid substance abuse and post-traumatic stress disorder: A case study. *Clinical Case Studies, 4*(3), 246–262.

Baxter Magolda, B. (1999). *Creating contexts for learning and self-authorship: Constructive-developmental pedagogy*. Nashville, TN: Vanderbilt University Press.

Baxter Magolda, B. (2001). *Making their own way: Narratives for transforming higher education to promote self-development*. Sterling, VA: Stylus.

Block, J., & Kremen, A. M. (1996). IQ and ego-resiliency: Conceptual and empirical connections and separateness. *Journal of Personality and Social Psychology, 70*, 349–361.

Bonanno, G. A. (2004). Loss, trauma, and human resilience: Have we underestimated the human capacity to thrive after extremely aversive events? *American Psychologist, 59*(1), 20–28.

Brown, K., & Ryan, R. (2003). The benefits of being present: Mindfulness and its role in psychological well-being. *Journal of Personality and Social Psychology, 84*(4), 822–848.

Capurso, V., Fabbro, F., & Crescentini, C. (2014). Mindful creativity: The influence of mindfulness meditation on creative thinking. *Frontiers in Psychology, 4,* 1020–1021.

Carp, J., Fitzgerald, K. D., Taylor, S. F., & Weissman, D. H. (2012). Removing the effect of response time on brain activity reveals developmental differences in conflict processing in the posterior medial prefrontal cortex. *NeuroImage, 59,* 853–860.

Chan, R., Shum, D., Toulopoulou, T., & Chen, E. (2008). Assessment of executive functions: Review of instruments and identification of critical issues. *Archives of Clinical Neuropsychology, 23*(2), 201–216.

Chiao, J., & Mathur, V. (2010). Intergroup empathy: How does race affect empathic neural responses? *Current Biology, 20*(11), R478–R480.

Chiesa, A., Calati, R., & Serretti, A. (2011). Does mindfulness training improve cognitive abilities? A systematic review of neuropsychological findings. *Clinical Psychology Review, 31*(3), 449–464.

Cikara, M., & Fiske, S. (2011). Bounded empathy: Neural responses to outgroup targets' (mis)fortunes. *Journal of Cognitive Neuroscience, 23*(12), 3791–3803.

Cohen, S., Janicki-Deverts, D., & Miller, G. (2007). Psychological stress and disease. *Journal of the American Medical Association, 298*(14), 1685–1687.

Converse, A. K., Ahlers, E. O., Travers, B. G., & Davidson, R. J. (2014). Tai chi training reduces self-report of inattention in healthy young adults. *Frontiers in Human Neuroscience, 8.* Retrieved from http://www.investigatinghealthyminds. org/ScientificPublications/2014/ConverseTaiChiFHN.pdf

Davidson, J., & McEwen, B. (2012). Social influences on neuroplasticity: Stress and interventions to promote well-being. *Nature Neuroscience, 15*(5), 689–695.

Evans, N. J., Forney, D. S., Guido, F., Patton, L. D., & Renn, K. A. (2010). *Student development in college: Theory, research, and practice* (2nd ed.). San Francisco, CA: Jossey-Bass.

Flook, L., Goldberg, S. B., Pinger, L., & Davidson, R. J. (2015). Promoting prosocial behavior and self-regulatory skills in preschool children through a mindfulness-based kindness curriculum. *Developmental Psychology, 51*(1), 44–51.

Goldin, P., & Gross, J. (2010). Effects of mindfulness-based stress reduction (MBSR) on emotion regulation in social anxiety disorder. *Emotion, 10*(1), 83–91.

Goldin, P. R., Hakimi, S., Manber, T., Canli, T., & Gross, J. J. (2009). Neural bases of social anxiety disorder: Emotional reactivity and cognitive regulation during social and physical threat. *Archives of General Psychiatry, 66,* 170–180.

Goldin, P., Manber-Ball, T., Werner, K., Heimberg, R., & Gross, J. J. (2009). Neural mechanisms of cognitive reappraisal of negative self-beliefs in social anxiety disorder. *Biological Psychiatry, 66,* 1091–1099.

Goldin, P. R., McRae, K., Ramel, W., & Gross, J. J. (2008). The neural bases of emotion regulation: Reappraisal and suppression of negative emotion. *Biological Psychiatry, 63*, 577–586.

Goldin, P. R., Ramel, W., & Gross, J. J. (2009). Mindfulness meditation training and self-referential processing in social anxiety disorder: Behavioral and neural effects. *Journal of Cognitive Psychotherapy, 23*, 242–257.

Goleman, D. (2001). *An EI-based theory of performance: The emotionally intelligent workplace: How to select for, measure, and improve emotional intelligence in individuals, groups, and organizations.* San Francisco, CA: Jossey-Bass.

Greenberg, J., Reiner, K., & Meiran, N. (2012). "Mind the trap": Mindfulness practice reduces cognitive rigidity. *PLOS ONE, 7*(5), e36206–e36207.

Grossman, P., Niemann, L., Schmidt, S., & Walach, H. (2004). Mindfulness-based stress reduction and health benefits. A meta-analysis. *Journal of Psychosomatic Research, 57*(1), 35–43.

Heeren, A., Van Broeck, N., & Philippot, P. (2009). The effects of mindfulness on executive processes and autobiographical memory specificity. *Behaviour Research and Therapy, 47*(5), 403–409.

Hocking, L. B., & Koenig, H. G. (1995). Anxiety in medically ill older patients: A review and update. *International Journal of Psychiatry in Medicine, 25*(3), 221–238.

Hölzel, B. K., Carmody, J., Vangel, M., Congleton, C., Yerramsetti, S., Gard, T., & Lazar, S. W. (2011). Mindfulness practice leads to increases in regional brain gray matter density. *Psychiatry Research: Neuroimaging, 191*(1), 36–43.

Hölzel, B. K., Lazar, S. W., Gard, T., Schuman-Olivier, Z., Vago, D. R., & Ott, U. (2011). How does mindfulness meditation work? Proposing mechanisms of action from a conceptual and neural perspective. *Perspectives on Psychological Science, 6*(6), 537–559.

Hutcherson, C. A., Goldin, P. R., Ramel, W., McRae, K., & Gross, J. J. (2008). Attention and emotion influence the relationship between extraversion and neural response. *Social Cognitive and Affective Neuroscience, 3*, 71–79.

Jain, S., Shapiro, S., Swanick, S., Roesch, S., Mills, P., Bell, I., & Schwartz, G. E. (2007). A randomized controlled trial of mindfulness meditation versus relaxation training: Effects on distress, positive states of mind, rumination, and distraction. *Annals of Behavioral Medicine, 33*(1), 11–21.

Jazaieri, H., Jinpa, G., McGonigal, K., Rosenberg, E., Finkelstein, J., Simon-Thomas, E., . . . Goldin, P. R. (2013). Enhancing compassion: A randomized controlled trial of a compassion cultivation training program. *Journal of Happiness Studies, 14*(4), 1113–1126.

Jha, A., Krompinger, J., & Baime, M. (2007). Mindfulness training modifies subsystems of attention. *Cognitive, Affective, & Behavioral Neuroscience, 7*(2), 109–119.

Kabat-Zinn, J. (2013). *Full catastrophe living, revised edition: How to cope with stress, pain and illness using mindfulness meditation.* New York, NY: Bantam Books.

Kaku, M. (2014). *The future of the mind: The scientific quest to understand, enhance, and empower the mind.* New York, NY: Random House.

Kandiko, C. B. (2012). Leadership and creativity in higher education: The role of interdisciplinarity. *London Review of Education, 10*(2), 191–200.

Karatsoreos, I., & McEwen, B. (2011). Psychobiological allostasis: Resistance, resilience and vulnerability. *Trends in Cognitive Sciences, 15*(12), 576–584.

Kaufman, J. C., & Sternberg, R. J. (2007). Resource review: Creativity. *Change, 39,* 55–58.

Kegan, R. (1982). *The evolving self: Problem and process in human development.* Cambridge, MA: Harvard University Press.

Kegan, R. (1994). *In over our heads: The mental complexity of modern life.* Cambridge, MA: Harvard University Press.

Kohlberg, L. (1969). *Stage and sequence: The cognitive-developmental approach to socialization.* New York, NY: Rand McNally.

Kozasa, E., Sato, J., Lacerda, S., Barreiros, M., Radvany, J., Russell, T., . . . & Amaro, E. (2012). Meditation training increases brain efficiency in an attention task. *NeuroImage, 59*(1), 745–749.

Langer, E. (2005). *On becoming an artist: Reinventing yourself through mindful creativity.* New York, NY: Ballantine Books.

Lazarus, R. (1993). From psychological stress to the emotions: A history of changing outlooks. *Annual Review of Psychology, 44*(1), 1–21.

Livingston, L. (2010). Teaching creativity in higher education. *Arts Education Policy Review, 111*(2), 59–62.

Lutz, A., Slagter, H., Dunne, J., & Davidson, R. (2008). Attention regulation and monitoring in meditation. *Trends in Cognitive Sciences, 12*(4), 163–169.

Mahone, E. M., Bruch, M. A., & Heimberg, R. G. (1993). Focus of attention and social anxiety: The role of negative self-thoughts and perceived positive attributes of the other. *Cognitive Therapy and Research, 17*(3), 209–224.

Mankus, A. M., Aldao, A., Kerns, C., Mayville, E. W., & Mennin, D. S. (2013). Mindfulness and heart rate variability in individuals with high and low generalized anxiety symptoms. *Behaviour Research and Therapy, 51*(7), 386–391.

McEwen, B. (2006). Protective and damaging effects of stress mediators: Central role of the brain. *Dialogues in Clinical Neuroscience, 8*(4), 367–381.

McEwen, B. (2009). The brain is the central organ of stress and adaptation. *NeuroImage, 47*(3), 911–913.

Moore, A., & Malinowski, P. (2009). Meditation, mindfulness and cognitive flexibility. *Consciousness & Cognition, 18*(1), 176–186.

Mrazek, M., Franklin, M., Phillips, D., Baird, B., & Schooler, J. (2013). Mindfulness training improves working memory capacity and GRE performance while reducing mind wandering. *Psychological Science, 24*(5), 776–781.

Multon, K. D., Brown, S. D., & Lent, R. W. (1991). Relation of self-efficacy beliefs to academic outcomes: A meta-analytic investigation. *Journal of Counseling Psychology, 38,* 30–38.

OECD. (2013). *OECD Skills Outlook 2013: First results from the survey of adult skills,* OECD Publishing. Retrieved from skills.oecd.org/documents/OECD_Skills_Outlook_2013.pdf

Orr, J. M., & Weissman, D. H. (2009). Anterior cingulate cortex makes two contributions to minimizing distraction. *Cerebral Cortex, 19*, 703–711.

Ostafin, B., & Kassman, K. (2012). Stepping out of history: Mindfulness improves insight problem solving. *Consciousness and Cognition, 21*(2), 1031–1036.

Pizzolato, J. E. (2008). Advisor, teacher, partner: Using the learning partnerships model to reshape academic advising. *About Campus, 13*(1), 18–25.

Pizzolato, J. E., & Ozaki, C. C. (2007). Moving toward self-authorship: Investigating outcomes of learning partnerships. *Journal of College Student Development, 48*(2), 196–214.

Plucker, J. A., & Makel, M. C. (2010). Assessment of creativity. In J. C. Kaufman & R. J. Sternberg (Eds.), *Cambridge handbook of creativity* (pp. 48–73). New York, NY: Cambridge University Press.

Posner, M. I., & Fan, J. (2004). *Attention as an organ system: Topics in integrative neuroscience: From cells to cognition.* Cambridge, UK: Cambridge University Press.

Ren, J., Huang, Z., Luo, J., Wei, G., Ying, X., Ding, Z., . . . & Luo, F. (2011). Meditation promotes insightful problem-solving by keeping people in a mindful and alert conscious state. *Science China. Life Sciences, 54*(10), 961–965.

Roemer, L., Orsillo, S. M., & Salters-Pedneault, K. (2008). Efficacy of an acceptance-based behavior therapy for generalized anxiety disorder: Evaluation in a randomized controlled trial. *Journal of Consulting and Clinical Psychology, 76*(6), 1083–1089.

Rosenzweig, S., Reibel, D., Greeson, J., Brainard, G., & Hojat, M. (2003). Mindfulness-based stress reduction lowers psychological distress in medical students. *Teaching and Learning in Medicine, 15*(2), 88–92.

Rubinstein, J. S., Meyer, D. E., & Evans, J. E. (2001). Executive control of cognitive processes in task switching. *Journal of Experimental Psychology: Human Perception and Performance, 27*(4), 763–797.

Scharmer, O. (2007). *Theory U: Leading from the future as it emerges.* San Francisco, CA: Berrett-Koehler.

Schunk, D. H. (1985). Self-efficacy and classroom learning. *Psychology in the Schools, 22*(2), 208–223.

Segal, Z. V., Williams, M. G., & Teasdale, J. D. (2013). *Mindfulness-based cognitive therapy for depression* (2nd ed.). New York, NY: Guilford Press.

Senge, P., Cambron-McCabe, N., Lucas, T., Smith, B., & Dutton, J. (2012). *Schools that learn: A fifth discipline field book for educators, parents, and everyone who cares about education.* New York, NY: Crown.

Shapiro, S., Schwartz, G., & Bonner, G. (1998). Effects of mindfulness-based stress reduction on medical and premedical students. *Journal of Behavioral Medicine, 21*(6), 581–599.

Shors, T. (2006). Stressful experience and learning across the lifespan. *Annual Review of Psychology, 57*, 55–85.

Singer, T., Seymour, B., O'Doherty, J., Kaube, H., Dolan, R., & Frith, C. D. (2004). Empathy for pain involves the affective but not sensory components of pain. *Science, 303*(5661), 1157–1162.

Singer, T., Seymour, B., O'Doherty, J., Stephan, K. E., Dolan, R., & Frith, C. D. (2006). Empathic neural responses are modulated by the perceived fairness of others. *Nature, 439*(7075), 466–469.

Stephan, W., & Finlay, K. (1999). The role of empathy in improving intergroup relations. *Journal of Social Issues, 55*(4), 729–743.

Taylor, E. W. (2008). Transformative learning theory. *New Directions for Adult and Continuing Education, 2008*(119), 5–15.

Todd, R., Cunningham, W., Anderson, A., & Thompson, E. (2012). Affect-biased attention as emotion regulation. *Trends in Cognitive Sciences, 16*(7), 365–372.

Tugade, M., & Fredrickson, B. (2004). Resilient individuals use positive emotions to bounce back from negative emotional experiences. *Journal of Personality and Social Psychology, 86*(2), 320–333.

Valentine, E., & Sweet, P. (1999). Meditation and attention: A comparison of the effects of concentrative and mindfulness meditation on sustained attention. *Mental Health, Religion & Culture, 2*(1), 59–70.

Weissman, D. H., & Carp, J. (2013). The congruency effect on the posterior medial frontal cortex is more consistent with time on task than with response conflict. *PLOS ONE, 8*(4), e62405.

Weissman, D. H., Gopalakrishnan, A., Hazlett, C., & Woldorff, M. (2005). Dorsal anterior cingulate cortex resolves conflict from distracting stimuli by boosting attention toward relevant events. *Cerebral Cortex, 15*(2), 229–237.

Weissman, D. H., Perkins, A. P., & Woldorff, M. G. (2008). Cognitive control in social situations: A role for the dorsolateral prefrontal cortex. *NeuroImage, 40,* 955–962.

Zautra, A., Hall, J., & Murray, K. (2010). Resilience: A new definition of health for people and communities. In J. R. Reich, A. J. Zautra, & J. S. Hall (Eds.), *Handbook of adult resilience* (pp. 3–30). New York, NY: Guilford Press.

Zeidan, F., Johnson, S. K., Diamond, B. J., David, Z., & Goolkasian, P. (2010). Mindfulness meditation improves cognition: Evidence of brief mental training. *Conscious Cognition, 19*(2), 597–605.

Zimmerman, B. J. (2000). Self-efficacy: An essential motive to learn. *Contemporary Educational Psychology, 25*(1), 82–91.

Editor

Marilee J. Bresciani Ludvik, PhD, serves as a professor of postsecondary educational leadership at San Diego State University. She is the founder of the Rushing to Yoga Foundation, which seeks to strengthen peace and compassion within higher education by training attention, emotion, and cognitive regulation skills among undergraduate students, graduate students, faculty, and administrators through integrative inquiry (www.integrativeinquiry.org).

Bresciani Ludvik's research has focused on the evaluation of student learning and development and the role leaders play in using evidence to improve student learning and development in higher education. Her most recent research explores the effectiveness of attention, emotion, and cognitive regulation training programs on the use of intuition and self-inquiry in evidence-based decision making and one's ability to think critically and act compassionately. Bresciani Ludvik has held faculty and higher education administration positions for more than 28 years. In those positions, she has conducted enrollment management research, quantitative and qualitative institutional research, course-embedded assessment, and academic and administrative program assessment. As assistant vice president for institutional assessment at Texas A&M University and as director of assessment at North Carolina State University, Bresciani Ludvik led university-wide initiatives to embed faculty-driven outcomes-based assessment in the curriculum. She has led reforms in outcomes-based assessment program review, assessment of general education, quality enhancement, and cocurricular assessment.

Bresciani Ludvik has been invited to present and publish her findings on assessment and is a lead author of six books on assessing student learning and outcomes-based assessment program review along with two books on self-inquiry and authenticity exploration. Bresciani Ludvik has developed and delivered several courses on assessment of student learning, as well as attention, emotion, and cognitive regulation.

In 2013, Bresciani Ludvik recieved the George D. Kuh Award for Outstanding Contribution to Literature and/or Research. The award recipient is nominated by peers (members of the National Association of Student Personnel Administrators) and honors individuals who have demonstrated a lifetime commitment to outstanding research and scholarship relating to higher education.

Bresciani Ludvik is a certified Search Inside Yourself Leadership Institute teacher, a certified yoga instructor who has trained with the Baron Baptiste Power Yoga Institute, and a certified meditation instructor trained by the Chopra Center for Well-Being. Furthermore, Bresciani Ludvik has been trained in the mindfulness-based stress reduction methodology by Jon Kabat-Zinn and Saki Santorelli. Her mantra is "I teach what I need to learn."

Bresciani Ludvik holds a doctorate in administration, curriculum, and instruction from the University of Nebraska and a master of arts in teaching from Hastings College. She can be reached at mbrescia@mail.sdsu.edu.

Contributors

Jacopo Annese is the director of the Brain Observatory, a San Diego–based neuroimaging laboratory and brain bank and the founder/CEO of the Institute for Brain and Society, a nonprofit organization dedicated to fostering mental health and social welfare through improved knowledge and awareness of the brain. He is also a faculty member in the department of radiology at the University of California–San Diego. He graduated from the University of Rome in Italy with a bachelor's and a master's degree in biology and zoology, respectively. He obtained a master's degree in neurological sciences at University College London, the United Kingdom. He completed the PhD program in cognitive neuroscience at Dartmouth College, New Hampshire.

Mark Baxter's work uses animal models to establish causal links between manipulations of defined neural circuits and behavioral and cognitive functions. After earning his PhD in neurobiology at the University of North Carolina at Chapel Hill and completing his postdoctoral training at the National Institute of Mental Health, he established an independent research program in neuropsychology and cognitive effects of neurochemical lesions, first as an assistant professor at Harvard University and then at Oxford. His research is funded by a senior fellowship from the Wellcome Trust. He now serves as a tenured faculty member at Mount Sinai School of Medicine and moved his laboratory from Oxford to New York in January 2010.

Anne Beffel is an artist and a professor at Michigan Technological University's (MTU) visual and performing arts department. Prior to joining the faculty at MTU, she taught studio courses at Syracuse University for 13 years. Currently she teaches creative processes to students from a wide range of disciplines. As an artist and teacher, she offers opportunities to project participants and students to pay attention to their surroundings and one another. Since earning her MA and MFA from the University of Iowa, her BFA from the University of Michigan, and participating in the Whitney Museum of American Art's Independent Studio Program in New York City, she has worked within contexts as diverse as the World Financial Center in Lower Manhattan shortly after 9/11; Saint John's Benedictine monastery in rural Minnesota; New York Downtown Hospital and surrounding streets, offices, and community centers; and the Wykoff toxic waste site on Bainbridge Island, Washington.

Bruce Bekkar served as a staff physician with Kaiser Permanente in San Diego from 1989 to 2013. He coauthored *Your Guy's Guide to Gynecology: A Resource for Men and Women* (North Star Publications, 2000), chosen as one of the Top 10 Books of the Year in 2001 by the Independent Publisher's Book Association. The book was also featured in numerous local and national television, radio, and print interviews. Bekkar's other passion, environmental activism, was inspired by his time spent living on the North County coast while earning his degree in biology at University of California–San Diego. After receiving his MD from the University of Southern California School of Medicine and completing a residency at Cedars-Sinai Medical Center, he returned to Del Mar and helped jump-start the first local chapter of the Surfrider Foundation. Most recently, he served on Del Mar's Sustainability Advisory Board and the city's Design Review Board. He also has served as a strategic adviser for the Equinox Center and as a community ambassador for SurfAid International. Bekkar additionally loves exercising and eating sustainably. He takes pleasure in telling himself he feels much younger than his 59 years of age.

Wendy Bracken has an MA in psychology and an EdD in educational leadership from San Diego State University (SDSU). She currently serves as a faculty member in the College of Education at SDSU, teaching doctoral research and writing support courses. Her research explores person–environment fit theories among underrepresented populations and examines training programs designed to enhance attention, emotion, and cognitive regulation. She also serves as the program coordinator for the SDSU Educational Leadership doctoral program. Previously, she coordinated the SDSU Human Research Protection Program, educating students, faculty, and staff about responsible conduct in research.

Laurie J. Cameron's focus is on developing resilient, compassionate leaders and cultures through consulting, teaching, and coaching. She teaches mindful leadership with the Executive MBA program at the Robert H. Smith School of Business at the University of Maryland, College Park, and is a senior fellow at the Center for the Advancement of Well-Being at George Mason University. She is also a certified teacher with the Search Inside Yourself Leadership Institute and a certified coach with the International Coach Federation (ICF). Formerly with Accenture, she founded PurposeBlue and serves clients in the United States, Europe, and Latin America. She studies mindfulness with teacher Thich Nhat Hanh. Cameron has a bachelor of arts in speech communication with an emphasis on organizational psychology and attitude change and persuasion from the University of Maryland, College Park.

Les P. Cook currently serves as the vice president for student affairs and advancement at Michigan Technological University (Michigan Tech). In this capacity, Cook is responsible for leading and helping to oversee student life, residential life, enrollment management and marketing, intercollegiate athletics and recreation, diversity programs, advancement, alumni relations, and the dean of students. Cook has a doctorate of education in educational leadership from Brigham Young University, a master of social science from Utah State University, and a bachelor of science in political science from Utah State University. Cook has been actively involved in a number of professional associations, including the National Association of Student Personnel Administrators, the National Orientation Director's Association, and the LeaderShape Institute. He currently serves as a faculty member for the LeaderShape Institute and the NASPA Foundation Board and sits on the editorial board for Student Affairs Today. Cook is involved in the Houghton community and is a member of the board of directors for the Keweenaw Community Foundation and the Michigan Tech Blue Line Club.

Matthew R. Evrard is working toward his doctorate in neural and behavioral science at the State University of New York (SUNY) Downstate Medical Center in Brooklyn, New York. His research interests seek to better elucidate the neural mechanisms that supersede learning and development, which can then be applied to improve areas of education and medicine. Evrard received his master of arts in postsecondary educational leadership at San Diego State University (SDSU), where his research, supervised by Marilee J. Bresciani Ludvik, focused on the role of attention, emotion, and cognitive regulation training to improve critical thinking dispositions. His bachelor of science is from SUNY in biopsychology. While enrolled at SDSU, Evrard worked at the University of California, San Diego, where he gained experience in neuroimaging, histology, microscopy, and experimental psychology. His diverse background has made him an invaluable asset in the assessment of integrative inquiry, a curriculum that has been shown to reduce students' stress and anxiety while increasing critical thinking dispositions.

Lisa Gates earned her PhD in communication from the University of Southern California and spent the early part of her career as a corporate management consultant. Throughout her academic career, she has won several awards for outstanding teaching and publishes in the areas of qualitative methods, organizational and health communication, leadership, and gender. She has taught at the University of Southern California; San Diego State University; and at San Diego Christian College, where she was founding chair of the department of communication. She currently is a lecturer and coordinator of the leadership minor and the masters in student affairs at San Diego State University.

Philippe Goldin earned a PhD in psychology at Rutgers University. He directed the clinically applied affective neuroscience laboratory at Stanford University for a decade and currently serves as an assistant professor and founding faculty in the Betty Irene Moore School of Nursing at the University of California Davis health system. His clinical research, funded by the National Institutes of Health, focuses on functional neuroimaging of emotion regulation mechanisms of mindfulness meditation, cognitive-behavioral therapy, and aerobic exercise in adults with anxiety disorders.

Christine L. Hoey's long interest in mind–body medicine has drawn her to using an integrative approach to healthcare. She is a board-certified family nurse practitioner and holds a BSN from Florida State University and an MSN from Duke University. Hoey has practiced maternal/child health and women's health in a variety of settings and published research on the medical costs and benefits of breast feeding. She continues to engage in studies centered on meditation, mindfulness, and nutrition as well as work with nonprofit organizations in San Diego.

Charles Iyoho currently serves as a research assistant in the doctoral program in community college leadership at San Diego State University where he explores the role of attention, emotion, and cognitive regulation on specific learning and development outcomes, particularly that of creative expression. Iyoho is also an adjunct professor of communication at National University. In the past, Iyoho served as a journalist for the *Marshall News Messenger*, a newspaper in Marshall, Texas. He was part of a team that won an Associated Press award for its coverage of the Ku Klux Klan. Iyoho received a graduate assistant fellowship while working toward his MA in communication at the University of Houston. He earned an academic scholarship to attend the University of Missouri–Columbia, where he studied Spanish and mass communication.

Emily Marx has served in student affairs at the University of California, San Diego for 14 years, most recently as the director of the Center for Student Involvement, with responsibility for student organization advising, Greek Life, communication and leadership development programs, community service initiatives, campus-wide events, and veterans' services. Marx has also served as adjunct faculty at San Diego State University, where she taught educational leadership. Her areas of academic interest include college student development, student engagement, leadership development, civic engagement, and service-learning and professional development in student affairs. She earned her doctorate in higher education leadership from the University of San Diego, where her dissertation research focused on new student affairs professionals' use of advising strategies that promote self-authorship among college students.

Patsy Tinsley McGill is a professor of strategic management in the College of Business at California State University–Monterey Bay, where she also serves as the capstone program director and faculty lead for assurance of learning. Her research focuses on understanding capstone as a transformative experience, improving high-stakes writing outcomes of students, and increasing educational effectiveness using technology. She earned her PhD in educational human resources development from Texas A&M University in College Station, Texas.

Shaila Mulholland is an assistant professor in the administration, rehabilitation, and postsecondary education department in the College of Education at San Diego State University. Her teaching and research interests focus on understanding the experiences of diverse students in postsecondary education. In addition, Mulholland is a classically trained pianist and performs as well as creates music in the San Diego community and beyond. She received a BA in biology and MS in higher education and student affairs from Indiana University Bloomington, and a PhD in higher education administration from New York University.

Sara Schairer is the founder and executive director of COMPASSION IT, a global social movement and nonprofit. A certified teacher of Stanford University's Compassion Cultivation Training, Schairer teaches at the University of California–San Diego's Center for Mindfulness and at various medical institutions. She speaks to audiences around the world and has presented at the Anthony Robbins Foundation's Global Youth Leadership Summit. Through COMPASSION IT and in partnership with the Botswana Ministries of Health and Education, Schairer led compassion training workshops in Gaborone. She is a proud graduate of the University of North Carolina at Chapel Hill.

Mark Tucker is an assistant professor in the administration, rehabilitation, and postsecondary education department at San Diego State University and a project coordinator with the university's Interwork Institute. Prior to joining the Interwork Institute, Tucker worked as a program coordinator for a Southern California–based nonprofit agency providing case management, crisis counseling, and vocational planning services. His areas of research interest include examining the relationships between individual, contextual, or case-service factors and vocational rehabilitation outcomes of transition-age youth and adults with disabilities. Tucker is a certified rehabilitation counselor; he holds an MS in rehabilitation counseling from San Diego State University and a PhD in human rehabilitation from the University of Northern Colorado.

Thomas Van Vleet is a leader in a new generation of scientific pioneers in brain plasticity research. As senior scientist and director of sponsored programs at Posit Science, Van Vleet leads the company's innovative clinical applications projects. Van Vleet has published more than 25 articles in leading peer-reviewed journals (e.g., *Brain* and *Progress in Brain Research*) and received numerous research awards from the National Institutes of Health (NIA, NINDS, NIMH), Department of Veteran Affairs, and the Defense Advanced Research Projects Ageency. His work has also been highlighted in the popular press, including the *New York Times* and *BBC News*.

J. Luke Wood is an associate professor of community college leadership and the director of the doctoral program concentration in community college leadership at San Diego State University. Wood teaches courses on assessment, evaluation, and quantitative research in the master's program in student affairs and in the doctoral program in community college leadership.

Wood is codirector of the Minority Male Community College Collaborative, a national project of the Interwork Institute at San Diego State University that partners with community colleges across the United States to enhance access, achievement, and success among minority male community college students. He is also chair-elect for the Council on Ethnic Participation for the Association for the Study of Higher Education, director of the Center for African American Research and Policy, and coeditor of the *Journal of Applied Research in the Community College.*

plausibility of, 59–63
strengthening neural connections
and, 62
stress as influencing, 146
students' potentials unlocked by,
55–56
well-being and resilience through, 154
neuropsychological analysis, 57–58
neuroscience
for advancing student success, 10–11
advertising field's turning to, 29
autopsy beginnings of, 33–34
benefits of mindfulness-based
practices and, 166
of compassion, 199–204, 213–14
compassion into action by, 210–13
higher education benefits of, 30
history and, 32–33
holistic learning and principles of,
18–19
incorporating higher education into,
27–28
integrating learning and
development, 237
learning and development at odds
with, 6
learning and development
connection to, 73–77
lens, 178
recent discoveries in, 1–2
summary of, 310–17
neuroscience research
INIQ training program and, 240–41
learning and development enhanced
by, 237–40, 314
statistics, 240–42
stress related, 74–75
neurotransmitters, 59–61
NMR. *See* nuclear magnetic resonance
Nobel Prize in Physiology and
Medicine, 42
nonlinear learning, xi, 13–14
nuclear magnetic resonance (NMR), 34
numeracy, 4, 316

obesity, 155–56
O'Brien, Bill, 310
OECD. *See* Organization for Economic
Cooperation and Development
O'Keefe, John, 42
online learning, 9
organizational change, 289–91
Organization for Economic
Cooperation and Development
(OECD), 4–5, 15, 238
organizations, decision makers in,
320–23
outcomes
declining higher education,
238
employers and learning, 5–6, 19
employers' demands of learning,
5–6, 19
essential learning, 99, 101–2
focus of outputs rather than, 18
INIQ learning and development,
242–44
INIQ methodology and related,
245–48
resilience and promoting positive,
151–54
self-authorship benefits and,
104–5
out-of-class experiences
integrating in-class with,
12–13
limitations for, 12
online learning as surrogate for, 9
students connecting in-class and,
12–13
oxygen, blood-borne, 224–26

pain, brain activation and, 200–201
parasympathetic system, 147
Park, H.-J., 33, 36–37
Parkinson's disease, 44–45
Parks, S. D., 105
PECTDI. *See* Postsecondary Education
Critical Thinking Dispositions
Inventory

pedagogies
    classrooms and effectiveness of,
        6–7, 20
    contemplative, 275–76, 279, 281
    modifications to approaches in,
        102–3
Perceived Stress Scale, 241
Perkins, D. N., 111
perseverance, 194–95
personal transformation, 121–22
person-environment fit, for student
    success, 2–3
perspectives, x–xi, 132, 270–71
Petrie, N., 10
PFC. *See* prefrontal cortex
pharmaceutical research, 66
physical exercise
    brain and, 226–27
    well-being and, 151
    for well-being and resilience, 154–55
physicians, balanced life and, 218–20
PIAAC. *See* Survey of Adult Skills
Pillemer, J., 181
Pink, Daniel, 134–36
Pittman, 9
play areas, company, 226–28
Plucker, J. A., 180–81
policies, 190
policymakers, 309–10, 323–26
*Policy paradox: The art of political
    decision making* (Stone), 190
portfolios, 13, 15, 20
Posner, M. I., 87
Postsecondary Education Critical
    Thinking Dispositions Inventory
    (PECTDI), 242
postsynaptic neurons, 61
post-traumatic stress disorder (PTSD),
    161
Poulin, Michael J., 209
prefrontal cortex (PFC), 224, 230
    location and function of, 43
    meditation and increased thickness
        of, 58
    prioritization and, 43

presencing, 305
present tense, 270–71, 285
presynaptic neurons, 61
prioritization, prefrontal cortex and, 43
problem-solving skills, 15, 226
pro-C creativity, 184–85
productivity
    less workday hours for increased,
        229, 269
    slowing down for increased, 269
"professional development day," 284
professionals
    insomnia and, 218–19
    life imbalance and, 219–20, 230
projects, 189–90
prosocial choices, 86
psychological well-being, 16–17
*The Psychology of Humor: An Integrative
    Approach* (Martin), 150
PTSD. *See* post-traumatic stress
    disorder
purpose, 136
Purpose in Life Scale, 105
Pyrz, Paul, 282

quadrant framework
    change quadrant model of, 302–3
    for strategic change, 301–3, 306

racism, 202–3
Ramon y Cajal, Santiago, 32, 57
rapid-prototyping processes, 303
Ratey, John, 151
Rath, Tom, 156
Raza, Rachel, 277
reflective learning, 13, 15, 20
reflective practice, 125
relationships, 156, 242–45
research
    brain and, 147
    CR and mindfulness training, 80–81
    creativity, 180–83
    CSUMB capstone course experience,
        125–26, 141–42
    four-Ps model tool for creativity, 180

person-environment fit for, 2–3
recognized, 2–5
SU. *See* Syracuse University
subcortical structures, 45
success. *See also* student success
AR and student, 75
collaboration and, 179, 309
communication and, 179
creativity and, 179
flexibility and, 179
goal of achieving career, 139
suffering, 197–98
support, 140
Survey of Adult Skills (PIAAC), 4
surveys, 132
global consumer engagement, 18
PIAAC and, 4
student stress, 145
sympathetic system, 146–47
synapses, 61
synaptic communication, 62–63
synaptic plasticity, 59
Syracuse University (SU), 274–81

Tagg, John, 122
Tan, Chade-Meng, 265, 284
Tang, Y. Y., 87
*Tattoos on the Heart: The Power of
Boundless Compassion* (Boyle), 211
teaching
community-based approach to, 122
CSUMB senior capstone for
management, 123–24
demands of whole student, 99–100,
315
INIQ as innovative approach to, 240
maximizing creativity, 189–90
self-authorship and, 101–2, 112–13,
117
through self-authorship lens, 101–2,
117
technology, 182
attention training and using, 245–46
neuroimaging, 33–37, 224

telomeres, 65
thalamus, 42
*Theory U: Leading from the future as it
emerges* (Scharmer), 310
Theory U Model, 298–99, 306
Thompson, W., 161
Thorndike, R. L., 272
threat, brain detection for, 76
TM. *See* Transcendental Meditation;
Transverse Myelitis
Toga, A. W., 38–39
tools, student inner development,
xiv–xv
training. *See also specific training*
benefits in combination of AR, ER,
CR, 74–77, 314
cognitive constructs' improvement,
16–17
CR and research for mindfulness,
80–81
for development of brain, 54–56
focus and attention span, 10
focused breathing, 79–82
focused movement as AR, ER, CR,
83
holistic learning and development
emotions, 250–51
holistic learning and development
self-regulation, 249–50
INIQ and brain association in,
256–57
INIQ program, 77–78, 83
psychological well-being, 16–17
self-compassion, 204–7, 214
skill-based, 87–88
technology and attention, 245–46
wisdom traditions and, 77
Transcendental Meditation (TM), 161
transformation
charting path to understanding and,
122–24
CSUMB capstone achievements of,
138–39
personal, 121–22

Sentipensante (Sensing/Thinking) Pedagogy

Educating for Wholeness, Social Justice and Liberation
Laura I. Rendón
Foreword by Mark Nepo

"Challenging, inspiring, beautifully written, and unusual, this book calls readers to find ways to link mind and heart—thinking and feeling—to transform teaching and learning in higher education. I commend this book to readers. Laura Rendón has illustrated how one can unite one's deep beliefs, values, and feelings with one's keen analytical and intellectual abilities." —*The Review of Higher Education*

22883 Quicksilver Drive
Sterling, VA 20166-2102

Subscribe to our e-mail alerts: www.Styluspub.com

Also available from Stylus

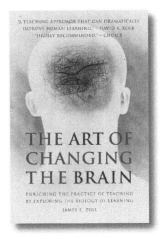

The Art of Changing the Brain

Enriching the Practice of Teaching by Exploring the Biology of Learning

James E. Zull

"This is the best book I have read about the brain and learning. Zull takes us on a fascinating and vivid tour of the brain, revealing the intricate structure of the organ designed by evolution to learn from experience. Using wonderful stories from his own experience filled with insight, humor, and occasional twinges of pain, this wise and humane educator and scientist describes his concept that teaching is the art of changing the brain. His perspective forms the foundation for a teaching approach that can dramatically improve human learning."—**David A. Kolb**, *Department of Organizational Behavior, Case Western Reserve University*

"Zull's years of experience as both professor of biology and director of a university teaching institute are apparent; the book is well written and appropriately technical for the audience interested in applying current knowledge about the brain to learning and instructing. Highly recommended."—**Choice**

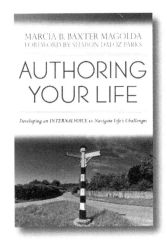

Authoring Your Life

Developing an Internal Voice to Navigate Life's Challenges

Marcia B. Baxter Magolda

Illustrated by Matthew Henry Hall

Foreword by Sharon Daloz Parks

"No one has carried the concept of 'self-authorship' forward more richly, or with greater use for the reader, than Marcia Baxter Magolda. Anyone interested in supporting their own, or others', adult development will benefit enormously from this book."—**Robert Kegan**, *Meehan Professor of Adult Learning, Harvard University, and coauthor of* Immunity to Change

"Given today's complex and ever-changing life demands, *Authoring Your Life* offers a timely, crucial map of possibilities for helping ourselves and others to grow and to meet the implicit and explicit demands of post-modern life."—**Ellie Drago-Severson**, *Associate Professor of Education Leadership, Teachers College, Columbia University; author of* Helping Teachers Learn *and* Leading Adult Learning

(Continues on preceding page)